Resourceful Reading
The New Empiricism, eResearch and Australian Literary Culture

Edited by Katherine Bode and Robert Dixon

SYDNEY UNIVERSITY PRESS

Published 2009 by Sydney University Press
SYDNEY UNIVERSITY PRESS
University of Sydney Library
www.sup.usyd.edu.au

© Individual authors 2009
© Sydney University Press 2009

Reproduction and Communication for other purposes
Except as permitted under the Act, no part of this edition may be reproduced, stored in a retrieval system, or communicated in any form or by any means without prior written permission. All requests for reproduction or communication should be made to Sydney University Press at the address below:

Sydney University Press
Fisher Library F03
University of Sydney NSW 2006 AUSTRALIA
Email: info@sup.usyd.edu.au

National Library of Australia Cataloguing-in-Publication entry

Title: Resourceful reading : the new empiricism, eResearch and
         Australian literary culture / editors, Robert Dixon, Katherine Bode.
ISBN: 9781920899455 (pbk.)
Notes: Includes index.
         Bibliography.
Subjects: Literature--Research--Australia.
         Australian literature--History and criticism.
         Internet research.
Other Authors/Contributors:
         Dixon, Robert.
         Bode, Katherine.
Dewey Number: 808

Cover design by Nathan Garvey

Contents

Contributors	v
Resourceful Reading: A New Empiricism in the Digital Age? *Katherine Bode and Robert Dixon*	1

Section 1: The State and Future of the Discipline

1	Structures, Networks, Institutions: The New Empiricism, Book History and Literary History *David Carter*	31
2	The Book, Scholarly Editing and the Electronic Edition *Paul Eggert*	53
3	Old Tricks for New Dogs: Resurrecting Bibliography and Literary History *Carol Hetherington*	70

Section 2: Case Studies

4	Australian Literature in the Translation Zone: Robert Dessaix and David Malouf *Robert Dixon*	87
5	Australian Literature in a World of Books: A Transnational History of Kylie Tennant's *The Battlers* *Roger Osborne*	105
6	Books in Selected Australian Newspapers, December 1930 *Robert Thomson and Leigh Dale*	119
7	Magical Numbers *Ivor Indyk*	142
8	Emerging Black Writing and the University of Queensland Press *Deborah Jordan*	156

9 Making Aboriginal History: The Cultural Mission in
   Australian Book Publishing and the Publication of Henry
   Reynolds's *The Other Side of the Frontier*   176
   Mark Davis
10 From British Domination to Multinational
   Conglomeration? A Revised History of Australian
   Novel Publishing, 1950–2007   194
   Katherine Bode
11 Squinting at a Sea of Dots: Visualising Australian
   Readerships Using Statistical Machine Learning   223
   Julieanne Lamond and Mark Reid
12 Is a Picture Worth 10,175 Australian Novels?   240
   Jason D. Ensor
13 Voices from the Past: Gender, Politics, and the Anthology   274
   Gillian Whitlock

Section 3: Project Reports
14 AustLit: Creating a Collaborative Research Space for
   Australian Literary Studies   299
   Kerry Kilner
15 A Place in Stories: A Report on the Literature of Tasmania
   Subset of the AustLit Database   315
   Tony Stagg and Philip Mead
16 AusStage: From Database of Performing Arts to a
   Performing Database of the Arts   325
   Neal Harvey, Helena Grehan and Joanne Tompkins
17 Constructing APRIL: The Australian Poetry Resources
   Internet Library   334
   John Tranter and Elizabeth Webby
18 An Australian Reading Experience Database, 1788–   340
   Patrick Buckridge

Index   348

Contributors

KATHERINE BODE is an ARC-funded Postdoctoral Research Fellow in the School of English, Journalism and European Languages at the University of Tasmania. Her current research investigates the critical potential of quantitative methods for analysing Australian literary and publishing history.

PATRICK BUCKRIDGE teaches Australian and world literature at Griffith University. He has active research interests in literary history, literary education and the history of reading and publishing. His most recent book, edited with Belinda McKay, is *By the Book: A Literary History of Queensland* (2007).

DAVID CARTER is Professor of Australian Literature and Cultural History at the University of Queensland. His most recent publications are *Making Books: Contemporary Australian Publishing* (2007), edited with Anne Galligan, and *Dispossession, Dreams and Diversity: Issues in Australian Studies* (2006).

LEIGH DALE teaches English literatures at the University of Wollongong, and is editor of the journal *Australian Literary Studies*. She is the author of *The English Men: Professing Literature in Australian Universities* (1997), soon to be revised as 'The Enchantment of English', and editor of several volumes of postcolonial criticism.

MARK DAVIS teaches in the Publishing and Communications Program in the School of Culture and Communication at the University of Melbourne. His most recent book is *The Land of Plenty: Australia in the 2000s* (2008).

ROBERT DIXON is Professor of Australian Literature at the University of Sydney. His most recent book, edited with Veronica Kelly, is *Impact of the Modern: Vernacular Modernities in Australia 1870s–1960s* (2008).

PAUL EGGERT is an ARC Professorial Fellow, based at the University of New South Wales at ADFA. He was founding general editor of the Academy Editions of Australian Literature, and chairs the AustLit Advisory Board. His Academy Edition (with Elizabeth Webby) of Rolf Boldrewood's *Robbery Under Arms* appeared in 2006 from the University of Queensland Press, and his book, *Securing the Past: Conservation in Art, Architecture and Literature*, was published by Cambridge University Press in 2009.

JASON ENSOR is a final year PhD candidate at the School of Media, Society and Culture, Curtin University of Technology. His research concerns Australian literary history and print cultures, particularly the influences of British-led publishing practices on the production of the novel in Australia. He is co-editor of *New Talents: Other Contact Zones* (2007).

HELENA GREHAN is a Senior Lecturer in English and Creative Arts at Murdoch University. She is the author of *Mapping Cultural Identity in Contemporary Australian Performance* (2001), and *Performance, Ethics and Spectatorship in a Global Age* (2009) as well as many scholarly articles on performance, representation and interculturalism.

NEAL HARVEY has worked with Joanne Tompkins and Helena Grehan on the bibliographic, editorial and repurposing stream of the AusStage project for two years. Neal has published papers on Australian theatre companies and on early adoption of new media technologies, and oversaw the beta phase development of the Ortelia project (www.ortelia.com) from 2002 to 2005. His PhD is under assessment through the University of Queensland and he currently lives in Melbourne, where he is the producer of the Elbow Room theatre ensemble.

CAROL HETHERINGTON is currently employed as Content Manager of the database AustLit: The Australian Literature Resource and as an editorial assistant for *Australian Literary Studies*. She has worked for many years as a research assistant and bibliographer with the English Department at the University of Queensland, and as a librarian in the Fryer Library of Australian Literature, University of Queensland.

IVOR INDYK is founding editor and publisher of *HEAT* magazine and the award-winning Giramondo Publishing, and Whitlam Professor in Writing and Society at the University of Western Sydney. A critic, essayist and reviewer, he has written a monograph on David Malouf, and essays on many aspects of Australian literature, art and architecture. He is currently engaged in research on a large ARC-funded project on Australian Literary Publishing and its Economies, 1965–1995.

DEBORAH JORDAN is a Research Fellow at the University of Queensland. She is currently working on the University of Queensland Press archives as part of the national project on Australian Literary Publishing and its Economies, 1965–1995, and the history of the book with Professor Ivor Indyk among others. She has worked as a professional historian, writer and scholar in the university, government and private sectors—in public history, maritime heritage and cultural history, especially women's history.

KERRY KILNER is an Arts Faculty Research Fellow at the University of Queensland and Director of AustLit: The Australian Literature Resource (www.austlit.edu.au). She is an associate editor and project manager of *The Bibliography of Australian Literature* (2004, 2007, 2008) and has been involved in Australian literary research and bibliographical compilation since 1993 when, at Monash University, she co-compiled the *List of Aus-*

tralian Writers (1995). Since then she has compiled a bibliography of Australian drama, *From Page to Stage* (2000, available through AustLit).

JULIEANNE LAMOND lectures in English in the School of Humanities at the Australian National University. Her areas of interest include Australian literature and film, and the cultural history of audiences and readerships.

PHILIP MEAD is a member of the AustLit Advisory Board, and coordinates the Literature of Tasmania Subset of AustLit, a bibliographical project that aims to record and map the historical depth and diversity of creative writing from and about Tasmania. He is the author of *Networked Language: History and Culture in Australian Poetry* (2008) and is currently Professor of Australian Literature at the University of Western Australia.

ROGER OSBORNE has conducted research in the fields of textual criticism, book history and print culture for more than ten years. He is co-editor of the Cambridge Edition of Joseph Conrad's *Under Western Eyes* and has published a number of articles on transnational print culture. He is currently the Project Manager of the Aus-e-Lit project at the University of Queensland and a researcher for the ARC-funded project, America Publishes Australia: Australian Books and American Publishers, 1890–2005.

MARK REID is a Postdoctoral Research Fellow in the statistical machine learning group of the Research School of Information Sciences and Engineering at the Australian National University. He is currently developing theoretical tools to better understand relationships between risk, divergence and information.

TONY STAGG joined the AustLit project in 2006, after completing his PhD, a multidisciplinary study focusing on the textual regeneration of Tasmanian history through the island's touristic bureaucracy. Under the guidance of Philip Mead, Tony together with colleague Ralph Spaulding constitutes the principal (and principally tenacious) archival bloodhounds for AustLit's Tasmanian Research Community, on a seemingly endless quest to uncover long-forgotten and often overlooked contributors to Tasmania's literary culture.

ROBERT THOMSON works as a researcher with AustLit.

JOANNE TOMPKINS is Professor of Drama in English, Media Studies, and Art History at the University of Queensland. She is the author of *Post Colonial Drama* (with Helen Gilbert, 1996), *Women's Intercultural Performance* (with Julie Holledge, 2000), and *Unsettling Space: Contestations in Contemporary Australian Theatre* (2006). She has been associated with AusStage since its inception and she also works with virtual reality models of cultural and heritage venues through the company Ortelia.

JOHN TRANTER has published more than twenty collections of verse. *Urban Myths: 210 Poems: New and Selected* won the 2006 Victorian state award for poetry, the 2007 New South Wales state award for poetry, the 2008 South Australian state award for poetry, and the 2008 South Australian Premier's Prize for the best book overall in 2006 and 2007. In 1992 he edited (with Philip Mead) the *Penguin Book of Modern Australian Poetry*. He is the editor of the free internet magazine *Jacket* (jacketmagazine.com) and in 2004 he initiated the Australian Poetry Resources Internet Library (april.edu.au).

ELIZABETH WEBBY was Professor of Australian Literature at the University of Sydney from 1990 until her retirement in March 2007. Her publications include *Early Australian Poetry* (1982), *Colonial Voices* (1989), *Modern Australian Plays* (1990), *The Cambridge Companion to Australian Literature* (2000) and, as joint editor, *Happy Endings* (1987), *Goodbye to Romance* (1989), *The Penguin Book of Australian Ballads* (1993), *Australian Feminism: A Companion* (1998) and the Academy Edition of Rolf Boldrewood's *Robbery Under Arms* (2006).

GILLIAN WHITLOCK is an ARC Professorial Fellow in the School of English, Media Studies and Art History at the University of Queensland. Her most recent book is *Soft Weapons: Autobiography in Transit* (2007) and she is currently working on a study of postcolonial life writing in an international frame.

Resourceful Reading: A New Empiricism in the Digital Age?

Katherine Bode and Robert Dixon

In a recent survey of eResearch and the humanities, Paul Longley Arthur invokes the famous title of C.P. Snow's 1959 Rede Lecture, 'The Two Cultures', to characterise the relationship between the arts and humanities, and the sciences and information technologies in Australia today. 'Quite suddenly,' he argues, 'at the end of the twentieth century, the digital environment began to trigger major changes in the knowledge economy, with the result that the humanities were thrown unexpectedly and involuntarily into a close relationship with technology. As one might expect in any forced marriage, it was not a case of love at first sight.'[1] Arthur describes a series of subsequent reactions to this 'forced marriage':

> from totally ignoring the other, through unashamedly raiding their wealth, to whole-heartedly embracing the exciting future they seem to offer. Whatever the reaction, it is clear that the humanities are now inescapably entangled with technology, for better or worse, and the two cultures are connecting more than ever before, notably in the new research activities and spaces signalled by the term 'e-research'.[2]

---

[1] C.P. Snow, 'The Two Cultures', The Rede Lecture, Senate House, Cambridge, 1959, cited in Paul Longley, Arthur, 'Virtual Strangers: e-Research and the Humanities', *Australian Cultural History* 27.1 (April 2009): 47.
[2] Ibid., pp. 47–48.

Arthur is by no means first to invoke Snow's two cultures. Since the 1960s, this phrase has stood as a 'popular shorthand' for a perceived 'rift—a matter of incomprehension tinged with hostility'[3]—between scientists and humanities scholars. In recent discussions, however, the gulf between the two cultures is most often used, as it is in Arthur's paper, as a statement about the past—albeit the very recent past—and as a starting point from which to identify and describe new metaphors of connection and collaboration between the arts and humanities, and the sciences and information technologies. The editors of a recent special issue of *American Literature* on Literature and Science contrast the 'two cultures' of the past with a new 'contact zone', a realm of entanglement where the arts and sciences are guests 'seated at the [same] table', and 'dynamic partners rather than ... hereditary enemies'.[4] In the same issue, Jay Clayton raises the possibility of a 'convergence' between the two scholarly spheres,[5] while elsewhere, Cathy Davidson speaks of the need to bring the 'two cultures' together with 'a real conversation, rather than a contest, across the humanities and sciences'.[6]

In presenting leading examples of research into Australian literary culture that employ empirical methods and digital technologies once associated with the sciences, *Resourceful Reading* demonstrates the potential and productivity of the conversation and connection these critics describe. The essays in this collection—by twenty-five leading scholars, archivists, publishing industry professionals and information technology

---

[3] Roger Kimball, '"The Two Cultures" Today: On the C.P. Snow–F.R. Leavis Controversy', *New Criterion* 12 (February 1994): 10.
[4] Wai Chee Dimock and Priscilla Wald, 'Literature and Science: Cultural Forms, Conceptual Exchanges', *American Literature* 74.4 (December 2002): 807–31.
[5] Jay Clayton, 'Convergence of the Two Cultures: A Geek's Guide to Contemporary Literature', *American Literature* 74.4 (December 2002): 706.
[6] Cathy N. Davidson, 'Humanities 2.0: Promise, Perils, Predictions', *PMLA* 123.3 (2008): 715.

specialists—provide an authoritative overview of the ways in which such methods and technologies are transforming research in Australian literary studies today. We want to begin, though, by complicating the idea that these two cultures have been, until recently, entirely separate. In recalling the long, and generally unrecognised, history of empirical and electronic investigations into literary culture—including Australian literary culture—we instead propose this 'contact zone' as longstanding, this 'conversation' as ongoing, and this sudden 'forced marriage' as an established relationship between research into literature and literary culture, and the empirical methods and information technologies supposedly exclusive to the sciences.

Until recently, this conversation has occurred in areas of research marginal, or largely unknown, to mainstream literary studies. The ways in which empirical and digital methods are becoming part of the mainstream conversation is one reason why we can now speak about a 'new empiricism' or 'empirical turn'.[7] In some cases, scholars are using empirical methods and digital technologies to ask and answer questions of long standing within literary studies. In others, these methods and technologies are being applied to new questions: questions that have become relevant to literary studies due to recent theoretically motivated shifts, particularly those contributing to the denaturalisation of the literary canon in the 1970s and 1980s. Empirical and eResearch methods are not thereby becoming *the* mainstream of literary studies—indeed, they have attracted some resistance both in Australia and in the United States as a distraction from 'evaluative criticism', which for Susan Lever remains 'the

---

[7] Cf. Terry Flew, 'The "New Empirics" in Internet Studies', in H. Brown, G. Lovink, H. Merrick, N. Rossiter, D. Teh and M. Wilson, eds, *Politics of a Digital Present* (Melbourne: Fibreculture Publications, 2001).

main game for a literary academic'[8]—but they do constitute an increasingly important domain of research in the discipline. To understand what is new about the way empirical and eResearch methods are now being taken up, it is best to begin with their separate histories in research into literature and literary culture.

Prehistories 1: Empiricism and Literary Studies

As it is widely understood, empirical research uses observation, experience and experiment, as opposed to theory, to access the presumed 'facts' and 'objects' of its inquiry, and is most commonly identified with scientific disciplines like chemistry, mathematics and medicine. While theory has occupied a privileged position in literary studies over the last thirty years, different forms of evidence- or information-based literary research preceded, persisted throughout, and emerged during this period.

For literary scholars, the most obvious and visible forms of empirical research are bibliography and scholarly editing. Research in both fields is fundamentally evidence- or fact-based: bibliography describes the material forms and publishing histories of literary works, while scholarly editing identifies and collates the different forms in which a literary work is published. These kinds of empirical research provided the infrastructure necessary for modern scholarship in literary studies. But they have often been characterised as subservient to the practice of literary criticism and, later, theory.

Speaking before the emergence of 'theory' as a separate pursuit within literary studies, G.A. Wilkes, in his inaugural lecture as Professor of Australian Literature at the University of Sydney in 1964, clearly demonstrates both the foundational importance, but also the perceived

---

[8] Susan Lever, 'Criticism and Fiction in Australia', *Overland* 193 (Summer 2008): 64–7, 67; see also Jane Gallop, 'The Historicization of Literary Studies and the Fate of Close Reading', *Profession* 121.5 (2007): 181–86.

subservience, of what he terms 'the associated disciplines and techniques—bibliographical, editorial, biographical':

> The University study of [Australian literature] means ... that it is brought into closer contact with the associated disciplines and techniques—bibliographical, editorial, biographical—on which the study of any literature at University level must rely. These may be disciplines that are transcended in the process of criticism and discrimination, but those further processes are apt to go awry ... in the absence of a foundation of this kind.[9]

As a further indicator of the perceived subservience of these 'associated fields', some of the most important early works of Australian scholarship were compiled not by literary scholars but by librarians, amateur bibliophiles and book collectors, including the foundational reference works by J.A. Ferguson, E. Morris Miller and H.M. Green.[10] As both Paul Eggert and Carol Hetherington argue in this collection, a primary condition of the success of 'new' empirical methods is overcoming 'the lingering effects', in Eggert's words, 'of the division of the

---

[9] G.A. Wilkes, *The University and Australian Literature: An Inaugural Lecture* (Sydney: Angus & Robertson, 1964), p. 20.
[10] J.A. Ferguson, *Bibliography of Australia* (Sydney: Angus & Robertson, 1941–69); E. Morris Miller, *Bibliography of Australian Literature 1795–1938* (Melbourne: Melbourne University Press, 1940); H.M. Green, *A History of Australian Literature* (Sydney: Angus & Robertson, 1961). More recent bibliographic projects in Australian literature include D.H. Borchardt and W. Kirsop, eds, *The Book in Australia* (Monash University Historical Monograph no. 16, 1988); and *The Bibliography of Australian Literature* edited by John Arnold and John Hay (Kew, Vic.: Australian Scholarly Publishing; St Lucia: University of Queensland Press, 2001–). Major outlets for bibliographic research include *La Trobe Journal* and *Script and Print*, the journal of the Bibliographical Society of Australia and New Zealand.

kingdom' of English departments between criticism and theory, and editing and bibliography.[11]

Emerging internationally within the discipline of history in the 1980s, the various histories of the book, publishing, print and reading represent another form of empirical research into literary culture. As the editors of *The Book History Reader* assert, this field inherited from bibliography 'the very recognition that a book is a result of a collaborative, albeit for bibliographers an often corrupting, process; and a detailed system for describing books on the basis of their production attributes which provided a universal standard for drawing attention to the material object rather than its contents'.[12] But rather than seeking to establish 'stable texts and precise textual intentions', book historians are concerned with the complex social life of books: the interactive processes whereby books are produced, distributed and consumed.[13] Statistical or quantitative research—a scientific tool, according to the paradigm of the two cultures—has been a central method in book history. Research into the history of the book in Australia—using empirical methods such as bibliographic description, publishing history and oral history interviews—includes *Australian Readers Remember* (1992), by Martyn Lyons and Lucy Taksa, and *A History of the Book in Australia, 1891–1945* (2001), edited by Martyn Lyons and John Arnold, one of three volumes (two published so far) arising from The History of the Book in Australia project, initiated in 1993.

Although book history draws on a core aspect of literary studies—bibliography—and although book historians are often housed in literature departments, until quite recently the theoretical orientation of

---

[11] Paul Eggert, 'The Book, Scholarly Editing and the Electronic Edition', p. 68.
[12] David Finkelstein and Alistair McCleery, 'Introduction', in David Finkelstein and Alistair McCleery, eds, *The Book History Reader*, 2nd ed. (London: Routledge, 2009), p. 2.
[13] Ibid., p. 3.

literary studies prompted harsh criticism from book historians, and led to a surprising disengagement between literary studies and histories of the book, publishing and print culture. Writing in 1996, Jonathan Rose describes the disenchantment of book historians with the more theoretically oriented literary studies, noting the contrast between Robert Darnton's 1986 vision of a future of 'fruitful collaboration between reader-response critics and historians of reading', and his 1994 perception that literary studies was built on unstable theoretical foundations: 'It is easy to issue programmatic statements. I think we need to work through the theoretical issues by incorporating them more thoroughly in more research of a concrete, empirical character.'[14] More pointedly, Nicolas Barker asserts, 'It is difficult not to regard the theorizing, the controversy, the construction of elaborate models of response, as activities detached from the texts to which they have been applied.'[15] Closer to home, the resistance to theory by empirical scholars was played out in debates at conferences of the Association for the Study of Australian Literature (ASAL) in the late 1970s and 1980s, and reflected in the *Meridian* editing debate of the mid-1980s.[16]

---

[14] Jonathan Rose, 'How Historians Teach the History of the Book', *Canadian Review of Comparative Literature—Revue Canadienne de Littérature Comparée* 23.1 (1996): 219. Rose is comparing Darnton's perspective in the following two publications: Robert Darnton, 'First Steps Toward a History of Reading', *Australian Journal of French Studies* 23 (1986): 5–30; and Krassimira Daskalova, 'Book History, the State of Play: An Interview with Robert Darnton', *SHARP News* 3 (1994): 2–4.
[15] Nicolas Barker, 'Intentionality and Reception Theory', in Nicolas Barker, ed., A *Potencie of Life: Books in Society* (London: British Library, 1993), p. 199.
[16] See articles on editing, theory and editorial theory in *Meridian: The La Trobe University English Review* by K.K. Ruthven, 4 (1985): 85–87; F.H. Mares, 4 (1985): 88–91; Stephanie Trigg, 5 (1986): 169–74; Paul Eggert, 5 (1986): 175–81; and Jenna Mead, 10 (1991): 81–88; and Paul Eggert, ed., *Editing in Australia* (Can-

If bibliography and scholarly editing were once regarded as subservient to literary criticism and theory, and if book history initially distanced itself from theoretically oriented forms of literary studies, another form of empirical research has been essentially invisible to literary scholars (as well as bibliographers and book historians). Since the 1960s, an interdisciplinary field called 'empirical literary studies' has investigated

> a broad range of topics: reading processes, the conditions of literary production and reception, literary education and socialization, the social and cultural contexts of literature, the effects of literature and other media, the role of institutions in the field of literature and the media, and the social history of literature.[17]

This area of study has its own journals, societies, and international conferences, and includes scholars from a variety of disciplines, including psychology, philosophy, education, history, medicine, linguistics and sociology.[18]

In his opening speech at the first International Society for the Empirical Study of Literature and Media conference in 1987, the founder of the society, Siegfried J. Schmidt, defined the empirical study of literature in terms reminiscent not only of book history's interest in the complex relations of production and consumption, but Franco Moretti's recent

---

berra: English Department, University College ADFA, 1990. Occasional Paper No. 17).

[17] Susanne Janssen and Nel van Dijk, 'Introduction', in Susanne Janssen and Nel van Dijk, eds, *The Empirical Study of Literature and The Media: Current Approaches and Perspectives* (Rotterdam: Waalwijk van Doorn, 1998), p. 7.

[18] Journals dedicated to 'empirical literary studies' include *Poetics: Journal of Empirical Research on Culture, the Media and the Arts* (1971–) and *Empirical Studies of the Arts* (1983–). Professional bodies in this interdisciplinary field include the International Society for the Empirical Study of Literature and Media (IGEL), founded in 1987, and the International Association of Empirical Aesthetics (IAEA), established in 1965 (www.science-of-aesthetics.org/index.html).

assertion of a shift of literary studies to 'distant reading': 'The focal shift from isolated literary texts to activities by producers, mediators, recipients and post-processors of literary phenomena in their respective social contexts can be regarded as the common denominator'.[19] Like the evidence-based research in bibliography and scholarly editing, and the more recent quantitative, data-based analyses prevalent in book history, the stated aim of empirical literary studies—'to carry on literary studies in a scientific way'[20]—challenges the view that the humanities and sciences have been two separate cultures.

Prehistories 2: eResearch and Literary Studies

The use of information technologies in literary research is also of longer standing than is generally acknowledged. Where Snow characterises literary scholars as 'natural luddites',[21] and Arthur more diplomatically depicts them as 'virtual strangers' to technology,[22] Susan Hockey identifies them as the first humanities researchers to employ information technologies, beginning more than fifty years ago.[23] But as with much empirical research, until recently the application of information technologies to literature has occurred in a discipline quite separate from mainstream literary studies: literary and linguistic computing, including computational stylistics. Almost since computers were invented, scholars in this discipline have used the technology to analyse literary texts (for example, to measure the frequency of certain words or word combinations, or to compare different editions of a text). While literary and

---

[19] Cited in Janssen and Dijk, 'Introduction', p. 7.
[20] Ibid., p. 10.
[21] Snow, p. 22.
[22] Arthur, p. 47.
[23] Susan Hockey, 'The History of Humanities Computing', in Susan Schreibman, Ray Siemens and John Unsworth, eds, *A Companion to the Digital Humanities* (Oxford: Blackwell Publishers, 2004), p. 3.

linguistic computing is an international discipline, one of its major centres, with some of its highest-profile researchers, is the Centre for Literary and Linguistic Computing at the University of Newcastle, Australia.[24]

The longstanding use of information technologies in the analysis of literary texts gives rise to some surprising historical facts: for instance, one of the first conferences hosted by IBM, in 1964, concerned Literary Data Processing.[25] The second Roberto Busa Award for 'outstanding achievement in the application of information technology to humanistic research', made jointly in the US and UK by the Association for Computing in the Humanities and the Association for Literary and Linguistic Computing, was awarded in 2001 to John Burrows, then director of the University of Newcastle's Centre for Literary and Linguistic Computing.[26] Although literary and linguistic computing has long been an established discipline—again with its own journals, associations and international conferences[27]—scholars in the field are well aware of, and frequently comment on, their marginal position in relation to mainstream literary studies. As Thomas Rommel laments,

> literary computing still remains a marginal pursuit ... rarely mak[ing] an impact on mainstream scholarship ... [E]ven the most sophisticated elec-

---

[24] www.newcastle.edu.au/school/hss/research/groups/cllc.
[25] Hockey, p. 7.
[26] 'Roberto Busa Award for 2001', www.newcastle.edu.au/centre/cllc/busaaward.html. See John Burrows, *Computation into Criticism: A Study of Jane Austen's Novels and an Experiment in Method* (Oxford: Clarendon Press, 1987).
[27] Computer-based analyses of literary texts have been a key feature of the journal *Computers and the Humanities* since its formation in the mid-1960s, and *Literary and Linguistic Computing* is entirely devoted to such research. The Association for Literary and Linguistic Computing (ALLC) and the Association for Computers and the Humanities (ACH) host regular international conferences.

tronic studies of canonical works of literature failed to be seen as contributions to the discourse of literary theory and method.[28]

Somewhat surprisingly—given the perception of eResearch as a new and entirely foreign interloper in literary studies—it is often information technologies that are enabling established or traditional research tasks and questions. eResearch—in the sense that Arthur defines it, as 'the *activity* of using new technology, rather than naming what appears to be a separate field, as indicated, for example, by the terms "digital humanities" or "humanities computing"'[29]—has been facilitating traditional forms of literary scholarship since the late 1980s and early 1990s. As Eggert notes, scholarly editing (notwithstanding initial teething issues) has been greatly assisted by digital technologies. Similarly, the digitalisation of library catalogues in the early 1990s, and significant capital investment in the creation of online bibliographies and archives in the late 1990s and 2000s, has facilitated traditional forms of literary scholarship by greatly expanding the material available to literary scholars.[30]

Since at least the beginning of the new millennium, there has been a concerted effort throughout the industrialised world to build capacity in eResearch, and this is now transforming the research environment in Australia and internationally. Key national funding bodies, including the

---

[28] Thomas Rommel, 'Literary Studies', in Susan Schreibman, Ray Siemens and John Unsworth, eds, *A Companion to the Digital Humanities* (Oxford: Blackwell Publishers, 2004), p. 92.

[29] Arthur, p. 51.

[30] An example is the *Waterloo Directory of English Newspapers and Periodicals 1800-1900*, a digital bibliography with advanced search facilities. The next generation is represented by NINES (Networked Infrastructure for Nineteenth-Century Electronic Scholarship), a federated, digitally organised Virtual Research Environment (VRE). See Patrick Leary, 'Googling the Victorians', *Journal of Victorian Culture* 10 (2005): 72-86; Jerome McGann, 'The Future is Digital', *Journal of Victorian Culture* 13 (2008): 80-88.

National Endowment for the Humanities in the United States, the British Research Councils, and Australia's various agencies for research, education and training, have driven this investment at a time when overall funding for the humanities has otherwise declined. The outcomes of investment in eResearch are significant, and in Australia include a number of key reports,[31] online databases,[32] and conferences.[33] In relation to Australian literary studies, a key development in eResearch infrastructure was the establishment of AustLit: The Resource for Australian Literature in 2002. This database was created with funding from the Australian Research Council, the Australian Academy of the Humanities and eleven Australian universities. Its mission was to consolidate all online resources and generate a comprehensive bibliography of Australian literature and its scholarship.[34]

---

[31] The Australian e-Humanities Research Network: Leveraging Digital Scholarship in the Humanities in 2004 (Australian Research Council, 2004; Report on the ARC Special Research Initiatives Scheme. www.ehum.edu.au/arc-report/opportunities.html); An Australian e-Research Strategy and Implementation Framework (Department of Education, Science and Training & Department of Communications, Information Technology and the Arts, Canberra: AGPS, 2006).

[32] For instance, in 2002, the Australian e-Humanities Gateway launched a major online database of Australian digital projects (www.ehum.ed.au).

[33] In 2007, the Academy of the Humanities based its annual symposium on the theme of Humanities Futures: New Methods and Technologies for Humanities Research (symposium.humanities.org.au). Also in 2007, the inaugural 'eResearch Australasia' conference was held at the University of Queensland. In its first year and subsequently, this conference has featured a number of papers from the humanities alongside eResearch investigations in the sciences and information technology (Humanities Technologies: Research Methods and ICT Use in Australian Humanities Research [2006–7]. See www.humanities.org.au/Policy/HumTech/default.htm).

[34] www.austlit.edu.au.

Research projects in Australian literature now frequently involve both new-empirical and eResearch techniques. Increasingly, the gathering and processing of information either draws upon new electronic archives and datasets, or uses eResearch techniques such as databasing, data mining, geo-spatial mapping and computer visualisation. This shift in research methods is accompanied and often enabled by the coming to maturity of databases such as AustLit and SETIS (Scholarly Electronic Text and Imaging Service), and the rise of new online projects such as the Australian Poetry Resource Internet Library (APRIL), AusStage and AusRED (the Australian Reading Experience Database). But as the Project Reports in Section 3 of this collection demonstrate, these large online projects do more than support research in Australian literary studies; they are changing the type of research conducted in the discipline. This suggests that eResearch in Australian literature may be at an important moment of transition. As Cathy Davidson argues, 'the first generation of digital humanities was all about data', while the next generation developments, facilitated by the capacities of Web 2.0, will see increased collaboration and repurposing of data through the creation of Virtual Research Environments (VREs).[35]

Commenting on these developments in 2007, David Carter noted 'a kind of "new empiricism"' as a direction of research developing 'precisely through engagement with theories of text and culture that point beyond literary autonomy'.[36] The ARC-funded Resourceful Reading project (2007–10) responds to and develops this new empiricism by using em-

---

[35] C.N. Davidson, 'Data Mining, Collaboration, and Institutional Infrastructure for Transforming Research and Teaching in the Human Sciences and Beyond', in David Theo Goldberg and Kevin D. Franklin, eds, *Socialising Cyberinfrastructure Watch* 3.2 (May 2007): 3–6. This quote p. 3.

[36] David Carter, 'After Postcolonialism', *Meanjin* 66.2 (2007): 118; see also Robert Dixon 'Australian Literature and the New Empiricism', *JASAL: The Colonial Present* (2008): 158–62.

pirical methods and digital archives to revise the legacy of theoretically driven literary history and criticism, and to generate new ways of writing literary history and reading texts.[37] The term 'resourceful reading' was meant deliberately to combine the information-rich, often computational techniques of what has come to be known, after Franco Moretti, as 'distant reading' with close reading's attention to the internal features of individual literary texts: their settings, idioms, themes and patterns of allusion. The chapters gathered here are intended to provide the first comprehensive account of the new empiricism and eResearch as they are converging in, and transforming, the field of Australian literary criticism and history in the twenty-first century. The essays range from synoptic accounts of the state of the discipline in its international contexts with a particular focus on future directions (Section 1), to exemplary applications of empirical methods by leading critics and scholars (Section 2), to reports on large-scale online projects that represent a significant future direction of literary studies in Australia (Section 3).

A New Empiricism? The State and Future of the Discipline

Given the prehistories of empirical and eResearch, it is obvious that defining the new empiricism is not as simple as pointing to the purportedly 'new' use of empirical or eResearch methods. What *is* new is their potential for application to questions of deep relevance to contemporary literary studies 'after theory'. Outside Australian literature, prominent examples of the new empirical turn include Franco Moretti's method of

---

[37] The Resourceful Reading project is an ARC Discovery Project funded from 2007 to 2010. The four investigators are Katherine Bode (University of Tasmania), Leigh Dale (University of Wollongong), Robert Dixon (University of Sydney) and Gillian Whitlock (University of Queensland).

'distant reading' and William St Clair's 'political economy of reading'.[38] These works herald a shift away from textual critique as the sole raison d'être of literary studies, and towards analysis of the political, economic, cultural and material contexts in which books are produced, circulated and received. But they present their findings in ways that are of interest to textual scholars and literary theorists alike.

The new empiricism might therefore be seen as a loose confluence of approaches and methods that bring a renewed recognition of the value of archival research, while also bringing information and datasets into conversation with questions that have been raised by theoretical work in literary studies during the last quarter century, especially through the application of eResearch methodologies such as databasing, data mining and geo-spatial mapping. These methods are valuable to the extent that they productively address in new ways some of the questions that mainstream literary studies has been unable to explore due to its investment in theoretical and textual analysis. The new empiricism expresses itself as a spectrum of work, from traditional forms of archival research to the mining and manipulation of data from new online datasets. While information can be used in traditional forms, eResearch enhances our access to that information as well as our ability to use it in new and innovative ways. At whatever point of the spectrum it might be located, such research brings theory into contact with the oxygen of rich data.

David Carter opens the collection with an overview of 'the different kinds of work on culture'—both in Australia and internationally—'that might be hidden in that not-quite innocent phase, "the new empiricism"'.

---

[38] Franco Moretti, *Graphs, Maps, Trees: Abstract Models for a Literary History* (London: Verso, 2005) (these essays originally appeared in *New Left Review* in 2003–04); William St Clair, *The Reading Nation in the Romantic Period* (Cambridge: Cambridge University Press, 2004), and 'The Political Economy of Reading', *The John Coffin Memorial Lecture in the History of the Book*, 12 May 2006, ies.sas.ac.uk/Publications/johncoffin/stclair.pdf.

In particular, he emphasises the status of the new empiricism as 'post-' rather than 'anti-theoretical':

> If the new cultural history has grown negatively out of a certain weariness with the subversive paradigm and the routines of contemporary critique … it has also grown positively out of engagement with cultural studies and poststructuralist critical theory, as much as with empirical forms of book history.[39]

In other words, and as the chapters in this collection demonstrate, while the new empiricism announces a shift from theoretically-driven criticism to information-driven histories of books, print cultures and reading, it nevertheless addresses some of the larger questions about production, distribution and reception, institutions and subjectivities, and cultural systems, networks and fields that have characterised post-structuralist theory as well as some versions of cultural studies. In situating books within a larger cultural, political and economic field, the new empiricism directs us beyond the 'intense investment in the *literariness* of the literary texts' that has characterised literary studies. It is this tactical deferral or suspension of 'our interest in the literary text' that allows the literary to 'emerge strategically in a new context, its cultural dynamics, meanings and effects better situated, and better *connected* to other media forms and social interactions'.[40]

While Carter emphasises what is 'new' about the new empiricism, Eggert and Hetherington demonstrate the continuing importance of established empirical practices in literary studies to these current disciplinary shifts. Their chapters point to a fundamental feature of the new empiricism—and of this collection: the way it brings together the essentially distinct, though occasionally entangled, traditions of literary scholarship and criticism. Literary scholarship has generally been seen as

---

[39] David Carter, 'Structures, Networks, Institutions', p. 42.
[40] Ibid., p. 36.

inferior to the primary act of literary criticism, and has often been carried out by non-academic personnel. This hierarchical division was exacerbated by the belated arrival and subsequent reification of theory in Australian literary studies from the 1980s. The new empiricism not only unites theory and criticism through historical, sociological and cultural approaches, but in its focus on evidence it brings the activities of scholarship to a new prominence.

Eggert discusses what he calls 'the oldest empirical form of literary scholarship': scholarly editing. Through an account of his involvement in the Colonial Texts Series and its development of systems for electronic scholarly editions, Eggert explores the 'different logics' of the book and the e-text. While he embraces the possibilities of new electronic editions, he also argues for the continuing importance of the printed scholarly edition. He then reflects on the conditions necessary for realising 'the benefits of empirical, electronically enabled methodologies in the literary field' and preventing the new empiricism becoming just another 'catastrophic', short-lived event in the history of literary studies. Among these conditions are the need to foster collaboration, to create an appropriate rewards structure for the different types of scholarly activity involved in new empirical and eResearch, and to maintain a 'continuous tension' between both 'the empirical and theoretical' and 'sensitised close reading'.[41] This is another version of resourceful reading. Overcoming longstanding divisions within literary studies is also the focus of Hetherington's chapter. Describing the marginalisation of bibliography since the 1970s—its virtual exclusion from university courses, funding eligibility and conference programs—she asserts the vital importance of 're-instat[ing] bibliography as the cornerstone of literary studies', including

---

[41] Eggert, pp. 53–69.

the undergraduate curriculum, if the 'possibilities of the digital and electronic revolutions in literary studies are to be fully realised'.[42]

The Case Studies

The second section of *Resourceful Reading* provides a series of exemplary case studies in the new empiricism and eResearch. These chapters investigate various aspects of what Robert Thomson and Leigh Dale describe as the 'ecology' of literary culture, and include studies in the history of the book, print culture, publishing history and histories of reading.[43] Although very different, they share a number of characteristics indicative of the new empiricism. All embody the shift from textual and ideological critique to a consideration of the place of books and print culture in their historical, economic and social contexts. For most, the consideration of these questions is enriched by archival research, often supplemented by digitally enabled forms of data mining or data analysis. For some, this trend is manifest in what Julieanne Lamond and Mark Reid describe as 'a shift in focus ... from canonical texts and authors towards an examination of Australian literature as a field, a network, a broader structure'.[44] However, in the double relation of literary studies to empirical methods that Carter describes, other chapters reposition canonical literary texts within publishing, print cultural and transnational networks and cultural contexts.

Many of these chapters use empirical methods to interrogate received findings about literary history produced in association with theoretically motivated forms of close reading, and to offer new interpretations of the place of books in relation to publishing and reading, and both Australian and transnational cultural formations. Gillian Whitlock's return to her

---

[42] Hetherington, p. 83.
[43] Thomson and Dale, p. 119.
[44] Lamond and Reid, p. 225.

own feminist work of the late 1980s is exemplary. Typically, the authors ask what Carter describes as 'those stubbornly particular "wise idiot" questions about books and texts, the radically simple questions we're now familiar with, but which reconfigure the field':[45] what books were actually available at the time, who published them, how much did they cost, how and where were they distributed, and what kinds of readers bought them?

A number of the case studies also contain warnings about potential pitfalls of the empirical turn. This is bound up with the question of whether the new empiricism is best understood as post-theoretical, as Carter and Dixon suggest, or a move beyond and 'after' the divisive moment of theory as Eggert, perhaps, implies. This is part of a wider perception that the moment of theory, which swept through the social sciences and humanities in the 1970s and 1980s, has now passed. It was announced initially in the 1990s, then more decisively in the 2000s.[46] And yet, as Colin Davis puts it in relation to the corpus of high theoretical texts and authors, 'we may come after them but we are not yet over them'.[47] Similarly, James Wood observes, 'No university teacher of literature has been untouched by theory; even its enemies speak some of its language'.[48] One of the legacies of theory is a continuing suspicion that a new empiricism might reinstate positivistic claims to objectivity that ignore the mediation of language, ideology, or the unconscious. Accordingly, Mark Davis perceives in some uses of empirical methods a 'temptation ... to rediscover social criticism as a search for "facts"' and to construct 'data' and 'theory' as antithetical.[49] His warning that 'Mere data

---

[45] Carter, p. 39.
[46] Cf. Thomas Docherty, *After Theory* (Edinburgh: Edinburgh University Press, 1996); Terry Eagleton, *After Theory* (New York: Basic Books, 2003).
[47] Colin Davis, *After Poststructuralism: Reading, Stories and Theory* (London: Routledge, 2004), p. 28.
[48] James Wood, 'Textual Harassment', *New Republic* (7, 14 July 2004): 28–35.
[49] Davis, p. 193.

... can't stand in for analysis of the institutional forces by which books are received, read, and sometimes remembered' is echoed by a number of other contributors, including Ivor Indyk and Jason Ensor, who point to possible affinities between empirical approaches to literary studies and the economic rationalism of political culture, which attempts to reduce questions of value to quantifiable data.

Ensor, along with Thomson and Dale, also raises concerns about the ways in which literary scholars collect and interpret data in the absence of established methodological and disciplinary protocols. In expressing their unease, these contributors refer to what might be described as the negative side of empiricism: the possibility that, as Hetherington identifies it, empirical studies might fall into the trap of dismissing 'theoretical abstraction in the belief that texts (or facts of history or biography) can "speak for themselves" without the intervention of analysis and interpretation'.[50] Such a version of empiricism would not be post-theoretical but constitute a return to earlier, more positivistic forms of literary scholarship. In placing the pitfalls of empirical analysis front and centre, these contributors demonstrate Eggert's point that 'humanities types ... will wish to understand the intellectual baggage that their methodological conceptions may contain'.[51]

The first two case studies explore, from different perspectives, the position of Australian literature in its transnational contexts. Robert Dixon applies the techniques of both close and distant reading to explore contemporary Australian literature in what Emily Apter calls 'the translation zone', 'a broad intellectual topography' in and between the spaces of national literatures.[52] While the 'translation zone' is a spatial metaphor, Dixon uses data mining to visualise the cultural and commercial econo-

---

[50] Hetherington, p. 70.
[51] Eggert, p. 60.
[52] Cited in Dixon, p. 88.

mies of that space. Is there a single translation zone, or are there multiple translation zones between Australian literature and other languages? Beyond English, does the reputation of an Australian book or writer spread from one foreign language to another, or are individual translations siloed, communicating back through English? How important is the agency of the author and the translator? More fundamentally, who *are* the often invisible translators of Australian literature?

Roger Osborne also situates Australian literature in a transnational context through a case study of the first edition of Kylie Tennant's novel, *The Battlers*, as it 'travelled the trade routes of a transnational print culture' from London to New York and then Sydney. He reflects on the various people who 'made *The Battlers*', and the 'multi-faceted cultural and economic network' in which this occurred. In this way, he illuminates the 'Australian presence in a transnational history of books' and enhances our understanding of 'how Australian fiction is positioned beyond our shores'.[53]

Thomson and Dale return us to Australia, but in a way that shifts the focus from the study of Australian literature to the study of literature in Australia.[54] By examining references to books (both Australian and non-Australian) in Australian newspapers in December 1930, they test existing accounts of interwar culture that have focused on subsequently canonical literature. In emphasising the important role economics and geography play in the creation of Australian literary culture, they reveal a very different picture to the prevalent canonical view, one that foregrounds 'the enormous diversity and range of books discussed in

---

[53] Osborne, p. 118.
[54] Cf. Robert Dixon, 'Australian Literature—International Contexts', *Southerly* 67.1–2 (2007): 23.

Australian newspapers', as well as the 'previously under-reported significance of the regional press'.[55]

Not surprisingly, given the importance of book history to the emergence of the new empiricism, a number of chapters in this section investigate the history of publishing using a wide range of empirical sources, including the AustLit database, library catalogues, and publishers' archives for data on print runs and sales figures. Ivor Indyk uses a case study of three Australian literary texts—Gerald Murnane's *Tamarisk Row*, Peter Skrzynecki's *Immigrant Chronicle* and Rosa Cappiello's *Oh Lucky Country*—to complicate what he calls the 'baseline reality of literary publishing—its unprofitability, its fundamentally uncommercial nature'. These three texts are exceptional in different ways: one lost money but has been published and republished in multiple editions; one was a belated commercial success after its adoption on high-school curricula; while the third received excellent reviews and was subsidised by two university presses, but had slow sales. Indyk suggests that the fate of these books is determined not solely by their literary appeal 'but the operation of public, educational or institutional forces, which suddenly change the scale of things, or produce unexpected surges of interest'. It is in relation to such factors 'that one has to seek the real sources of the literary economy'.[56]

Deborah Jordan presents a history of the University of Queensland Press's publishing of Indigenous and Black writers in the context of the David Unaipon Award and the subsequent formation of its Black Australian Writers Series. The 'case of Indigenous authors' challenged 'notions of value and difference, of motivation and intention, of agency and reception'.[57] Through archival research, Jordan develops a thick institutional

---

[55] Thomson and Dale, p. 120.
[56] Indyk, p. 147.
[57] Jordan, p. 157.

history of the personalities, as well as the political, aesthetic and economic factors involved in establishing a canon in Aboriginal writing. The tension between a publisher's social responsibilities and commercial imperatives is also the focus of Mark Davis's chapter. Drawing on the Penguin archives, among other sources, Davis examines the complex pre- and post-publication history of Henry Reynolds's landmark book, *The Other Side of the Frontier* (1981), in the context of the 'rise and decline', from the 1960s to the mid-1990s, of what he calls the 'cultural mission' in Australian book publishing.[58]

Katherine Bode takes a quantitative approach to Australian publishing history in second half of the twentieth century. In contrast to the prevalent view of a British-dominated industry, she argues that Australian novel publishing in the 1950s and 1960s was dominated by a handful of Australian mass-market publishers. In the 1970s and 1980s, the number and diversity of Australian publishers of Australian novels increased, confirming the general perception of these decades as a nationalist period in Australian publishing history, but this growth was accompanied by the entry of multinational conglomerates into the field, a phenomenon commonly identified with the 1990s and 2000s.

The use of digitally enabled quantitative analysis is also a feature of the two final chapters in this section, which additionally employ more sophisticated eResearch methods and visualisation techniques. They represent the point at which eResearch moves, in Arthur's words, beyond 'the *activity* of using new technology' to something like a newly distinctive field of 'humanities computing'.[59] Ensor argues that eResearch methods are producing a 'new ontology' of Australian literary history. Due to the newness of this endeavour and the methodological uncertainties it involves, he advocates the creation of an eResearch charter,

---

[58] Davis, p. 178.
[59] Arthur, pp. 50–51.

providing a best-practice model for computer-assisted research that articulates 'consensus on meaningful standards for experimental evidence provided by data mining' and builds a bridge between new empirical methods and the 'aims, objectives and methods of Australian literary history'.[60] Whether such a charter could—or even should—aim to regulate the diverse manifestations of eResearch exemplified in this collection is a matter for future debate.

Lamond and Reid employ techniques from statistical machine learning to develop a new history of reading in Australia. By applying these techniques to datasets derived from the Australian Common Reader project, they create a visual summary of the database that reveals culturally significant patterns in the readership data. In this process, eResearch methods alter the kinds of questions literary scholars are able to ask of data, while answering them frequently involves a turn from the quantitative back to the qualitative—to the specific texts and readers, and the specialised skills of the literary critic.

The Project Reports

The project reports in Section 3 record the current state of development of the most important large-scale eResearch projects in Australian literature today: namely, AustLit, including its new Aus-e-Lit project and the Literature of Tasmania subset of the database; the Australian Poetry Resource Internet Library (APRIL); AusStage; and the Australian Reading Experience Database (AusRED). Reports on research infrastructure projects are not usually included in publications of this kind. However, as the reports demonstrate, and as many of the previous chapters confirm, the future of new-empirical approaches to research in Australian literary culture is inherently bound up with the success of these large-scale online initiatives. While they typically began as infrastructure projects, serving

---

[60] Ensor, p. 249.

the classical functions of supporting and enhancing the research projects to which they are articulated, they are now at a point of transformation where they are developing research agendas of their own. This represents a dramatic and historic displacement of the hierarchisation of criticism, research and scholarship prevailing since the 1950s. Rather than merely being supplementary to 'pure' research projects, in other words, these online initiatives are increasingly behaving like research projects in their own right. One consequence of this shift—as Anthony Gibbons predicted in his widely influential definition of 'Mode 2' research—is the coming together around a central 'problem' of the different kinds of personnel represented by the contributors to this book, who include academic scholars, archivists, librarians and IT professionals.[61] Our inclusion of these project reports is therefore a sign of the transformation of research in Australian literary culture in the digital age. It is also a further instance of the difficulty of defining eResearch as either 'the *activity* of using new technology' or a distinct field of 'humanities computing'.[62]

Austlit, the oldest and most mature of the projects reported here, has become a foundational tool for research in Australian literary studies and is now an integral component of many successful applications for Australian Research Council Discovery Projects, including Resourceful Reading (Dale, Dixon, Bode and Whitlock), America Publishes Australia (Carter) and Australian Literary Publishing and its Economies, 1965–1995 (Carter and Indyk). Kerry Kilner reflects on the changing nature of research in an eResearch environment, and on the impact AustLit has had on Australian literary studies. She also speculates on the potential of the proposed Aus-e-Lit project to further transform research practice by adapting 'traditional scholarly activities' to the digital environment.

---

[61] See Robert Dixon, 'Boundary Work: Australian Literary Studies in the Field of Knowledge Production', *JASAL* 3 (2004): 27–43.
[62] Arthur, pp. 50–51.

Tony Stagg and Philip Mead describe a bibliographic and geographic subset of AustLit dedicated to the literature of Tasmania. The intersection of theoretical perspectives, historical inflections, database methodologies and limitations, visualisation technologies, cognitive mapping and insider knowledge implicated in the creation of their AustLit subset is a further example of the coming together of the previously separate spheres of scholarship, criticism and theory in the creation of eResearch infrastructure. Their discussion also reflects the way that changing technology is motivating methodological and theoretical debate from inside research projects and not merely as a supplement to them.

The other online initiatives detailed in these reports are not yet as established as AustLit, but promise to have as significant an impact on research practice in Australian literary and cultural studies. APRIL, discussed here by its creators, John Tranter and Elizabeth Webby, brings together a wide range of contemporary and earlier Australian poetry, as well as critical and contextual materials, to readers via the internet, and is poised to develop new research questions. Neal Harvey, Helena Grehan and Joanne Tompkins describe AusStage, an online database of live, Australian theatre performances and event-related data. In bringing such data together with 'the wider sociological and historical context in which the event existed', AusStage enables a new, empirical research practice in Australian theatre studies—one that will make 'research in the performing arts ... more dynamic and far-reaching'.[63] This potential to transform research by uniting the particular and the general will also be a feature of AusRED, the Australian Reading Experience Database. As Patrick Buckridge explains, once launched, it will significantly expand research into the history of readers and reading in Australia as an emerging field related to yet distinct from the history of writers and writing. It will also

---

[63] Harvey, Grehan and Tompkins, p. 326.

function interoperably with other national REDs, such as the British Reading Experience Database, to enable transnational studies of reading.

Implicit in all of these reports on large-scale eResearch infrastructure initiatives, and in some of the essays in the preceding sections, are implications for the management and policies of research funding and reward: that is, the problematic distinction in research funding criteria between 'pure research' and 'scholarship', which may well reflect earlier assumptions about the hierarchisation of research practice. The potential for these large-scale eResearch initiatives to secure adequate levels of funding, to access research—as distinct from research infrastructure— funding, and for their outputs to be recognised as contributing to a research track record, are perhaps destined to become major issues in determining how well the new empiricism fares in the future, and how successfully collaborative research can be effected and sustained.

The essays in *Resourceful Reading* were first presented as papers at the conference 'Resourceful Reading: The New Empiricism, eResearch and Australian Literary Culture', convened by the editors at the University of Sydney on 4–5 December 2008. The conference was hosted by Australian Literature at the University of Sydney with additional financial support from an ARC Discovery Project grant on which Leigh Dale, Robert Dixon and Gillian Whitlock are chief investigators, and Katherine Bode an Australian Postdoctoral Fellow. We wish to acknowledge the contribution of these institutions, and the intellectual generosity and enthusiasm of delegates to the conference. The editors acknowledge the contributions of staff at Sydney University Press, Susan Murray-Smith, Agata Mrva-Montoya, and Maisie Dubosarsky, and the editorial and administrative assistance given by Jacinta van den Berg, Elaine Minor and Nathan Garvey of the School of Letters, Art and Media at the University of Sydney.

Section 1

The State and Future of the Discipline

1
Structures, Networks, Institutions: The New Empiricism, Book History and Literary History

David Carter

To begin with I have to plead guilty, not only to using the term 'the new empiricism' in public, but to doing so with intent in the presence of high theory and textual politics. By re-claiming an unfashionable term and claiming for it the power to renew literary studies, the point was not just to observe the arrival of a new set of interests into the field but more polemically to break with dominant practices of ideology critique or 'cultural pathology'. By declaring that the new had become old, something older (whether empiricism or simply history) could suddenly look new again. At stake, at least in part, were precisely the kind of political interventions that theoretically driven literary analysis typically claimed but which it located primarily within the text or as an essential quality of textuality itself in ways that were at once too narrow and too ambitious. The other, more significant part was to argue for a very different way of conceiving the literary field and the kinds of research and research questions that were likely to produce new knowledge about it: not in a world of texts but in a world of books and print and ordinary readers.

On one level, this was a modest call for a more pragmatic, historical or sociological approach to literary studies. On another level, though, the purpose was to announce a paradigm shift, a more fundamental reorientation of objectives and methods: from negative critique to positive explanation, from deconstructive hermeneutics to constitutive description, from textual politics to cultural history. It was time to address what Kay Ferres and I once called the 'public life of literature'; that is, to develop a positive account of literature's being in the public sphere, in the marketplace, and as a cultural industry.[1] Instead of aiming for a higher level of theoretical purity, it was time to aim lower and take on the messy historical circumstances through which, in my shorthand version, books get to readers and readers get to books (a shorthand that immediately gives rise to a whole further set of questions and qualifications beyond the book).

From this point in time it is possible to trace a range of prior and parallel developments leading to calls for a new empiricism and revisionist histories: the emergence of the *new* book history and studies of reading; the kind of intellectual history that puts the sociology of print at the centre of its explanations; the rise of cultural history across the new humanities (not least in the discipline of history itself); various projects bouncing off Pierre Bourdieu's model of the field of cultural production; more recently, the political economy approach, indeed the application of business models, in William St Clair's work; the kinds of large-scale cultural mapping and modelling practised by Franco Moretti and the revisions of comparative or world literature with which he's also associated; from a rather different direction, the institutional and policy turns in cultural studies and some of its work on popular culture and consumption; and perhaps across all of these, the various 'after theory' narratives that have appeared with some regularity over the last decade or so (again I probably have to plead guilty).[2] There are elements of the 'after

---

[1] David Carter and Kay Ferres, 'The Public Life of Literature', in Tony Bennett and David Carter, eds, *Culture in Australia: Policies, Publics and Programs* (Cambridge: Cambridge University Press, 2001), pp. 140–60.
[2] See for example Adrian Johns, *The Nature of the Book: Print and Knowledge in the Making* (Chicago: University of Chicago Press, 1998); Peter D. McDonald,

theory' narrative I support and others I hope to resist, as will become clear.

There is now a mass of material on book, print or publishing history even just for the modern period, although the twentieth century is still light on compared, say, to the rich archive on Victorian books and reading. Publishing or print culture studies for Australia remain patchy, but we can point to a steadily growing body of work and significant new projects under way. Book history and especially the history of reading can still feel new, still with that sense of excitement that goes with discovering new questions and methodologies, new archives and, indeed, new facts. But perhaps the field is already moving into its second generation, having undergone its own kind of interdisciplinary and cultural turn. There's now an *Introduction*, a *Reader* and a *Companion* to book history, all published in the last few years; and predictably enough there's already been a symposium called 'What *Was* the History of the Book?', although the retrospectivity here refers to a founding moment not the end of the enterprise.[3] The assumptions and methods of this work have altered the course of the mainstream, not just in the various national

---

British Literary Culture and Publishing Practice 1880-1914 (Cambridge: Cambridge University Press, 1997); William St Clair, *The Reading Nation in the Romantic Period* (Cambridge: Cambridge University Press, 2004); Franco Moretti, *Graphs, Maps, Trees: Abstract Models for a Literary History* (London: Verso, 2005); Tony Bennett, Michael Emmison and John Frow, *Accounting for Tastes: Australian Everyday Cultures* (Cambridge: Cambridge University Press, 1999); Terry Eagleton, *After Theory* (London: Lane, 2003); David Carter, 'After Postcolonialism', *Meanjin* 66.2 (2007): 114-19.

[3] David Finkelstein and Alistair McCleery, *An Introduction to Book History* (London: Routledge, 2005); David Finkelstein and Alistair McCleery, *The Book History Reader* (London: Routledge, 2002; 2nd ed., 2006); Simon Eliot and Jonathan Rose, eds, *A Companion to the History of the Book* (Malden, MA: Blackwell, 2007); 'Symposium: What Was the History of the Book?', *Modern Intellectual History* 4.3 (2007): 491-544.

histories of the book, which might never stray far from the reference shelves, but in general publications such as *The Oxford English Literary History*, in particular its twentieth-century volumes.[4]

In short, without in the least wanting to lose that sense of discovery—the feeling that we really are on to something new, something that's just beginning to be explored—we can assume that the moment for polemics has passed and the task is now to tease out the range of different kinds of work on culture that might be hidden in that not-quite innocent phrase 'the new empiricism' and to look again at their relation to literary history. If there is a new empiricism, is it new (or for that matter empirical) strictly in terms of method or simply in comparison to what came before? There are questions about both adjective and noun, about old and new methodologies and the kinds of knowledge they might bring into focus. These give rise, in turn, to a series of further questions about the object or objectives of our research, not least because *new* objects appear in our field of vision. Is the object of our research still literature or is it books, publishing, or print culture? Is what we're doing still *literary* history or is it book history, the history of reading, or something else again—the history of cultures or subjectivities? Are we still talking about 'literary studies' or is the literary simply dispersed into all the other studies? There is no single, theoretically pure answer to these questions, but nor do I think we need one (a principled position not merely a pragmatic one). Book history or print culture studies, I want to argue, can best be described as agnostic towards literature.

Even so, in writing the present chapter, I was very conscious of sliding back and forth between literary history and book history, and then again

---

[4] Chris Baldick, 'The Modern Movement', *The Oxford English Literary History Vol. 10, 1910–1940* (Oxford: Oxford University Press, 2004); Randall Stevenson, 'The Last of England?', *The Oxford English Literary History Vol. 12, 1960–2000* (Oxford: Oxford University Press, 2004).

between each of these and *cultural* history, in terms of what it was I was attempting to map out. I don't think this is just a reflection of my own ambivalent relation to literary studies, for it manifests a more positive, constitutive ambivalence or multiplicity produced by the intersection of literary studies, critical theory and more empirically inflected kinds of book or print culture studies. Indeed, it is exactly a practice of sliding or shifting frames I want to argue for.

Publishing or print culture studies, of course, are not necessarily interested in the literary at all; there are other kinds of print, reading, and social or economic relations to be considered. And there are clearly kinds of literary studies that don't much need book history: textual analysis in its ethico-formalist, psycho-cultural or meta-linguistic modes; perhaps in its more teacherly modes too.[5] Because of the irreducibly wide range of interests and purposes to which literature is connected, even in the narrowest definitions, claims for a new method or critical paradigm can never be global or more than modestly prescriptive. However positivist or sociological we try to be, the moment of interpretation will always arrive; literary 'appreciation' is something we will still want to teach in one form or another; and there are good reasons to keep returning to the canonical works. Further, *pace* Moretti perhaps, I think literary history *can* be written as a history of exceptional texts; those texts made even more exceptional, as Moretti suggests, by close reading. In less ironic terms, we might say that literary history can be written as the history of the most significant innovations in form, subject, or literary subjectivity. We might even recruit Paul de Man to argue that to 'become good literary historians, we must remember that what we usually call literary

---

[5] For an interesting 'post-theoretical' defence of close reading see Jane Gallop, 'The Historicization of Literary Studies and the Fate of Close Reading', *Profession* (2007): 181–86. Gallop reminds us that as historians, even cultural historians, literary critics are mostly amateurs (183); and the new criticism in the classroom, at least, was 'a great leveler of cultural capital' (184).

history has little or nothing to do with literature and that what we call literary interpretation—provided it is good interpretation—is in fact literary history'.[6] Good close reading is always potentially good cultural history.

But at this point in time, because of what has been left undone, the *reverse* equation is far more persuasive, far more likely to produce new knowledge. That is, if we are interested in more than the exceptional texts and their serial textuality, if we're interested in how literature and literariness circulate in a wider world of books and print, then we also need the histories of ordinary literature and ordinary readers, of the everyday, the ephemeral, the institutionalised, not merely the moments of excess and subversion. To know these, in turn, we need new empirical research, both on the scale of the micro-histories of particular editions, publishers or reading occasions and on the macro-scale of transnational histories or the long historical projections of 'distant reading'.

For those of us still committed to literary history, this means, I think, locating the literary *within* and *against* the social histories of publishing, distribution and consumption. It means having to defer or suspend our interest in the literary at the tactical level, as it were, in order for it to emerge strategically in a new context, its cultural dynamics, meanings and effects better situated, and better *connected* to other media forms and social interactions. As Martyn Lyons has written, 'the history of the book, or the history of print culture ... is a great leveller'—not because it devalues literariness or interpretability but simply because of its primary empirical interest in the material artefacts of print culture, the conditions of their production, and their social consequences.[7] But this negative (or

---

[6] Paul de Man, 'Literary History and Literary Modernity', in *Blindness and Insight: Essays in the Rhetoric of Contemporary Criticism* (New York: Oxford University Press, 1971), p. 165.

[7] Martyn Lyons, 'Introduction', in Martyn Lyons and John Arnold, eds, *A History*

better *positive*) charge is precisely what makes the enterprise feel new, with the capacity to transform both the methodologies and objectives of literary study, for it puts 'the radical situatedness of texts, as material and institutional forms, at the centre of historical inquiry'.[8] Further, however myopic or microscopically empirical its particular concerns, or alternatively, however large-scale and abstract, it is precisely this kind of interest that connects book history to critical theory rather than sets them in opposition.

My search for some new illumination on that old question, 'What is literary history?', uncovered one essay with the disturbing title, 'Is Literary History the History of Everything?'; the point, of course, is a serious one.[9] More immediately relevant to the present argument is Peter McDonald's 'Ideas of the Book and Histories of Literature: After Theory?', an essay from which I quoted above and to which I'll return. McDonald's essay, significantly enough, was published in a special 2006 issue of *PMLA* on 'The History of the Book and the Idea of Literature', another sign of the changing chronotope. My research also took me to Volume Three of *The History of the Book in Canada*, which provided the following encouraging aphorism: 'Literary history used to be impossible to write; lately it has become much harder'.[10] But perhaps, in some ways, a bit easier too.

---

of the Book in Australia, 1891–1945: A National Culture in a Colonised Market (St Lucia: University of Queensland Press, 2001), p. xiv.

[8] Peter McDonald, 'Ideas of the Book and Histories of Literature: *After Theory?*', *PMLA* 121.1 (January 2006): 222.

[9] David Simpson, 'Is Literary History the History of Everything? The Case for "Antiquarian" History', *SubStance* 28.1, Issue 88 (1999): 5–16.

[10] Lawrence Lipking quoted in Carole Gerson and Jacques Michon, 'Coda', in Carole Gerson and Jacques Michon, eds, *History of the Book in Canada Volume III, 1918–1980* (Toronto: University of Toronto Press, 2004), p. 515.

Either way I'm more than happy to claim the label of 'the new empiricism' for the raft of large and small, new and renewed approaches to the study of books, print, publishing, reading, writing and literature that have emerged over the last decade or so. The idea of a new empirical turn remains important as a way of announcing a break from those forms of textual politics and literary history that depend, after all, on their intense investment in the *literariness* of the literary text and/or on some version of the text-culture homology. (The latter is something John Frow finds in Moretti's work, alongside or rather inside his practice of large-scale quantitative analysis.[11]) Rather than homologies, book history soon tells us that transformations in the different domains affecting texts—in publishing technologies, reading practices or generic systems—do not follow the same historical cycles or geographical spread as each other, let alone those of other social phenomena. In other words, as one of its moves, the force of empirical research is to disaggregate the idea of culture and *merely cultural explanations* for changes in genre, style, print forms or institutions. This is true even where, as in Moretti's work, the disaggregation or 'under-generalisation' supports a second move, in his case to a form of inspired hyper-generalisation. The bridge is the use of quantitative data: 'shifting literary history away from its attention to exceptional moments—the tiny minority of texts that constitute events within the literary series—to a study of its routine configurations, using large masses of data to chart patterns of production, circulation and consumption and thereby dispensing both with the individual texts and its readings, and with the ideological functions of the proper name'.[12]

Despite what is undoubtedly inspiring and challenging in Moretti's grand project, it is clearly only one deployment of empirical methods.

---

[11] John Frow, 'Thinking the Novel', *New Left Review* 49 (January–February 2008): 139.
[12] Ibid., p. 139.

Others will quite properly remain linked to the disaggregated detail, to the bits of the machine and the grit in its machinery: the life spans of particular texts and editions, localised bookselling practices, the structures of particular publishing houses or print markets, and so on. Charting titles or genres is only one small part of what quantitative research might want to pursue; gender, ethnicity, occupation, education and location can all be mapped. And book history itself, of course, is only one form that studies newly oriented towards the empirical or historical might take; biography or studies of careers come to mind. Nonetheless, the idea of the new empiricism captures nicely the force of asking those stubbornly particular 'wise idiot' questions about books and texts, the radically simple questions we're now familiar with but which still retain their capacity to suddenly reconfigure the field: who was actually reading these books, when and how? In what form and format did they reach their readers? How, when and why were they published? How many, how often, and how much? Where could they be bought or borrowed? When did *this* kind of reading become available, and to whom? And what did it mean to be *this* kind of writer at this point in time?

From one end, the 'new empirical' agenda is driven directly by the issue of how we go about answering these sorts of questions, working from the bottom up. What kinds of information do we need, how can we find it, in the first instance, and how do we then go about processing it? Here the arguments for quantitative research, digitally stored datasets and computational analysis—alongside serious time in the archives—are irresistible. Once we start asking the dumb questions, the *obvious* questions once you finally think of them, it is remarkable how much we discover we simply do not know about print runs, sales, reprints, bookselling, distribution, educational settings, pedagogy, periodicals, the social embedding of writing careers, and much more.

At the same time, as Robert Dixon remarked in a seminar on William St Clair's work, it is important not to make a fetish of empiricism; nor, we might add, of the material object. What makes St Clair's work impressive as literary and intellectual history is not just the level of detail and mass of information, but the modelling of book production and distribution it offers, from the dynamics of the publishing business and the crucial role of the copyright regime to the temporal and hence hierarchical divisions in reading experience he charts across the eighteenth and nineteenth centuries. The horizon of his research, after all, is a history of *mentalités*. Frow's somewhat sceptical response to Moretti points in a similar direction: 'such analysis is, in the long run, only useful to the extent that it can open up for us something of the way readers engaged with the novel: how it helped shape their world of sense and emotion, how it spoke to them, how they interpreted and put to use the words they consumed'; and in the short or long run this means an engagement with the complex, localised histories of form and reception.[13] Closer to my own interests, McDonald reminds us that 'What circulates in the culture ... is neither an author's work nor simply the book historian's material document but a *highly institutionalised ... symbolic form*'.[14] From the *other* end, then, the research agenda will still be driven by—or driven towards—theoretical models: models of cultural production and transmission, of subjectivities and institutions, and even, at times, of literary form or textuality. As Leah Price puts it: 'Far from replacing hermeneutics by pedantry, book history insists that every aspect of a literary work bears interpretation—even, or especially, those that look most contingent'; the task, then, is 'to situate the study of material culture as a player in theoretical debates rather than as a bolt-hole from which to wait them out'.[15]

For this reason, if there has been a paradigm shift, I'd want to describe it in terms of a shift from theoretically driven critique to theoretically informed cultural history rather than as a shift from 'theory' to 'empiri-

---

[13] Ibid., p. 140.
[14] McDonald, 'Ideas of the Book', p. 225. My emphasis.
[15] Leah Price, 'Introduction: Reading Matter', *PMLA* 121.1 (January 2006): 11, 15.

cism' *tout court*. The 'cultural' in 'cultural history' here may be understood in two senses: first, as a complex of institutional, industry and commercial settings (for books, print, reading, literariness), and, second, as 'subjectivities' (in the sense St Clair and Frow suggest). While publishing and bibliographical studies will always contribute to cultural history at some level, individual instances are often left to stand as isolated cases without being 'made over' into cultural history; that is, into the kind of knowledge that affects our understanding of the field, its structuring relations or temporal variations. We've had both publishing history and literary history, but we're still learning how to bring them together beyond the individual case: perhaps even more so with studies of reading.

As Roger Osborne wrote to me, in the process of mapping out the contours of our current project on American publishers of Australian books, there's still a lot of 'old' empiricism to be done in the process of doing the new empiricism. That is, the models depend upon reliable primary data and the foundational scholarship needed to produce them, much of which is still in process. Nonetheless, I think there are various senses in which the new empiricism—or perhaps I should say the new cultural history—*can* be defined as new. First, in its engagement with quantitative analysis across relatively large datasets and historical periods, for the most part made possible, indeed 'thinkable', through the collecting, modelling and analytical capacities of e-technologies. (While this is not an essential attribute it has been the case for all the recent Australian examples I can bring to mind.) Second, it has emerged after an 'anti-empirical' phase in critical theory in which empiricism was seen to be part of the package you got when you bought the dominant ideology; it seeks to address questions either not asked or not answered by that theory. But thirdly, it is also, in a positive sense, *post*-theory rather than anti-theory; that is, its logics have developed precisely through engagement with theories of text and culture that point us beyond literary autonomy. David Greetham, for example, a US textual scholar (in the bibliographical sense of the term), sees the history of the book not as earth-bound empiricism but as a manifestation of the 'postmodernist dispersal of the subject as an originary figure and its replacement by materiality, economics and power'.[16] Above all, what should make the new practices new is their capacity to reconfigure our understanding of the literary field—its structures and dynamics, its 'political economy', its temporalities—not just by supplying new information but through bringing a whole new set of objects and agents into view, working a kind of reversal of background and foreground, inside and outside, in the relation between text and context.

I want to insist on the post-theory point, although it won't apply to every individual trajectory or every kind of empirical work, as it represents the most productive way of understanding the relationship of the new studies of print culture to literary studies, and indeed to a range of other intellectual fields after the 'cultural turn'. If the new cultural history has grown negatively out of a certain weariness with the subversive paradigm and the routines of contemporary critique (the feeling that they had lost their capacity to generate new knowledge), it has also grown positively out of engagement with cultural studies and poststructuralist critical theory, as much as with empirical forms of book history. Theories of textuality or discourse, even the 'death of the author', always carried within them a double imperative. If the primary uptake was to extend textuality beyond literature until it covered the whole world as text, there was always another take possible, pointing us beyond the autonomy of the literary text in the opposite direction, to the worldly conditions of its existence, to its 'structured and structuring' determinations. This was a harder lesson for literary studies to learn, even for Marxist critics, because it was more disruptive of aesthetic autonomy. In my own case, I can think of a number of quite different pathways intersecting at various

---

[16] David Greetham, 'What is Textual Scholarship?', in Eliot and Rose, eds, *A Companion to the History of the Book*, p. 29.

points into the present: the experience of working on non-canonical texts (minor periodicals and bad socialist realist novels); the influence of Marxist literary theory with its invocation of the 'conditions of production and reception' (although this was mostly parlayed into ideology critique); meeting the poststructuralist assault on canonical ethico-formalist criticism; engaging with postcolonial literary theory and wanting to ask: if literary works could be subversive, who were they subversive for and under what conditions?; and finally, encountering the cultural industries model and studies of cultural consumption: what would happen, I was not the first to wonder, if we did the same for books?

As Katherine Bode put it when arguing for the application of quantitative analysis in Australian literary studies, poststructuralist and postmodernist theories 'reconstituted the literary text as inherently part of a system'.[17] If that has been taken primarily to mean a discursive system—and if 'discourse' has all-too-easily been folded back into literary textuality—we certainly do not want to lose this sense of structured and structuring discourses and of relations (discursive and extra-discursive) within a system; we might though want to relocate those systems and make them less text-like. What links much of the new work, and certainly the major signpost texts along the way, is precisely this engagement with structures or systems: the sense that books and readings are produced within a system, an economy, a field, a network, a circuit, a culture, a community; indeed within a 'structure of structures'.[18] There's a history to

---

[17] Katherine Bode, 'Beyond the Colonial Present: Quantitative Analysis, "Resourceful Reading" and Australian Literary Studies', *JASAL Special Issue: The Colonial Present* (2008): 184.

[18] This phrase comes from mis-remembering the discussion of literary history, formalism and institutions in John Frow's *Marxism and Literary History* (Oxford: Basil Blackwell, 1986), pp. 93–94, 177. The correct phrase is 'the system of systems' derived from Jurij Tynjanov, but perhaps the mis-remembered version

be written just on the competing metaphors that have been put forward to make the same kind of point about the relational, systemic or 'networked' nature of the field.

The new book or print history is, in this particular sense, 'poststructuralist', however impatient it might be with theory. In terms of explaining historical change, it will favour a model of periodic structural reorganisation rather than of gradual evolution (the sudden, uneven leap version of evolutionary theory rather than the slow gradualist one). Of course, the different metaphors will suggest different models. A network is probably imagined as looser, more fluid and unpredictable, than, say, Bourdieu's sense of a field, although that too is a model of dynamics.[19] Nonetheless the general point remains, whether the focus is on publishing, policy, genres, circulation or reading habits, and among critics or historians with very different time-scales and social maps in view. In Moretti's terms, 'it *isn't* a sum of individual cases: it's a collective system, that should be grasped as such, as a whole'.[20] Or St Clair, from his very different perspective, urging us to 'conceive of a culture as a complex developing system with many independent but interacting agents, including authors and readers, into which the writing, publication, and subsequent reading of a printed text were interventions'.[21] Closer to home, we can cite Paul Eggert's argument concerning late-nineteenth-century fiction in Australia, that 'only a modelling of the marketplace forces that acknowledged the competing agencies of authors, publishers, booksellers, libraries and reviewers could allow the tale of shifting tastes to be fully told'; or Tim Dolin's discussion of the way readers' responses to

---

better captures the sense of 'structured and structuring' relations in the cultural field.
[19] Pierre Bourdieu, *The Field of Cultural Production: Essays on Art and Literature*, trans. and ed. Randal Johnson (London: Polity, 1993).
[20] Moretti, *Graphs, Maps, Trees*, p. 4.
[21] St Clair, *The Reading Nation*, p. 6.

a particular text are 'shaped by its arrival into a dense network of texts and meanings'.[22] Perhaps this interest in structures and networks is why many of us keep returning to Bourdieu, even though the model of the field of cultural production always delivers less for specific analyses than it promises.[23]

In slightly different terms we might understand the task as that of building an *institutional* history of Australian literature or, rather, of literature in Australia. Such an institutional history seems to me to be the point of counting titles, following editions, mapping the spread of the periodical press, or searching for evidence of reading practices. The institutional, we might say, is the point at which empirical histories become cultural or social or intellectual history. It can be driven in one direction down to the histories of particular texts, publishers or reading communities, and in the other direction outwards towards a history of *mentalités*, national institutions or transnational networks. At both levels it will rely on extensive empirical research. As Simon During has suggested in the context of a debate on 'post-European' literatures:

> When we think of literatures from other places and times outside the protocols and values of close reading and aesthetic judgement (and even if we wish to defend these things) we need thick descriptions of these literature's institutionality. This requires precisely empiricist (often sociological) methods—even if we know in advance that these methods will present us with less reality and truth than we hope for or, indeed, need.[24]

---

[22] Paul Eggert, 'Australian Classics and the Price of Books: The Puzzle of the 1890s', *JASAL Special Issue: The Colonial Present* (2008): 131; Tim Dolin, 'First Steps Toward a History of the Mid-Victorian Novel in Colonial Australia', *Australian Literary Studies* 22.3 (May 2006): 291.

[23] See, for example, Ken Gelder, *Popular Fiction: The Logics and Practices of a Literary Field* (London: Routledge, 2004) and McDonald, *British Literary Culture*.

[24] Simon During, 'Comparative Literature', *ELH* 72.2 (2004): 317.

As well as studies of concrete institutions such as publishing houses, reading communities, writers' associations, schools and universities, censorship and patronage regimes, I take this call for institutional history to include studies such as Patrick Buckridge's of 'literary appreciation' or 'bookishness', or During's own earlier attempt at a history of 'literary sensibility' in colonial Australia; examples I've chosen because they *are* focused on the literary, even literature in a narrow sense, but not in the ways we associate with text-centred critique.[25] Or drawing on a rather different source, Lawrence Rainey criticises accounts of modernism that 'draw on arguments derived solely from the reading of literary texts':

> a procedure that evinces excessive faith in our capacity to specify the essence and social significance of isolated formal devices and to collate them with complex ideological and social formations, slighting the institutions that mediate between works and readerships, or between readerships and particular social structures. To focus on those institutions, instead, is to view Modernism as more than a series of texts or a set of ideas that found expression in them. It becomes a social reality, a configuration of agents and practices that converge in the production, marketing, and publicization of an idiom.[26]

While this kind of history will almost certainly have a 'de-canonising' or at least a relativising effect through dispersing literariness more

---

[25] Patrick Buckridge, 'The Age of Appreciation: Reading and Teaching Classic Literature in Australia in the Early Twentieth Century', *Australian Literary Studies* 22.3 (May 2006): 342–56 and 'Bookishness and Australian Literature', *Script and Print* 30.4 (2006): 223–36; Simon During, 'Out of England: Literary Subjectivity in the Australian Colonies, 1788–1867', in Judith Ryan and Chris Wallace-Crabbe, eds, *Imagining Australia: Literature and Culture in the New New World* (Cambridge, Mass.: Harvard University Press, 2004), pp. 3–21.

[26] Lawrence Rainey, 'The Cultural Economy of Modernism', in Michael Levenson, ed., *The Cambridge Companion to Modernism* (Cambridge: Cambridge University Press, 1999), p. 34.

broadly, it will not be motivated by the kinds of *anti*-canonical critique that drove earlier textual politics but rather by the desire for 'thick descriptions' of material and institutional forms, and the empirical and sociological methods for their investigation. In *that* process, questions of ideological or discursive effects might return, but in their 'radical situatedness' rather than their (or the critic's) radical textual politics.

Because of literature's peculiar cultural force, it helps to move outside the literary to see some of these points more clearly: through an analogy with television for example. It would certainly be possible to write the history of Australian television as a history of locally made programs, for there is now sufficient historical density and internal referencing, indeed what we might call traditions or canons, to make this worth doing; it could be canonising or anti-canonical. But such a history would represent only a small part of the meanings of 'television in Australia'. Even to explain the nature of local programs would require a 'thick' institutional history which would, inevitably, involve an account of Australian television's place within an international English-language television system. The meaning of any particular program or viewing occasion will be significantly determined by its location within this international system, and any account of audiences or consumption would need to begin from the fact that for most Australians most of the time, television will mean watching programs made elsewhere. Television in Australia is routinely local, national and international, if not quite all at once then certainly in sequence.[27] Arguably, its effects are both powerfully 'Australianising' and powerfully 'de-localising'. The point for the present argument is that this is a lot more like the situation of books and reading in Australian society than our models of Australian literature suggest.

---

[27] Tom O'Regan, *Australian Television Culture* (Sydney: Allen & Unwin, 1993), ch. 4.

To return to my earlier questions about literary history then, I now think of this work as involving a kind of double movement. The first move is the deferral or suspension of our interest in literature: dissolving or integrating the literary back into a more heterogeneous field of books, newspapers and magazines, back into a crowded media marketplace or print economy (as in a different kind of work, literary discourses have been folded back into broader discursive economies); in short, running literature back through its institutional contexts and social networks. In this gesture even the rarest texts become infected with ordinariness, while ordinary texts and ordinary readers become thoroughly significant. But the second move works in the opposite direction, lifting the literary back up again, as it were, such that the literary text (or oeuvre or career) re-emerges, now as one among many in a network of texts and readings, 'relatively autonomous' but bearing all the traces of the institutional history that defines its distinctive place within that field or economy (or in a historical sequence or geopolitical array of fields and economies). In a different register of cultural history, we can imagine a similar process for our interests in the national: deferring or denying these in histories of particular institutions outside the frame of a developing national culture or consciousness, in order that the national might re-emerge, better situated, understood relationally as a 'field within a field', one set of institutional structures among others.

This sense of a double movement (which of course is not necessarily sequential) is manifested in the double aspect of critical theory itself; and perhaps this in turn reflects the double face of literature. In the article mentioned earlier, Peter McDonald makes a case for the productive intersection of poststructuralist theory and interdisciplinary book history, and does so partly through resisting the 'after theory' narrative as a simple story of rise and fall. He distinguishes between two traditions in what he calls 'anti-essentialist' thinking on literature, by which he means the broad poststructuralist consensus against the idea of literature as a stable entity with essential, universal or normative characteristics. On one side are the 'sceptical anti-essentialists', including Stanley Fish and Bourdieu, who, in their different ways, stress the role of social or ideological forces, both agents and institutions, in defining and protecting particular versions of the literary. The literary thus becomes ideologically charged, giving rise in one direction to what I've been calling textual politics. On the other side are those he calls '*enchanted* anti-essentialists': enchanted, that is, by writing's own always 'excessive' energies (a strand he finds in Barthes and Blanchot; Derrida, unsurprisingly, presents a more complicated case). Enchanted anti-essentialism is invested in the belief 'that a particular piece of writing, in performing its distinctive literariness, might simultaneously disturb or subvert *a priori* ideas of the literary'.[28]

To find ourselves back with literary subversion or textual excess might seem to be about as far from empirical work and cultural materialism as it's possible to travel. But McDonald's argument is, first, that it is simply not possible to choose between the two anti-essentialisms, that literature requires 'a pure appreciation of the distinctiveness of specific texts [but one] that does not ignore their impure situatedness in larger social, political, and institutional histories' (222); and second, that this latter dimension is precisely where critical theory and book history intersect: 'both enterprises have, in their largely separate ways, highlighted the book's historical and cultural specificity ... as an artefact of particular technologies, legal histories, ideologies, and institutional practices' (223). This is not a compromise position but a way of pushing the two logics together. Bourdieu's concept of the field, McDonald argues, offers 'the most effective link between book history and theoretical reflections on literature' (225), although it is inadequate for dealing with the power of 'writing' to transform the field 'by exceeding or subverting its determinations' (226).

---

[28] McDonald, 'Ideas of the Book', p. 219. Subsequent references in text.

While my immediate response to that final formulation is to ask the materialist and book history questions—under what conditions, when and where, for whom, and with what effects?—McDonald's arguments parallel my own sense of the double nature of literary history, of literary history as *cultural* history, and the 'reforming role' of empirical book history within that model. McDonald himself illustrates his argument through close reference to the material form of three different editions of J.M. Coetzee's *Waiting for the Barbarians*, each edition, he argues, representing a 'particular kind of spatiotemporal event':

> That *Waiting for the Barbarian* ... appeared in English under three imprints between 1980 and 1982 is not a merely bibliographic fact. The Secker and Warburg, Penguin, and Ravan Press editions—the last was the imprint of the most important anti-apartheid publisher in South Africa—all situated it in very different social, political, critical and institutional histories, modifying its identity as a literary work in different national contexts or legally agreed transnational markets accordingly. (225)

The key point, again, is to place 'the radical situatedness of texts, as material and institutional forms, at the centre of historical inquiry' (222).

Dealing with the questions at this level of abstraction, with the emphasis on structures and systems, risks sounding as if I'm advocating a kind of 'super-history'—literary history indeed as the history of everything, all mapped within a single model of the field, the economy, the structure of structures. The point is rather that this sense of structures, institutions and networks will operate at *every* level, informing the most particularist case study; this, for example, is one implication of Bourdieu's model of the field, and it can be taken as an imperative towards disaggregation as well as towards large-scale modelling or 'systematisation'. Although in practice (or polemics) they often function as opposites, the value of *both* micro-histories and macro-histories should not need to be spelt out: the former revealing the contingencies of the individual case, the fine-grained detail of publication, availability and 're-printability', or the encounters of individual readers and reading communities (the details in fact that might resist systematic explanation); the latter seeking patterns over a long historical sweep or a large mass of disparate instances (structures that 'contain' the multiplicity and fragmentation of detail). My emphasis on structures, institutions and networks might best be seen as mediating between these two levels, drawing them back in together, as it were, as cultural history.

We've been better served in this respect by work on colonial culture than by that on the twentieth century, as if there's an inverse relation between the presence of canonical texts and authors on the one hand and the presence of 'thick' cultural history on the other. (Perhaps literature's new entanglements in policy, new marketisation and engagements with new media will mean that for the present century institutional contexts once again become unavoidable.) Despite all the gaps, work on colonial newspapers and magazines, reading societies, libraries, commercial theatre and professional networks has given us a relatively dense institutional history, as in the absence of canonical texts and a securely national context critics are forced to become historians and sociologists and to work across imperial and transnational networks. For the twentieth century this is still patchy. We still lack published book-length studies of the twentieth-century *Bulletin* and the twentieth-century Angus & Robertson.

Whether the focus is broad and distant or narrow and close-up, the implication of what I've been arguing is a history that's played across three intersecting scales—the history of Australian literature, the history of literature in Australia, and the history of books or print in (or 'through') Australian society. The study of reading or consumption will cut across all three; but in order to avoid the sense that reading is merely the end-point of production and circulation, merely a secondary effect, it also needs to be conceived separately, as originary and constitutive not merely as a destination. Indeed I suspect that studies of reading have the greatest potential to transform the field: as Dolin suggests, inviting us to rethink 'our assumptions about the constitutive role of fiction in culture

… because they resituate that constitutive role in the act of consumption as well as the act of production'; or Buckridge's argument that the 'reading culture' should be understood as an autonomous culture, quite distinct from the 'writing culture' upon which most literary studies and history have concentrated.[29] Reader-centred histories, like industry or institutional histories, will rarely find 'national cultural' or 'psychocultural' explanations sufficient; they will reveal the ways in which cultures are *not* language-like, not like novels or psyches writ large. In other words, even if studies of reading do not radically transform our understanding of 'Australian literature' narrowly defined, they are likely to alter our sense of its capacity to explain or stand in for Australian culture more broadly.

I hope it's clear that these ambitions stop well short of asking for a history of everything, that they point down and inwards as well as upwards and beyond. A renewed literary history, pulled through the practices of book history or print culture studies, will not only offer us a richer, institutionally dense cultural history of Australian books and reading, it might also provide better arguments for literary studies per se, even for the canon, at least in the curatorial sense that Robert Dixon has recently proposed.[30] Agnosticism towards literature in theory does not contradict a commitment to literary studies in practice.

---

[29] Dolin, 'First Steps', p. 276; Patrick Buckridge, 'Reading the Classics in Australia: Great Books Anthologies, 1890–1960', *Bibliographical Society of Australia and New Zealand Bulletin* 23.1 (1999): 47.

[30] Robert Dixon, 'Australian Literature—International Contexts', *Southerly* 67.1–2 (2007): 17.

2
The Book, Scholarly Editing and the Electronic Edition

Paul Eggert

Scholarly editing is our oldest empirical form of literary scholarship. The first chief librarian at Alexandria, Zenodotus of Ephesus (c. 325–c. 234 BC) developed, for his editions, a system of marginal markings of spurious lines in the competing manuscript recensions of originally oral works that the library was acquiring. The man who was probably his successor, Aristarchus of Samothrace (c. 220–c. 145 BC), tried to reduce the subjective element involved in the judgement of what was spurious and what authentic by introducing technical considerations of the manuscripts' palaeographic and codicological characteristics. Two millennia later, Nicholas Rowe's editorially emended edition of the works of Shakespeare, based on the Fourth Folio, was published in 1709; and later in the century the need for systematic collation of the earlier printings was gradually recognised. Three centuries later again, bringing a modern critical edition through the final stages of production—after the editorial work is supposedly finished—involves, more elaborately than in 1709, some months of work, proofreading and rechecking the several thousand internal cross-references and the hundreds of quotations in the front and end matter. So why bother with scholarly editions, I am sometimes asked, now that we can access e-texts at the touch of a few keystrokes? This chapter is at one level an extended answer to that innocent query. It is also a reflection on the different logics of the book and e-text, differences that we need to appreciate as we move forward into new modes of production and publication of literary scholarship.

The particular experience of getting the Academy Edition of *Robbery Under Arms* finished and to the printer in 2005–06 is still fresh in my mind. Computer and paper had gone hand in hand at every stage. The identification of the work's various versions, and of their relationship to one another, was a bibliographical enquiry that had taken a few years to resolve properly. It was aided by the inputting of the serial and book versions. The computer-collating of these versions gave me, as textual editor, the basic information from which to plot, and thus to understand, the complexities of the text's transmission over time. This in turn led me to an argument about the choice of copy-text and to a basically historical form of apparatus, recording how that first serialised version fared over many years of abridgement, new typesettings, regularising and bowdlerising. Settling that textual evidence down into a readable text and compiling a specially devised apparatus was of course time-consuming. But every variant recording served either to challenge or to confirm the editorial route I had chosen: all editions have this sort of automatic feedback-loop in their apparatus. It is essential to the editor and can be important to the reader who wants to engage with the history of the work and its successive receptions over the decades. Already one answer to the innocent query with which I started is obvious: texts on Project Gutenberg and nearly all of those collected within the Scholarly Electronic Text and Image Service at the University of Sydney Library (SETIS) have not been subject to scrutiny of this kind.

The scholarly editor feels a keen responsibility to present the evidence reliably, always keeping in mind the inherent logic of the book, which dictates the need both for economy and clarity. One considers keenly the rationale for and the effect of presenting textual apparatus at foot of page as opposed to the end of the book. Different reading experiences result. But, having made one's decision about this and many other matters, one then has to follow through. Being systematic—as opposed to whimsically preferring this variant from this source today and that one from that source tomorrow, because it 'reads better'—is necessary if the edition is to be of use as something other than an expression of the editor's aesthetic tastes. Scholarly editions are expensive to produce and to buy, so they must have long shelf lives in the library. So that necessitates, in those final months of production, a thorough checking that the editorial conventions—some of them traditional, and perhaps some innovative that had had to be specially devised, and later adapted and re-adapted—have in fact been used consistently. The editor must also check (as in the case of the *Robbery Under Arms* edition) that copy-editorial conventions for expression in front and end matter have actually been followed; that the volume's explanatory notes, historical background essay, the stage and screen adaptations essay and the appendix on Australianisms and slang (all of which Elizabeth Webby prepared), the essay on places in the novel (which Julieanne Lamond contributed), as well as the accompanying maps, the textual apparatus, both foot-of-page and end-of-volume *and* the extensive introduction all had no mistakes or extraneous matter remaining that did not support the volume as a whole. We needed to ensure as best we could that nothing had been said twice and that everything was correctly and fully cross-referenced: that this book was, in short, a unified piece of scholarship.

The anxiety of finding error, illogic, redundancy or infelicity is what keeps you going through this process. The scholarly edition, you have become all too aware, is a complex reference book *about* the work you have edited, as well as being, you hope and trust, a reliable presentation of the text of the work. It is, in other words, a meta-book: a book about a book, where both books are present in the same, inevitably bulky volume. When it at length arrives, and you have the printed scholarly edition in your hands for the first time, it seems like a miraculous simplification and clarification of the mass of photocopies of the early printings—with different paginations and texts, some abridged, some not—with which you had been struggling for all too long. You realise as you turn the pages of the scholarly edition that this knowledge-machine *works*, as you'd prayed it would. Is not your editorial passion a response to the book form itself, which you only have one chance to get right?

What is the alternative? If we are to take, instead, the emerging electronic-texts route we will have to accept the working logic of that environment just as we and our predecessors have always internalised the working and production logic of the book. The shift from the scroll to the codex gradually brought out increasingly ingenious forms of cross-referencing, and many forms of reference book today consist of small chunks of text cross-referenced to other small chunks. Therefore one might say, from the perspective of today, that the default position with reference books was always already electronic, the moment scrolls were superseded. Today, we are moving on once again, changing medium, if more slowly than the frenzied futurologists of the early 1990s predicted when the internet was first invented. This is especially the case with reference books such as dictionaries and encyclopaedias, but even there the printed and electronic forms seem to be surviving in complementary forms, carving out their different markets, serving different users' needs.

Scholarly editions work in a densely cross-referenced way, and they mostly deal in texts of greater than screen length. Thus they are harder to develop electronically than forms with smaller text-chunks such as lightly cross-referenced dictionaries. This fact produces difficulties. Page-and-line-number referencing systems, such as printed scholarly editions use, are sensitive to page layout and choice of font. Since print pages are not ideal for computer presentation, a basic problem faces anyone trying to generate two forms of edition from the same set of XML files (eXtensible Markup Language files).[1] If intended for print production they are usu-

---

[1] The comments in this paragraph have benefited from an email discussion with John Lavagnino, co-general editor of *The Collected Works of Thomas Middleton*

ally encoded in terms of their future appearance in print: that is, encoded according to whether the encoded text chunk is meant to be, for example, a speech heading, section head or apparatus entry. Each of these categories of text is then styled according to a separate set of instructions about the appearance of all instances of the category. This serves the print-production need for achieving the desired layout of the page, and in principle it allows the text that has been thus encoded to be used for another purpose. The encoding has to be enhanced for the new purpose, while leaving the text alone.

While pdfs of the printed pages can be readily produced without enhancement and made available electronically with ease, an electronic edition needs to observe a different, non-book logic if its potential is to be realised. For a start, something less page-bound is desirable, with its own linkings, and smarter search capacities than pdfs can afford. A lot of metadata need to be added if this is to happen. (The danger of adding metadata to already checked and rechecked text files is discussed below.) At the moment some university presses with a backlist of scholarly editions, or in the business of producing new ones, are struggling with this very problem.

What is implied for the scholarly editor by the additional phase of encoding is in effect two production lines for editions that are otherwise joined at the hip. This is a significant matter, since keeping the two in perfect synch when complex proofs are being checked becomes very difficult indeed. Although this is not an insuperable problem, the modern production process begins to mimic the originally divided textual situations that the scholarly edition was meant to clarify, record and resolve. This is not ideal.

(Oxford: Oxford University Press, 2007) and information from Sarah Stanton at Cambridge University Press. I also thank Ian Donaldson, co-general editor of the forthcoming *Cambridge Ben Jonson*, for his kind assistance.

Print editions will remain, I predict, but will be more readily understood as inevitably only a partial expression of the work. In particular, print on demand, as the technology improves, will serve a wider variety of needs than it can at present. Electronic editions themselves, as experimentation continues, will be different from the grand experiments we are probably all familiar with, such as the William Blake Archive and the Rossetti Archive hosted at the Institute for Advanced Technology in the Humanities at the University of Virginia. These archives have in some ways duplicated the production logic of the book. Here, editors create and fix. Readers read and are able to launch sophisticated queries of the website that books do not allow; but readers do not in any essential way control the materials or their organisation. We can therefore think of these archives as an impressive first stage, a 1990s stage, in electronic scholarly editing that we need to move beyond if we are to benefit fully from observing the inherent logic of the electronic domain.

That logic, it seems to me, is to be fundamentally collaborative and open-ended in the production of knowledge. It is to accommodate our humanities traditions while becoming, to use the convenient German term, more *wissenschaftlich* (that is, systematic and rigorous: as opposed to *scientific* in the English sense, with its implication of thorough objectivity). Scholarly editors and editorial theorists have ample reason—just as literary and cultural critics do—to be grateful for the (extended) moment of high theory: it licensed all of us to think afresh about text. But, thriving on paradox as it did, it also hindered some practical ways of seeing and dealing with literary phenomena. *Yes*, we participate in what we know; and *yes*, objectivity is strictly speaking beyond us; and *yes*, forms of power can be implicated in what we say and inflect how we say it. But does that familiar poststructuralist dilemma mean that texts can *only* be thought of as traces of circulating discourses? Or that rigorous, empirical forms of collaborative enquiry about texts are impossible?

If we look back over the last thirty years of literary studies what we see is a series of, in the geological sense of the word, *catastrophic* events. As I put it in an essay I wrote in 1997, published in 1999:

> In the humanities and social sciences, knowledge is not accumulative and progressive as it is in the sciences. Paradigm shifts in scientific practice are rare, but thinking in the humanities is marked by the emergence of new perspectives and vocabularies which reconfigure the existing landscape of thought, introducing topographies which first alienate and then annex, by redefinition, parts of the old one until the entire territory be covered, and swamps and backwaters that were overlooked under the old dispensation are brought into connection with the new mainstream. A previously untapped power of explanation is enjoyed; intellectual muscles are flexed. But it all happens with too great a rush: as the older concepts are rejected much that had been accounted for is pushed aside. Enduring habits of thought, pockets of resistance, which the latest intellectual movement has overlooked sooner or later return, in a self-reinvented form, to disturb the new, always multi-faceted, potentially conflict-ridden, never-quite-achieved consensus.[2]

This, I take it, is what the so-called new empiricism in Australian literary studies, which the present volume is proclaiming, is doing right now. But will it be possible for us be a little steadier and less hyped so as to avoid being retrospectively cast as merely the latest in the series of catastrophes I have just described? Can we achieve this? And can we avoid the triumphalism, with the career-ending, or career-diverting, effects that it had on some academics in English departments who came to believe that the expertise they had to offer was no longer wanted?

Certainly we can try. I see two reasons to be optimistic. For a start, researchers, if their work is genuinely empirical, are very interested in advancing the enabling conditions of their methodologies. But also, if

---

[2] Paul Eggert, 'Where Are We Now with Authorship and the Work?', *Yearbook of English Studies, Special Issue: Text as Evidence* 29 (1999): 88–102, 88.

they are humanities types, they will wish to understand the intellectual baggage that their methodological conceptions may contain. That is one thing, and we are good at discursive analysis of this kind. For a second thing, empirical research is typically hard work. Those who do it want it to last, or at least some parts of it to last: and such work can best do that by remaining part of ongoing research agendas. Here is where my crystal ball—whose cover I have just removed—tells me that the electronic enablement of humanities research offers real hope, at last. I look at it this way, through a series of conditionals.

If our enquiry is collaborative; and *if* we have suitable electronic platforms to host that enquiry, able automatically to interrogate relevant information and bibliographical and scanned and ocr'd newspaper resources, as well as all extant textual versions and documentary images of the work we may be studying; and *if* all of this can be brought together coherently onto our desktop or onto what I call the electronic worksite; and *if* we are then able to link our interpretation or argument or mapping at every point to the texts (in whatever medium) on which we are commenting; and *if* we are able to leave our results and the traces of our activity across this worksite of relevant materials so that others may follow if they find our track through it persuasive or suggestive; and if *they* are able, as a part of their research in turn to leave their track across the worksite visible and their contribution available for successors to learn from or to dispute—if *all* of these desiderata come to pass, and *if*, finally but crucially, the Australian federal government, prompted by a host of research deputy vice-chancellors, agree that such collaborative, electronically hosted and facilitated scholarship *counts* for funding purposes—in other words, if appropriate reward systems are put in place—then and only then will we realise the benefits of empirical, electronically enabled methodologies in the literary field on other than the boutique scale that we presently enjoy.

Only when my scenario is fulfilled will we be able to fuse empirical results with the more creative energies and intuitive insights that have always enlivened our common endeavour but which have generally gone empirically untested. We tend to be too tolerant of the new truth-claim that introduces a seductive new terminology able to generalise the established field away from under us. Keeping the empirical and the theoretical in continuous tension will lead, I believe, to a healthier outcome.[3] Electronic worksites, by virtue of their collaborative methodologies, may create the climate of expectation for this to happen, perhaps indeed the assumption that it must happen. Knowledge creation will, I hope, become more accumulative rather than catastrophic in its rhythms of inevitable change.

If this is sounding like visionary preaching, the sobering antidote is ready to hand: *who* is going to set up this grand infrastructure, even if the time is propitious, now that, institutionally speaking at least, the moment of high theory is over? The funding signs are more promising for the humanities in Australia than they were only three years ago. We have been getting funding from the small Australian Research Council infrastructure schemes (RIEF, then LIEF) since the mid-1990s for the AustLit database, first at the University of New South Wales at the Australian Defence Force Academy (ADFA) and more recently, as a consortium of university partners, via the University of Queensland. And now at last, in its support for the Aus-e-Lit project from 2008, the much bigger infrastructure funding scheme (National Collaborative Research Infrastructure Strategy: NCRIS) has begun to act on its stated obligation to support the development of infrastructure for humanities eResearch. Let us hope that this is only a beginning.

---

[3] Cf. David Hoover's commentary on Jerome McGann's *Radiant Textuality: Literature after the World Wide Web* (New York: Palgrave, 2001): 'Hot-Air Textuality: Literature after Jerome McGann', *Text and Technology* 14 (2005): 71–103; and Hoover's 'The End of the Irrelevant Text: Electronic Texts, Linguistics and Literary Theory', *Digital Humanities Quarterly* 1.2 (2007): not paginated.

Electronic Scholarly Editions and the Worksite

If I look back over the last fifteen years to 1993, when I first became involved (rather amateurishly) in the development of systems for electronic scholarly editions, my first conclusion is that, together with my stalwart collaborators Chris Tiffin and Graham Barwell, we got into the business too early. The original idea was to take advantage of the computerised transcriptions of the versions of the works being edited for the Academy Editions of Australian Literature project at the Australian Scholarly Editions Centre at ADFA. Editorial theorists in the 1980s, of whom I was one, had been getting increasingly irritated with the restrictions on the reporting in scholarly editions of versions of the work that varied from the one that was established by the editor, on the basis of final authorial intention, for the reading text. The basic source of textual authority—authorial intention—had gone unchallenged since the founding period of the New Bibliography in the early part of the twentieth century, and the Greg-Bowers methodology it finally induced for scholarly editions had been concreted into position by the early 1960s. What if, we dared to think, we could open the work up, so that the reader could, as it were, enter the same waters of textuality in which the editor had been immersed when preparing the edition?

It turned out to be easier said than done. The Text-Encoding Initiative (TEI) had only just been enunciated and promised a permanence for the encoding of humanities texts. This was crucial since, as we were learning, there was no point in pouring time and money into schemes of presentation and collation if they depended on transient software and operating systems. This seems so obvious now, but in the early 1990s we had to learn it.

Peter Shillingsburg had visited ADFA's forerunner college, Duntroon, in 1984 and 1985. His textual collation program Computer Assisted Scholarly Editing (CASE) had been funded by a grant from the US government's National Endowment for the Humanities; it was intended to assist his edition of the novels of Thackeray. CASE was ported to the

ADFA mainframe computer, and then to successive ones as each was replaced. By 1995, Phill Berrie, a Macintosh programmer at ADFA, had joined our team and had ported what was by then PC-CASE for the Mac. The funding I was able to secure for the electronic project was on-again, off-again and the programming assistance it paid for was always only part-time. Nor was there funding for more than one programmer, a fact which finally scuppered further development of the project in 2005. It remains an orphan, but its main ideas have filtered through into the wider digital humanities debate.

In the early 1990s, there was no software available for the Mac that could read SGML, the standardised general markup language for documents, of which the TEI is a more specialised dialect for the humanities. Also we noticed that TEI was itself soon subject to periodic rewritings. It is up to version 5 at the moment. This was shifting ground. What scholarly editorial work could responsibly be done in these circumstances?

By then our programmer Phill Berrie was enrolled in a MSc. For his thesis—working with me (bizarrely, as I thought at the time) as one of his advisers, and even reading Gaskell's *New Introduction to Bibliography*—he hit on the brilliant idea that we could guarantee the accuracy of all our text versions via a checksum algorithm if only we divided up the digital information in our text files into content on the one hand and markup on the other. This was counter-intuitive because the 1990s paradigm—into which, it has to be said, digital text collections around the world including SETIS have invested a lot of energy and money—was and still is that markup should be stored in-line within the text file.

After some initial experiments in which we learned more than we achieved, we moved on to re-purposing the text-files that were being used to create the print Academy Edition of Marcus Clarke's great convict novel from the 1870s, *His Natural Life*. The print edition appeared in 2001 and the electronic edition in iterations between 2002 and 2004.

At first we thought we were creating an electronic equivalent to the scholarly edition, only with more information: facsimiles of the early editions, transcriptions and ancillary information. If the reader did not agree with the editorial policy then at least all the information on which the edited text had been based would be readily available. Creating this textual assembly turned out to be a much bigger job than we thought, but users now had access to a preceding, much longer serialised version from which the novel itself had been adapted by the author and much reduced in length. This version could not be contained within the print edition. But users still stood essentially outside the archive, just as they did with the printed edition; and we had to admit that, given sufficient volumes, we could have provided in book form what we were providing electronically anyway. Ours was an act of gathering, collating, organising and making accessible electronically the related, but otherwise dispersed, materials. The e-edition (an e-archive, really) is still operational on the Scholarly Editions Centre website (at www.unsw.adfa.edu.au/JITM). Our interest was solely in functionality, not appearance: no professional screen-design work was done to enhance the look of it. With the printed Academy Editions on the other hand, we had been able to draw on hundreds of years of experience with typesetting, layout, volume division and cross-referencing systems. It had been possible—more or less—to imagine the finished product in considerable detail from the start, even though, as I have confessed, some praying went with it. With the electronic edition, praying was just about all that we collaborators—three English literature academics—could do.

The main, underlying function of the system that Phill Berrie came up with was that, whenever the user turned to the e-edition, the act of tailoring the visualisation of one of its versions on screen, or of bringing explanatory notes to bear on it, simultaneously authenticated the text of the version the user had called up. The necessary markup for the visualisation was stored separately from the text in stand-off files and was introduced just in time. Hence the name we adopted for it, Just In Time Markup (JITM). If the text file had been corrupted in any way the user was told. The system still works.

Authentication is crucial to scholarly editing. A text's hard-won authenticity must be able to be guaranteed over time, despite the introduction of new operating systems and software. But with standard in-line markup being added to the text file to incorporate new dimensions of interpretation, there is a constant danger of unintended change. Achieving automatic authentication was the main aim of JITM. But what we realised, once the authentication routine had been perfected, was that we had done something that might have a wider application than we had originally intended. By splitting off text from interpretation of it (which is what markup essentially is) we had laid the groundwork for collaborative interpretation of the text that could be stored separately from it and would not endanger its accuracy. We next set out to demonstrate this with the Jerilderie Letter project. It was published in 2005 at the same address and remains available; I have discussed it in detail elsewhere in the context of an argument about arranging collaborative literary eResearch around what I call the 'worksite'.[4]

Scholarly Editing as a Model for Empirical Literary Research?

So why bother with printed scholarly editions? went the innocent enquiry with which I began this chapter. The answer may be clearer now. They embody their preceding empirical research about the life of a particular work or works in a peculiarly focused if not fully comprehensive

---

[4] Paul Eggert, 'Text-Encoding, Theories of the Text, and the "Work-site"', *Literary and Linguistic Computing* 20 (2005): 425–35; revised and extended as 'The Book, E-Text and the "Work-Site"', in Marilyn Deegan and Kathryn Sutherland, eds, *Text Editing, Print, and the Digital World* (London: Ashgate, 2009), pp. 63–82. See also Phill Berrie, Paul Eggert, Graham Barwell and Chris Tiffin, 'Authenticating Electronic Editions', in Lou Burnard, Katherine O'Brien O'Keeffe and John Unsworth, eds, *Electronic Textual Editing* (New York: Modern Language Association, 2006), pp. 436–48.

form. They facilitate the awareness that one cannot so much read a literary work as read *in* it, that each text of the work and each material embodiment are necessarily only partial expressions of that ongoing life. Based on study of the textual documents, scholarly editions return us to indefeasible evidence of the textual agency of the author and of others: a sobering realisation after the grand diversion away from the notion of authorship of the last thirty years.

But they can't do everything. Because scholarly editing is so time-consuming and can be flattening in its after-effects, editors usually have little energy left over to pursue the literary-critical meanings of the new textual and other information that they have brought to the table. If they did so, literary research would be enriched with the kinds of evidence about textual evolution that New Criticism, with its eye on the finished Verbal Icon, could not endure, and that Foucauldian and other discursive criticism typically sees as irrelevant because of the now standard view of meaning-production as essentially unauthored and in circulation, as unbounded by human intention.

Yet when editors have reflected on the wider meaning of textual variation in the works they have edited, the focus has yielded arguments of peculiar richness in the literary debate. The printing of two *King Lears* in the Oxford Shakespeare of 1986 emerged from a growing editorial and text-critical sensitivity towards evidence of authorial revision in the early printings. The idea of a 'performance Shakespeare' and a counteracting 'materialist Shakespeare' grew out of reactions to the existing editorial tradition. The Clarendon edition of Hardy's *Tess of the D'Urbervilles* of 1983 included a most sensitive essay by Juliet Grindle and Simon Gatrell on the meaning of Hardy's own punctuation in the manuscript, and the benefit of allowing it to prevail in the edited text, as against the deadening effect of the regularised forms in which Hardy's wordings had previously been presented. Kathryn Sutherland's recent book *Jane Austen's Textual Lives* recovers the social milieu in which Austen's writing took place, inspired by female companionship, and then read aloud within the family setting while the works were still in unpublished manuscript form. She finds reflections of this early life in the punctuation of the first edition of *Mansfield Park* of 1814. These traces were partially obliterated when a second edition was typeset in 1816; and Austen's scholarly editor of the 1920s, R.W. Chapman, perpetuated the changes. Sutherland argues that the reading voice can be heard more clearly in the 1814 typesetting; and this is no trivial matter for a novelist who is generally credited with having invented for the English novel the subtleties of free indirect style, with its range of ironic possibilities and deft shifts of focus.[5] Marta Werner's attention to the original form of domestic publication of Emily Dickinson's poems—written on scraps of paper and envelopes, thus dictating those characteristically short lines and idiosyncratic punctuation—also yields a richness of interpretation that their later regularised public forms blunted and refused.[6] There has been far too little of this kind of attention paid to Australian literature. We have remained the poor cousin, although a reading of the introductions of the

---

[5] Nevertheless, Chapman's understanding of the meaning-laden nature of the typography and design of editions contemporary with their author, the importance of not regularising old spelling and punctuation, and of the inevitable deterioration of a text subject to frequent resettings puts him (surprisingly) in the more modern camps of W.W. Greg and Jerome McGann. Cf. R.W. Chapman, 'Old Books and Modern Reprints' and 'The Textual Criticism of English Classics', in his *The Portrait of a Scholar and Other Essays Written in Macedonia, 1916-1918* (London: Oxford University Press, 1922), pp. 48-65 and 65-79.

[6] See: essays in Gary Taylor and Michael Warren, eds, *The Division of the Kingdoms: Shakespeare's Two Versions of King Lear* (Oxford: Clarendon Press, 1983); 'Some Features of the Manuscript Punctuation', in Juliet Grindle and Simon Gatrell's edition of Thomas Hardy, *Tess of the d'Urbervilles* (Oxford: Clarendon Press, 1983), pp. 88-99; Kathryn Sutherland, *Jane Austen's Textual Lives: From Aeschylus to Bollywood* (Oxford: Oxford University Press, 2005); and Marta Werner, *Emily Dickinson's Open Folios: Scenes of Reading, Surfaces of Writing* (Ann Arbor: University of Michigan Press, 1995).

Academy Editions and of some of the Colonial Texts Series volumes will show that an essential start has been made.

What stops more from being done? I believe it is the lingering effects of the division of the kingdom that English departments entrenched in the immediate postwar period. Critics thought of editorial and even biographical scholarship as a world well lost; and the scholars narrowed their enterprise to avoid conflict with the organising tropes of the critics.[7] The situation, which must have entailed a great waste of opportunities and intellectual energy, was inimical to collaboration across the divide. One major form of scholarship—the critical edition—was normally presented as complete, thorough, finished: in book form. Yet nearly all the critical editions were collaborative in their preparation (at least between general editor and editor; but usually more scholars were involved, and many were typically thanked in extended acknowledgements pages). On the other hand, criticism was rarely collaborative.

If one puts one's habitual scepticism aside, the future prospect I broached above seems to hold out an opportunity for a regathering of the flock into a single fold. I do not say this because I believe there will be a sudden, Christmassy outburst of goodwill. Rather, I would point to the inherent logic of the electronic organisation of cultural materials: both of our access to them, and of the necessary curation (as it is called) of this data. Here, for instance, is one likely effect: our obligation as literary scholars and critics will change as ignorance of the resources hidden in

---

[7] The locus classicus is the exchange between F.R. Leavis and F.W. Bateson in the early 1950s, conducted in the journals they edited: *Scrutiny* (Cambridge) and *Essays in Criticism* (Oxford). The essays (which are reprinted together with a 'Rejoinder' by Leavis and a 'Postscript' by Bateson, in Leavis's *A Selection from Scrutiny* [Cambridge: Cambridge University Press, 1968, vol. 2]) are, respectively: Bateson, 'The Function of Criticism at the Present Time', *Essays in Criticism* 3 (1953): 1–27; and Leavis, 'The Responsible Critic: Or the Function of Criticism at any Time', *Scrutiny* 19 (1952–53): 162–83.

newspapers and manuscript collections becomes a thing of the past. There will be data against which to test at least some aspects of the heady generalisation: if it survives the test it will be the stronger for it. The capacity to risk offering it, though, is essential. Literary research will always need the sensitised close reading, as well as the grand synoptic overview that changes the view of the field from above. But because, in an electronic environment, viable contributions will be able to be more fractionated than before, and offered in relation to a tradition of earlier contributions, the opportunity for cross-fertilisation of the various forms of literary enquiry may become better than it has ever been.

3
Old Tricks for New Dogs: Resurrecting Bibliography and Literary History

Carol Hetherington

Few would argue with the observation made in the *Concise Oxford Dictionary of Literary Terms* that the term 'empiricism' 'as used in modern literary theory ... usually has an unfavourable sense, referring to those critical approaches that dismiss theoretical abstraction in the belief that texts (or facts of history or biography) can "speak for themselves" without the intervention of analysis and interpretation'. The *Dictionary* further defines 'one who pursues any inquiry within the limits of empiricism, or who regards theory as a distraction ... [as] an empiricist'. In these terms, bibliographers must surely be the most empirical of researchers in the field of literary studies and, like others of an empirical inclination, they have been, to say the least, unfashionable in Australia for several decades. Their discipline is barely represented in university courses, is considered ineligible for research funding, and has been conspicuously absent from conference programs. Indeed the principles, practices and tools of bibliography are little understood by a generation of researchers.

The work of Australian bibliography, set in motion in the 1940s by the legendary Morris Miller, came to a halt in the late 1970s, stalled by concentration on new critical and theoretical approaches to literature, until it was revived in the 1990s by the collaborative projects that resulted in the formation of AustLit. The relatively recent shift of focus to book history, reading and readership, and print culture studies has given new impetus to empirical research. But this shift has also exposed gaps and inaccuracies in the story of what we as a society read and wrote—gaps that result to a significant degree from this focus away from bibliographical research.

AustLit: The Australian Literature Resource is an electronic bibliography which preserves the richness of the Australian bibliographic tradition in a contemporary format, continuing, updating and enhancing its work. It is both a research tool and a research repository and provides a unique opportunity for data analyses that have the potential to open up new perspectives on Australian literary history. To be meaningful, these evidence-based studies must be able to draw on informed and meticulously compiled data. Such data can only be produced by trained bibliographers. In this chapter I want to argue for the need to reinstate bibliography as the cornerstone of literary studies, with central importance not only in literary scholarship but in teaching, specifically in the undergraduate curriculum.

The Resourceful Reading conference itself arose out of a perception about 'New Directions', described by Robert Dixon and David Carter at an ASAL mini-conference in February 2007. At the 2008 ASAL conference in Wollongong, Paul Eggert summarised their views thus:

> Their proposal was ... that the Literary Theory movement in Australia had run out of steam. They argued that new forms of empirical research, including databases and data mining, as well as the recent resurgence of book history, when taken together with the return of older forms such as literary histories, author biographies, scholarly editions and descriptive bibliographies, potentially offer ways of understanding literary works afresh by more densely locating them in the various contexts from which they arose.

So in a climate where empiricism is newly respectable, is it time for bibliographers to come in from the cold? What do we mean by the term bibliography? D.F. McKenzie defines it as 'the discipline that studies texts as recorded forms, and the processes of their transmission including their production and reception'.[1] I use it to include enumerative, descriptive, analytical and annotative bibliography; it also involves book history and basic biographical and literary research. Bibliography has not always been relegated to the fringe and deemed an 'ancient madness'.[2] E. Morris Miller's *Australian Literature* (1940), updated and extended to 1950 by Frederick Macartney, was the first modern attempt at a comprehensive bibliography of Australian literature. Miller's breathtakingly simple and optimistic intention was to 'place on record the extent of Australian authorship',[3] a task that he (and others) saw as an essential foundation for the study of the national literature. Writing in 1940, Miller says the 'development of literature in Australia has reached the stage when the demand for criticism has become impelling ... criticism cannot accomplish its purpose without the aid of bibliography'.[4] Nobody disagreed.

Bibliographical studies in Australia have never been so highly regarded since. When I wrote the abstract for this chapter, I was cautious in my references to the academic climate that has prevailed in Australian literary studies for the last few decades. After all, I was acting as an apologist for my own field from a position outside the academy. I chose restrained language, using the terms 'unfashionable' and 'unfavourable'. I should have been bolder. Well-respected academics overseas do not use such timid language, notably Jerome McGann, a prominent critic of the

---

[1] D.F. McKenzie, *Bibliography and the Sociology of Texts* (Cambridge: Cambridge University Press, 1999), p. 12.
[2] David Leon Higden, 'Ancient Madness or Contemporary Wisdom? A New Literary Research Methods Course', *Profession* (2002): 143.
[3] E. Morris Miller, *Australian Literature From its Beginnings to 1935: A Descriptive and Bibliographical Survey of Books by Australian Authors in Poetry, Drama, Fiction, Criticism and Anthology with Subsidiary Entries to 1938* (Melbourne: Melbourne University Press, 1940), p. 9.
[4] Ibid., p. 1.

regard in which bibliography has been held for several decades. He speaks of a 'widespread malaise' in humanities education, 'a system of apartheid' in 'literary and cultural studies' with editing, bibliography and textual studies regarded 'as menial, if somehow also necessary'.[5] Others, such as Philip Cohen, have no hesitation in using terms such as 'aggressively marginalized'.[6]

Although the status of bibliography progressively declined from the 1960s, it has nevertheless continued in reasonably vigorous health, maintaining a dogged presence even if consigned to the sidelines. There was no attempt to carry on the updating of the comprehensive bibliography of Miller and Macartney until the Bibliography of Australian Literature project (begun in 1990s), but a rich and diverse range of smaller, specialist scholarly bibliographies regularly appeared. Examples include several series of bibliographies such as the *Australian Literary Studies* annual bibliography, begun in 1964, *The Year's Work in English Studies* entries and the Victorian Fiction Research Guides series (1979–2002); Gregory Hubble's *The Australian Novel: A Title Checklist 1900–1970* (1970); Grahame Johnston's *Annals of Australian Literature* (1970), revised by Joy Hooton and Harry Heseltine (1992); and numerous bibliographies devoted to specific forms, genres and individual authors.[7] They are

---

[5] Jerome McGann, 'A Note on the Current State of Humanities Scholarship', *Critical Inquiry* 30 (Winter 2004): 409.

[6] Philip Cohen, 'Is There a Text in This Discipline? Textual Scholarship and American Literary Studies', *American Literary History* 8.4 (Winter 1996): 728.

[7] Other examples include Stephen Torre's *The Australian Short Story 1940–1980: A Bibliography* (Sydney: Hale & Iremonger, 1984); John Loder's *Australian Crime Fiction: A Bibliography 1857–1993* (Port Melbourne: Thorpe in association with National Centre for Australian Studies, 1994); Marcie Muir and Kerry White's *Australian Children's Literature* (Melbourne: Melbourne University Press, 1992); Sneja Gunew et al., eds, *A Bibliography of Australian Multicultural Writers* (Geelong: Centre for Studies in Literary Education, Humanities, Deakin University, 1992); Debra Adelaide's *Bibliography of Australian Women's Literature* (Port

testimony to the commitment of scholars who have persevered in editorial and bibliographic work despite scant return in terms of professional reward or credit.

The most important single development in Australian literary bibliography since Morris Miller has been the formation of AustLit in 1999. This brought together in a single electronic format a range of print bibliographies and electronic initiatives.[8] The literary community clearly recognised the ability of electronic bibliographies to overcome restrictions of time, space and format, thus allowing continual and progressive updating, correction and revision, multiple access points to data and ease of linkage and cross-referencing. Funding bodies obviously found 'developing electronic resources' more exciting and acceptable, more 'relevant' than 'bibliography'. And AustLit has continued to attract substantial funding, although the term 'bibliography' is not prominent in grant applications.

But AustLit *is* primarily a bibliographic resource, albeit a new and sophisticated one which has extended, and can continue to extend, the scope of bibliography. It has crossed from the one-dimensionality of older bibliographic records to the granularity of 'layered' records, and can describe contents as well as contexts and relationships. AustLit's imple-

---

Melbourne: Thorpe in association with National Centre for Australian Studies, 1991); Hugh Anderson, Ma Zuyi and Chen Zhengfa's *Australian Writing Translated into Chinese, 1954–1988* (Ascot Vale, Vic.: Red Rooster Press, 1989); Alan Lawson's bibliography of *Patrick White* (Melbourne: Oxford University Press, 1974); Ian Sysons's unpublished index to *Realist Writer*; Elizabeth Webby's annotated bibliography *Early Australian Poetry* (Sydney: Hale & Iremonger, 1982), which lists poetry published in newspapers before 1850; and Toni Johnson-Woods's *Index to Serials in Australian Periodicals and Newspapers: Nineteenth Century* (Canberra: Mulini Press, 2001); Brian Hubber and Vivian Smith's *Patrick White: A Bibliography* (New Castle, Del.: Oak Knoll Press, 2004).
[8] Details of the formation of AustLit are available on its website, www.austlit.edu.au/about/history [Accessed 22 February 2009].

mentation of a new bibliographical data-model, the Functional Requirements for Bibliographic Records (FRBR),[9] allows for a rich contextualisation of literary works, and dissolves the boundaries between critical and creative literature, and between biographical and bibliographical information. It also provides information on publishing history and reception by tracking individual texts, in a detailed and descriptive way, from creation and production to revision and reception. The series of grants to AustLit, and to individual researchers, each year since 2002 has ensured the continued development and expansion of the resource such that AustLit itself has become a reference work-in-progress. As details of new research are added they illuminate and develop other information already contained within the resource or recently added to it. New federated searching functions under development, and planned links to other online resources such as the National Library's People Australia service, will continue to enhance its usefulness. A growing body of digitised material housed both within AustLit and in other institutional repositories, and the development of collaborative research functionality within AustLit, are opening up further exciting possibilities.

At the end of 2008 we have at our disposal a unique bio-bibliographic resource for Australian literary studies, print culture studies and book history. It is particularly valuable for literary-historical research and contains the raw material to answer a wide variety of research questions. Fortunately bibliographical data are immune from fashion. They are not subject to prejudices and trends. However, the fact that nobody asks a question does not mean the question is not important or the answer is

---

[9] The FRBR model was developed by the International Federation of Library Associations in 1998. Their website is available at www.ifla.org/VII/s13/frbr/frbr.htm [Accessed 22 February 2009]. AustLit's was the first full-scale implementation of the model and details of this are available on the AustLit website, www.austlit.edu.au/about/metadata [Accessed 22 February 2009].

not available in the bibliographic data. This is well illustrated by the case of Australian crime fiction. The literary gatekeepers of the 1940s and 1950s—Vance and Nettie Palmer and Frederick Macartney to name a few—passionately wanted to establish a national high culture, as did the first promoters of Australian Literature in universities. They usually saw no place in literary history for popular fiction and it was ignored in discussions, articles and syllabi. When English medievalist Stephen Knight took up a position in Australia and turned his attention to crime fiction, he found that its presence had 'melted into invisibility', conspicuously absent from 'histories and general accounts of Australian literature'.[10] He turned back to Miller and Macartney and Hubble and found that despite 'the little the historians may say about ... Australian crime fiction, a different narrative is found, albeit in unstructured form, in the bibliographies'.[11] Many other narratives exist within AustLit waiting to be recovered and articulated. Two that suggest themselves are the role of newspapers and their editors in Australian culture and the nature and extent of serialised fiction by Australian authors in the early twentieth century. The bringing together of information from numerous small bibliographic projects into the one larger resource has enabled a truer picture of some issues to emerge, exposing gaps and inaccuracies in the story of our literature and providing the opportunity to bring to the fore information previously overlooked or unavailable. For example, following a bibliographic paper trail through AustLit has shown that the American publication of Australian literature was much greater than had previously been supposed; this is presently the focus of David Carter's 2006 ARC-funded project, *America Publishes Australia: Australian Books and American Publishers, 1890–2005*.

---

[10] Stephen Knight, 'The Case of the Missing Genre: In Search of Australian Crime Fiction', *Southerly* 48.3 (1998): 235.
[11] Ibid., p. 235.

Is there cause, then, for anything but optimism when unparalleled resources exist to facilitate and support research and to house the results of that research, when new approaches and areas of research are opening up, when Australian literature is being given a new emphasis in schools and universities, and when the field of scholarly editing in the digital environment is developing? This should mean that our excellent resources will be used to their full potential.

But at this exciting point, some sobering questions asked by concerned scholars overseas are worth considering in the Australian context. I quote McGann again:

> In the next fifty years the entirety of our inherited archive of cultural works will have to be re-edited within a network of digital storage, access, and dissemination ... Now ask yourself these questions: Who will be carrying out this work? Who will do it? Who should do it? Just when we will be needing young people well trained in the histories of textual transmission and the theory and practice of scholarly editing ... language study, textual scholarship and bibliography ... [these] three core disciplines preserve but a ghostly presence in most of our PhD programs.[12]

These are questions I find particularly relevant to AustLit. Since 2002, nearly forty individuals have been employed within AustLit. We have had great difficulty in finding suitable personnel to carry out the foundational research work, whether that work be specialist research projects, retrospective bibliographic coverage, or day-to-day indexing of current publications. Teaching someone the mechanics of the database is quite simple—it is a well-designed, user-friendly tool. However, when it comes to the literary and bibliographical skills and the knowledge range required, throughout this six-year period we have rarely found anybody who has been able to bring a full complement of the necessary skills to the more complex tasks. Broadly summarised these are: an understand-

---

[12] Jerome McGann, 'A Note', p. 410.

ing of bibliographic principles, knowledge of and interest in Australian literature, and a knowledge of and proficiency in using a comprehensive range of electronic and print resources in the field of literary studies. Enquiries to my academic friends and colleagues about possible recruits elicits the response: 'I don't know anyone who can do that type of work', 'We don't teach that sort of thing'.

Literature departments and library schools have not produced a body of trained bibliographers ready to engage with the demands of a resource like AustLit. Because of this, the training task at AustLit has been expensive and time-consuming, exacerbated by the need to produce results quickly and a fluctuating funding situation which has resulted in many short-term contracts. And there is the added problem that quite a few graduates whose studies have focused on literary theory and interpretative criticism find the work uninteresting and lacking in relevance and status. If this sounds like a grumble, it is, but it is prompted by a situation the effects of which are not confined, and will not be confined, to AustLit. As McGann's comments indicate, the discipline of literary studies needs bibliographic researchers.

Bibliographic training is far wider than a simple understanding of referencing styles and documentation protocols. Being able to compose an accurate list of works cited for an article, or to follow the Chicago or MLA style manuals accurately, is relatively simple. We need researchers who are aware of major Australian literary figures and periods or know how to find this information and who have been trained to have scholarly habit of mind and an appreciation of the need for detail, accuracy and verification. We need researchers with specific skills: researchers who understand terms such as edition, impression, reprint and facsimile; who know something about copyright; who know the difference, and can describe it, between a digital reproduction and an electronic encoded text; who can interpret library catalogues and their conventions; who have a common vocabulary with which to describe printed works, and understand such descriptions—who know a recto from a verso, a vignette from a frontispiece, an epigraph from a half-title and the different meanings of the term colophon.

Some of the skills I have mentioned may seem trivial or arcane: a matter merely of terminology or belonging to scholarship of a previous era. On the contrary, as the following examples illustrate, ignorance in these areas can lead to quite serious errors and omissions. All of these examples come from my experience at AustLit and all involve researchers with degrees and often higher degrees. In one instance, unfamiliarity with the octavo symbol (8°) in a British Library catalogue record led to the assumption that an edition had 80 pages; a small mistake perhaps, but not when it led to the assumption that this particular publication, being lesser in extent than other editions of the same work, must be an abbreviated edition. Similarly, a forty-six-page edition was identified as an abbreviated edition because of inattention to its quarto size and ignorance of the nineteenth-century practice of publishing novels in double-column format.[13] Another researcher, confusing a common meaning of the term vignette (defined by the Oxford Dictionary as 'a brief verbal description of a person, place, etc.') with the specific bibliographic one (a borderless illustration shading off at the edges) argued that a work described as having a vignette must include some type of brief introduction, preface or authorial musing. Other problems have arisen because of unfamiliarity with book production and book history leading to the inability to interpret the often confusing publishing information on the versos of title pages—for example, assuming that the phrase 'First published in the United States in XXXX' means that the American edition was the first edition, rather than just the first American edition.

Today we have unprecedented access to online catalogues in a variety of languages and researchers need to understand cataloguing conventions

---

[13] This was an American edition of Ada Cambridge's *A Mere Chance* (New York: George Munro, 1882).

if they are to interpret records correctly. There are internationally agreed cataloguing standards but they allow for local variation: a book listed in an Australian library as published in London and Sydney may be listed in an American library as published in London and New York. These are not two different editions; they are the same edition differently described.[14] Another misunderstood cataloguing convention is the use of the letter 'c' to denote the copyright date in records created before the use of the copyright symbol (©) became common. When this has been misunderstood as meaning *circa* and rendered as such, a precise date becomes an approximate one introducing ambiguity regarding the date of publication and the authority of the text.

These instances are not just specific examples of particular, rather embarrassing ignorance, unfamiliarity or error; they are indicative of a generic lack of training in the field. Importantly, they all relate to the key tasks of identification and differentiation of texts. Relatively little attention has been paid to variant texts of Australian literary works and where that has occurred (in the work of the Scholarly Editions Centre and of individuals like the late Elizabeth Perkins) it has usually been for pre-twentieth and early twentieth-century literary works. There has been little awareness of textual variations in more contemporary literature; these are more common than is often supposed—for example, Christopher Koch has revised and rewritten parts of several of his earlier works, there are substantial differences between editions of Kate Grenville's *Lilian's Story* and between the American and British editions of Prichard's *Haxby's Circus*, and a chapter is missing from some editions of Carey's *Oscar and Lucinda*.[15] Establishing an authoritative text is central to liter-

---

[14] For a publication which lists multiple places of publication, the Anglo-American Cataloguing Rules stipulate that the first named place be recorded, with the option of adding a local place of publication as well.

[15] For more detail see my 'Authors, Editors, Publishers: Katharine Susannah Prichard and W.W. Norton', *Australian Literary Studies* 22.4 (2006): 417–31 and

ary and print culture studies, and as both historic and contemporary texts become ever more widely available in digitised form, the need to be able to identify and describe them accurately becomes more evident.

We need people with the background to create resources such as AustLit, as well as a body of researchers who know how to use them: if it is difficult for AustLit to find personnel with the knowledge and experience to continue building this resource, there is also a question mark over the abilities of similarly trained researchers to interpret our data and to take advantage of the research opportunities it offers. The problem is, to quote Ann Hawkins, 'a pedagogical one'.[16]

Ann Hawkins's 2006 book *Teaching Bibliography, Textual Criticism, and Book History* contains more than twenty essays discussing aspects of the problem with reference to courses in literature departments and library schools in the United States. Two courses in bibliography and literary research available at American universities caught my attention particularly. I was delighted to find how closely the core elements of these courses aligned with the type of training we have tried to give the researchers at AustLit. The course described by Maura Ives in Integrating 'Bibliography' and Literary Research, offered at Texas A&M University, has six main elements: MLA documentation format; print and electronic reference sources in English and the humanities; the special characteristics of humanities research; the history of books and printing; enumerative, analytical and descriptive bibliography; and editorial theory and practice.[17]

'AustLit: A Resource for Print Culture Research', *Journal of Publishing* 1.1 (2005): 115-27.
[16] Ann R. Hawkins, ed., *Teaching Bibliography, Textual Criticism, and Book History* (London, Pickering & Chatto, 2006), p. 7.
[17] Maura Ives, 'Integrating "Bibliography" and Literary Research', in Ann R. Hawkins, ed., *Teaching Bibliography, Textual Criticism, and Book History* (London: Pickering and Chatto, 2006), pp.117-23.

Apart from the editing component, and finer detail of the earlier history of books and printing, this is almost exactly the type of task and training we have needed to give people employed at AustLit. For assessment in this course, students must produce a comprehensive research guide, including a descriptive bibliography, for an author (not contemporary) together with an edition proposal. It is essentially a practical course. A similar course proposed at the University of Kentucky by Milton scholar John T. Shawcross is a full fourteen-week course with three class periods per week. Shawcross emphasises 'resources for information, the significance of past "knowledge", the revision of past knowledge by updated study, and sources of correct up-to-date information'[18]; he also stresses the importance of setting up a text and assessing its accuracy and stability, and of teaching students to question the reliability of texts. He claims that many of his students have found the course 'meaningful for … [their] future work, teaching, publication and oral presentations' and that 'conversely, others whose later teaching and writing would have benefited from such study have come to regret the lack of such a course'.[19]

I know there have been comparable research methods courses in Australian universities in the past. Is it not time to revive this type of course in literature departments, and for library schools to re-introduce book history and cataloguing to their courses? Ives is adamant that courses be practical, arguing that 'sending students on a few library "treasure hunts" is equivalent to teaching writing through grammar drills', asserting that 'only research develops research skills'.[20] It might be possible to integrate such courses into AustLit by requiring that elements

---

[18] John T. Shawcross, 'The Bibliography and Research Course', in Ann R. Hawkins, ed., *Teaching Bibliography, Textual Criticism, and Book History* (London: Pickering & Chatto, 2006), p. 109.
[19] Ibid., p. 109.
[20] Maura Ives, 'Integrating "Bibliography" and Literary Research', p. 118.

of the research tasks be submitted within the database, providing a real hands-on experience—benefiting the student and enriching the resource.

We can hardly comfort ourselves, as Jerome McGann pretends to: 'OK, then, what's the problem? Our traditional departments *have* managed to keep around a few old-fashioned editorial and bibliographic types. Let's hope that their brains aren't completely fried.'[21] Speaking as an old-fashioned bibliographic type, conscious of my contemporaries in the field retiring at a record rate, I think the time has arrived to start teaching old bibliographic tricks to a new generation if the possibilities of the digital and electronic revolutions in literary studies are to be fully realised.

---

[21] Jerome McGann, 'Literary Scholarship and the Digital Future', *Chronicle of Higher Education* 49.16 (13 December 2002): B7.

Section 2

Case Studies

4
Australian Literature in the Translation Zone: Robert Dessaix and David Malouf

Robert Dixon

Translate ... v.t. [L. *translatus*, used as past part. of *transferre*, to transfer ...] **1.** To bear or change from one place, condition, etc., to another. **2.** Specif.: **a** To remove to heaven;—originally implying without death. **b** To remove (remains) for reinterring ... **3.** To turn into one's own or another language; broadly, to carry over from one medium or sphere (into another). **4.** To transport or ravish; enrapture. **5.** *Mech.* To impart translation to. **6.** *Teleg.* To repeat or forward (a message) by translation.[1]

I have argued recently for the value of thinking about Australian writing as belonging not just to the nation but also to an expanded field in which national literatures come into being in complex and competitive relations between what Pascale Casanova calls 'the literary province' and 'world literary space'.[2] In a recent overview of Australian literature, Graham

---

[1] *Webster's Collegiate Dictionary*, 5th ed. (Springfield, Mass.: Merriam, 1942), p. 1061.
[2] Pascale Casanova, *The World Republic of Letters* (Cambridge, Mass.: Harvard University Press, 2004); Robert Dixon, 'Australian Fiction and *The World Repub-*

Huggan also concludes, 'it is now generally recognized ... that national literatures are globally produced, often by expatriate or diasporic writers who ... may still choose to market their "Australianness" ... both for a domestic audience and a larger audience elsewhere'.[3] Central to the cultural economy of this expanded field is the role of the translator, so often rendered 'invisible', as Lawrence Venuti has observed.[4] Australian writers and Australian literature have never been confined to the boundaries of the nation, but are implicated in what Emily Apter calls 'the translation zone', which she describes as 'a broad intellectual topography that is neither the property of a single nation, nor an amorphous condition associated with postnationalism, but rather a zone of critical engagement that connects the "l" and the "n" of transLation and transNation'.[5] Literary influences, intellectual formations, careers in writing, and the processes of editing, publication, translation, reception and reputation-making take place both within and beyond the nation, and in more than one language. What might a transnational practice of Australian literary criticism that aimed to overcome the translator's invisibility look like? What kinds of research questions would it ask? What kinds of data and readings would we need to develop a transnational perspective, to see Australian literature in the translation zone?

My approach to these questions is part of the larger collaborative project, supported by the Australian Research Council, called the

---

lic of Letters: 1890–1950', in Peter Pierce, ed., *The Cambridge History of Australian Literature* (Cambridge: Cambridge University Press, 2009).

[3] Graham Huggan, *Australian Literature: Postcolonialism, Racism and Transnationalism* (Oxford: Oxford University Press, 2007), p. 11.

[4] Lawrence Venuti, *The Translator's Invisibility: A History of Translation*. 2nd ed. (London and New York: Routledge, 2008).

[5] Emily S. Apter, *The Translation Zone: A New Comparative Literature* (Princeton: Princeton University Press, 2006), p. 5.

Resourceful Reading project.[6] It recognises that there has been a significant investment in the creation of digital information resources in Australia in recent years, but argues that literary scholars have scarcely begun to learn how to use the new datasets in their research methodologies, which often remain centred on the techniques of 'close reading'. One alternative is Franco Moretti's method of 'distant reading', in which large quantities of contextual information are applied to questions in literary history, often with the aid of computer-assisted analysis.[7] Another influential approach, especially in the fields of book history and publishing studies, is what William St Clair calls 'the political economy of reading'.[8] What books were actually available at the time and in what quantities? Who published them, how much did they cost? How and where were they distributed, and what kinds of readers bought them?

The term 'resourceful reading' is meant deliberately to combine the information-rich, computer-assisted techniques of distant reading with close reading's attention to the internal features of individual literary texts: their settings, themes and patterns of allusion, for example. This chapter is meant as an outline of such an approach with a particular focus on the field of literary translation. I will look very briefly at two case studies of contemporary Australian writers 'in the translation zone', Robert Dessaix and David Malouf, and especially Dessaix's exemplary

---

[6] My co-investigators are Dr Katherine Bode (University of Tasmania), Professor Leigh Dale (University of Wollongong) and Professor Gillian Whitlock (University of Queensland).
[7] Franco Moretti, *Graphs, Maps, Trees: Abstract Models for a Literary History* (London and New York: Verso, 2005).
[8] William St Clair, *The Reading Nation in the Romantic Period* (Cambridge: Cambridge University Press, 2004) and 'The Political Economy of Reading', *The John Coffin Memorial Lecture in the History of the Book*, ies.sas.ac.uk/Publications/johncoffin/stclair.pdf [Accessed 20 July 2009].

Night Letters (1996).[9] What can such an approach tell us about that 'broad intellectual topography' in and between the spaces of national literatures that Apter calls 'the translation zone'?

Close Reading: Night Letters

Paolo Bartoloni, Dessaix's Italian translator, has said that it was the 'innate hybridity' of *Night Letters* which inspired him to translate it: 'Dessaix's book is inherently between Australia and Europe, and its language is an interesting mixture of local vernacular and international idiom'.[10] Ostensibly a series of letters written from Venice by a man identified only as R, who has been diagnosed with a fatal illness, to Peter, his correspondent in Melbourne, *Night Letters* is indeed about translation in all of the senses indicated in the dictionary definition cited at the head of this chapter. It is about translation in the sense of travel, transformation, translocation, and exultation, hence the recurring references throughout to travellers and travel writing: to Laurence Sterne, Marco Polo, Giacomo Casanova, D.H. Lawrence and Bruce Chatwin, among others. As Noel Henricksen observes, 'Dessaix's fiction and his philosophy of travel are analogous, both obsessed with ostensible impulsiveness, eruption of the unexpected, and the possibility of quasi-religious transformation nurtured by the exotic'.[11]

The connection between translation and travel is picked up in Russell West-Pavlov's claim that 'translation in the broadest sense is an operation

---

[9] Robert Dessaix, *Night Letters: A Journey Through Switzerland and Italy*, edited and annotated by Ignor Miazmov (Sydney: Pan Macmillan, 1996). (All subsequent references appear in parentheses in the text.)
[10] Paolo Bartoloni, 'On Translating', *Southerly* 63.1 (2003): 90–1.
[11] Noel Henricksen, 'Allusion in Robert Dessaix's *Night Letters*', *Southerly* 67.3 (2007): 191–205, 192.

which establishes continuity across a space of discontinuity'.[12] He notes that 'alongside the several translators who figure in the narrative, [*Night Letters*] ... as a whole offers an image of "translation" in the spatial sense as it is ostensibly a collection of letters, and in the literary and cultural sense as it constantly has recourse to much[-]transmitted and translated texts (the Gospels, Dante, Mann, as well as Lermontov and Tolstoy) to weave the fabric of its own symbolic work'.[13]

Just as travel can be the spatial realisation of linguistic translation, so the processes of both reading and writing in *Night Letters* are citational, a dense and playful intertextuality carried across with often dazzling immediacy from one text and culture to another. In the context of so much Renaissance art, like the Tintorettos that cover the ceiling and walls of the 'magnificent baroque hall' of Venice's Scuola Grande di S. Giovanni Evangelista (32), Dessaix's aesthetic of travel/translation/citation is 'baroque' in the sense of its dramatic juxtapositions between one cultural or textual space and another. R provides both Renaissance and postmodern instances of the phenomenon. Travelling through Venice at night, he is shot from its maze-like back streets into the plenitude of St Mark's Square:

> On the first night I couldn't resist following that zigzagging route from the station across to the Rialto Bridge and then on to St Mark's Square. Do you know what it reminded me of at night? Those enchanted mazes I used to be taken to at Christmas as a child in one or other of the big departments stores ... everything glinting and gleaming in the beautiful, but menacing darkness, I couldn't bear to come out. Then, with the wave of some wand—boom! You're out of the maze and in St Mark's Square, vast and magnificent to the point of absurdity. (4)

---

[12] Russell West-Pavlov, *Transcultural Graffiti: Diasporic Writing and the Teaching of Literary Studies* (Amsterdam and New York: Rodopi, 2005), p. 97.
[13] Ibid., p. 102.

A similar juxtaposition in time and space is effected for the antipodean air traveller, who pops through, again as if by magical agency, from the new world into the old, like Alice through the looking glass:

> there is still a kind of magic for the antipodean traveller in setting off from home in the late afternoon one day, blundering about for an hour or two at some South-East Asian airport in the middle of an interminable night, to arrive as the sun comes up next morning in Europe. (14–15)

Another example is R's journey from the north of Europe to the south through the St Gotthard tunnel:

> It comes upon you suddenly, too, when you take the train from Zurich: one moment you're in the North, with its doleful, tired cities and tamed farmlands, you slide through the fog into the St Gotthard tunnel, and when you emerge into the light on the other side you're in the South. It's like waking up on the other side of the looking-glass. (33)

This baroque aesthetic of citational reading and writing, of textual translation as a form of cultural and even spiritual transportation, is a central organising principle in *Night Letters*, especially in R's reading of Dante's *Divine Comedy* as he journeys through contemporary European analogues of purgatory, hell and paradise in search of some way to come to terms with death, the ultimate act of translation. The novel abounds not only in bravura and vertiginous citations from the canonical literatures of many cultures, but also in references to translation and multilingual encounters, some of them witty and delightfully self-effacing for those who know of Dessaix's previous career as a lecturer in Russian, as in Rachael Berg's presumption that R would not speak Russian (67), or his praise of her excellent English: 'I *am* English', she replies (24). Learning another language, such as Greek, is like 'forging onwards into some unknown world' (77).

The conflation of linguistic translation, foreign travel and quasi-religious exultation is also associated with its sense of erotic seduction. West-Pavlov suggests that 'What is at stake for Dessaix's terminally ill narrator is the transformation of selfhood through a mode of storytelling based upon translation both as textual and spatial principles.[14] R comments, 'I needed a story, probably because the story of my own life is in danger of petering out in a series of incomplete sentences' (153). Listening to Rachel Berg's story about the erotic amulet, R finds himself 'seduced' in the sense of being transported to a series of exotic locations, including the extravagantly baroque Winter Palace in St Petersburg: 'In my mind by this time I was deep inside the Winter Palace in St Petersburg. The tang of the waxed parquet flooring was pinching my nostrils. I had been seduced' (61).

The cities and locations R elects to visit, like the St Gotthard tunnel, Locarno and Venice, are the switching points of transnational cultural flows, 'swarming' with foreign travellers and their many languages (112). Historically, some of them have long been points of cultural transmission where the European self and its others seek both seduction and redemption through translation, even to the point of mutual contamination. In contemporary Venice, Germans on holiday seek a kind of secular 're-demption' (151), but in the old Venice, at the crossroads of Occident and Orient, Europeans risked seduction by the other, as 'translation' becomes a form of 'ravishment':

> With the desire for spices and silks and gold came a sense of the seductiveness of what lay behind those things—the cultures, the religions, the secrets, the ways of living. And it was all covered in a cloak of erotic pleasure because, at root, Venice knew she was trembling on the brink of ravishment. Musn't touch! To touch could be fatal! And so the priests thundered and the Church called lewd anything that was not Catholic—Jews were lascivious and ridden with syphilis, Turks were fornicators and rapists, Orientals practised monstrous sexual rites and so on. The outsider is *always* in the final analysis a sexual threat *because he is so desirable*. (133–4)

---

[14] Ibid., p. 102.

The purpose of travel and of travel writing, as R understands them, is to seek 'translation' of the self in the form of redemptive change, and this can become a kind of limit experience which can either be resisted or to which one can surrender. In the letter from Venice dated 17 April, R reports to Peter a lengthy discussion with his fellow hotel guest, the German cultural historian Professor Eschenbaum, on the varieties of foreign travel. It is the purpose of travel writing, Eschenbaum argues, to record and perform this translation of the self. There is a distinction to be drawn between Marco Polo and Casanova. Marco Polo travelled the world to record opportunities for foreign trade, but did not attend to the way his experiences changed him: 'he left Italy as an Italian teenager and returned to Italy twenty years later as Italian as he'd left it' (246); he is 'a failed traveller', as West-Pavlov observes.[15] Casanova, on the other hand, travelled to force himself into new experiences, and wrote about how these changed him. West-Pavlov argues that 'the transmission of the self through time and space is to be understood as a constant process of interrogation, just as translation can be construed not as reconstituting, but rather questioning an original'.[16] Eschenbaum explains that Casanova 'discovered paradise *in the travelling*'. In this sense, Casanova is the first truly modern traveller, echoing his contemporary, Sterne, in formulating the idea of sentimental travel: 'The sentimental traveller travels simply in order to observe the motion of his own sensibilities' (243).

In the end, R not so much rejects Europe for Australia, as he feels compelled to translate himself back to the Antipodes. In doing so, he experiences a moment of 'exultation' (272)—translation in its quasi-religious sense of rapture. Although *Night Letters* celebrates the transformative value of travel/translation, it finally grounds R's experience of Europe—his viewing of its art and architecture, and his

---

[15] Ibid., p. 103.
[16] Ibid., p. 103.

reading of its literature—in a revelation of his own provincial or, as he calls it, 'antipodean' perspective (269). This is what Apter means by her insistence that 'the translation zone' is not 'an amorphous condition associated with postnationalism, but rather a zone of critical engagement'. In his final letter from Venice, R informs Peter that he has decided to 'move on', or more specifically, return home. West-Pavolv suggests that this decision is largely motivated by his anxiety arising from the fact that Professor Eschenbaum is beaten up by the hotel staff late one night upon returning from a gay club in his own quest for limit experiences: 'it is precisely this event which motivates the narrator to move on from Venice'.[17] But R also explains that he has become 'saturated with Europe' (270) in the way one feels when looking at grandparents' photo albums. Above all, he has come to recognise the difference in perspective that occurs when Europeans and antipodeans enter each other's cultures: 'you know they really haven't the faintest idea about, let alone respect for, the things that move you and they're never going to change' (270).

No contemporary Australian writer could be less provincial or cultural nationalist than Robert Dessaix, and R is quick to explain that he hasn't 'been dreaming of gum-trees or koalas', but he does 'feel a pull this morning back to a place where I think I can live more diversely than here' (270). The 'pull' caused by this sense of difference is evident in his experience of both seeing Europe and reading its literature. As he reaches the third and final phase of his travels, modelled on the three-part structure of the *Divine Comedy*, which he has been reading at the urging of Professor Eschenbaum, he arrives in Venice, the potential resolution point of his journey, only to find that his antipodean perspective has been reactivated by his foreign travels. Surprisingly, he reveals that his Italian is inadequate to allow him to read Dante in Italian and that he is using an English translation: 'How I wish I could read that in Italian. How I wish I

---

[17] Ibid., p. 104.

could talk to somebody about it at my own level' (264). In the end, he confesses, 'I wasn't really prepared for *Paradise*' (262):

> I spent most of the morning reading it ... but it's overwhelming ... I did feel I'd put myself to sea in a boat which was far too small—I kept peering back over my shoulder longingly at the shore. You need such erudition ... to make the slightest sense of it, that it almost seems to be an impertinence to be reading it at all ... It's all too much. (262)

In his penultimate view of Venice, R is conscious of the scene before him as a simulacrum, a sign rather than something felt as real, and this arises from his antipodean perspective, as the banalities of home intrude on the foreign scene before the eye. R's vantage point is the courtyard of the Venice Guggenheim, an eighteenth-century *palazzo* 'revamped in the taste of Peggy Guggenheim (Modern Gracious)'—and itself, therefore, a provincial 'translation' from the Italian—whose institutional function is to display European art for foreign visitors:

> Just across the canal from me to the right was one of the world's greatest sights: the extravagant pink confection of the Doge's Palace, the swarm of ferries and gondolas at the edge of the Piazzetta San Marco, the gleaming white loggia of the Marciana Library, the soaring red bulk of the *campanile* on St Mark's Square—bordering on the sublime, like an hallucination or bubble of memory, but curiously lifeless. Perhaps it was just my sombre mood. For an hour or so I gazed across at it but didn't see it. I could just as well have been at home, staring at my irises. (Which really should be dug up and separated, I've just remembered, or else they'll hardly flower at all next summer—do you know if it's been done?) (265–66)

In this passage, in which R is contemplating the elusiveness of hope and its sources in what, for him, is a post-religious world, it is precisely the experience of being 'in translation' in Europe that prompts his desire for reverse translation to the Antipodes, from the sublime to the banal or the vernacular. In this way, he accidentally discovers an emblem of hope—the seasonal regeneration of the irises in his home garden—and thereby 'translation' in the sense of exultation. The final entry is a postcard to Peter briefly announcing that he is once again 'in translation': 'I'm on the way' (273).

Distant Reading 1: Robert Dessaix in the Translation Zone

Apter's 'translation zone' is of course a spatial metaphor. But to understand how that space operates we need to move beyond a close reading of such 'innately hybrid texts' as *Night Letters* to explore its cultural economy. A resourceful reading approach can begin to populate Apter's metaphoric space with real data. Is there, for example, a single translation zone, or are there as many translation zones beyond Australian literature as there are other languages and translators? Beyond English, does the reputation of an Australian book or writer spread from one foreign language to another, or are they siloed, communicating back through English? Is the impact of successive translations cumulative throughout a writer's oeuvre, or is each translation a new beginning? How important are paratextual phenomena and events? How important is the agency of the author and translator in relation to other personnel, including authors' and publishers' agents, publishers, editors, and publishers' scouts, in commissioning translations? Increasingly, it seems that overseas rights and translation contracts are initiated by publishers and their scouts at events such as the Frankfurt and London trade fairs. Are these commercial arrangements similar throughout the world or do they vary from one culture to another? As if confirming Venuti's claim for the translator's 'invisibility', there is to date no systematic, empirically informed account of this translation zone in Australian literary scholarship.

As we have seen, Paulo Bartoloni points to the content, especially the range of allusions to European literature, 'the innate hybridity of *Night Letters*', as one reason for his being attracted to Dessaix. By contrast, in their article 'Robert Dessaix's Journey into French', Ninette Boothroyd and Michelle Royer argue that factors external to the text were critical in Dessaix's French reception. They argue that 'The role of the media, the reputation of the publisher and its editorial line, the stereotypes attached to the country in which the book originated and specific events occurring at the time of publication can be considered to be part of the translation process as these factors form the context in which the book is read".[18]

On 7 January 2000, a special Australian edition of the French cultural television program, *Bouillon de culture*, hosted by the influential media personality Bernard Pivot, was aired in France. The show had been filmed at the Quay restaurant at Circular Quay, overlooking Sydney Harbour, and brought together a panel of French-speaking Australians to discuss Australian life and culture. The panellists were Robert Dessaix, Dominique Gerard, Margaret Sankey, Marion Potts, Djon Mundine, Nathan Waks and Chris Cody. Dessaix made a strong impression with his fluent French and erudite manner, and Pivot was clearly enthusiastic about his work. According to one account:

> The excitable book-owl Pivot went into flights of ecstasy over Dessaix's first book to appear in French, 1994's *A Mother's Disgrace* ... How could such a gifted writer be ignored for so long in France, asked Pivot in mock horror. '*Je comprends*', answered Dessaix in his impeccable, laid-back French. 'You want books about kangaroos and wombats, I don't know anything about those exotic creatures, I live in a city like you.'[19]

For Boothroyd and Royer it is Pivot's advocacy and the context of the Sydney Olympic Games that best explain the high French sales of Dessaix's earlier book, *A Mother's Disgrace* (1994): they 'launched the process of [cultural] translation by providing the audience with a cultural context

---

[18] Ninette Boothroyd and Michelle Royer, 'Robert Dessaix's Journey into French', *Southerly* 63.1 (2003): 95–96.
[19] Scott Steedman, 'Of Wombats and Live TV', *Paris Voice: The Magazine for English-Speaking Parisians* (April 2000), parisvoice.com/00/apr/html/books/books.cfm [Accessed 20 July 2009].

in which to read the work'. It placed French readers in a position that allowed easier access and understanding of the book and gave readers a strong motivation to discover an unknown Australian writer. The publisher, Reflet, 'aimed to publish an author rather than a book', and it is clear that Dessaix made a great impression on Pivot's French audience: 'an Australian writer who could speak French almost perfectly, was erudite and had a very European outlook, not to mention a French name, was a very attractive combination'.[20]

Boothroyd and Royer's argument is that Dessaix's television appearance paved the way for the successful French translation of *A Mother's Disgrace*, which then supported the subsequent success of French translations of his other novels. I started my investigation of Dessaix in the translation zone with the assumption that translations of his work into other Europe languages had branched out, as it were, from the French publications. But the data provided by the AustLit data base suggest another interpretation.[21] As I was following the translation of Dessaix's works into other languages, I noticed that the novels had been translated into other languages much more widely than *A Mother's Disgrace*, and in some—such as German and Italian—this had all happened well before Dessaix's *succès d'estime* in France.

The first of Dessaix's works to be translated was not *A Mother's Disgrace* but *Night Letters*, which was translated into German by Wolf Koehler as *Briefe aus dere Nacht*, and published in Frankfurt in 1997. This was followed by Bartoloni's translation of *Night Letters* into Italian, published in Rome in 1998, and a Finnish translation published in Helsinki in 1999. Bartoloni is an academic at the University of Sydney, and in 1999 he and Dessaix were awarded $4000 by the Australia Council to travel to Italy to promote the book. In the same year, he published an

---

[20] Boothroyd and Royer, 'Robert Dessaix's Journey into French', p. 95.
[21] Unless otherwise stated, data for distant readings are derived from AustLit.

interview with Dessaix in the American journal *Antipodes*.²² *Night Letters* had therefore been translated into several European languages prior to Dessaix's spectacular debut on French television to promote *A Mother's Disgrace* in January 2000.

It has been easiest to find information on Dessaix's work in French, especially but not only because of Boothroyd and Royer's article, and he does seem to have been most successful there. But it is not clear from the data whether these different translation zones are isolated or connected: that is, whether Dessaix's success in France influenced further translations, whether the initial publication of *Night Letters* in German had any influence on the French translation of *A Mother's Disgrace*, or whether either or both of these influenced translations into Finish, Dutch and other languages. The chronology of translation suggests that the 'innate' factors, such as the content and textual allusions, may initially be more appealing to potential translators than contextual factors such as the author's appearance on television or his chance association with the Olympics, but that these may contribute to subsequent reception.

Another factor is Dessaix's own role in the journey of his texts into French. In 2002, without actually publishing anything in French, Dessaix was made a Chevalier dans L'Ordre des Arts et Lettres for services to French culture. Dessaix participates actively in creating networks for the translation of his writing: he has travelled extensively on the circuit of launches in support of the translation of his works into other languages. This suggests that literary celebrity confers some additional agency on authors within the translation zone, especially when they are fluent in the target language or languages, and are willing and able to travel abroad and to make promotional appearances.

---

²² Paolo Bartoloni, 'A Conversation with Robert Dessaix', *Antipodes* 13 (1999): 21–24.

Distant Reading 2: David Malouf in the Translation Zone

While Boothroyd and Royer's account of Dessaix's journey into French stresses the role of the author's media profile and events in the public sphere, the comparable case of David Malouf points to the importance of advocacy by individual translators. Since the 1980s, Malouf's early works had been translated into European languages including French, German, Dutch, Italian and Swedish, though initially each of them appears to have been an isolated project with a different translator and publisher, even when a second or third work was translated into the same language. As one would expect, there was increased international interest in and translation of Malouf's work after *Remembering Babylon* (1994) received the Prix Femina Best Foreign Novel (France 1994), the Prix Baudelaire (France 1995), and the International IMPAC Dublin Literary Award (1996), after which he tended to be taken up by a single translator-advocate in each language who then systematically translated and even re-translated his works. Malouf's main translator-advocates have been Robert Pepin in French and Franca Cavagnoli in Italian.

The first of Malouf's works to be translated into French was *An Imaginary Life*, in 1983 by Marie-Claude Peugeot as *L'enfant du pays barbare*. This was followed by *Harland et son domaine* (*Harland's Half Acre*) translated by Antoinette Roubichou-Stretz in 1986. The first of Robert Pepin's translations, *Ce vaste monde* (*The Great World*), was published in 1991 by Albin Michel of Paris, who had earlier published Roubichou-Stretz's translation of *Harland's Half Acre*. In that same year, 1991, Pepin's translation of *The Great World* won the Prix Femina Étranger Award for the best foreign novel. After *Remembering Babylon* won the Prix Femina Étranger in 1994, it was republished in that year by the Librairie Générale Française as *Ce vaste monde: roman*. In 1995, it was translated by Pepin as *Je me souviens de Babylone*, and won the Prix Baudelaire de Traduction. Pepin has since translated and even re-translated a number of other books which have greatly enhanced Malouf's reputation in France. *Je me souviens de Babylone*, originally published by Albin Michel in Paris in 1995, was republished by Librairie Générale Française in 1997; *Dernière conversation dans la nuit: roman* (*The Conversation at Curlew Creek*) was published by Albin Michel in 1998 and again republished by the Librairie Générale Française in 2000. Pepin's translation of *Dream Stuff* (*L'étoffe des rêves: nouvelles*) was published by Albin Michel in 2003.

When Judith Rodriguez interviewed Pepin during a visit to Australia in 1998, she asked, 'Do you ever ask for a book you like?' He replied, 'In France it doesn't happen, because we get the book before publication, with the copyright taken care of by the publisher ... As an editor, from 200 books sampled per year, I choose about three.'[23] Pepin's telling remark, 'it doesn't happen', tends to confirm the overriding power of publishing houses to initiate translation projects as separate commercial arrangements rather than their being a direct expression of the intellectual and aesthetic interests of the translator in following through the works of an individual author or group of national authors.

In Italian, the role of Franca Cavangnoli as Malouf's translator-advocate has been similarly important. Cavagnoli lectures in Translation Studies at Università degli Studi di Milano and at ISIT Milan. A novelist herself, she has translated into Italian works by such internationally established writers as Toni Morrison, Nadine Gordimer, Jamaica Kincaid, V.S. Naipaul and J.M. Coetzee. While there is evidence of some early interest in Malouf in Italy, Cavagnoli seems to have played a major role in the translation and publication of his most important works from the mid-1990s. A bilingual Italian-English edition of Malouf's poetry, *Un poeta australiano*, translated by Pietro Spinucci, was published by Bulzoni of Rome in 1987. Spinucci was also the author of the first book-length

---

[23] Judith Rodriguez, 'The French Version', interview with Robert Pepin, *ALiTrA: Journal of the Australian Literary Translator's Association* (Summer 1998): 1–3.

study in Italian of the novels of Patrick White, a work which Malouf reviewed in *Australian Literary Studies* in 1985.[24] *An Imaginary Life* was translated into Italian in 1994 by Sabrina Pirri and Raffaele Giannetti, and published by Nuova Immagine in Sienna. After *Remembering Babylon* won the IMPAC Award in 1996, Franca Cavagnoli translated a succession of Malouf's novels, all published by Frassinelli, who is also the Italian publisher of Peter Carey and Thomas Keneally: these were *Ritorno a Babilonia* (*Remembering Babylon*) (1997), *Conversazioni a Curlow Creek* (1998), *Nel mondo grande* (*The Great World*) (2000), *La materia dei sogni* (*Dream Stuff*) (2002) and *Vola via* (*Fly Away Peter*) (2004). Cavagnoli's role as an advocate for Malouf's work in Italian is suggested by the fact that she wrote a new preface for the 2001 republication by Frasinelli of *Una vita immaginaria*.

The same pattern holds in the case of Malouf's translation into German. The first was *Das Wolfkind* (*An Imaginary Life*) by Helga Herborth in 1987. *Harland's Half Acre* was translated as *Verspieltes Land* by Erhard Schuttpelz in 1989 and *The Great World* as *Die grosse Welt* by Götz Burghardt in 1991. Following the IMPAC Dublin Literary Award for *Remembering Babylon*, Schuttpelz's translation of *Harland's Half Acre* was republished, though by a different publisher. In that same year, Adelheid Dormagen's translation of *Remembering Babylon* (*Jenseits von Babylon*), appeared. Like Pepin in France and Cavangnoli in Italy, Dormagen then emerged as Malouf's leading German translator. *Die Nachtwache am Curlow Creek* was published in 1997, and *Südlicher Himmel: erzahlungen* (*Antipodes*) in 1999. There have also been reprints of Herborth's translation, *Das Wolfkind* in 1998, and Dormagen's *Babylon* in 1999, and *Curlow Creek* in 2001.

This preliminary study of Australian literature in translation suggests that the technique of resourceful reading—a combination of close and

---

[24] *Australian Literary Studies* 12.1 (May 1985): 152.

distant readings—can shed light on the cultural and industrial factors that make up what Emily Apter has suggestively called the translation zone. It can begin to populate the translation zone with data that reveal its complex economies and the differently effective roles of its personnel, including authors, translators, agents, publishers, editors and publishers' scouts. Key factors include the formal and aesthetic qualities of some texts that have been singled out for multiple translations, including their content and patterns of allusion to other languages and literatures; the role of the author's celebrity and the visibility of translator-advocates in championing a particular work or author for a particular readership; and the effects of extra-textual events, such as television broadcasts, international cultural or sporting events, and literary prizes in promoting both an awareness of the author and a sympathetic understanding of their country of origin. What is less clear are the spatial, temporal and economic arrangements of translation as a literary and commercial practice, and the extent to which individual instances of translation are connected across an author's body of work, or between one language and another. A major factor remains the sheer commercial power of a publishing house to commission translations independently of the initiatives of authors and translators, whose role appears at times to have been relatively reactive. The cases of Dessaix and Malouf suggest that the translation zone is a loose aggregation of all of these separate phenomena—a field of cultural production in Bourdieu's sense—whose relations need to be gradually pieced together by careful empirical research. It is also apparent that these diverse phenomena can be crystallised around a single event, such as Dessaix's appearance on French television or Malouf's winning of the International IMPAC Dublin Literary Award, to produce signal 'translation events'—such as the success of *A Mother's Disgrace* and *Remembering Babylon*—which in turn have the capacity to reconfigure the ecology of the translation zone and promote the emergence of what might be called master translator-advocates.

5
Australian Literature in a World of Books: A Transnational History of Kylie Tennant's *The Battlers**

Roger Osborne

In his introduction to *A History of the Book in Australia, 1890–1945*, Martyn Lyons declares that one of the primary goals of Australian book history is to determine who 'made the books that make Australian literature'.[1] But due to the common perception that Australian publishing was a 'tale of three cities' with London dominating the smaller local markets of Sydney and Melbourne,[2] most makers of Australian literature in the United States of America have escaped the attention of book historians.

---

* Research for this chapter was supported by Professor David Carter's ARC-funded project, America Publishes Australia: Australian Books and American Publishers, 1890–2005. Professor Carter's continued support and advice was essential to the completion of the paper.

[1] Martyn Lyons and John Arnold, eds, *A History of the Book in Australia: A National Culture in A Colonised Market* (St Lucia: University of Queensland Press, 2001), p. xv.

[2] Richard Nile and David Walker, 'Marketing the Literary Imagination: Production of Australian Literature, 1915–1965', in L.T. Hergenhan and Bruce Bennett, eds, *The Penguin New Literary History of Australia* (Ringwood: Penguin, 1988), p. 286.

Recent work done by AustLit indexers for the *Bibliography of Australian Literature* has produced a more complete picture of overseas editions, showing that a considerable percentage of Australian novels were published in the United States. This bibliographical evidence encourages more intensive research into American editions of Australian novels, but any comprehensive analysis of the phenomenon is limited by the dearth and dispersal of contextual evidence. Nevertheless, as such evidence is identified, transcribed and analysed, we can form an idea of the transnational trajectory taken by Australian novels by concentrating on single case studies that offer an abundance of evidence. Drawing on the large collection of papers held at the National Library of Australia, this chapter explores the first editions of Kylie Tennant's novel *The Battlers* in New York, London and Sydney during the 1940s. From its beginning as a typescript that slowly accumulated in the inner suburbs of Sydney, Kylie Tennant's novel eventually travelled the trade routes of a transnational print culture, engaging some of the most prominent figures in world publishing. Many people *made* Kylie Tennant's novel *The Battlers*. Acknowledging this leads us towards a deeper understanding of the Australian presence in a transnational history of books.

Like most Australian novelists seeking to make a living from their writing and still reach at least a few Australian readers, Kylie Tennant looked to London as the most appropriate place to send her novels. When she sat down to write *The Battlers* in her Dulwich Hill home in Sydney's inner western suburbs, she had already won one of Australia's major literary prizes and she was contracted to the London publisher Gollancz for her next novel. In the spring of 1938 she had spent several months on the track with unemployed and itinerant workers of rural New South Wales, collecting data that would inform the social realism that characterised her fiction. After her return to Sydney in December 1938, she spent the next twelve months turning her experience into fiction despite the distraction of domestic interruption and her involvement in the Christian Socialist Movement. The novel was finished by the time she moved to the country town of Muswellbrook in January 1940 and typescripts were prepared for transmission to prospective publishers. One copy of this typescript moved along the busy shipping routes from Sydney headed toward a London destination.

As several studies have shown, such literary export was common for Australian novels at the time. It was also common for Australian novels to reach a publisher in the United States after first succeeding in the British marketplace for books. This situation was consolidated by the restrictions of international copyright law. The 1886 Berne Convention established reciprocal copyright arrangements between many countries, but for much of the twentieth century authors and publishers foreign to the United States received no copyright protection within that country unless their textual product was fully manufactured within the borders of that country. Most publishers were reluctant to risk such an investment and so only successful authors were guaranteed attention in New York. Indeed, the prominent British publisher Stanley Unwin estimated that less than 5 percent of British books were also printed in a separate American edition.[3]

Those books that were published as an American edition were unlikely to be exported outside of the United States due to trade restrictions imposed by the British Traditional Market Agreement.[4] Unofficial for many years and formalised in 1947, the British Traditional Market Agreement effectively divided the market for books in English between the United States and its territories and Britain's well-established colonial network. Any book published in the United States could not be sold in the British territories and vice versa. Although it was officially

---

[3] Stanley Unwin, *The Truth About Publishing* (London: George Allen & Unwin, 1960), p. 72.
[4] The most comprehensive discussion of the agreement can be found in Mary Nell Bryant's 'English Language Publication and the British Traditional Market Agreement', *Library Quarterly* 49.4 (October 1979): 371–98.

dismantled in 1976 after anti-trust action in the USA, the agreement continues unofficially to this day. For most Australian novels published overseas, the restrictions imposed by copyright law and trade barriers narrowed the channels along which they travelled towards publication in British, American and Australian markets. If an Australia author wanted to succeed overseas, the route to New York via London was rarely avoided.

Reaching New York from London, Sydney or Melbourne required the services of an enthusiastic publisher or literary agent. Australian novelists were represented by a variety of London firms including A.P. Watt & Son, James Pinker, Curtis Brown Ltd, and the New York firm, Paul R. Reynolds. No literary agent had a monopoly on Australian novelists and Paul Reynolds's memory of Australian writing in the interwar period suggests that few sought to keep anything resembling an Australian list. In his 1971 autobiography Reynolds wrote, 'Thirty years ago Australia was an insignificant country with almost no writers who were published in America'.[5] Nevertheless, Australians took the American market seriously and several efforts were made in the 1940s to address an increasing American interest in Australia because of the military presence in the Pacific during World War II. W.G. Cousins of Angus & Robertson engaged the services of the Leland Hayward agency, which succeeded in finding publishers for a number of novelists, including Henry Lamond, Eve Langley, Xavier Herbert and Arthur Upfield. But this association faltered when the New York Agency was taken over by a larger entertainment agency, becoming, in the process, much less interested in books.[6] Attempts were made to promote Australian writing in 1948 when

---

[5] Paul Reynolds, *The Middle Man: The Adventures of a Literary Agent* (New York: Morrow, 1972), p. 142.

[6] Neil James, 'Spheres of Influence: Angus & Robertson and Australian Literature from the Thirties to the Sixties' (Unpublished PhD Thesis, University of Sydney, 2000), pp. 268–70.

the Australian Government Trade Commissioner displayed a selection of Australian books at the Rockefeller Center.[7] The display included American editions of Joseph Furphy's *Such is Life*, Kylie Tennant's *The Battlers*, Eleanor Dark's *The Timeless Land*, Norman Lindsay's *Age of Consent*, John Ewers's *Written in Sand*, Joan Colebrook's *The Northerner*, Jon Cleary's *You Can't See Around Corners* and Patrick White's *The Aunt's Story*. But, despite such initiatives, Australian writing was rarely offered in large doses.

The difficulty of reaching an American audience directly from Australia is seen in the story of the Noëlle Brennan literary agency, set up in 1946 as an experiment of the New York agency, A. Watkins Inc. Armitage Watkins developed an interest in Australia through his work during World War II. Graduating from Yale in 1928, he worked for the educational publishers Charles E. Merrill & Company during the 1930s and was an intelligence officer for some time during World War II before joining the Office of War Information as a publishing consultant. He was soon elevated to assistant chief of the Publication Division and ended his career with the military as the liaison officer of the Overseas Branch dealing with foreign correspondents in Washington and New York.

While in these positions, Watkins became interested in Australia and made a concerted effort to find Australian writers suitable for the American magazine market and publishing industry. To achieve this, he engaged Noëlle Brennan and Dorothy Cubis as representatives in Sydney. Brennan and Cubis worked together in government departments and at the ABC, the former with experience in journalism and the latter holding a first class honours degree in modern history and English literature from the University of Sydney. On 1 October 1946, the Noëlle Brennan literary

---

[7] Office of the Australian Government Trade Commissioner, press release dated 17 November 1948, C. Hartley Grattan Papers, Harry Ransom Research Center, University of Texas, Austin.

agency opened for business in Rushcutters Bay, hoping to gather a list of Australian writers who might fulfil Armitage's 'wish to further the activities of Australian writers, bringing about closer understanding between the two countries'.[8]

This enterprise appears to have been a complete failure, with few of the hundreds of submissions promising to fulfil Armitage's wish. Notices about the new agency appeared in local magazines and newspapers, and manuscripts began to appear in large numbers at the conclusion of the *Sydney Morning Herald* novel competition. From the perspective of the twenty-first century, Brennan was going to have extreme difficulties with the manuscripts she handled. Few made any lasting impact on Australian literature, let alone the American magazine and book markets. She spoke with enthusiasm of minor writers such as Frank Sarao, Edith McKay, V. Atherton and Art Hausler, several of whose work had appeared in the annual *Coast to Coast* short story anthologies. Stories and novels that included scenes familiar to American servicemen were promoted, but the tendency of Australian short stories to meet the requirements of a *Bulletin* sketch made it difficult to attract the interest of American magazine editors who sought a much longer form. A letter to Watkins from Charles Scribner's Sons, dated 7 February 1947, shows that disappointment was widespread: 'This sounds as though they had been sending you the same kind of manuscripts as we have been getting from there which we hoped would have been weeded out at the other end'. These included novels and short stories by E.M. England, Lyndall Hadow, V.J.A. O'Connor and Mary Pinney, none of which seem to have found much success outside of Australia.

---

[8] Letter from Brennan to Watkins, 26 February 1947, Watkins, Loomis Papers, Columbia University, 'Australia' file. All subsequent references in my discussion of the Watkins experiment are drawn from this source.

By 6 June 1947 Armitage was signalling the failure of the enterprise, writing that 'The quality is so wide of the mark, in almost every case, that were the stories submitted to us by local residents of the United States we would quickly decline them'. Rejections were reported all round with an assessment that Australian writers were out-of-date. American readers were 'becoming too sophisticated' for fiction like England's contrived romance, *Strange Sequence*, and publishers were not willing to take a chance on anything that could not sell at least 8000 copies. To Watkins, Cecil Mann's short story collection *The River* appeared to be 'a raison d'être for our Australian experiment', but Mann only showed *future* promise with his humour, technique and characterisation. His stories offered 'very little to American readers'. To support his position, Watkins enclosed a typewritten draft of an article by the Australian expatriate Alwyn Lee which reported that the New York agency was 'embarrassed' to be in 'possession of some hundred Australian novels and some three hundred Australian short stories'. Hoping to uncover another Henry Handel Richardson (who had tremendous success in the 1930s with American editions of the Richard Mahony trilogy), Watkins was extremely disappointed to find only 'literary fashions of thought and style which disappeared [in America] a generation ago', particularly what seemed to be the old-fashioned 'Australian specialties' of 'sentimental and dialect stories'. Watkins's experiment was a failure and the Noëlle Brennan literary agency appears to have folded due to the New Yorker's growing disappointment.

It is not known how far Kylie Tennant hoped her novel would travel when she posted the typescript to her London publisher, but, as these brief notes demonstrate, the pathways open to her literary work were well established. The Australia–London–New York trajectory for Australian novels was so distinct by the 1940s that C. Hartley Grattan, a strong American advocate for Australian literature, remarked

> Australian writers have long thought that London was a bottleneck as far as 'dinkum' Australian books are concerned and have looked to New York

with hope. Now that New York is opening up, it seems that only what gets through the London barricade can get here.⁹

Exploring the journey of *The Battlers* along this trajectory provides a useful example for comparison with other cases as they emerge. The abundance of contextual evidence that informs this exploration will help to understand the movement of the many books that lack such primary evidence.

*   *   *

With an option on Tennant's next novel after publishing *Foveaux* in 1939, the London publisher Victor Gollancz received a typescript and accepted *The Battlers* on 25 June 1940.[10] No contract for *The Battlers* is extant, but a Gollancz statement reveals that Tennant agreed to a 10 percent royalty on the first 2000 copies, rising to 15 percent after that. Tennant was paid an agreed £40 advance when the novel was published on 9 January 1941, a sum that was halved after commissions, taxes and other charges were subtracted. By 25 March, 2561 copies had been sold in London and 457 copies had been sent overseas, most to Australia. Royalties were halved by the usual subtractions, leaving Tennant with £45 11s 10d. Like any other author, Tennant could have made more money more quickly by writing short stories for magazines, but the novel was her chosen form. The London publisher Michael Joseph once told prospective novelists that sales in the order of 2000–3000 copies was considered good in the trade.[11] In London, *The Battlers* was a good seller.

---

[9] In Laurie Hergenhan, *No Casual Traveller: Hartley Grattan and Australia–US Connections* (St Lucia: University of Queensland Press, 1995), p. 191.

[10] All evidence supporting the textual history of *The Battlers* in the following discussion is found in the Kylie Tennant Papers, National Library of Australia, MS10043.

[11] Michael Joseph, *Complete Writing for Profit* (London: Hutchinson, 1930), p. 586.

In 1941, a small but significant fee for securing copyright in the United States was included in a royalty statement from Tennant's literary agent Curtis Brown, revealing that *The Battlers* had made a trans-Atlantic crossing and was being considered for publication in New York. Tennant's earlier novels had not attracted any American interest. In 1940 *Fouveaux* was rejected by Bobbs-Merrill, Houghton Mifflin, Harpers, Putnams, Carrick & Evans, Macmillan, Morrow, Knopf, Penn Publishing, Viking and Doubleday Doran. But with the support and enthusiasm of Curtis Brown Ltd in London, *The Battlers* was sent to the United States with a strong stamp of cultural authority. With brisk sales in London from the outset, *The Battlers* caught the attention of Curtis Brown, Snr, who wrote to Tennant to congratulate her and forecast a bright future: 'I can't quite see *The Battlers* adding to your riches with film or second-serial rights; but I can foresee another book from you that will achieve both serial and film rights'. Such support from the head of one of London's biggest agencies was extremely fortunate, but a handwritten addendum to the typed letter showed even further devotion: 'I am sending copy of this letter to our New York Office. We must find an American publisher for this book.' The New York office worked fast, but had little good news to report when writing to Tennant just one week later. The novel had been rejected by four publishers, including Little Brown, Duell, Sloan & Pearce and Lippincott. An extract from Lippincott's response revealed that publisher's reasons: 'The weakness of the thing as I see it is that it is a picaresque narrative without any plotting beyond the sequence of adventures through which the characters go'. Lippincott acknowledged that it was 'an eminently publishable book' but didn't think that 'it would do much in the way of sales'. What level of sales Lippincott expected from their publications is not known, but Curtis Brown eventually found a publisher that was willing to take the risk.

Macmillan had published several of Eleanor Dark's novels and had accepted the best-selling *The Timeless Land* when *The Battlers* arrived for their consideration. There is no evidence to suggest that these two novels were accepted to provide an Australian focus for the American publisher. Indeed there is no mention of the other novel in either Dark's or Tennant's business correspondence. The novels were not advertised together and the selection of *The Timeless Land* by the Book-of-the-Month Club gave Eleanor Dark a much greater profile. Nevertheless, Tennant was granted a $250 advance on 25 July 1941, losing almost $100 of this to taxes, commission and miscellaneous fees. Macmillan might not have expected *The Battlers* to sell too many copies and, based on a later contract, probably offered 10 percent royalty on the first 5000 copies. It is not known how many copies were printed, but a modest sale of 1126 copies had been achieved by 30 April 1942. Sales quickly dropped off and only 477 copies were sold in the following twelve months. After sales repaid the Macmillan advance, additional royalties reached close to $160 in the two years after publication. Like its British counterpart, the American edition of *The Battlers* was a moderate success and Macmillan remained the American publisher of Tennant's novels throughout the 1940s.

Until she established Sirius Publications in 1945, Tennant probably had more readers in New York than in the whole of Australia. She had entered the novel for the S.H. Prior Memorial Prize and was one of three winners announced in *The Bulletin* on 16 October 1940, sharing the prize with Eve Langley's *The Pea-Pickers* and Malcolm Henry Ellis's biography of Lachlan Macquarie. Submitted as 'The Brown Van' under the *nom de plume* Antiene, it was accepted by Angus & Robertson's Beatrice Davis (one of the judges) on the condition that it was reduced to three-quarters of its original length. No evidence of Tennant's response exists, but her contract with Gollancz must have strengthened her resolve to reject the Australian offer and accept the limited number of copies that the British publisher would deliver to Australian readers.

With fewer than 500 copies of *The Battlers* sent to the British colonial market, Tennant had little hope of building a wide readership in her own country. When copies of her works became unprocurable in Australia, she established the Sirius Publishing Company with her husband and father, each contributing £100. Editions of 5000–7000 copies were planned and *The Battlers* was the first of these in 1945, printed on cheap wartime paper. Seven thousand copies were printed and 5750 had been sold by 31 December 1945, earning Tennant a £70 royalty and bringing the publishing company a gross profit that approached £200. Similar results followed with editions of *Ride on Stranger* and *Foveaux*, but no more books were published and the company ceased operation in the late 1940s.

Thanks to Kylie Tennant's collection of reviews pasted in several scrapbooks we have a very good idea of how and where *The Battlers* was reviewed.[12] In Great Britain the English edition was reviewed widely in newspapers and magazines. The book was frequently reviewed as a social document rather than a work of fiction because of what reviewers saw as Tennant's objective view of a little-known segment of Australian culture. Comparisons to Steinbeck's *Grapes of Wrath* appear occasionally, but this is often done to distinguish Tennant's humour from the grim polemic of the American novel. Readers were warned about the language contained in the book with one reviewer suggesting that *The Battlers* described 'the most disreputable, foul-mouthed folk imaginable'. Alternatively, George Orwell, writing for the *New Statesman*, criticised Tennant's 'feminine coyness about bad language', suggesting that some readers sought a more earthy view of life on the track. But the morality of the characters attracted some British reviewers' disgust. The novelist Frank Swinnerton suggested that the novel is a 'remarkable insight into the ways of those for whom the battle of life is always a flight from discipline and restraint'. According to Swinnerton, Tennant's characters are 'all weak in the wits and would be better dead'. Other reviewers were much kinder, suggesting

---

[12] The Kylie Tennant Papers include several scrapbooks that contain cuttings sent from various clipping agencies in England and the United States. All reviews were transcribed from this source.

that the novel provided a timely portrait by describing the background of Australian soldiers at battle in World War II. The individual encounters with single copies of the book as seen in these reviews demonstrates the cultural work that *The Battlers* was made to perform in newspapers and magazines across Great Britain. What these reviews say about the British attitude to Australia is debatable, but a tone of Imperial superiority over colonial subjects is often apparent.

The novel was reviewed across the United States. With its promotional material telling book-buyers that *The Battlers* was 'a really first-rate novel, a sort of Australian *Grapes of Wrath*', Macmillan set the tone for many American reviewers. The reviewer for Boston's *Morning Globe* offered a standard opinion: 'Steinbeck is a master of scorn and fury. Tennant is a good writer with a story to tell.' Tennant's storytelling was widely praised with only a few baulking at the novel's potential obscurity to American readers. The *New York Times*'s Ralph Thompson suggested the need for a glossary (a necessity occasionally suggested by American reviewers of Australian novels), but he stressed that 'as a story, it is conventional enough and none too remarkable, but it is almost solid with local color and amusing detail, and the atmosphere is the genuine atmosphere of back country New South Wales'. Indeed, a number of reviewers detected something familiar in this atmosphere. The colloquial language of the characters reminded the Boston *Post*'s George Smart 'of the rich colloquial language of the American frontier', the Kansas City *Star* noted that '*The Battlers* seems to confirm ... that of all other people, the Australians are most akin to Americans', and Beatrice Murphy of Washington DC's *Afro American* explained that in Dick Tyrell's relationship with brown-skinned Mary Burns, 'We are once more reminded that the so-called "race-problem" is not exclusively an American problem'. A number of reviewers described the novel by looking to England for another familiar comparison. The reviewer for the New Bedford *Standard Times* was neither the first nor the last to compare the picaresque quality of *The Battlers* with J.B. Priestley's *The Good Companions*, a bestseller in Great

Britain and the United States in 1929. American reviews contained no warnings about bad language and many expressed a sympathy for the characters that was absent from many English reviews. In the United States *The Battlers* was frequently regarded as a depiction of 'Okies from Down Under', but the novel would never emulate the sales of Steinbeck's famous novel.

Australian reviews of the English edition frequently echoed British and American opinion. The Melbourne *Age* said the novel was 'too sordid and squalid, too restricted in range' to hold interest and the Adelaide *Mail* did not recommend the book to those 'squeamish about language'. Comparisons with Steinbeck and Priestley also appeared in the Australian press and Frank Dalby Davison suggested that the novel was reminiscent of 'Gorki, leavened with a dash of Lawson's humour'. Perhaps the strongest opinion of the novel came from an anonymous *Bulletin* 'Red Page' reviewer who said the novel was about escape 'into a world of color, freedom and virility, providing ... a vicarious satisfaction for the eternal hunger for the primitive'. Four years after this initial response, the first Australian edition seemed to escape without notice, but *The Battlers* was presented to Australian readers with a wide cross-section of overseas reviews on the dust jacket, drawing readers' attention to positive responses in other nations and giving these responses a cultural value higher than their Australian counterparts.

Each edition of *The Battlers* was manufactured in separate nations for different groups of readers, but they maintain a connection through their association with an idea of the work that we know as Kylie Tennant's *The Battlers*. The first edition of *The Battlers* is an English one, a familiar phenomenon in Australian book history in which London provided opportunities for Australian writers that a local publishing industry could not. The second edition of *The Battlers* is an American one, a less familiar phenomenon in Australian book history, but one that many Australian writers sought to achieve. The third edition of *The Battlers* is an Australian one, bringing the novel full circle to be produced in the country of its composition and setting. Copies of these books can be found in libraries and antiquarian bookshops throughout the countries in which they were produced, extending the idea of the work across national borders to very specific locations, building a multi-faceted cultural and economic network that incorporates the diverse worlds of authors, publishers, printers, booksellers, lenders and readers.

My copy of the American edition of *The Battlers* was sent to me from the Russian Hill Bookstore on Polk Street in San Francisco, removing it from American print culture to become an artefact in the hands of an Australian book historian. Printed in New York by American Book-Stratford Press, it travelled almost 5000 kilometres across the United States before this unceremonious export to the Antipodes. This trajectory reminds me of the initial movement of Kylie Tennant's manuscript from Sydney to London before arriving in New York with the support of Curtis Brown. If we are to determine who made the books that make Australian literature, such movements should be incorporated into our idea of the literary work. While the American edition of *The Battlers* might not have contributed to the development of Australian literature within the borders of Australia's literary culture, it stands beside the English and Australian edition as a physical manifestation of our idea of the work. Australian book history is much more than a 'tale of three cities'. If we are to better understand how Australian fiction is positioned beyond our shores, we must begin to consider Australia's contribution to a transnational history of books. The transnational history of Kylie Tennant's *The Battlers* is a good topic to start the conversation.

6
Books in Selected Australian Newspapers, December 1930

Robert Thomson and Leigh Dale

This essay reports on an element of the Resourceful Reading inquiry, a project which aims to bring large-scale empirical data collection and analysis to the study of Australian literature. Our 1930 subproject is targeted specifically on the collection of data from Australian newspapers. Central to our inquiry is the recognition that, just as commercial literary culture has played a relatively minor part in academic criticism and the teaching of literature in universities, conversely, academia is on the fringes of the ecology of literature.[1] The term 'ecology' is used, here, as a term useful for implying the complex interactions and highly localised nature of print culture.

In focusing on newspapers this study takes up a line from John Barnes's review of Bruce Bennett's *Cross Currents: Magazines and Newspapers in Australian Literature*. Noting the attention given to the discussion of literature in newspapers in the nineteenth century, Barnes wonders

---

[1] See Carol Hetherington, 'Little Australians? Some Questions about National Identity and the National Literature', *Antipodes* 21.1 (2007): 11–15. The term 'intellectual ecology' is from Joseph Jones, *Radical Cousins: Nineteenth Century American and Australian Writers* (St Lucia: University of Queensland Press, 1976), p. 13.

whether this medium might not be important for Australian literature in the twentieth.[2] However, our study reconfigures the elements of most existing discussions. Rather than considering literature in newspapers— the publication of creative works—we are examining the ways in which books are represented as cultural and commercial objects. Information of three main kinds has been gathered: reviews, 'notes' (usually one-paragraph summaries) and advertisements.[3] While a key aim is to identify these materials for the AustLit database, and in particular to supplement AustLit's listings of book reviews, our process of gathering data on books regardless of the author's nationality avoids the problem of presuming either the subordinate or superior place of the national. We are also testing existing narrative accounts of interwar literary culture, which have focused on 'literature' considered as canonical (or potentially canonical) texts. Finally, the choice of 1930 reflects a desire to reconsider the interwar period, often neglected, and to do so in ways that foreground the economic aspects of literary culture.

This chapter deals with the pilot phase (year one of four) of the project, which focused on the month of December and which established conventions for the collection and classification of material. As will become clear, our findings in relation to Australian literature point to the previously under-reported significance of the regional press, as well as the enormous diversity and range of books discussed in Australian newspapers: for the period under discussion, there were 5400 mentions of

---

[2] 'Charting the Current: Periodicals and Australian Literature', *Westerly* 28.2 (June 1983): 69. See, for example, Elizabeth Webby, '"Blushing Unseen": Australian Literature Published in Regional Newspapers of the 1840s', *BSANZ Bulletin* 24.1 (2000): 73–80 and W. Bunbury, 'Newspapers and Literature in Western Australia, 1829–1859', *Westerly* 23.1 (March 1978): 65–83.

[3] Difficulties have arisen in separating notes and reviews from each other and from advertisements. An advertisement is counted each time it appears, a repeated review only if it appears in a different publication.

nearly 1700 individual titles, in our thirty-two selected newspapers. We began by selecting newspapers on the basis of the size of the populations they served—the six largest cities in the country and significant regional centres—and then added a handful of country newspapers (Table 1). Robert Thomson scanned each page of each newspaper for literary materials: columns, advertisements, essays, reviews, poems, serials, etc., with new Australian data—such as publication details of an essay by Katharine Susannah Prichard in the *Kalgoorlie Miner*—added to AustLit, and all data collected in tabular form.

Table 1 Selected Newspaper Sources

Town or City[a]	Publication	Published
Geelong	*Geelong Advertiser*	Monday–Saturday
MARYBOROUGH (Queensland)	*Maryborough Chronicle*	Monday–Saturday
ADELAIDE	*Advertiser*	Monday–Saturday
MELBOURNE	*Age*	Monday–Saturday
MELBOURNE	*Argus*	Monday–Saturday
Armidale	*Armidale Express*	Monday, Wednesday, Friday
Ballarat	*Ballarat Courier*	Monday–Saturday
BENDIGO	*Bendigo Advertiser*	Monday–Saturday
Albury	*Border Morning Mail*	Monday–Saturday
BRISBANE	*Brisbane Courier*	Monday–Saturday
Grafton	*Daily Examiner*	Monday–Saturday
SYDNEY	*Daily Guardian* [see also *Sunday Guardian*]	Monday–Saturday
MACKAY	*Daily Mercury*	Monday–Saturday
LAUNCESTON	*Examiner*	Monday–Saturday
MELBOURNE	*Herald*	Monday–Saturday
Kalgoorlie	*Kalgoorlie Miner*	Monday–Saturday
Lithgow	*Lithgow Mercury*	Monday, Wednesday–

Town or City[a]	Publication	Published
		Friday
Maryborough (Victoria)	*Maryborough Advertiser*	Monday, Wednesday, Friday
HOBART	*Mercury*	Monday–Saturday
ROCKHAMPTON	*Morning Bulletin*	Monday–Saturday
Mudgee	*Mudgee Guardian*	Monday, Thursday
ADELAIDE	*News*	Monday–Saturday
Port Fairy	*Port Fairy Gazette*	Monday, Thursday
SYDNEY	*Sun*	Weekly
SYDNEY	*Sunday Guardian* [see also *Daily Guardian*]	Sunday
SYDNEY	*Sydney Morning Herald*	Monday–Saturday
BRISBANE	*Telegraph*	Monday–Saturday
TOOWOOMBA	*Toowoomba Chronicle*	Monday–Saturday
TOWNSVILLE	*Townsville Daily Bulletin*	Monday–Saturday
Port Augusta	*Transcontinental*	Friday
Warwick	*Warwick Daily News*	Monday–Saturday
PERTH	*West Australian*	Monday–Saturday
Yass	*Yass Tribune-Courier*	Monday, Thursday

[a] Caps: population >30,000; small caps: population 15–30,000; ordinary font: population <15,000.

Significant demographic differences between states affected the size and scope of newspapers: Queensland, Tasmania and Victoria had substantial regional centres, less demographically subordinate to the state capital. By contrast, New South Wales was distinctive in having the largest city in Australia, Sydney, with a population of around 1.2 million, but no regional centre with more than 15,000. South Australia and Western Australia likewise had no large regional centres. The circulation of different newspapers therefore varied greatly, from more than 100,000 per day for the large metropolitan publications to perhaps a few thousand a week for a small country paper. Nevertheless, we acknowledge, as Gordon Beavan demonstrates in his lively essay 'A Critique of Newspaper History', that circulation is a crude measure which should be balanced by reference to page numbers and frequency if a longitudinal study is being carried out.[4]

In this period, all newspapers balanced local with national and international coverage, while country readers often had the choice of a recent city paper, delivered by rail.[5] Another influence on content was rival technology, changes which would ultimately make the carriage of non-local news unviable for country publications.[6] An advertisement on the front page of the 1 December issue of Launceston's *Examiner* encouraged readers to ready themselves for the impending launch of radio station 7LA by purchasing a Radiola 'Specially constructed to receive this powerful station'. Cinema was a popular medium: on the same day, a two-column, front-page advertisement in the *Maryborough Advertiser* carries 'An Apology / from the / Town Hall Talkies / to the many intending patrons who were turned away on Saturday night / House packed to capacity / Never enthusiasm like it before', while myriad other stories testify to the popularity of films and their stars. But in the period under discussion, most newspapers clearly aimed to provide a 'complete' news

---

[4] *BSANZ Bulletin* 17.1 (1993): 5-15. Before the introduction of septic systems and sewerage, recycling (with pages torn to an appropriate size) was a major incentive for purchase of a newspaper.

[5] See Beverley Smith, 'Heyday of the Goldfields: 1. The New Journalism', *Westerly* 3 (September 1976): 58 on coverage and Rod Kirkpatrick, *Sworn to no Master: A History of the Provincial Press in Queensland to 1930* (Toowoomba: Darling Downs Institute Press, 1984), p. 300 on rail.

[6] Leigh Edmonds, 'Reading and Listening: How Radio Changed the Dimboola Banner', *BSANZ Bulletin* 23.4 (1994): 249-58.

service to their readers, covering local, metropolitan, national and international news.

Beavan emphasises the importance of geography to the selection of news stories and range of advertising that connects a specific audience to their region and each other. This is something like what Benedict Anderson has called 'imagined communities', populations which find themselves addressed by and represented in print sources such as newspapers and novels, and which consequently regard themselves as having a kind of commonality.[7] Thinking regionally (rather than nationally, as Anderson does), we find that geography, in concert with transport, limits the scope of timely distribution of newspapers, thence the range of businesses for whom it is viable to advertise and thus the audience it is viable to address. These kinds of factors—essentially economic and geographical—have not usually been at the forefront of the mind of scholars interested in the reception of specific literary works. In most literary criticism, newspapers are used mainly as a source of contemporary reviews, with little attention to the local context of that review, or to the significance of other kinds of literary materials which might appear beside it. There are, however, some important exceptions to this trend in Australian literary studies, particularly in relation to the nineteenth century (as Barnes noted). The work of Elizabeth Webby is important here, but neither Webby's findings nor her methods have informed formations of the field as they might have been expected to do, given their weight and significance.[8]

---

[7] *Imagined Communities: Reflections on the Origin and Spread of Nationalism* (London: Verso, 1983; rev. ed., London: Verso, 1991).

[8] For example, 'Australian Literature and the Reading Public in the Eighteen-Twenties', *Southerly* 29.1 (1969): 17–42; 'English Literature in Early Australia: 1840–1849 (Part One)', *Southerly* 36.2 (1976): 200–22; and 'English Literature in Early Australia: 1840–1849 (Part Two)', *Southerly* 36.3 (1976): 297–317.

The relative lack of discussion of the impact of the Depression on Australian literature is perhaps even more surprising. Perhaps the most influential study of this period is Drusilla Modjeska's *Exiles at Home: Australian Women Writers, 1925-1945*, in which Modjeska argues that middle-class women writers were more or less insulated from the disastrous economic conditions. Thus she concludes that it is fascism, not the economic situation, which 'was the over-riding issue of that period'.[9] But her account nevertheless demonstrates that writers were deeply affected, their often straitened circumstances making them acutely aware, for example, of the struggle between 'literature' and other forms—cinema, radio, and genre fiction and magazines, generally regarded as corrupting—for the attention of consumers.[10] Many newspapers published in December 1930 ran stories related explicitly or implicitly to the spread of poverty, and while there is some sense that books were seen as usefully distracting, especially for children, our analysis does not support the view that writers and their work more generally were 'insulated' from economic conditions in any way. Indeed, this would seem unlikely at a time when, for example, 6000 people in Queensland had registered for unemployment benefits, and the state government of New South Wales prepared to sack 600 married women teachers on the grounds that 'their husbands were capable of supporting them'.[11]

The choice of December for the pilot was suggested by senior AustLit researchers: we were hoping to collect 'retrospectives' which discussed the year's best books, as well as Christmas advertisements, and thereby to collect large amounts of data quickly. This did happen, but there was one unanticipated effect: advertising focused heavily on children's annuals, as

---

[9] Drusilla Modjeska, *Exiles at Home: Australian Women Writers, 1925-1945* (London: Sirius/Angus & Robertson, 1981), p. 13.
[10] Ibid., pp. 194, 252.
[11] 'Married Women Teachers', *Sydney Morning Herald*, 23 December 1930, p. 8.

department stores and specialist retailers appealed to Christmas shoppers.[12] *Warne's Pleasure Book for Girls* might now raise an eyebrow, but in December 1930 this was one of around 135 annuals to choose from. The premium annuals, *The Boys'* and *Girls' Own*, were generally priced at fifteen shillings, nearly 20 percent of the minimum weekly male earnings, almost 40 percent of same for women.[13] Their price is perhaps why these titles survive as the iconic examples of the annual as a genre and as a publishing phenomenon.[14] By contrast, popular fiction retailed for one or two shillings, while the prices of rag books, bumper books and novelty books for children were measured in pence.[15] Advertisements placed by 'quality' department stores or specialist literary booksellers often ignored or gave only glancing attention to these much cheaper items, but Sydney's *Sun* was happily hyperbolic in promoting the *No. 7 Sunbeam's Book*: 'Depression flees! … There is not one father, who, buying a "Sunbeams Book" for his boy or girl, doesn't first read every one of its 32 pages with glee. He feels years younger after following Ginger [Meggs] through these hectic adventures.'[16] Almost no other titles achieve the commercial prominence of any one of two dozen leading children's annuals, but most Australian works achieved a certain density of exposure. Among others,

---

[12] There were 734 separate advertisements, notes or reviews—overwhelmingly advertisements—for annuals, although not all annuals were for children.
[13] The basic weekly wage was reduced to £3/17/- (men) and £1/19/- (women).
[14] Very high prices are rare although Macmillan did run a large advertisement in the *Argus* for 'exquisitely bound' editions. The copywriter stumbled, though, for the volumes included *Collected Poems*, *Later Poems*, and *Plays in Prose and Verse* by 'Yates', and the poetry of Dickens. *Argus*, 13 December 1930, p. 6.
[15] Rag books were the size of exercise books (or smaller) and had about ten pages, made of strong white cloth doubled over and bound at the spine with brightly coloured tape. They had gaudy pictures with a line or so of text in large letters on each page; children of pre-school age received them from Santa Claus. We thank Doris Dale for this information.
[16] 'Depression Flees!', *Sun*, 21 December 1930, p. 21.

Vance Palmer's novel *The Passage* was prominent, and Mervyn Skipper's children's book *The White Man's Garden*.[17]

As is the case today, nonfiction seems to have constituted a significant portion of the market, with particular notice given to books by and about male sporting stars. John Johnston's handbooks on meat inspection featured heavily in advertisements, but books by Clarrie Grimmett, Charlie McCartney, M.A. Noble, Geoffrey Tebbutt and 'Plum' Warner on cricket, and Walter Lindrum on billiards, were often referred to in advertisements or notices. Many books about the Australian military forces in World War I were noted, advertised or reviewed, and these took many forms: official histories of campaigns or battalions, individual volumes from multi-volume series (including the official history of Australia's participation in the war), memoirs or novels, military analysis or personal reflections. Travel writing seems to have been a popular interest, and perhaps a slightly larger than normal number of titles with words like 'vagabond' or 'tramp' in were noted. As we might expect, there was some interest in books on economics, finance and banking, including self-help manuals for employers and employees. But in the period covered by the pilot Edward Shann's study *An Economic History of Australia* received only notes, and then only in Adelaide, Perth and Melbourne. Perhaps Shann's work seemed too academic, a fate that might also have befallen W.K. Hancock's *Australia*, which gained some attention in Melbourne and Perth but, like Shann's book, cut little ice in the northern states or country areas. We can note that a similar level of attention was given to Ida Rentoul Outhwaite's *Bunny and Brownie*, a book which history has, rightly or wrongly, judged less influential—likewise J.R. Adams's *Defence at Auction Bridge*, Barbara Cartland's *For What?* and Baroness Emmuska Orczy's *Marivosa*. Further evidence that the reception of specific books and authors could have a

---

[17] Our findings on the length of time for which a book remained 'current' are necessarily very limited during this phase of the research.

quite peculiar regional weighting is that Orczy, author of the Scarlet Pimpernel stories, seems to have been especially popular in New South Wales and in the regions. Why, one wonders, did cities other than Sydney spurn Sir Percy?

In general our data suggest that the book trade in Australia was dominated by the British Empire publishing network, and particularly by English publishers. This presumably reflects the configuration of trade and commerce within the English-speaking world, the division into British and American spheres by copyright law, and the way in which publishers operated within these spheres. While there are quite a number of books by American authors, the snapshot reveals a general absence of Australian books published in the United States (the references to *Ultima Thule*, published in 1929, are a notable exception here). The children's westerns advertised in the *Mudgee Guardian* by local department store Loneragan's might be an exception, although even this evidence is not conclusive as the British Library catalogue indicates that most were published in England by Cassell.[18] While Australian literature and writers were certainly viewed favourably, and could be seen as 'significant' or 'important', in terms of space they occupied a lesser position in the scheme of things than their British counterparts.

The big Australian authors of December 1930 were both Sydney journalists: John Dalley, whose *Only the Morning* was the single most mentioned Australian novel, and Nina Murdoch, whose books were widely advertised. *Miss Emily in Black Lace: A Christmas Tale in which the Heroine is Plain and Perilously Near Forty and the Good Fairy has Bushy Eyebrows and Green Eyes* was for younger readers, while *Seventh Heaven: A Joyous Discovery of Europe* was the first of Murdoch's four travel books

---

[18] 'Loneragan's Big Gulgong Store', *Mudgee Guardian*, 22 December 1930, p. 8, although Loneragan's main store was actually in Mudgee, where their competitors were Kellett's and, to some extent, Roth's.

published that decade. Sacked from her newspaper job (with other married women) in 1930, Murdoch moved into radio and among other things founded *The Argonauts*, an extraordinarily successful ABC radio program for children.[19] For Dalley, it seems possible that his novel about the rise to fame and fortune in England of a young man from Sydney captured the dreams if not the reality for readers of his time, while being featured in advertisements placed by one Sydney bookshop, Angus & Robertson—coincidentally, her publisher—was sufficient to make Murdoch statistically exceptional.[20] What is crucial, here, is that energetic promotion by an individual or a single bookseller (possibly the same thing) means that a book could be projected into the public arena.

These findings—of commercial interest in children's writing, popular novels, classics and nonfiction works, and the occasional emphasis on popular Australian books—will cause no surprise; nor are our conclusions about the dominance of British publishing houses and authors at odds with existing accounts. We turn now to those findings which do trouble received understandings of literary culture, the first of which is the regional specificity evident in the presentation of books, noted in the case of Orczy and others. Our data confirm the presence of a well-established and fairly widespread culture of reviewing within the Australian press in 1930, but this is not confined to the metropolitan newspapers, nor do all metropolitan papers carry such material. Newspapers in country towns have offered an outlet for original criticism and commentary, and an active writer could give

---

[19] AustLit, Nina Murdoch biographical notes, accessed 4 March 2009. Her AustLit record indicates she published widely as a poet, work that has received some mention, but the prose has attracted no interest.
[20] AustLit, John Bede Dalley biographical notes (which quote E. Morris Miller's summary of the novel), accessed 4 March 2009. 'Books for Christmas' [Angus & Robertson, Advertisement], *Sydney Morning Herald*, 13 December 1930, p. 10, featured *Seventh Heaven* as 'The Best 7/6 Christmas Gift Book', calling it 'the best book of its kind we have read for many years'.

considerable weight to local content; recycling of reviews from other sources appears to have been rare.[21]

Some regional centres had a definite (though not necessarily distinct) literary culture, produced by people such as schoolteachers, lawyers and others who brought their literary education and interests to the regions they moved to or had always lived in, a cadre of critics, reviewers and booksellers who operated in non-metropolitan Australia. Past studies have tended to use specialist periodicals or literary societies, usually metropolitan, as markers of the breadth and depth of literary culture in Australia, but our findings suggest that ideas about sources of literary discussion might be challenged to some extent. Apart from advertisements, reviews and notes, quite a few newspapers had a designated space, that is, the literary page/s, which also contained literary essays, literary criticism, literary chit-chat and other material, including poems and anecdotes. We can conclude that many editors and journalists felt confident that books themselves were news, but it is difficult to be conclusive about whether newspapers were significant players without knowing more about the relative influence of, say, libraries, schools, or adult education or literary societies in specific areas. It does seem reasonable to conclude that books were a valued commodity in many communities,

---

[21] Three reviews from the *Age* appeared also in the *Kalgoorlie Miner*, only one with acknowledgement of prior publication. The repeated appearance of the Kalgoorlie paper can lead to suspicion about editorial proprieties at that publication, but if we are taking that view then the puzzle is the *Miner*'s review of H.W. Miller's *The Paris Gun*, which was published in New South Wales twelve days after it had appeared in the west. See '*The Paris Gun*', *Kalgoorlie Miner*, 18 December 1930, p. 7 and *Daily Examiner*, 30 December 1930, p. 1; '*The Mayerling Mystery*', *Age*, 6 December 1930, p. 17 and *Kalgoorlie Miner*, 26 December 1930, p. 2; '*Master Minds of Modern Science*', *Age*, 6 December 1930, p. 17 and *Kalgoorlie Miner* 20 December 1930, p. 2, the source of which is acknowledged; and '*Bapu Gandhi*', *Age*, 13 December 1930, p. 6 and *Kalgoorlie Miner* 31 December 1930, p. 1.

and that for many readers, their newspaper was a key source of information about them.[22]

In terms of literary content, the newspapers can be divided into three groups, shown in the Tables 2, 3 and 4. The first group, of newspapers with very little material, can be divided into two sets: those with virtually no reviews or advertisements (although they might have run a serial), and those with very little literary material by way of reviews or advertisements but which nevertheless had a literary column of some description. To some extent this subdivision is arbitrary, for one could reasonably contend that the *Mercury*'s 'notes' constitute more significant literary content than the one 'review'—here, the term is used generously—published in each of the *Armidale Express* and the *Lithgow Mercury*. But the *Express* did run a weekly 'Poet's Corner', and the *Lithgow Mercury* a monthly 'Australianities' column, so perhaps the more notable point is the inclusion of Adelaide's *Advertiser* in this group. But we should also note that the amount of information about books is in general extremely high by today's standards. The next category is large newspapers, these exclusively metropolitan, with substantial coverage of books. Among these, four newspapers attracted large amounts of advertising: the *West Australian* (the largest advertiser measured in terms of individual titles mentioned), the *Argus*, the *Sydney Morning Herald* and the *Sun* (Sydney). In terms of book reviews, the order is quite different: the *Age*, the *Herald*, the *Sun*, the *Brisbane Courier* and the *Sydney Morning Herald*, all of which managed to publish what now seem like prodigious numbers of book reviews. The balance of advertising to reviewing varied widely in these newspapers, but what they did have in common is that none appears to have given emphasis to books by Austra-

---

[22] Concomitantly, nor can we take the absence of evidence as proof of the lack of importance of books in any given community, given the brief period covered by the pilot.

lian authors. Indeed, the *Age* and the *Herald* seem to have downplayed them.

The third group of newspapers, mostly published in larger country towns, are the most interesting for scholars of Australian literature because they gave disproportionate emphasis to books by Australian authors. The largest number of reviews of Australian books appeared in the *Age* and the *Sun*, but these tend to be of nonfiction works; contrastingly, the largest reviewers of Australian publications *proportionately* were the *Ballarat Courier*, the *Daily Examiner* in Grafton, Rockhampton's *Morning Bulletin* and Townsville's *Daily Bulletin*. Interestingly, the only metropolitan newspaper which emphasised Australian content in this way was the *Sunday Guardian* in Sydney.[23] Notably, the *Morning Bulletin* in December 1930 reviewed only Australian books; the *Ballarat Courier* did equal numbers of Australian and other. Looking more closely at these reviews, we can qualify our excitement a little: some were thinly disguised advertisements, for works ranging from *Miss Emily* to D.P. Macdonald's *Your Marriage* to *The B.P. Magazine*. The only book reviewed in December by these newspapers which would now be called 'literary' was Charlotte Dick's novel *Huon Bell*, although various works for children—*The Gang on Wheels*, *Miss Emily in Black Lace*, *Old Eko's Notebook*, *Pick and the Duffers* and *There Came a Call*—present a more complicated case.

These works for younger readers, and the ubiquitous annuals (particularly commercial ones) were the most frequently reviewed books by Australian authors (assuming that Australian annuals published only local writers, which is unlikely). But there are substantial discussions of

---

[23] The *Geelong Advertiser* and the *Kalgoorlie Miner* are also close to making this list, for which the cut-off was a minimum of four reviews of books by Australian writers, but both reviewed only nonfiction works.

Table 2 Newspapers with Minimal Coverage of Books

Group 1A:	Reviews (% Aust.)	Adverts (% Aust.)	Notes (% Aust.)	Library List (% Aust.)
Transcontinental				
Border Morning Mail			1 (100%)	
Warwick Daily News	1 (100%)			
Yass Tribune-Courier	1 (100%)			
News	2 (100%)		4 (75%)	
Port Fairy Gazette	3 (33.5%)			
Daily Guardian	3 (66.5%)			
Daily Mercury	4 (50%)		2 (0%)	
Mudgee Guardian	20 (10%)			
Mercury	66 (13.5%)	27 (7.5%)		

Group 1B: Few reviews				
Armidale Express	1 (100%)			58 (7%)
Lithgow Mercury	1 (100%)		43 (9.5%)	
Maryborough Advertiser	3 (100%)			
Maryborough Chronicle	5 (20%)	9 (22%)		
Toowoomba Chronicle	8 (12.5%)	48 (12.5%)		
Bendigo Advertiser	16 (12.5%)			
Kalgoorlie Miner	19 (16%)	37 (0%)	2 (50%)	
Advertiser (Adelaide)	21 (9.5%)	85 (6%)	134 (12%)	

Table 3 Newspapers with Substantial Coverage of Books

	Reviews (% Aust.)	Adverts (% Aust.)	Notes (% Aust.)	Library List (% Aust.)
Age	113 (10%)	122 (30.5%)	180 (9%)	
Herald	87 (9%)	37 (32.5%)	123 (18%)	30 (6.5%)
Sun	75 (12%)	227 (17.5%)	181 (6%)	
Argus	68 (12%)	375 (16%)	229 (12%)	
Brisbane Courier	67 (7.5%)	58 (5%)	82 (8.5%)	
Sydney Morning Herald	67 (10.5%)	276 (16.5%)	141 (8%)	99 (11%)
Telegraph	56 (10.5%)	61 (5%)		
West Australian	48 (12.5%)	404 (8.5%)	210 (11%)	

Table 4 Newspapers which Prioritised Works by Australian Writers

	Reviews (% Aust.)	Adverts (% Aust.)	Notes (% Aust.)	Library List (% Aust.)
Morning Bulletin	5 (100%)	22 (13.5%)	1 (0%)	
Daily Examiner	6 (66.5%)	1 (100%)	5 (100%)	
Sunday Guardian	14 (28.5%)		1 (0%)	
Townsville Daily Bulletin	16 (37.5%)	57 (14%)	11 (27%)	5 (0%)
Ballarat Courier	18 (50%)	54 (11%)		
Geelong Advertiser	21 (24%)	3 (0%)		
Examiner	30 (13.5%)	2 (50%)	5 (0%)	

literary topics by Freda Barrymore in the *Townsville Daily Bulletin*, 'C.J. Staughton' in the *Ballarat Courier*, and, just possibly, Nettie Palmer in Rockhampton's *Morning Bulletin* (a series of essays on 'Australian Prose Literature', 'Lawson's Place in Australian Literature', 'Marcus Clarke' and 'Andrew Barton Paterson', each of which has Palmer's distinctive self-confidence and reach).[24] These writers and publications seem to present a fruitful area for further investigation; reviews in the *Sunday Guardian* and the *Examiner* are also more than cursory.

The specificity of literary culture can be demonstrated through brief reference to advertising. Although five newspapers carried no advertisements for books, and a further eleven named fewer than ten titles, most newspapers carried large advertisements in the run-up to Christmas. The *West Australian* advertised more books than any other paper in Australia in December 1930, but this was the effect of a 'department store war' which pitted Boans against Foy & Gibson's, and to a lesser extent, Bairds—Foy & Gibson's also advertised in Brisbane.[25] For such retailers, children's annuals were merely one among many kinds of commodities featured in dramatic and often illustrated multi-column advertisements targeting Christmas shoppers. By contrast to the situation in Perth, book advertising in Sydney newspapers was dominated by two specialist booksellers, Dymocks and Angus & Robertson, who offered a considerable variety of stock. Even so, an apparently fierce antagonism has a certain

---

[24] 'C.J. Staughton' was the pen name of Ballarat solicitor (subsequently Victorian premier) Tom Hollway and Ballarat schoolteacher (subsequently politician) E.H. Montgomery. The essays in the *Morning Bulletin* appeared on 6 December, 13 December (Lawson), 20 December (Clarke), and 27 December (Paterson), always on p. 6.
[25] 'Boans Unequalled Christmas Bargain Carnival', *West Australian*, 2 December 1930, p. 5; [Foy and Gibson's], *West Australian*, 3 December 1930, p. 13; 4 December 1930, p. 19; [Bairds], *West Australian*, 18 December 1930, p. 10.

balletic quality: both advertised on the same page of the same paper on the same day four times over the month of December.[26]

Melbourne's *Argus*, by comparison, benefited from an eclectic list of advertisers, although it was the only one of the three Melbourne papers surveyed to do so. Advertisements were placed by Prahran merchant Read's; three booksellers, A.H. Spencer, H.A. Evans and Mullens; the publisher Macmillan; the department stores Foy & Gibson and Mac-Clellan & Co. (who seem to have advertised in tandem), and Myer's; and the distributor Gordon and Gotch.[27] The *Argus* was also distinctive in carrying something like 'literary classifieds', brief, one-column advertisements for small bookshops, textbooks, the newspaper's own publications, and hard-to-get works like 'Marie Stopes's Books—*Married Love* 2/9, *Wise Parenthood* 3/9 [and] *Hornibrook's Practical Birth Control*'.[28] Several of the bookshops which took less than a column inch in these classifieds early in December placed larger advertisements just

---

[26] Dymocks ran 'Give Books This Xmas', *Sun*, 14 December 1930, p. 27 and 21 December 1930, p. 29; Angus & Robertson offered 'Books for Christmas', *Sun*, 14 December 1930, p. 27 and, more aggressively, 'The Best Books for Christmas Presents are at Angus & Robertson's', 21 December 1930, p. 29. The latter ads appeared in the *Sydney Morning Herald* under the same titles on 13 December 1930, p. 10 and 20 December 1930, p. 10 (with minor changes); those for Dymocks were heavily revised.

[27] 'A Wonderful List of Books, Xmas Cards, &c.', [Read's], 1 December 1930, p. 13; 'A.H. Spencer Pty Ltd / New, Secondhand and Rare Booksellers', 6 December 1930, p. 6 and 20 December 1930, p. 7; 'H.A. Evans and Son', '"Mullens" / Booksellers – Stationers – Librarians', 13 December 1930, p. 6, and 20 December 1930, p. 6, and 'The Best Novels Make the Best Gifts', 22 December 1930, p. 5; 'Macmillan's Cardinal Series / of Beautiful Leather Bindings', 13 December 1930, p. 6; [Foy & Gibson; Maclellan & Co.], 13 December 1930, p. 9 and 17 December 1930, p. 15, and [Myer], 13 December 1930, p. 8; 'The Children's Encyclopedia', 13 December 1930, p. 24 and 'Books are ideal Gifts' [Gordon and Gotch], p. 27.

[28] See the *Argus*, 6 December 1930, p. 6 and 22 December 1930, p. 4.

before Christmas, one cannily offering to buy textbooks in a period when many were likely to be searching for cash.[29]

In Melbourne, Perth and Sydney we can see quite different lineaments. The *Argus* is distinguished by the variety of its book advertisers—which was surely peeving for their competitor the *Age*, which published nearly twice as many reviews, although perhaps the *Age* preferred to be augustly non-commercial about books. The *West Australian* was the beneficiary of competition between department stores, who limited their advertising to a particular genre and market: annuals for children. Two of Sydney's newspapers likewise benefited from a very specific rivalry, this time between specialist booksellers, Angus & Robertson and Dymocks—both of which, remarkably, remain significant presences in the Australian retail market in the early twenty-first century. The specificity of advertising patterns also prevails in country centres, where one bookshop or department store often monopolised the advertising of books, and indeed where local department store rivalries could also break into print advertising. The difference is that country newspapers were much less likely to get advertising from publishers or distributors, although nowhere in our sample does this advertising outweigh that by retailers. This might suggest that the ordering and advertising of books by large, non-specialist retailers played a more central role in affecting what was available and what was read, particularly by children, than might have been thought.

As the study proceeds, we are exploring the question of whether the press in non-metropolitan areas has had a disproportionate role in the promotion of Australian literature, in a period normally thought to have been unkind to local writers and writing. There is emerging evidence of some useful and certainly sustained discussion of contemporary writers, and we might wonder how many of those involved in 'discovering' or

---

[29] 'College, High School, and University / Books Bought at / Hanley's Book Exchange', *Argus*, 20 December 1930, p. 6.

promoting the idea of national literature in the 1950s, for example, contributed to such publications (as Palmer did) in the interwar years, or grew up reading newspapers in which the discussion of Australian literature was frequent and detailed?[30] And this raises a slightly different question: did the assumptions about the significance of local and/or national writing—often manifested in particular emphasis being given in reviews to questions of place and authenticity—interlock with formations of identity in country areas? (Could this still be the case?) Of course, asking such questions risks being seen as ignoring the weight of the metropolitan press. For smaller newspapers, limited audience perforce means limited income from advertising, thence limited page space. In these circumstances it is more difficult, perhaps impossible, for such publications and such places to cultivate a sense that a book is being 'talked about' and valued, notwithstanding the efforts of critics to take books seriously, to encourage readers to do the same, and to put those opinions onto a larger stage. For the scale of the larger metropolitan papers meant that the representation of books worked differently there, aesthetically and commercially. In the *Argus*, for example, the sheer size of the paper meant that a title could be advertised, reviewed, library listed and noted several times over a period of weeks, helping to build up a sense of currency through cross-reference.

Thinking about Anderson's imagined communities, we can say that readers in non-metropolitan areas were much more likely than their metropolitan contemporaries to encounter a kind of dissonance—reading advertisements placed by stores to which they had only very irregular or mail order access, for example, or stories about places they did not personally know. In turn, metropolitan readers were perhaps less likely (and probably less able) to purchase a newspaper which did not

---

[30] For similar arguments see Roe, 'My Brilliant Career and 1890s Goulburn', *Australian Literary Studies* 20.4 (2002): 359–69.

address them directly. Ironically it might be precisely the *lack* of encounter with publications that did not address them—a certain insularity, we might provocatively say—that made metropolitan readers more culturally self-confident. Just as paradoxically, it is perhaps the *commercial* as much as the 'intellectual' density of urban areas that allowed for a sense to develop that certain books were or could be aesthetic (as much as commercial) objects. Certainly the fact of being in a rural or regional area did not mean that literary culture could not exist, in Australia or elsewhere;[31] this is slightly different to the notion of an 'aesthetics of region' that has dominated use of that idea in criticism so far and gives a new slant to that intersection of place and representation of place in literature that makes the aesthetics of a work like Miles Franklin's *My Brilliant Career* so complex and seemingly contradictory. As Jill Roe has argued, there was good reason for the young Franklin to feel, in some ways at least, closely connected to the literary and political debates of her time.[32]

If there is unexpected geographical variation in the discussion of books, we can also say with certainty that books were not just one kind of cultural or commercial capital: they were sources of practical guidance, of consolation or titillation; they were display items, disposable items, childminders and commercial bait. The Book Trade Co-Operative's Christmas advertising campaign encouraged readers to 'Give Books This Christmas' because 'They Cement Friendships'. Likewise, individual retailers pro-

---

[31] J.E. Traue cites William J. Gilmore's *Reading Becomes a Necessity of Life* (1998) as showing that the American state of 'Vermont transformed itself, with a little help from the outside world, into a modern, commercial, industrial and print-intensive economy while still remaining essentially a rural society'. See 'Fiction, Public Libraries and the Reading Public in Colonial New Zealand', *BSANZ Bulletin* 28.4 (2002): 86.
[32] For work of this kind on an earlier period see Jill Roe, '*My Brilliant Career* and 1890s Goulburn'.

moted their stock of annuals as 'reward books', prizes for success in school or community activities.[33] Readers seem to have wanted detail: just under 20 percent of those described in some fashion are reviewed, a remarkable proportion. Australian books constitute about 10–15 percent of the material in each of advertisements, notes and reviews, but that figure conceals huge variations in the data, as indicated in the tables above. These variations constitute a complication for those seeking to use the paradigm of a national literature or literary culture. And this variety brings us to a related point about temporality: readers even in the same region would not necessarily encounter the same books if they used different newspapers for information about possible purchases or library loans. The extraordinary number of books in circulation is daunting not only for researchers but readers. Which was the best, for example, of *Advanced Auction Bridge, Auction Bridge, Complete Bridge for Thinkers, Cornerstones of Auction Bridge, Defence at Auction Bridge, More Lenz on Bridge, Taylor and Hervey on Auction Bridge* or *The Complete Auction Bridge Player*—or would readers have been better off with Murray Sinclair's *Queer Partners*? This very proliferation of books paradoxically makes it more difficult for individual titles to stand out nationally. That there was a total of eight items on Henry Handel Richardson's monumental novel *The Fortunes of Richard Mahony* (including on *Ultima Thule*, volume three) might seem like horrible neglect, but this level of notice was well above average for a literary novel.[34]

---

[33] The trade ad appears in several papers: see for example, the *Sydney Morning Herald*, 6 December 1930, p. 10, although 'Give Books this Christmas' was also picked up by Dymocks for their own advertisement. For 'reward books' see 'Gobbett and Booth', *Toowoomba Chronicle*, 2 December 1930, p. 2.

[34] This is particularly so when bearing in mind that we have so far sampled only a small proportion of Australian papers being published at this time—thirty-two. More than double that number were being published in Queensland alone, although total numbers dropped in the 1920s (from around 100 to 77). In *Sworn to*

The initial collection of data for the 1930 component of the Resourceful Reading project also indicates that scholars will need to be wary about how we constitute our search terms in newly emerging electronic resources. In its simplest terms, the data produced from such searches will be misleading if collection is restricted to authors and texts of existing interest, which is to say, canonical rather than popular. And how can we know which categories are significant until we have already structured the data by designing parameters for its collection? Should we be noting the nationality of the authors of books, their gender, their publisher or their star sign? If we do not know that the most mentioned book of December 1930 is not Virginia Woolf's *A Room of One's Own* but Jeffery Farnol's *Over the Hills*, then without painstaking collection from a wide range of sources, Farnol will not be searched for. He will thereby remain invisible to those who do not remember him in situ.

No Master (Toowoomba: Darling Downs Institute Press, 1984) Rod Kirkpatrick attributes this drop to economic decline, while noting that some were able to take advantage of the circumstances. The Dunn family in Rockhampton, for example, bought the town's evening paper and published it within their own *Morning Bulletin* (300).

7
Magical Numbers*

Ivor Indyk

On 29 April 1982 Peter Blocksidge wrote a memo to Keith McDonald, the finance manager of the University of Queensland Press (UQP), about the so-called MIX System then in use at the press, a computer program designed to determine, in advance, whether a proposed book would be likely to make money or lose money, and therefore to allow decisions about publication to be based on a firm empirical footing.[1]

The programmer was concerned with two values in particular, purchase units or PUs—which would determine whether the cost of the book would be appropriate or not; and gross profit units, or GPUs—which would determine whether the book would make enough profit to make its publication worthwhile.

The formula for the calculation of the purchase unit was the actual cost of production (PC), divided by the model cost for that kind of book (MC), providing of course that no special conditions apply:

---

*I would like to acknowledge the invaluable assistance given by Dr Deborah Jordan in the gathering of information from the University of Queensland Press and University of Queensland archives in relation to the publishing activities described in this essay.

[1] Memo to Keith McDonald, 29 April 1982, UQP Archives.

$$PU = \frac{PC}{MC}$$

This seems straightforward, but immediately complications set in. Many literary titles published in Australia attract subsidies from government funding agencies and other sources—these should be included in the calculation of the production cost, because they reduce that cost, and therefore the outcome of the calculation. On the other hand, there are variables, like author's royalties and related expenses, which also have to be factored in, because they increase the production cost. And so the equation becomes more complex:

$$PU = \frac{PC - \sum_{i=1}^{n} \text{Special conditions amount}}{MC}$$

where subsidies are recorded as positive and author's royalties as negative, so as to count as reductions or additions respectively.

Gross profit units should be easier—after all gross profit is simply the difference between the revenue a book might bring in—its sales value—and its cost:

$$GPU = \frac{SV - R - PC}{GPD}$$

where SV is sales value, R is author's royalty, PC is production cost as original defined, and GPD or gross profit dollars is the ideal income predicted for this category of book.

Already this looks complicated, and PC has yet to be modified in the way indicated in the second equation above. But worse is to come. SV may also be effected by variables, since discounting is an essential part of the selling process, and by no means a constant, depending as it does on the selling point of the book. So the equation to determine likely profit comes to depend on a fraction like this:

143

$$\frac{3 \text{ years Sales} \times \text{RRP} \times (1-\frac{\text{Discount}}{100}) + \sum_{i=1}^{n}\text{Special conditions value} - R - PC - \sum_{i=1}^{n}\text{Special conditions amount}}{GPD}$$

And even then it is not complete, because R—the author's royalties—is a percentage of the selling price of the book, and both the percentage and the selling price are variables, and so R should be replaced by SV x Royalty rate, and SV in turn replaced by everything that stands to the left of R in the equation above.

Hopeless, completely hopeless. There are 'special conditions' everywhere in the equation. The only thing that is constant is GPD, which is what the press would like the book to earn—what it will actually earn remains so uncertain as to be virtually indeterminable from an empirical point of view.

And so it turned out. The attempt to fix the earning power of books in mathematical equations enshrined in a software program was short-lived and soon forgotten. There is no mention of the MIX program, nor its programmer, in *UQP: The Writer's Press 1948–1998*, the official history of the University of Queensland Press.[2]

It is important to note that this effort at empiricism came out of a sense of crisis. In 1981, a special University of Queensland committee appointed to review the operations of UQP handed down its report to the university Senate.[3] The press had been losing a lot of money, as a result of the expansion of its publishing program after 1972. The number of books published annually had doubled from forty to eighty titles, with the intention of creating a back list which would, in time, generate enough income to produce working capital for the publication of new titles. The

---

[2] Craig Munro, ed., *UQP: The Writer's Press* (St Lucia: University of Queensland Press, 1998).

[3] Report of the Committee Appointed to Review the Operations of the University of Queensland Press [20 August 1981], University of Queensland Senate Correspondence 1.10.8 to 10.12.81, Fryer Library, LG704.S44.

university had undertaken to subsidise this expansion by lending the press $50,000 per annum (with interest), but it had not been enough. By 1977 the press owed the university $700,000, with unsold stock (the much-desired but unprofitable back list) valued at another $700,000. The university wrote off $400,000 of this debt in 1977, but by 1980 the amount owing was around $2,000,000, with unsold stock now worth $1,000,000. The press's annual losses and stock write-offs were around $400,000 per annum.

And yet—and this is one of the great ironies of literary publishing, at least in Australia—it was precisely during this decade, from 1972 to 1982–83, that UQP's publishing program laid the foundations for what has since come to be regarded as a renaissance in Australian literature. It was certainly one of its most productive periods. During this decade, UQP made a decisive impact on contemporary Australian poetry with its Paperback Poets series, and on Australian fiction with its Paperback Prose; it introduced other new series, which were ahead of their time, Asian and Pacific Writing, and Contemporary Russian Writing, and the Portable Australian Authors which helped to consolidate Australian literature as a university discipline by providing source material alongside key texts by classic authors. The authors it published at this time include many of the key figures of the coming literary generation, Michael Dransfield, Rodney Hall, David Malouf, Tom Shapcott, Roger McDonald, Vicki Vidiikas, Peter Skrzynecki, Peter Carey, Murray Bail, Michael Wilding, Alan Wearne, Martin Johnston, and then later Barbara Hanrahan, Thea Astley, Olga Masters, Fay Zwicky, Elizabeth Jolley, Dmitris Tsaloumas and Angelo Loukakis. They were important authors, but even though some sold well by literary standards at this time, and many others simply paid their way, they did little to stem the press's losses.

The 1981 report commissioned by the university recommended a plan for the future which involved an appropriate mix of the various categories of titles published by the press (hence the MIX program with its nine categories, PUs and GPDs, and dedicated programmer), and installed a finance officer, Keith McDonald, as assistant manager to the charismatic Frank Thompson, to keep an eye on the practical side of things.

The report was notable for another conclusion, remarkable even now in its frank appreciation of the uneconomical nature of scholarly and literary publishing, 'that given all the conditions now existing, the Press can never reach viability'. As it noted, 'The Press Development Plan was therefore seen by the committee as a basis rather for minimizing the Press loss, than for seeking to achieve a profit'.

What is one to make of the empirical evidence, in relation to literary publishing then, when the sales figures are generally low, and give no indication of the cultural value of the titles in question? The undoubted significance of UQP's publishing program in the 1970s was achieved at great financial cost, which was borne partly by the writers and editors involved, but most obviously by the University of Queensland. The titles in the Paperback Poets series might sell between 500 and 1000 copies: often they sold fewer than 500. Michael Dransfield, who was the most popular poet of this period, sold around 3000 copies each of his two collections, *The Inspector of Tides* and *Streets of the Long Voyage*—but he was the only poet to achieve these sorts of numbers.[4]

The situation was no different at Angus & Robertson, which had the other important poetry imprint at this time. Sales figures for the second half of the 1970s have David Campbell's three collections, *Devil's Rock*, *Words with a Black Orpington* and *Man in the Honeysuckle*, selling around 700 copies each—the last of these was a posthumous publication, and his death led to an increase in demand, so a second print run of 600 copies was produced in 1980. There were similar figures for Vincent

---

[4] I am indebted to Craig Munro and Sam Martin for the recovery of these sales figures and estimates from the royalty cards and publishing schedules in the UQP Archives.

Buckley's *Golden Builders*, Les Murray's *Ethnic Radio* and Geoffrey Lehmann's *Ross's Poems*; 500 for John Tranter's *Red Movie*; 400 for Robert Gray's *Grass Script*; 200 for Jennifer Maiden's *Border Loss*. Les Murray had a similar position at A&R to Dransfield at UQP—yet his landmark collection *The People's Otherworld* sold only 3000 copies over five printings in four years in the early 1980s; and his most controversial individual collection, *The Boys who Sold the Funeral*, sold under 2000 copies.

On the other hand, Murray's various selecteds, published under the title *The Vernacular Republic* (1976, 1982), sold around 23,000 copies in the ten years from 1976. An essentially unprofitable poetry list was effectively subsidised by these selecteds, though only if they were listed on high-school syllabi. Similar volumes by Kenneth Slessor, A.D. Hope and Judith Wright sold in their tens of thousands, regularly, year after year. Without such a listing, it was a similar story as for individual collections: Christopher Brennan's selected sold 3500 copies over eight years before going out of print; Chris Wallace-Crabbe 1100 copies over ten years; Bruce Beaver 800 copies; Geoffrey Lehmann 550; Robert Adamson 1200.[5]

These low figures simply reiterate what one soon comes to recognise, from empirical research, as the baseline reality of literary publishing—its unprofitability, its fundamentally uncommercial nature. It is in what goes on behind or to the side of the figures, elsewhere in the list, or in the publishing program, or in the society at large, those invisible inputs, not the literary appeal of the work in itself, but the operation of public, educational or institutional forces, which suddenly change the scale of things, or produce unexpected surges of interest, that one has to seek the real sources of the literary economy.

---

[5] These figures are drawn from Mitchell Library, Angus & Robertson Archives No. 3, Boxes 144–48 ('Old Royalty Cards') and 207–13 ('Production Record Cards').

In fiction at UQP in the 1970s and 1980s, the print runs were larger than for poetry—around 2500 copies—still not large enough to make a significant profit, even if the print run sold out—and again, profitability depended on particular authors, in this period Peter Carey and Michael Wilding, whose short story collection *The Fat Man in History* and novel *Living Together* sold around 10,000 and 6000 copies respectively in the five years after they appeared. Carey's fiction would become the mainstay of UQP's economy in the 1980s, particularly after *Oscar and Lucinda* won the Booker Prize in 1988 and the Miles Franklin Award in 1989, and subsequently sold in the hundreds of thousands.

It was a similar story with Penguin's much vaunted fiction list in the 1980s: though there were many memorable books, the profitability of the list was owing to a handful of titles, nearly all of which had high-school settings: Randolph Stow's *Merry Go Round in the Sea*, David Malouf's *Johnno* and *Fly Away Peter*, Jessica Anderson's *Tirra Lirra by the River*, Nicholas Jose's *Paper Nautilus*, Helen Garner's *Monkey Grip*, Tim Winton's *Cloudstreet* and Ruth Park's *Harp in the South* and, of course, A.B. Facey's *A Fortunate Life* (nonfiction). Each of these titles also owed its success to its relation to significant aspects of Australian life, in terms of landscape or place, social history or representative types—they had taken on an iconic status, and their adoption into school and university curricula was as much a recognition of this status as it was part of the process which bestowed this aura upon them.

Another example: during the 1980s, Currency Press presided over a golden age in Australian drama, publishing many fine plays by contemporary dramatists—Alex Buzo, Peter Kenna, Jack Hibberd, John Romeril, Dorothy Hewett—alongside Australian classics like *The Sunny South* and *The Summer of the Seventeenth Doll*. But its financial viability depended on one single author—David Williamson—and then on only two of his plays, *The Club* and *The Removalists*, the first of which played on the centrality of football to Australian life, the second on police violence.[6]

It's in this context that I would like to tell the story of three Australian literary titles: one began the progress towards iconic status twenty years after it was first published and had gone out of print; the other two have never achieved large sales despite being grounded in significant moments and aspects of Australian life.

Gerald Murnane has been hailed by many critics, in Australia and overseas, as a classic Australian author. His first work of fiction, *Tamarisk Row*, was published by Heinemann in hardback in 1974. Out of a print run of 3000 hardback copies, 1200 were sold in Australia, 860 were exported to the UK, never to be heard of again, and 787 were remaindered. Angus & Robertson published a paperback edition of 5000 copies in their popular Arkon series in 1976, and only 1100 sold in the next three years, before it was remaindered in 1979. They did a second paperback edition of 3000 copies in their more literary Sirius imprint in 1983, and this time the result was worse, only 465 copies sold over the next three years. There the matter rested for twenty-five years. In 2008 Giramondo republished *Tamarisk Row* in an edition of 1000 copies. It has sold 540 copies.[7]

It is remarkable that a title that has never made anyone any money (Murnane himself claims to have never been paid royalties on any of his books)—indeed has lost a considerable amount of money—should have been published and republished in four separate editions. Clearly there is a conviction shared by its publishers, and its small coterie of readers, that *Tamarisk Row* is a significant work of Australian literature. From a commercial point of view, its publication looks like an exercise in folly.

---

[6] Currency Press papers, National Library of Australia, MS 8084, Records of Currency Press, Box 99, 'Financial Papers, Royalty Totals, 1977–88', Folders 1 and 2.
[7] Sales figures for *Tamarisk Row* provided by Gerald Murnane; Angus & Robertson Archives No. 3, Box 147; Ivor Indyk for Giramondo Publishing.

By contrast, the story of Peter Skrzynecki's poetry collection *Immigrant Chronicle* is one of commercial success, though that success was a very long time coming. The manuscript was sent to Roger McDonald, the poetry editor at UQP, in June 1973. By this time, UQP's Paperback Poets series had established a strong literary reputation, and some of its first eighteen titles—in particular, David Malouf's *Bicycle* and Michael Dransfield's *Streets of the Long Voyage* and *The Inspector of Tides*—had sold out their 1500-copy print runs and been reprinted. McDonald held the manuscript for twelve months to allow Skrzynecki to strengthen it with new poems. A number of titles were suggested by the author—'All the King's Horses', 'Dearest and Most Dead', 'The Speaking Walls'—none of which would have suited the role for which it was destined. McDonald saw straight away, as did his reader Judith Rodriguez, that the most compelling poems in the collection were on the themes of migration and family.

> [Skrzynecki] is a lone representative, on the Australian poetry scene, of the assimilation of post-war migration into the mainstream of this country's intellectual life, and for this reason is a poet of special interest. His poems are largely poems of reflection and observation, but in the course of their 'meditations' on experience they touch on the peculiar pathos of immigrant families: able to put their roots down only so far into the soil of a new land, stunned into an acceptance of the raw shabbiness of inner suburbia that their good luck in surviving the holocaust has handed them.[8]

McDonald's report would form the basis of the blurb on the back of *Immigrant Chronicle* when it came to be published in November 1975.

---

[8] Roger McDonald, note headed '"Immigrant Chronicle" Peter Skrzynecki', February 1975, Peter Skrzynecki editorial file, UQP Archives. The following sales figures are drawn from this file, the UQP royalty card file, and from discussions with the author.

The collection did relatively well—it sold half its print of 2000 copies—but then it went to sleep. It didn't wake again until it was set for the 1991-92 NSW Higher School Certificate examination, in the 2 Unit General course, the most popular of the HSC's English courses. UQP started with a modest reprint of 1000 copies in July 1991, and then quickly produced four more reprints over the next three years, a total of 17,000 copies, with an additional fifth reprint of 9000 copies planned for July 1994. Skrzynecki wrote to his editor Sue Abbey in February 1993 to say that he was touring the far north coast of New South Wales and would have visited ten high schools by the end of the following week; this was immediately after a tour of high schools in the central west of the state. He estimated an audience of around a thousand students. By then UQP had experienced the power of a high-school adoption, particularly in the 'general' courses, but they geared up too quickly. *Immigrant Chronicle* went off the HSC syllabus in 1994, leaving the press with nearly 7000 copies in stock, even before the planned July reprint. This could easily have turned into a disaster, because only 900 copies sold over the next five years. Then, in 2003-04 *Immigrant Chronicle* returned to the 2 Unit General Course. Since then the book has sold over 40,000 copies, one of the largest selling poetry books in the recent history of Australian literature.

If the history of *Tamarisk Row* demonstrates the unalloyed persistence of the Australian literary classic against all common sense—at least of the commercial variety—and *Immigrant Chronicle* the power of educational adoption, Rosa Cappiello's *Oh Lucky Country* owes its existence in English at all to a combination of intellectual goodwill—not easily quantifiable as an input in the economy of publishing—and institutional subsidy. The book had aroused considerable interest in Australia while still in its original Italian (it was published by Feltrinelli in 1981 under the title *Paese fortunato*) both because it was a popular success in Italy (it supposedly sold 70,000 copies in its first month) and because it had won the prestigious Premio Calabria. In Sydney, where it was set, it had also scandalised the local Italian-speaking community with its depiction of Australian life, and its sexual and scatological perspectives. That couldn't be bad for its prospects. But what is remarkable is the extent to which informed critical opinion argued in advance for the translation of the novel. Reviewing *Paese fortunato* at length in the *Age Monthly Review* in October 1982, Franco Schiavoni concluded, 'I have no doubt that *Lucky Country* is a work of considerable maturity and value, deserving an immediate translation, possibly by an Irishman brought up in Leopold Bloom country, and also a film transposition. It is in many ways an uncomfortable text; yet, it unquestionably deserves an important place in Australian letters.'

The translation took three years to organise. UQP's fiction editor, D'Arcy Randall, was conscientious in seeking out the right translator, taking far more time over it than commercial considerations would normally allow. An American, she had previously worked at Louisiana State University Press, which had a distinguished list of works published in translation. She was also committed to rectifying what she perceived as a masculine bias in UQP's fiction list, a commitment that led to the publication of novels by Barbara Hanrahan, Elizabeth Jolley, Olga Masters and Kate Grenville, alongside *Oh Lucky Country*.[9]

The Literature Board of the Australia Council offered Cappiello a General Writer's Grant (she was the first author of non-English speaking background to receive a Literature Board grant), and a writer-in-residence position at the University of Wollongong, where she was able to work closely with the chosen translator, Gaetano Rando, who was himself a lecturer in Italian at the university. Two universities were therefore actively engaged in subsidising the publication of *Oh Lucky Country*, the University of Queensland through the extra work required by its press to bring a translated work to publication, which in this case went well be-

---

[9] Interview with D'Arcy Randall, Sydney, 22 November 2008.

yond the normal commercial constraints, and the University of Wollongong, through its support of the author's residency, and Dr Rando's translation of the novel which, because he was an academic, could be undertaken for considerably less than the normal commercial rate. The Literature Board also made a contribution to the translation fees, and subsidised the publication costs—its total support for the book must have been over $20,000 with the grant, the residency, the translation and publication subsidies.

Oh Lucky Country was published in December 1984, three years after UQP was first told about the book, in a hardback edition of 3000 copies. The critical response was amazing, for a book by a migrant, written originally in a language other than English. The coverage alone was impressive: the major newspapers, journals, review magazines and the women's press and magazines. There was barely a dissenting voice. The most impressive response was Helen Garner's in the journal *Helix*, because it was a recognition and, implicitly, an identification, unconditionally offered, across the divide so powerfully felt then, between the Anglo-Australian mainstream and the migrant writer ('writing from the margins' as the theorists would have it). Garner took her hat off to the translator, 'and then I throw it in the air for the exhilaration that this fabulous, furious woman provokes in me'.

> This is the very opposite of the soft-centred family tales we have come to expect in this genre. These women are the bad girls. They fight back. They manipulate men and each other, they fuck for whatever it can get for them, they con people, they lie and cheat, they hate each other, they turn on each other, they close ranks in rare bursts of solidarity, they slave, they sponge—their work is a purge, a flux, never still, always frantic, exaggerated, violent, melodramatic.
>
> People who are afraid of giving offence to their adopted country should steer clear of the swash-buckling Cappiello. The book rolls along

on a level of rhetoric that leaves the reader breathless with shock and laughter. She's so full of energy and rage she's terrifying.[10]

Yet of that first hardback edition of 3000 copies, fewer than 1300 copies were sold. The remainder had their boards removed, and were reissued as a paperback edition two years later, in 1986. This edition took five years to sell out. A reprint of 1000 copies was ordered in February 1991. But not without some hesitation. Whichever way the sums were done, the reprint would show a loss—even if offered at the highest possible price, even if production overheads were not included in the estimate of costs. 'This really is sad, every copy sold is at a loss. The loss exceeds the O/H 50% of PPB [i.e., the allowance made for overheads]', the finance manager of UQP noted on the costing sheet. 'Remove O/Hd [overhead],' Laurie Muller, the general manager, wrote at the bottom of the sheet. 'Special title, must be kept in print.' What this meant, in effect, was that UQP was paying to keep the book in print because of its cultural significance.[11]

This second paperback edition sold between 100 and 200 copies a year—in 1994 over 300 copies were sold—and by 1997 it had sold out. This time the decision to reprint was harder to make. UQP's agreement with Feltrinelli had lapsed. Cappiello, not having heard from UQP for several years, was resentful and suspicious of her publisher's intentions. She had a reputation of being difficult to deal with ('pathologically misanthropic' was how one member of the press put it). Once again the sums could not be made to add up. They considered a reprint of only 500 copies, or fewer, 50–100 copies print on demand. Finally Laurie Muller, who had saved the book in 1991, pronounced the sentence. 'The ongoing demand for the above title is small,' he wrote in a memorandum dated 23

---

[10] *Helix* 21–22 (Spring 1985): 110–11.
[11] This account of the publishing history of *Oh Lucky Country* is drawn from the Rosa Cappiello editorial file in the UQP Archives.

July 1996, '230 p.a. and only 86 in the past 12 months. We have exhausted its potential. As Rosa is uncooperative it is not worth the anxiety and hostility involved to negotiate a new licence. It is now O/P permanently.'

Previously the will had been there, when the numbers weren't. Now the will wasn't there. *Oh Lucky Country* had sold 4000 copies over a period of twelve years. That's not so bad for a literary title, not so good from a commercial point of view. In the final count the numbers, or rather the lack of numbers, carried the day.[12]

---

[12] It is important not to end on a negative note. The literary title can never be pronounced dead. Since 2003 *Oh Lucky Country* has been available print on demand from the Sydney University Press eStore in its Classic Australian Works series. In 2004, twenty-four copies were sold; in the four years 2005–08 fifteen copies were sold. (Information provided by Sydney University Press.)

8
Emerging Black Writing and the University of Queensland Press*

Deborah Jordan

2009 saw the twentieth anniversary of the David Unaipon Award, the important national prize for Indigenous writing established by the University of Queensland Press (UQP) in 1988. The Black Australian Writers (BAW) series followed in 1990, leading to the publication of prize-winning and highly commended submissions. It is vital that the rich tapestry of these emerging Indigenous voices is celebrated for their subjects and achievement;[1] the focus here is, however, on the responsibilities and function of the publisher in the cultural field in the conception and implementation of the prize and series. Critical to their success was a suspension of belief about cultural values for Indigenous and Black writing. UQP did respond to critiques by the Aboriginal and Torres Strait

---

* Thanks for initial discussions with staff of the Aboriginal and Torres Strait Islander Studies Unit (www.uq.edu.au/departments/unit.html?unit=31) and Yvette Holt of Black Words of AustLit. I would like to thank the staff of UQP and the publisher Madonna Duffy in particular for access to and permission to quote from the UQP Archives.

[1] For an initial selection see *Fresh Cuttings A Celebration of Fiction and Poetry from UQP's Black Writing Series* selected by Sue Abbey and Sandra Phillips (St Lucia: University of Queensland Press, 2003).

community and others. UQP began, then, to make a substantial contribution to the production of a rich and diverse lode of Indigenous literature. In any publisher's archive there are rich resources for the new empiricism and, as Robert Dixon has called for, new 'fact-driven questions'.[2] As part of a wider study of Australian Literary Publishing and its Economies, 1965–1995,[3] both 'visible' and 'invisible' economies are being addressed. The UQP archive contains editorial files, production files and the normal paraphernalia of business history, all of which lend themselves to materialist readings especially. Yet Black writing raises complex issues about cultural value and prestige, politics of authenticity and author recognition, copyright and intellectual property issues, and whiteness, let alone Indigenous cultural and literary expression and Aboriginal cosmologies. It is a contested terrain and challenges a number of divides in literary history, even that between literary and trade fiction, and 'high' and 'popular' culture. The case of Indigenous authors and their publishing histories challenge notions of value and difference, of motivation and intention, of agency and reception. How do we include 'the hidden emotional territory' which as David Marriott warns can be easily 'voided' by positivist objectivity.[4]

What can the history of the book, drawing on publishers' archives, contribute to ongoing debates in Australian literature over emergence of 'classics', the process of canon formation, even the 'death' and subjectivity

---

[2] Robert Dixon, 'Australian Literature and the New Empiricism: A Response to Paul Eggert, "Australian Classics and the Price of Books"', *JASAL* 9 (2008): 158.
[3] This research arises from a wider project on economies of literary publishing in Australia from 1965 to 1995 with Ivor Indyk, Louise Poland, Bruce Sims, Mark Davis, Craig Munro, Jessica Raschke, Jacinta Van Den Berg, John Arnold and David Carter. My special thanks to Bruce Sims and Louise Poland for comments on this essay.
[4] David Marriott, 'Black Cultural Studies', *Year's Work in Critical and Cultural Theory* 16 (2008): 284.

of the author, or Australian literature in its global frame? Black writers were initially defined by UQP to include Aboriginal or Torres Strait Islander, South Seas Islander and also Australian African writers and others. This allowed them to sidestep initially ongoing complex issues of authentication. Nor can these issues be addressed here.[5] Our focus is not on either the authors themselves or readings of their texts, albeit a fascinating field. Contemporary literary and biographical criticism of Aboriginal Literature is developing in its own right; a recent exponent Estelle Castro, for instance, shifts the way we think about Aboriginal ontologies and epistemologies which are woven within the texts.[6]

UQP has been described as the most prolific publisher of Aboriginal and Torres Strait Islander writers worldwide.[7] UQP is an independent publisher which emerged from a focus on the merely scholarly and meeting the requirements of a university in the 1960s under the management of the publisher—the 'larrikin' publisher—Frank Thompson with his visionary and adventurous program. Thompson himself sees some of the press's successes emerging from the cultural divides in Queensland between the old Oxbridge Catholics and the democratic avant-garde. Complex changes were taking place economically, socially and culturally,

---

[5] This important issue became more urgent in the mid-1990s. For a current definition of 'Black' see BlackWords, www.austlit.edu.au/specialistDatasets/BlackWords. Anita Heiss gives a working definition of 'Aboriginal Literature' in 'Indigenous Book Publishing', in David Carter and Anne Galligan, eds, *Making Books: Contemporary Australian Publishing* (St Lucia: University of Queensland Press, 2007), p. 256.

[6] 'Tradition, Creation and Recognition in Aboriginal Literature of the Twentieth and Twenty-First Centuries', PhD thesis, EMSAH University of Queensland /Institut du Monde Anglophone, 2008.

[7] Sandra Phillips 'Publishing Indigenous Writers', in Craig Munro, ed., *UQP: The Writer's Press 1948–1998* (St Lucia: University of Queensland Press, 1998), p. 150. See also Louise Poland, 'An Enduring Record: Aboriginal Publishing in Australia 1988–1998', *British Australian Studies* 16.2 (Winter 2001): 84.

creating a different space for writers, readers and listeners in the 1960s. The changing provisions for Australian copyright and foreign rights enhanced the prospects for independent Australian publishing.

In *UQP: The Writer's Press 1948-1998*, a collection of essays by those closely connected with the press, Craig Munro provides a chronicle of their extraordinary achievements. Not only did the press publish the writings of Peter Carey, David Malouf, Janette Turner Hospital, Michael Dransfield, and Judith Rodriquez among hundreds of others, they fostered multicultural writers such as the tempestuous Rosa Cappiello and reprinted Australian classics by Steele Rudd and Vance Palmer. Under the superb editorial skills of D'Arcy Randall and Rosanne Fitzgibbon, women writers such as Elizabeth Jolley, Olga Masters and Barbara Hanrahan emerged from the shadows. The press also published a number of periodicals and journals, important in generating understandings of writing in Australia. A number of series—in Australian drama, poetry, short-stories, Portable Authors—begun by the press with Thompson, were to be continued by Laurie Muller, who followed Thompson as publisher in the mid-1980s.

A major paradigm shift was taking place in white literary thinking recognising that Australia, the 'land was neither new nor strange'.[8] The Indigenous voice was just beginning to be listened for and find publication in Australia; at the same time the "death" of the author was being proclaimed by French theorists Michel Foucault and Roland Barthes in the northern hemisphere. In Brisbane, Thompson's friend, Brian Clousten of Jacaranda Press, published *We are Going* by Kath Walker [Oodgeroo Noonuccal] in 1964. The book did very well. Given that so much of Australian writing has been shown to depend on the construc-

---

[8] Alan Lawson, D. Blair and Marcie Muir, 'English Language and Literature', in D.H. Borchardt, ed., *Australians: A Guide to Sources* (Sydney: Fairfax, Syme & Weldon Associates, 1987), p. 400.

tion of the Aboriginal person as Other, and as illiterate Other, its publication was an important challenge to the mainstream. The upwelling of publishing was part of an international shift, marked by, as Lydia Wevers finds, Indigenous presses, websites, academic courses and journals.[9]

How do we compare the rich outpouring of new writing in, for instance, Africa from 1972 to 1984 to Australian and UQP publishing programs? Those newly independent countries in Africa of the late 1950s whose curricula were fashioned on European models and traditions wanted to replace European educational literature by Africans for Africans much earlier.[10] In Australia, the halcyon publishing years were more often about inclusion of Australian authors rather than British in Australian curricula at all levels, reaffirmed by the Whitlam era and the subsidies of the Literature Board. UQP was late to create an Indigenous list. From the mid-1970s, Thompson's gaze was overseas; he was dedicated to building up an international market for UQP authors.[11]

While we might suspect openness to Indigenous authors at UQP, only one book has been identified from this early period. It took UQP until 1978 to bring out Kevin Gilbert's *People are Legends*, which was produced in hardback and paperback editions. Gilbert was a high-profile Aboriginal leader, activist, dramatist and writer. In 1971 he had disowned the publication of an earlier version of his poetry, *End of Dream-Time*, because of editorial alterations without his permission; this is a significant and ongoing area of concern in Indigenous writing and one that the press was to continue to address. *People are Legends* was the authorised collection. Unit costs were down because of the Literature Board subsidy

---

[9] Lydia Wevers, 'Globalising Indigenes: Postcolonial Fiction from Australia, New Zealand and the Pacific', *JASAL* 5 (2006): 123.
[10] Becky Clarke, 'The African Writers Series—Celebrating Forty Years of Publishing Distinction', *Research in African Literatures* 34.2 (Summer 2003): 164, passim.
[11] Thompson had been devastated when, after the success of *Johnno*, David Malouf left UQP and found an overseas publisher.

for publication and the book had 'strong sales' of over 1600 copies by 1985.[12] UQP cover material read:

> The voice of the living Australian Aboriginal is rarely heard: but in Gilbert's writings the authentic cry of the dispossessed resounds ... Kevin Gilbert believes Australia is capable of giving justice to Aboriginals and will do so—'if we can bridge that gap of non-understanding of our situation and rights in the matter'.[13]

UQP was not initially at the forefront of publishing Indigenous writers in Australia. David Headon suggests the field was opened up for the best part of a decade through the commitment of Aboriginal Studies Press (established in 1964), Allen & Unwin, Fremantle Arts Centre Press, Magabala (1987), Currency, and to a lesser extent Penguin, Rigby and Angus & Robertson.[14] Anita Heiss names others such as the IAD Press (1972), and the University of Western Australia Press. Munro highlights the importance of BlackBooks.[15] Yet the 'limited representation' of Indigenous people in both specialist and mainstream publishing is 'striking', finds Poland.[16] Given the developing general and educational markets, can we ask like Heiss about the nature of publishers' commitment to supporting Indigenous writing. Is it simply the publishers' ability to iden-

---

[12] Craig Munro has prepared invaluable data on sales figures and print runs for UQP poetry, and this study draws on those.
[13] Former UQP website, www.uqp.com.au, quoted 'Kevin John Gilbert' blackwebs.photoaccess.org.au/~kevingilbert/books/books.html [Accessed 30 February 2009].
[14] David Headon 'A Hectic, Bountiful Decade for Aboriginal Literature', *Canberra Times*, 6 October 1990, p. 38. UQP Archives.
[15] C. Munro, 'Indigenous Writers', in Craig Munro and Robyn Sheahan-Bright, eds, *Paper Empires: A History of the Book in Australia, 1946–2005* (St Lucia: University of Queensland Press, 2006), p. 152.
[16] Poland, 'An Enduring Record', p. 87

tify and market specific Indigenous titles?[17] Australian publishing of Indigenous titles was not the wholesale internationalisation of postcolonial literature by overseas publishing conglomerates as in Africa[18] and elsewhere. Black Australian writing had become commercially viable when UQP first became more involved (as evidenced by the spectacular successes of *My Place* by Sally Morgan first published by Freemantle Arts Centre Press in 1987). Not independent from commerce, UQP did help to shape values removed from it.

By the mid-1980s, UQP had a different publisher, that was Laurie Muller, who was and is committed to the pursuit of a strong Australian Studies list. Muller's was a very different managerial regime from Thompson's. Despite this, however, they seemingly took a very similar approach to the publication of their first volume of Black poetry. *Love Poems and Other Revolutionary Actions* by Dr Roberta Sykes came out in 1988. Just as Gilbert's poems had not been a first edition, Sykes's *Love Poems* had initially been published in 1979 by a small independent press.

UQP approached Sykes. Like Gilbert, she had been extremely prominent in the Black Rights movement of the 1970s. She was poet, writer, political leader, and after her return from Harvard, public intellectual.[19] Just at the time UQP was looking at the options of publishing Sykes's poetry, there was a change of poetry editors. When the new poetry editor, Sue Abbey, read the original volume, she argued that it was 'ridiculous' to pass judgement on work based on Black experience and attitude.[20] Abbey's vision was a relatively rare one in the Australian publishing industry. Not everyone in the press agreed with her on the importance of

---

[17] Heiss, passim.
[18] Compare Robert Fraser, *Book History Through Postcolonial Eyes: Rewriting the Script* (London and New York: Routledge, 2008), p. 185.
[19] Roberta Sykes, *Australian Women Archives Project*, www.womenaustralia.info/biogs/AWE1199b.htm [Accessed 20 February 2009].
[20] Internal memo [n.d.], Bobbi Sykes File, UQP Archives.

Black writing being assessed on its own terms, not in some tradition of English literature. An internal memo argued a different case for the importance of publishing Sykes's poems in terms of their 'topical value as commentary'.[21] The previous poetry editor, Martin Duwell, believed it stood up, reasonably well. Judith Wright was much more enthusiastic, writing, 'Bobbi Sykes is ... one of those "fighters and singers" whose voices and songs we are at last beginning to listen to. She and her compatriot writers are a new energising factor in the writing of the world.'[22]

Can *Love Poems and Other Revolutionary Actions* be seen as a pivotal bridging publication in opening up UQP to Indigenous authors or is the timing of its of publication more haphazard? Included in the UQP poetry series, edited by Nicola Evans and with a foreword by the high profile Indigenous leader Pat O'Shane, *Love Poems* was launched on 5 September 1988. Partly through educational adoptions as a HSC textbook in Victoria, the support of the Aboriginal and feminist communities, and even the marketing strategies and hard work of Sykes herself, the volume was very successful. On an international author tour, funded not by UQP but the Department of Foreign Affairs, Sykes ensured the book was available and then generated considerable interest among buyers. It was one of UQP's best-selling books of poetry. The second print run of 6000 copies came out a year later. A German language edition was published[23] and the requests for permissions to include some of the poems in anthologies started arriving.

UQP set up the David Unaipon Award the same year in 1988. It is a prestigious national literary award for a manuscript by an unpublished Indigenous author. The Bicentenary of the 'founding' of Australia in 1988 focused the white Australian public's attention on the myths of origins as

---

[21] Internal Memo 27 April 1988, Bobbi Sykes File, UQP Archives.
[22] Judith Wright to Craig Munro, 3 June 1988, Bobbi Sykes File, UQP Archives. Sykes had requested a recommendation for the cover to be sent straight to UQP.
[23] WURF in 1990.

perhaps never before, and also provided an opportunity for Indigenous people and their supporters to take a public stance; in 1987 the mainstream had been forced to confront the scandalous findings of the Royal Commission into Deaths in Custody. In Queensland, it was the final extraordinary years of the extremely conservative Joh Bjelke-Petersen National Party government. The polarised community and its cultural politics were a critical context for the formation of the award. While UQP might be selling tens of thousands of copies of Peter Carey's *Illywhacker* worldwide, others such as Ross Fitzgerald's contested history of Queensland had to be withdrawn from sale. Given the embattled nature of the more progressive forces in Queensland, UQP was partly honed in adversity.

Queensland's history of race relations was well theorised and documented by a group of then young Queensland historians through UQP— that is Raymond Evans, Lyndall Ryan, Kay Saunders, Bill Thorpe and Kathryn Cronin. UQP's scholarly and general publications on Aboriginal and Torres Islander subjects was long and distinguished, including those by John Mulvaney and Jennifer Isaacs among others. Under Thompson's management UQP was especially responsive to the publication of Black overseas authors, primarily through its Asia and Pacific series, which included *A Heap of Ashes*, the first English translation of Pramoedya Ananta Toer, now recognised as one of Indonesia's greatest writers. Ulli Beier selected *Black Writing from New Guinea*. After Thompson left UQP in the early 1980s, he went on to work for the Aboriginal Studies Press, employed to revitalise it. There were some attempts at joint publication with UQP, which, however, did not eventuate. When Heiss asked Craig Munro about the foundation of the Unaipon Award, he indicated the important intertextual discursive processes at play, and the politics of author recognition:

> the bi-centenary that galvanised us into feeling more political about it, and feeling that we could make a conscious change in philosophy where we published on Aboriginal topics, we would where possible seek books

by Aboriginal writers, whatever the subject matter or whatever the style of book ... we thought it wasn't just an accident that all of our books in the areas of broad Aboriginal studies had been by non-Aboriginal people.[24]

Under the general editorship of Tony Hassall in a new series Studies in Australian Literature, J.J. Healy's thesis had been turned into *Literature and the Aborigine* and reprinted. Adam Shoemaker also had his doctoral research published as *Black Words, White Page: Aboriginal Literature, 1929-1988*. Both books challenged paradigms in Australian literature. With Jack Davis, Stephen Muecke and Mudgeroo, Shoemaker compiled a selection of Aboriginal and Torres Strait Islander writings. They all actively supported the establishment of a prize, raising the idea in their original manuscript proposal to the Aboriginal Arts Board.[25]

Prizes have increasing currency in the economy of prestige and, while they serve a multitude of purposes as icons and markers, artistic achievement is assumed to be a competition or contest.[26] Despite some expressed ambivalence about the Vogel prize—for UQP saw its role in developing supportive relationships with its authors but 'lost' Gillian Mears when she won the prize to Allen & Unwin—Muller and Munro established the prize for an unpublished manuscript. There was a special Aboriginal and Torres Strait Islander bicentennial fund which had allocated monies to Davis, Muecke, Mudgeroo and Shoemaker for their compilation; part of the grant money was given by them for the inaugural prize. Heading Abbey's argument about the crucial importance of Indige-

---

[24] Anita M. Heiss, *Dhuuluu-Yala = To Talk Straight: Publishing Indigenous Literature* (Canberra: Aboriginal Studies Press, 2003), p. 148.
[25] 'Foreword', Jack Davis, Stephen Muecke, Mudrooroo Narogin and Adam Shoemaker, eds, *Paperbark: A Collection of Black Australian Writings* (St Lucia: University of Queensland Press, 1990), p. xi.
[26] James E. Fisher, *The Economy of Prestige Prizes, Awards, and the Circulation of Cultural Value* (Cambridge, Mass.: Harvard University Press, 2005), p. 4.

nous voices being assessed by Indigenous critics, the centrality of culturally appropriate judgements was enshrined with the formation of the judging panel. The judges were all established Black writers—Oodgeroo Noonuccal, poet; Jack Davis, playwright; Mudrooroo Narogin, novelist. They had ultimate say on the winner (and resulting publication).

In 1989, their first choice was Graeme Dixon's *Holocaust Island*. Opening up UQP to Indigenous authors, as Maggie Nolan finds, opened up new kinds of knowledge and new kinds of readers.[27] When Muller read the manuscript he was impressed: 'This is a talent here we should evaluate a little further'.[28] UQP paid Davis to edit the book. The press printed 1500 copies. When attempting to calculate the optimum number of copies to be printed to cover the costs of cover artwork, overheads, editing and printing, the accountant's scrawl reads:

> Difficulty of making figures work for this kind of book. Unit cost is 4.06 ie gross profit of only 40%. If we sell 1400 we will have done well.[29]

The Literature Board subsidy for publication came in to help cover production costs. Launched by Davis at Shenton House, held during Aboriginal Week and celebrated with dancing, the poems were taken up by community. *Holocaust Island* 'sets a standard and begins a new tradition in Australian writing and publishing' proclaimed Kevin Brophy.[30] 'The three judges,' he continued, 'have chosen a book that stands clearly stranded between a devastated and largely forgotten cultural past and the

---

[27] 'Bitin' Back: Indigenous Writing in Queensland', in Patrick Buckridge and Belinda McKay, eds, *By the Book: A Literary History of Queensland* (St Lucia: University of Queensland Press, 2007), p. 277.
[28] Graeme Dixon File, UQP Archives.
[29] Graeme Dixon File, UQP Archives.
[30] Kevin Brophy, 'Exploring Black Identity', *Australian Book Review* (November 1990): 12.

Table 1 David Unaipon Award Winners

Title	Author	Year
Every Secret Thing	Marie Munkara	2008
Skin Painting	Elizabeth Eileen Hodgson	2007
Me, Antman, and Fleabag	Gayle Kennedy	2006
Anonymous Premonition	Yvette Holt	2005
Swallow the Air	Tara June Winch	2004
Whispers of this Wik Woman	Fiona Doyle	2003
Home	Larissa Behrendt	2002
The Mish	Robert Lowe	2001
Bitin' Back	Vivienne Cleven	1999
Of Muse; Meandering and Midnight	Samuel Wagan Watson	1998
Is that You Ruthie?	Ruth Hegarty	1997
When Darkness Falls	John Bodey	1996
Black Angels, Red Blood	Steven McCarthy	1995
Warrigal's Way	Warrigal (Edward) Anderson	1994
The Sausage Tree	Valda Gee and Rosalie Medcraft	1993
Bridge of Triangles	John Muk Muk Burke	1992
Sweet Water ... Stolen Land	Philip McLaren	1991
Broken Dreams	Bill Dodd	1990
Caprice: A Stockman's Daughter	Doris (Garimara) Pilkington	1989
Holocaust Island	Graeme Dixon	1989

brutal, racist face of modern Australia.' '[T]he poems of *Holocaust Island* rendered,' wrote Headon.³¹ The UQP marketing staff believed: 'This dynamic collection of poetry is sure to attract strong literary acclaim and plenty of the right kind of attention'.³² The book actually was a poetry bestseller, selling well over 1000 copies.

The Unaipon Award taps into the creativity of the Indigenous writing community, finds Sandra Phillips. Through the numerous dynamic Aboriginal writers' organisations, journals and magazines, poetry readings and international conferences developed over the previous decade, contemporary Aboriginal story-telling and writing was 'outing' and visible. Phillips, one of UQP's Indigenous editors from 1995, recalled that between twenty and thirty manuscripts were entered every year in the early 1990s.³³ Louise Poland discussed with her both the implications of the prize in vital feedback to aspiring authors and, on the other hand, the important ramifications for the press itself. The submissions became the primary source in the press for manuscript appraisal of Indigenous authors and the press could offer publication for some of them. The press, as a result, had a 'very clear insight' into contemporary Indigenous literature.³⁴

The first print run of *Paperbark: A Collection of Black Australian Writings,* UQP's very successful anthology, was heavily subsided in 1990. Shoemaker, Davis, Muecke and Mudgeroo's compilation of Aboriginal and Torres Strait Islander writing took six years. Although the editors sought a comprehensive volume, several authors refused inclusion because the book was to be funded by the Aboriginal and Torres Strait

---

³¹ Headon, 'Aboriginal Literature', p. 38.
³² UQP Marketing Plans August, Production File, Graeme Dixon *Holocaust Island*, UQP Archive.
³³ Phillips in Munro, ed., *UQP: The Writer's Press 1948–1998*, p. 152.
³⁴ Phillips quoted by Heiss in Carter and Galligan, eds, *Making Books*, p. 260.

Islander bicentennial fund.[35] So highly conflicted were the bicentennial celebrations that 'a flexible approach' was allowed in the acknowledgement of financial support; the citation page would do, not necessarily on the cover.[36] It sold well with a second print run in November of that year and had a total of four reprints of 26,000 copies. Sales representatives reported that reception across the states varied. It did well in all states except Victoria where booksellers only took two or three copies; in New South Wales 'Most bookshops supported this because it's Australian' and threes and fives were taken 'except in the country where they aren't as fond of books by or on Aboriginals'.[37]

The establishment of a Black Writers series was recommended by Shoemaker, who prepared a position paper. In 1990, the year UQP had generated the greatest profit since its inception, the BAW series began. It includes the Unaipon Award winners and 'highly commended' entrants achieving publication. Bobbi Sykes's *Love Poems and Other Revolutionary Actions* was also included. Oodgeroo, Davis and Mudrooroo and later Mary Graham were the editorial consultants. First series editors were Munro and Clare Forster. Abbey recalled the difference between the urgency of publication of the winning Unaipon manuscript which had to be done within a year, and those commended manuscripts accepted for publication which could be more carefully worked on.[38] Different protocols and procedures could be developed.

The third title in the Black Australian Writers series is a case in point. Joe McGinness's memoir as an Aboriginal leader, activist and unionist from the 1920s submitted in 1989, was originally titled 'Struggle Against Colonial Suppression'. A second title was proposed by the press but rejected because of its negative implications, and the book was finally

---

[35] Headon, 'Aboriginal Literature', p. 38.
[36] Paperbark Files, UQP Archives.
[37] Paperbark Files, UQP Archives.
[38] Sue Abbey, interview with author, December 2008.

published as *Son of Alyandabu: My Fight for Aboriginal Rights* in 1991, two years later. 'Some of my own people are inclined to think that's the law and you can't change the law,' McGinness told journalist Kay Dibben. His was an extraordinary story, as he was centrally placed in many of the key struggles in Australia—on Palm Island, about mining claims and leases, stolen wages, and the 1967 referendum on Aboriginal citizenship. 'We've got moral laws,' he continued, 'you have to live under and laws of the country and then political interpretation of those laws—everyone's got a different idea.'[39] Because he was a first-time author, $1000 to $1200 was allocated for editing. Historical and legal research had to be done, too, and legal costs paid for advice as to acceptable defamation risks. Four thousand paperback copies were printed.

Memoirs, autobiographies and biographies are strongly represented in the early series. In 1990 Doris Pilkington was awarded the Unaipon Award for her fiction manuscript *Caprice: A Stockman's Daughter*, the first in a proposed trilogy that went on to include *Follow the Rabbit-Proof Fence*. The prize had been raised from $2000 to $5000 by the Queensland Minister of Arts. Ruby Langford Ginibi's *My Bundjalong People,* a rich autobiographical account, resulted when Ginibi inquired about any further Black writing anthology. Herb Wharton's autobiographical novel *Unbranded* resulted from his highly commended poetry manuscript. Bill Dodd drew on his own experiences in a moving but hopeful account in *Broken Dreams*. Rosalie Medcraft and Valda Gee's *The Sausage Tree*, even if it was a 'born again Aboriginal story', helped fill in the 'aching gaps', argued Terry Whitebeach, that still remain for many.[40] Was readers' awareness of Indigeneity raised through the publication of such life stories? Especially women's narratives? How do we situate Indigenous

---

[39] 'Unfinished Struggle', *Sunday Sun*, 7 April 1991, p. 4. UQP Archives.
[40] Terry Whitebeach, 'Recent Writing by Indigenous Women', *Australian Women's Book Review* 10 (1998): 3.

writing in relationship to the halcyon days of Australian publishing from the 1960s to the mid-1990s? Phillips refuses the distinction between men's and women's autobiography but she does write of the importance of a 'full range of biographical telling' in a need for 'our' identity as a people.

Authors are historical agents of auto/biographical and cultural criticism and change. Such is the logic of the press and its publications. 'What difference does it make who is speaking?' asked Foucault.[41] 'The difference it makes, in terms of the voices I can persuade you are speaking,' answers the feminist critic Cheryl Walker, 'occupies a crucial position in the ongoing discussion of difference itself.'[42] The publisher's archives provide evidence of the economic disparity between many Blacks and whites, but in general authors are impoverished often needing publishers' advances. The archives gives little insight into questions of difference, only glimpses into the complexity of Indigenous 'subjectivities' and their representations of community, their responsibilities and the importance of opening up the space of listening. They are important questions, but any explanations about the Indigenous 'outing' are to be found beyond the archives, both in the agency of the Indigenous communities and writers, that is their commitment and passion, even the social protest movements of the 1970s and the changing readerships through the power of the consumer. On an initial reading, the archives seem silent on two key players—that is, Oodgeroo Noonuccal and Jack Davis. Oodgeroo was never published by UQP so there is little documentation relating to her involvement. Davis, as a senior Aboriginal figure, rarely penned a letter to the press despite his *A Black Life* being kept in print. Both people were pivotal in the establishment and operation of the award and series.

---

[41] Quoted in Cheryl Walker, 'Feminist Literary Criticism and the Author', *Critical Inquiry* 16.3 (Spring 1990): 571. She refers to his essay 'What is an Author?'.

[42] Walker, 'Feminist Literary Criticism', p. 571.

Mudgeroo and Shoemaker's involvement is much clearer in their frequent, generous readers' reports for the press.

Indigenous titles continued to sell extremely well—most going into reprints (and many of these early titles still in print). Editors and the press did not always agree with the findings of the judges as to the quality of a manuscript, despite being committed, as they were, to its publication. An award winner was not necessarily included in the BAW series. Publicity could be minimal, with few review copies being sent out if the press did not like the book. Notes were made in-house gauging the extent a new author could 'withstand vigorous editing'. When Philip McLaren, film and television script writer and producer,[43] won the Unaipon Award in 1992, the potential commercial success of his novel took careful negotiations between in-house editor (who wanted the manuscript edited to read as a thriller) the freelance editor (whose style was very different and did not see the novel as a detective story) and the experienced but 'unknown' author (whose ideas were clear about inclusion of European as well as Indigenous content). The novel, *Sweet Water ... Stolen Land*, went on to sell very well with a further second print run of 3000 copies in 1993, and film options were taken up, but not foreign publishing rights. A detailed breakdown of sales showed that it was selling best through Dymocks, George Street, central Sydney. It had also been picked up by department stores such as David Jones and Myer.[44]

Different costing for editors—whether in-house or freelance—tracks the commitment to, and difficulties, the press had in working with Aboriginal and Torres Strait first-time authors. When *My Bundjalong Country* was solicited by Abbey it had been rejected by three other publishing houses primarily, she thought, because of the high editorial costs likely.

---

[43] Official Phillip McLaren homepage, www.geocities.com/pmclaren.geo/index.html [Accessed 20 February 2009].
[44] Title Inquiry October 1993, UQP Archives. Magabala Books republished it in 2001.

Abbey termed it the 'white reader's problem'. Abbey noted that $4000 editorial costs were not unusual in the BAW series; they were often nearly as high as printing costs. The different fees charged by professional white editors and emerging Aboriginal editors (several of whom are key figures in the Aboriginal community) warrant further study, so too the nature and extent of editorial changes by white editors. Ginibi thought her book was being prettified to make more readily saleable.[45] Mary Graham was editorial consultant for Pilkington's *Caprice* and very significant in shaping the final product.[46] One of the senior readers urged pruning to allow an emphasis on the Black Australian voice, to cut sections relying on non-Aboriginal historical authorities. When Ginibi challenged why Shoemaker was involved in Aboriginal reviewing, Clare Forster explained her belief that it is good that whites and Blacks could work together on such worthwhile projects.

'It does make a difference that you are Black, that you are a woman, that you are a mother, that you might be thirty, or twenty, or forty, or fifty, or ten—all these things count,' said Cliff Watego to Roberta Sykes in a poetry reading soon after *Love Poems* was published.[47] In the early days Black poetry was associated with political protest, and poetry collections not in this genre faced a difficult journey. But conditions had changed by the time Sykes's second volume of poetry was published by UQP. Associated technologies of the publishing industry were more critical. Sykes's *Eclipse* only had an initial print run of 500 copies, despite earlier plans for 2000 at publishing meetings in the press in late 1995. A print run of 3000 copies would have solved the problem of making a loss on the book.[48]

---

[45] Heiss, *Dhuuluu-Yala*, chapter 5, discusses the editorial experience of many of UQP's Indigenous writers.
[46] Clare Forster to Carole Ferrier, 5 September 1991, UQP Archives.
[47] 'Roberta Sykes with Cliff Watego', in Gerry Turcotte, *Writers in Action: The Writer's Choice Evenings* (Paddington, NSW: Currency Press, 1990), p. 34.
[48] Eclipse Editorial File, UQP Archives.

Print runs in the UQP poetry series were decimated as Docutech, the new print-on-demand printing, became operational. That year Mudrooroo's *Pacific Highway* had the largest print run of 650; only 180 copies of another poet; 300 was standard. *Eclipse* was sold out in the month of publication and was reprinted. Lisa Bellear's *Dreaming in Urban Areas* was printed five times from 1996 to 1998, each time with small runs.

The press privileged the literary. We can see the seeds of the emerging canon in these early days, in the importance the press accorded to literary authors such as Graeme Dixon and John Muk Muk Burke. Abbey believed that Burke's book *Bridge of Triangles* was invaluable because of its literary and poetic qualities. While readers of literary fiction now amount to, finds Fraser, 'a respectable, nay a desirable market in the global economy',[49] UQP's market in the early 1990s was mainly confined to the national. Part of the attraction of Indigenous texts for a globalised culture dealing in discursive or ideological mirages may be, argues Lydia Wevers, the revisioning they force, and the hope they offer of imagining the world locally, specifically, but also radically re-drawn. With now over thirty books in its BAW series, the indefinably Indigenous based in memoirs, biographies and autobiographies is still dominant. Has the press narrowed the gap as much as possible between these fields with literary fiction?

In the dynamic and changing fortunes of UQP, the Unaipon Award continues to serve a vital function in the cultural politics of Indigenous publishing, as too does its Black Australian Writers series. In its formation of a Black judging panel and commitment to follow through with publication, in its acceptance of manuscripts of any genre, in English or any Indigenous language, the award (and resulting series) grew from the principled stand by a powerful press in its heyday. By the mid-1990s proof of Indigeneity was required, and UQP's first Indigenous editor,

---

[49] Fraser, *Book History*, p. 185.

Phillips was appointed with an awareness of what, as Heiss sees, is essential 'cultural and intellectual property rights and issues'.[50] In the early heady years of the Unaipon Award, with the diverse range, genre and quality of applicants, the autonomy of the Black judges allowed them a very broad understanding of Indigeneity. There were occasions when the judges were in conflict with the press. In this convulsing 'outing', whether coming of age or the 'ongoing journey of creative expression', as Phillips casts it,[51] with the recuperation of agency as a profound claim of Indigeneity, the press provided, and continues to provide in modified form, the material conditions of possibility. The complex history of the Unaipon Award will always challenge the certainties of empiricism.

---

[50] Heiss, *Dhuuluu-Yala*, p. 82.
[51] Phillips in Munro, ed., *UQP: The Writer's Press 1948–1998*, p. 157.

9
Making Aboriginal History: The Cultural Mission in Australian Book Publishing and the Publication of Henry Reynolds's *The Other Side of the Frontier*

Mark Davis

Dear Sir,

I would like you to consider my manuscript entitled The Other Side of the Frontier which is subtitled The Aboriginal Response to the Invasion of Australia.[1]

Henry Reynolds's *The Other Side of the Frontier*, which was published by Penguin Books in 1982, two years after Reynolds invited them to consider his manuscript, is considered a landmark book in Australian history because it told frontier history from an Aboriginal point of view. As Humphrey McQueen wrote in his review of the book, 'This is the most important book ever on Aboriginal–European contact'.[2] Yet while the book is now regarded as a classic, it had a complex pre-publication his-

---

[1] Henry Reynolds to Penguin Books, letter, 20 August 1980, Penguin file.
[2] Humphrey McQueen, 'The Conquest of Australia', *National Times*. Undated newspaper review of James Cook University edition, Penguin file.

tory. With his cover letter Reynolds had submitted 'five chapters or about 45,000 words which is the core of the book', and told Penguin that

> I am attracted to Penguin because I want the book to come out reasonably quickly and cheaply and have a wide circulation. I believe it is an important book politically with immediate bearing on the current white-Aboriginal situation.

The manuscript, he added, had been read by Professor C.D. Rowley, who 'recommended that I send it to you', and who 'went so far as to say that it will be one of the best books yet written on Australian history'.[3] But Penguin's editors were initially unimpressed. 'I don't think this book is for us', one wrote, 'I don't like his style very much', before recommending that the book might better be published by Longman as an educational title.[4] An internal memo provided an assessment of the manuscript:

> Henry Reynolds, from his letter, strikes me as quite presumptuous, but he does have a lot of interesting information here. He's not organized [sic] it well—it's very episodic and jumps around from issue to issue and from one geographical area to another. Perhaps the introduction and conclusion would put his general thesis into better perspective. Professor Rowley is certainly one of the best people in the field, but I still don't like Reynolds presentation much.

The memo then canvasses the likely contractual difficulties in publishing the book given that Reynolds had already signed a contract with another publisher, ANU Press. The memo continues:

> However, all that aside, the question remains: do we want a new analysis of Aboriginal history since the coming of white man?[5]

---

[3] Henry Reynolds, letter to Penguin Books, 20 August 1980, Penguin file.
[4] Undated internal note, Penguin file.
[5] Internal memo to Brian Johns, 5 September 1980, Penguin file.

In what follows I want to do three things. First, with reference to the large Penguin archival file for *The Other Side of the Frontier*, I want to briefly document the process by which in-house understandings of the manuscript changed through the publication process, from scepticism to embrace of the manuscript, and the decision-making process that led to it being published. On the one hand this process was relentlessly commercial. On the other hand, during the process the manuscript went from being yet another 'analysis of Aboriginal history since the coming of white man' to being understood as a different type of history altogether.

I also want to consider the publication of *The Other Side of the Frontier* in the context of what might be called the 'cultural mission' in Australian book publishing. My argument, briefly, is that between the late-1950s and the mid-1990s Australian culture went through a particular transformative phase that had peaked by the late 1980s; a period marked by extraordinary energy and reforming, often nationalist, zeal. This was, as Hilary McPhee has since put it, following Penguin founder Allen Lane, a 'creative phase' that would seek to replace the former culture where everything British was absorbed more or less without question.[6] This new mood could be seen in the growing influence of the novels of Patrick White in the 1950s, the proud nationalism of *Meanjin* and *Overland*, the founding of *Nation* and the *Observer* in 1958, or the confidence with which books such as Robin Boyd's *The Australian Ugliness*, Donald Horne's *The Lucky Country*, or Robert Hughes's *The Art of Australia*, were published through the 1960s and found mass audiences—94,000, 250,000 and 56,000 copies respectively in their various Penguin editions—or the willingness of publishers, during the 1970s and 1980s, to put before the public books about topical issues such as feminism and Aboriginal issues, apparently because the social movements to which they were connected were thought as important as the economic reasons

---

[6] Hilary McPhee, *Other People's Words* (Sydney: Picador, 2001), p. 62.

for publishing them. In the rise and decline of this cultural mission it is possible to see, in turn, a transformation in the shape of the Australian public sphere, first, as a combination of nationalism, aversion to British dominance and progressive social movements reshaped Australian cultural life, and then as the very notion of a unitary public sphere began to collapse and fragment through the 1990s in an era of globalisation, marketisation and corporate publishing models, and as the nature of social movements and the contexts in which they operate changed.

Finally, I want to reflect briefly on the new empiricism, and whatever lessons for new methodological approaches might be gleaned from an examination of the publishing history of *The Other Side of the Frontier*.

*   *   *

At issue, here, then, are the micro and macro aspects surrounding the publication Reynolds's book—the in-house reception of the manuscript and the wider culture into which it was published—which, of course, interact.

In the first instance, there was little early acceptance of Reynolds's manuscript. Reynolds has described how he initially sent the manuscript to several publishers, 'whose negative responses', he later said,

> were deeply disappointing. One publisher observed that there were already too many books about the Aborigines; the other that my manuscript had left out many significant themes and that it would need substantial revision.[7]

One reason for their disinterest, as a letter Penguin sent Reynolds two months after his initial approach to them made clear, was that the market for such books was already highly competitive, with several books such as Geoffrey Blainey's *A Land Half Won* having recently been published. The

---

[7] Henry Reynolds, 'New Introduction', *The Other Side of the Frontier: Aboriginal Resistance to the European Invasion of Australia* (Sydney: UNSW Press, 2006), p. 1.

same letter requests substantial revisions to make the book more palatable for a trade audience, before Penguin would consider publication.[8] Four months later, in February 1981, having not heard from Reynolds, they returned the manuscript. Reynolds, in the meantime, disappointed with the response to his manuscript, had made the decision to publish the book himself. As he later wrote, 'Feeling that the readers had not appreciated how innovative the work was', the decision was made to publish it out of his university department. The response from readers was instantaneous: 'The venture was far more successful than we could have imagined. For weeks the departmental office was overwhelmed by orders from all around the country.'[9]

This success reactivated Penguin's interest in the book. An internal note in the archive records that the 'boys at International Bookshop' in Melbourne had buttonholed a senior Penguin figure and asked 'why don't Penguin buy this from James Cook'; and that it was 'selling like hot scones despite high cost' and 'poor production'.[10] In October 1981, having sold most of the 1000 copies of the James Cook University edition, Reynolds sent a copy of the book to Penguin with the suggestion that they publish a second edition. A few weeks later he sent a second letter pointing out that the book had received a favourable review from Humphrey McQueen in the *National Times* and saying that 'the first edition is already half gone. We will have to decide in the next few weeks if to go ahead ourselves and print several thousand more copies.'[11] An internal Penguin memo makes mention of Reynolds's second letter and the positive review and suggests that the book would be worth publishing on the condition that revisions be requested to 'make it easier for the general reader to understand'. The writer adds, 'I think we could get the book

---

[8] Editor letter to Henry Reynolds, letter, 9 October 1980, Penguin file.
[9] Reynolds, 'New Introduction', p. 1.
[10] Internal memo to Brian Johns, 5 March 1981, Penguin file.
[11] Henry Reynolds, letter to Penguin Books, 19 October 1981, Penguin file.

fairly cheaply—Reynolds is not interested in making money', and points out that his previous book published by Cassell had sold over 18,000 copies, of which 5000 were because of Victorian HSC setting. A hand-scrawled note on the bottom of the memo says 'RT says let's do it. 5000 top.'[12]

This, then, is how the decision to publish was made. That the decision-making process was relentlessly commercial tends to undercut the notion that there was somehow a 'golden age' in which publishers operated less commercially than they do now. This impression is confirmed by the businesslike tone of the letter of offer that Penguin sent Reynolds. While such letters are by nature formal, this one is notable for the complete absence of any mention of the virtues of the book that Penguin proposed to acquire. Its main topic of business is instead the royalty rate that was to be offered, which Reynolds, in a subsequent letter, no less hard-nosed than his publisher, contested and was able to renegotiate.[13]

But this isn't to suggest that while Penguin's motives were commercial, there was no understanding of the book or appreciation of its importance. As the archive makes clear, early in the process outside evidence of the likely cultural value of the manuscript was especially important in Penguin's decision to publish it. The endorsement of the book by C.D. Rowley and by booksellers, the Humphrey McQueen review and an offer from Fontana to Reynolds to publish the book in their McQueen-edited politics series were all important factors in its being published. As the archive and recent comments by then-Penguin editor Jackie Yowell and publisher Brian Johns make clear, through the publishing process there was a growing understanding in-house that the book was more than just another 'analysis of Aboriginal history since the coming of white man'.

---

[12] Internal memo to RT, BJ, 30 October 1981, Penguin file.
[13] Editor letter to Henry Reynolds, 17 November 1981, Penguin file.

The Other Side of the Frontier, as Reynolds has said he later realised, took an approach that 'closely paralleled the contemporaneous work' of the subaltern studies group and in particular the work of Ranajit Guha and his concern with 'the failure of traditional history to acknowledge the subaltern as the maker of his own destiny'.[14] Reynolds was also influenced by the work of E.P. Thompson, 'with his commitment to writing history "from below"'.[15] The whole idea of the book, as he wrote in its conclusion, was 'to turn Australian history not upside down, but inside out'.[16] Another influence was Aboriginal people themselves. Reynolds recounts one moment in the genesis of the book when,

> I was visiting a Murray Islander elder with my friends Noel Loos and Eddie Mabo. The old man narrated in characteristic Island style with a loud, commanding voice. He retold stories that he had heard as a child: tales of European castaways, shipwrecks, pearl-diving and the arrival of the London Missionary Society's teachers in 1871. One of the stories was about the appearance of a sailing ship off Murray Island. The old man vividly described the scene. His ancestors were scrutinising the ship and its occupants. They had seen Europeans at the rail just as interested in them. Indeed they were looking through telescopes or what out informant called 'white man's eyes'. I think that may have been the moment when the idea of *The Other Side of the Frontier* first took root.[17]

One can see, through the correspondence in the archive, a growing understanding that the book represented a quantum shift in Aboriginal history because for the first time the history of white settlement was being told in published form from an Aboriginal point of view. What began as a testy correspondence between author and publisher gradually

---

[14] Reynolds, 'New Introduction', p. 4.
[15] Ibid., p. 4.
[16] Henry Reynolds, *The Other Side of the Frontier: Aboriginal Resistance to the European Invasion of Australia* (Ringwood: Penguin, 1982), p. 198.
[17] Reynolds, 'New Introduction', p. 3.

becomes less formal, even jocular, and as the content of the book is grappled with the main task of the editor becomes one of how to best foreground the shift in thinking that the book represented. It is instructive to compare the text of the James Cook edition with the first Penguin edition, to note the changes to the book made by Penguin to recast it for a popular market. The subtitle is changed from the equivocal *An Interpretation of the Aboriginal Response to the Invasion and Settlement of Australia*, to the more confident *Aboriginal Resistance to the European Invasion of Australia*. C.D. Rowley's 'Preface' is expanded slightly to provide a stronger explanatory context for the book, and the introduction is tightened and its focus shifted away from the long process of scholarship that lead to the book and towards its likely impact. Subheadings are introduced to the chapters, authorial 'signposting' is considerably reduced, and the number of footnotes is cut by half to two-thirds in most chapters. The main text, however, in most chapters, stands more or less unchanged, a few editorial tweaks aside.[18] So far as the publishing decision-making process is concerned, then, commerce and ideology were deeply intertwined. The things that made the book radical, and that were missed at first by the Penguin editors, were ultimately the things that made it publishable and saleable.

But I want to turn now briefly to the environment in which the book was published, and to the broader question of its place in the cultural mission in Australian book publishing.

The Other Side of the Frontier, as the Penguin editors' somewhat jaundiced response to the possibility of publishing 'a new analysis of Aboriginal history' suggests, was published in the wake of a series of

---

[18] Henry Reynolds, *The Other Side of the Frontier: An Interpretation of the Aboriginal Response to the Invasion and Settlement of Australia* (Townsville: History Department James Cook University, 1981); Henry Reynolds, *The Other Side of the Frontier: Aboriginal Resistance to the European Invasion of Australia* (Ringwood: Penguin, 1982).

popular and successful books at a time when broad-scale Aboriginal histories were almost fashionable. From the 1960s to the mid-1990s Australian trade publishers made it their business to publish nonfiction books about Aborigines for general readers with an enthusiasm that is these days mostly the preserve of a few select independent publishers, university presses and specialist Aboriginal presses. Many of these books found large popular audiences and made a lasting and important cultural and political impact.

It is striking to note the differences between the Aboriginal publishing programs of the 1970s and 1980s and those of today. As one prominent nonfiction publisher recently told me, anything about Aborigines is now considered 'box office poison'. Yet, in the 1970s, for example, Penguin published popular editions of Kenneth Maddock's *The Australian Aborigines* (1972) and C.D. Rowley's *The Destruction of Aboriginal Society* (1972), *Outcasts in White Australia* (1972), and *The Remote Aborigines* (1972), along with Humphrey McQueen's *Aborigines, Race and Racism* (1974), and Kevin Gilbert's *Living Black* (1977). Penguin began to computerise in the late 1960s and a surprising amount of sales data from the 1970s and 1980s survives intact. Together the Rowley books sold almost 50,000 copies. *Living Black* went on to sell almost 25,000 copies through many reprints.[19] Today any nonfiction book that sells 3000–5000 copies is regarded as successful by most small- to medium-sized publishers. The 1980s saw a new edition of Maddock's *The Australian Aborigines* (1982), and the publication of his *Your Land is our Land* (1983), as well as *The Other Side of the Frontier*, Charles Rowley's *Recovery: The Politics of Aboriginal Reform* (1986), Reynolds's *Law of the Land* (1987), and Ruby

---

[19] All Penguin sales figures in this essay are drawn from company records, kindly made available by Penguin for the ARC research project, Australian Literary Publishing and its Economies, 1965–1995, in which I am an investigator and from which this chapter flows.

Langford Ginibi's *Don't Take your Love to Town* (1988), which sold almost 32,000 copies. In the 1990s Penguin published a new edition of *The Other Side of the Frontier* (1990), Geoffrey Bardon's *Papunya Tula* (1991), Frank Brennan's *Sharing the Country* (1992), and Reynolds's *Fate of a Free People* (1995), though by then sales of individual Aboriginal-related titles had begun to fall, and while sales were strong by today's standards none sold more than 10,000 copies.

Other publishers were no less ambitious. Between the 1960s and 1990s Angus & Robertson, the pre-eminent Australian nonfiction publisher until the rise of Penguin, mined its back list to publish new editions of staples such as Colin Simpson's *Adam in Ochre: Inside Aboriginal Australia*, and A.P. Elkin's *The Australian Aborigines: How to Understand Them*, both of which went through many editions, and Charles P. Mountford's *Brown Men and Red Sand: Journeyings in Wild Australia* (1974, [c. 1948]). They also published originals such as Oodgeroo Noonuccal's *Stradbroke Dreamtime* (1972), Kevin Gilbert's *Because a White Man'll Never Do It* (1973), James Miller's *Koori, A Will to Win: The Heroic Resistance, Survival and Triumph of Black Australia* (1985), Burnum Burnum's *Burnum Burnum's Aboriginal Australia: A Traveller's Guide* (edited by David Stewart, 1988), Al Grassby and Marji Hill's *Six Australian Battlefields: The Black Resistance to Invasion and the White Struggle Against Colonial Oppression* (1988), and Ruby Langford Ginibi's *Real Deadly* (1992).

In the 1960s and 1970s Sun Books published Roland Robinson's *Aboriginal Myths and Legends* (1966), a new edition of Clive Turnbull's 1948 classic *Black War: The Extermination of the Tasmanian Aborigines* (1974) and Geoffrey Blainey's *Triumph of the Nomads* (1976).[20] Through the

---

[20] *Black War* was first published in Melbourne by Cheshire in 1948. Cheshire-Lansdowne republished it in 1965, and Sun Books brought it back into print in 1974.

1980s McPhee Gribble published books such as Phillip Toyne and Daniel Vachon's *Growing up the Country: The Pitjantjatjara Struggle for their Land* (1984), which sold over 6000 copies, Elsie Roughsey's *An Aboriginal Mother Tells of the Old and the New* (1984), which sold over 14,000 copies, Gary Presland's *Land of the Kulin* (1985), which sold 3500 copies before being re-titled *Aboriginal Melbourne* and republished in 1994, and Tony Dingle's *Aboriginal Economy* (1988), which sold 5000 copies.[21] In 1982 Allen & Unwin Australia, then four years old, published Richard Broome's *Aboriginal Australians* (1982). They followed this up with Diane Bell's *Daughters of the Dreaming* (1983), Henry Reynolds's *Frontier* (1987), Robert Hall's *The Black Diggers: Aborigines and Torres Strait Islanders in the Second World War* (1989) and Henry Reynolds's *Dispossession* (1989).

Perhaps the most prolific publisher in the area was Rigby. Through the 1960s and 1970s this Adelaide-based publisher published around thirty-five nonfiction titles on Aboriginal matters. They include Victor Hall's *Dreamtime Justice* (1962), Douglas Lockwood's *I, the Aboriginal*, (1962) (in fact a biography of Waipuldanya [Phillip Roberts] despite Lockwood's appropriation of the first person in the title for his own use, which went through several editions and sold over 85,000 copies),[22] Charles Duguid's *No Dying Race* (1963) (which went through several editions), Ainslie Roberts and Charles P. Mountford's *The Dreamtime: Australian Aboriginal Myths in Paintings* (1965) (which went through many editions), Charles P. Mountford's *The Aborigines and their Country* (1969), Aldo Massola's *Journey to Aboriginal Victoria* (1969), Rex and Bernice Battarbee's *Modern Aboriginal Paintings* (1971), Patsy Adam Smith's *No Tribesman* (1971), Charles Duguid's *Doctor and the Aborigines*

---

[21] McPhee Gribble sales figures taken from Penguin records.
[22] Adam Shoemaker, *Black Words, White Page: Aboriginal Literature 1929–1988*, 3rd ed. (Canberra: ANU E Press, 2004), pp. 93–94.

(1972), Alan Marshall's *These Were my Tribesmen* (1972), Michael Terry's *War of the Warramullas* (1974), Louis A. Allen's *Time Before Morning: Art and Myth of the Australian Aborigines* (1976), Charles P. Mountford's *Nomads of the Australian Desert* (1976), Frank Hardy's, *The Unlucky Australians* (1976) (first published by Nelson in 1968), Charles P. Mountford's *Ayers Rock: Its People, their Beliefs and their Art* (1977), Ella Simon's *Through my Eyes* (1978), Graham Jenkin's *Conquest of the Ngarrindjeri* (1979), Bobbie Hardy's *The World Owes me Nothing* (1979), Keith Cole's, *The Aborigines of Arnhem Land* (1979), and Geoffrey Bardon's *Aboriginal Art of the Western Desert* (1979).

As some of the above sales figures show, the appetite for such books among publishers was in many cases matched by an appetite among readers. *The Other Side of the Frontier* was a popular bestseller that, according the Penguin's records, sold over 30,000 copies. As an illustration of how successful the cultural mission was in commercial terms, it is worth noting that during this same period books such as Anne Summers's *Damned Whores and God's Police*, Miriam Dixson's *The Real Matilda* and Jan Mercer's *The Other Half: Women in Australian Society* clocked up similarly impressive figures (57,000, 26,000, and 21,000 copies respectively). A large-scale longitudinal analysis of the National Library catalogue database gives an idea of the rise and decline of the cultural mission in Australian book publishing with respect to Aboriginal-related nonfiction.[23] Broadly speaking, between the 1960s and the late 1980s a small group of publishers—Rigby, Angus & Robertson, Penguin and, through the 1980s, Allen & Unwin, McPhee Gribble and UQP—

---

[23] Between November 2008 and April 2009 searches were conducted for all non-fiction books held by the NLA published between 1960 and 2008 that had Aboriginal or Aborigine in their title or subject field, excluding those primarily for educational use or for children. The results were then tabulated year-on-year by publisher. The data were then cross-checked against other databases and historical research in the area.

published the lion's share of nonfiction books by or about Aborigines, with a strong emphasis on books with a strong social reformist agenda that was at the heart of the cultural mission. But when imprints such as Rigby, McPhee Gribble and Angus & Robertson were absorbed by multinationals through the 1990s, their Aboriginal-related nonfiction lists were either not maintained by their new owners or else the emphasis of the lists changed. The Rigby list declined significantly after it was taken over by James Hardie in 1979, and while the imprint was kept alive by Reed Books after they bought it in the early 1990s, it was as an educational imprint. The interest in the area showed by Angus & Robertson was to some extent continued by HarperCollins after they took over the firm in 1989, but their output was comparatively sporadic (the average number of Aboriginal-related titles published halved from around a title a year under Angus & Robertson in the decade prior) and was marked by a shift of emphasis towards spiritualism and celebrity-based books. Penguin's publishing in the area peaked in the second half of the 1980s (with seven new titles published between 1985 and 1989, compared to five in the next decade) and the emphasis of their publishing in the area has also changed since the 1970s and 1980s.

Since the 1980s Aboriginal nonfiction publishing has, broadly speaking, split into two streams. On the one hand the cause was maintained by independents and university presses such as Allen & Unwin, FAC Press, UNSW Press and UQP, and specialist Aboriginal houses such as IAD Press, Magabala Books, Aboriginal Studies Press and Black Inc. Publishing. These books are often issues-driven, documentary and/or (auto) biographical, and/or localised in their ambit. As such, in some ways they continue the cultural mission, albeit to a smaller audience than such books enjoyed in the 1970s and 1980s, though as Anita Heiss has written, new concerns around ideas of specificity and identity have inflected the ways lists are constructed.[24] Typical titles are: Colin Tatz, *Genocide in Australia* (Aboriginal Studies Press, 1999); Gillian Hutcherson, *Gong-Wapitja: Women and Art from Yirrkala, Northeast Arnhem Land* (Aboriginal Studies Press, 1998); Jackie Huggins, *Sister Girl: The Writings of Aboriginal Activist and Historian Jackie Huggins* (University of Queensland Press, 1998); Susan Magarey (Ed.), *Human Rights and Reconciliation* (University of Queensland Press, 1999); Rosalind Kidd, *Black Lives, Government Lies* (UNSW Press, 2000); Anna Haebich, *Broken Circles: Fragmenting Indigenous Families 1800–2000* (Fremantle Arts Centre Press, 2000); Ruby Langford Ginibi, *Haunted By the Past* (Allen & Unwin, 1999); Gillian Cowlishaw, *Rednecks, Eggheads and Blackfellas: A Study of Racial Power and Intimacy in Australia* (Allen & Unwin, 1999); Peter Read, *A Rape of the Soul so Profound: The Return of the Stolen Generations* (Allen & Unwin, 1999); Magdalene Williams, *This is my Word = Ngay Janijirr ngank* (Magabala Books, 1999; edited by Pat Torres); Cilka Zagar, *Goodbye Riverbank: The Barwon-Namoi People Tell their Story* (Magabala Books, 2000); Sally Babidge, *Written True, Not Gammon!: A History of Aboriginal Charters Towers* (Black Ink., 2007; with consultation and editorial assistance from Patricia Dallachy and Valerie Alberts); and Rowena MacDonald, *Between Two Worlds: The Commonwealth Government and the Removal of Aboriginal Children of Part Descent in the Northern Territory* (IAD Press, 1995).

The multinationals, meanwhile, more inclined to follow audiences than issues and legally bound to the interests of their shareholders, have published constantly if sporadically in the area, but with a different focus. While autobiography and biography have always been staples of Aboriginal nonfiction publishing, often by or about 'ordinary', unknown people, increasingly the subjects of such books are celebrities in other fields, as

---

[24] Anita M. Heiss, *Dhuuluu-Yala = To Talk Straight: Publishing Indigenous Literature* (Canberra: Aboriginal Studies Press, 2003).

exemplified by books such as Cathy Freeman's *Cathy: Her own Story* (Penguin, 2003), media personality Stan Grant's *The Tears of Strangers: A Memoir* (HarperCollins, 2002) and *Dizzy: The Jason Gillespie Story as Told to Lawrie Colliver* (HarperSports, 2007). Since the 1980s the Penguin Aboriginal issues list has almost single-handedly been carried by Reynolds, most recently in reprints of *The Law of the Land* (1987, 1992, 2003) and *Why Weren't we Told?: A Personal Search for the Truth About our History* (2000). This has been done with a characteristically hard-nosed understanding of the commercial realities of trade publishing. One might note, for example, the packaging of Chloe Hooper's *The Tall Man* (2008) which, while it deals explicitly with an Aboriginal death in custody, makes no mention or hint of Aborigines on its front cover.

At its height the cultural mission, as I've called it, was never simply altruistic. It was commercially driven. As John Hooker, who was Penguin publisher from 1969 to 1978, has said, 'it was a time when radical politics made money'.[25] Hooker's radical politics, it should also be noted, made him enemies. After he published Kevin Gilbert's *Living Black* he heard that conservatives on the British Penguin board thought that he was 'a bit too radical', and that he was even a 'nigger lover'.[26] The cultural mission was driven, too, by the availability of a public. This public was never simply called into being by the books: it existed in tandem with the books, having been called into being by nationalist fervour, social movements, the optimism of the Whitlam era, and the belief that books were an important form of media for engendering social change. As such, the cultural mission demands to be understood as a particular moment in the shaping of the Australian public sphere. New publics were being created and with them, audiences.

---

[25] Geoffrey Dutton, *A Rare Bird: Penguin Books in Australia 1946–96* (Ringwood: Penguin, 1996), p. 97.
[26] Ibid., p. 106.

We might speculate on the reasons for the decline of the cultural mission. One possibility is that the very plurality embraced by books such as *The Other Side of the Frontier* carried the seeds of its undoing. The decline of the cultural mission in the early 1990s marked an era when the consequences of Aboriginal social agency had become deeply problematised. After the Black power struggles of the 1960s, the land rights struggles of the 1980s, the protests of the 1988 Bicentennial of white settlement, and the Mabo and Wik cases of the early 1990s it became less easy to understand Aborigines as passive objects for white liberal concern. Instead, as I've argued elsewhere, they have been more often cast as disruptive to the patterns of white political and economic consensus.[27] 1988 and the Bicentennial, which is when the cultural mission peaked, arguably mark a point after which telling the story of the other and speaking for the other in simple, unitary terms is no longer possible. *The Other Side of the Frontier*, as such, stands near the beginning of a process of giving voice to the other in histories published for a popular audience that has since been challenged by conservative authors such as Keith Windschuttle, whose *Fabrication of Australian History* (2002) discounts Aboriginal accounts of their own histories and attacks the legacy of the radical historians of the 1970s and 1980s. At the same time, the increasing emphasis on celebrity and a turning away by readers from accounts of struggles for social justice towards the personal is consistent with a broad depoliticisation of culture described by many critics, and with a culture where, as I've argued elsewhere, information systems, belief systems and social identities are increasingly fragmented and the cultural imperatives of book production and consumption have fundamentally changed.[28] The

---

[27] Mark Davis, *The Land of Plenty: Australia in the 2000s* (Melbourne: Melbourne University Press, 2008).
[28] Wendy Brown, 'American Nightmare: Neoliberalism, Neoconservatism and De-Democratization', *Political Theory* 34.6 (December 2006): 696; Mark Davis, 'The Decline of the Literary Paradigm in Australian Publishing', in David Carter and

decline of the cultural mission is hence also a crisis in nationalism, and arguably marks a shift in the logic of the Australian public sphere as top-down modes of cultural authority were destabilised by the growth of digitally networked cultures and communities, and by the construction and calling into being of different types of publics; multiple, superficially deracinated, global in outlook, and formed by disjunctive global cultural flows as much as by national ethics of reform, in a world that reaches beyond the printed page to the screen.

But in closing let me reflect very briefly on the new empiricism. Like many who work in the area of publishing studies, I am wary of analysis that understands books as more or less autonomous textual instances, rather than as objects with production and market histories. As such I welcome the scholarly trend towards the use of data and information about how books are published, distributed, and sold, by whom, and in what quantity. Yet it's perhaps because I am a scholar working in the area of publishing studies, and having worked in publishing for two decades, that I would urge caution. Much as it might be tempting to argue that information about the relationship between books and the marketplace, and the availability of certain titles, can yield more insight about the cultural impact of books than 'ideological and discursive explanation[s]', it is important to remember, as those who work in the publishing industry are constantly reminded, availability and audiences don't necessarily go together.[29] To take this point further, many readily available books don't find audiences but are canonised, while others find them but lack canonical status. Mere data, in other words, can't stand in for analysis of the institutional forces by which books are received, read, and sometimes

---

Anne Galligan, eds, *Making Books: Contemporary Australian Publishing* (St Lucia: University of Queensland Press, 2007), pp. 116–31.

[29] Paul Eggert, 'Australian Classics and the Price of Books: The Puzzle of the 1890s', *JASAL Special Issue: The Colonial Present* (2008): 130–57.

remembered. Similarly, even as we focus on the dynamics of supply and demand, we should be wary of any tendency to believe that markets are somehow outside the circuits of institutional meaning-making. Scholarship that assumes the primacy of market forces is perhaps more ideological than it might want to admit. The risk in thinking that raw data are somehow value-free is a kind of market fundamentalism, even market populism, as if markets occasion a perfect democracy of consumption. In the new empiricism there is a temptation, too, to that sort of binarism that invites critics to think empiricism against those theoretical frameworks for analysing texts and their reception that have been so influential since the 1970s, as part of their own cultural mission, and to rediscover social criticism as a search for 'facts'. As I hope the publication history of *The Other Side of the Frontier* shows, the commercial facts of a book's publication and its ideological content and the social context into which it is published are deeply interdependent. No single aspect of a work can be extracted from this ideological web. Books, quite simply, are always, in their every aspect, political objects. Rather than understand data and 'theory' as antithetical, we might embark on the more difficult task of understanding how the empirical facts of book production and the ideological frameworks in which books are published and gain audiences (or not) are in fact inextricably intertwined.

Seeking to understand the cultural mission in Australian book publishing is itself an example of this sort of project. For a time certain types of audience existed, then more or less evaporated. Rather than understand this as simply an occasion for regret, it might be understood in terms of changes to the Australian public sphere. All the changes that took place between the 1950s and the mid-1990s; the changing shape of markets, changes in the way that books were published, and in what numbers, and by whom; were nothing if not ideological. They demand to be understood not merely in terms of the data mining that enables such trends to be perceived, but as very specific social histories.

10
From British Domination to Multinational Conglomeration? A Revised History of Australian Novel Publishing, 1950–2007

Katherine Bode

Recent collections like *Making Books* and *Paper Empires* map an increasingly detailed history of contemporary Australian publishing.[1] Three generally accepted phases of that history are described. From the British-dominated trade of the 1950s and 1960s there emerged, in the 1970s and 1980s, an energetic and independent local publishing industry. In the 1990s, this 'golden age of Australian publishing and the promotion of Australian literature'[2] ended as multinational conglomerates entered, and came to dominate, the Australian book market. As Brigid Magner asserts, 'Transnational corporations have now begun to assume the role formerly

---

[1] David Carter and Anne Galligan, eds, *Making Books: Contemporary Australian Publishing* (St Lucia: University of Queensland Press, 2007) and Craig Munro and Robyn Sheahan-Bright, eds, *Paper Empires: A History of the Book in Australia, 1946–2005* (St Lucia: University of Queensland Press, 2006).
[2] Elizabeth Webby, 'Australian Literature and the Marketplace', in Alison Bartlett, Robert Dixon and Christopher Lee, eds, *Australian Literature and the Public Sphere: Refereed Proceedings of the 1998 ASAL Conference* (Toowoomba: Association for the Study of Australian Literature, 1999), p. 16.

occupied by British publishing companies'.[3] While describing trends in the publishing industry as a whole—including general, educational and trade publishing, and the reprinting of local and overseas books by Australian companies as well as the production of original titles—the basic shape of this history is generally assumed applicable to all aspects of publishing. This is not the case, however, for a particularly high-profile part of that industry: publishing new Australian novels. Using the AustLit database[4] I compiled a list of publishers of new Australian novels from 1950 to 2007, and ranked them according to the number of titles they produced per decade. The tables in the Appendix show the top ten publishers of Australian novel titles for each decade, the approximate number these publishers produced, and the proportion of the decade's total novel output this represents.[5] This data reveals not British domination leading to multinational conglomeration but a concentrated and

---

[3] Brigid Magner, 'Anglo-Australian Relations in the Book Trade', in Munro and Sheahan-Bright, eds, *Paper Empires*, p. 9.
[4] AustLit: The Australian Literary Resource (www.austlit.edu.au), 2002–. I collected the data for this study from AustLit in July 2008. My dataset includes all publications categorised by AustLit as novels, except those works designated 'Non-AustLit Novels' and the non-Australian titles included in AustLit's Banned Novels subset. As with any dataset, the results of this study are approximate. AustLit probably does not contain every Australian novel published from 1950 to 2007 and, as AustLit is regularly updated, the results I present may not be identical to current database records. Nevertheless, the dataset I have collected is certainly large enough and full enough to render the impact of small omissions and errors statistically negligible, and the random nature of errors and omissions in AustLit means broad trends will remain constant regardless of minor changes. The viability of this study is further supported by the relative completeness of records on Australian novels (compared to other fictional forms in AustLit).
[5] In interpreting these results it is vital to note that the companies listed in the Appendix often published under a number of imprints. For example, the results for Horwitz includes novels produced by Transport Publishing Co., Stag, Scripts, Gold Star, Horwitz Grahame and, from 1965, Ure Smith.

Australian-dominated industry opening up to an increasing diversity of publishers, Australian and other.

I chose to focus on Australian novels because of the significant and illuminating hinge this fictional form provides between debates about cultural nationalism on the one hand, and publishing on the other. The historic relationship of the novel and nationalism[6] was explicitly fostered in Australia by critics like the Palmers who, in the 1920s and 1930s, emphasised the importance of the novel to national identity.[7] This established relationship between the novel and Australian nationalism accounts for, and in recent times has been compounded by, the strong associations drawn between the fate of this fictional form and the fate of the Australian publishing industry. At present, this association is most commonly expressed in the idea that both industry and book are dying.[8] I aim to resist and complicate this narrative of decline, while exploring some of the complex ways in which both novel and industry are Janus-faced: turned to the national and the transnational, the cultural and the commercial.

---

[6] Benedict Anderson, *Imagined Communities: Reflections on the Origin and Spread of Nationalism* (London: Verso, 1983).

[7] As Carter notes: 'Against the general elevation of poetry, Palmer's commitment to the novel was symptomatic of the modern form of nationalism and was shared with a generation of literary nationalists who emerged in the 1930s'. See David Carter, 'Critics, Writers, Intellectuals: Australian Literature and its Criticism', in Elizabeth Webby, ed., *The Cambridge Companion to Australian Literature* (Cambridge: Cambridge University Press, 2000), p. 267.

[8] See, for example, Michael Wilding, 'Michael Wilding on Australian Publishing in a Global Environment', *Antipodes* 14 (2000): 152–54; David Myers, 'Getting Published in Australia', *Quadrant* (December 2004): 66–67; Nathan Hollier, 'Between Denial and Despair: Understanding the Decline of Literary Publishing', *Southern Review* 40.1 (2007): 62–77.

British Domination: 1950–70

Craig Munro and John Curtain begin a chapter on Australian publishing 'After the War', with the observation:

> The history of the book in Australia may be characterised as the movement of durable cultural goods over very large distances. Raw material was dispatched to Britain in the form of stories and other texts to be converted into books at the industrial heart of Empire. These were then shipped back to the Antipodes along with numerous other books to satisfy the prodigious appetites of Australian readers. Local publishing was a sideline undertaken by enterprising printers and booksellers.[9]

Contrary to this accepted view, five of the top six publishers of Australian novels in the 1950s, and three of the top five in the 1960s, were Australian. In order of their ranking, these companies are: Horwitz, Cleveland, Action Comics, Calvert and Angus & Robertson in the 1950s, and Cleveland, Horwitz and Calvert in the 1960s.[10] This finding does not deny that British publishers exported a huge volume of books to Australia.[11] But it does challenge the idea that Australian books only or even predominantly became material objects in Britain. It also contradicts Curtain's related argument that, 'In 1953 there were only three Australian publishers—A&R, MUP and F.W. Cheshire—who produced more than 10 titles

---

[9] Craig Munro and John Curtain, 'After the War', in Munro and Sheahan-Bright, eds, *Paper Empires*, p. 3.
[10] Other Australian companies in this top-ten list include the mass-market publisher Webster Publications (at number nine in the 1950s) and Angus & Robertson (at number eight in the 1960s).
[11] See Elizabeth Webby, 'Colonial Writers and Readers', in Elizabeth Webby, ed., *The Cambridge Companion to Australian Literature* (Cambridge: Cambridge University Press, 2000), p. 54; Munro and Curtain, 'After the War', pp. 3–5; and Richard Nile, *The Making of the Australian Literary Imagination* (St Lucia: University of Queensland Press, 2002), p. 27.

per annum'.[12] In fact, Cleveland and Horwitz published around 400 novel titles each in the 1950s, and significantly more than that in the 1960s.

The top five Australian publishers of the 1950s were responsible for approximately 61 percent of Australian novels that decade; in the following decade, the top three Australian companies published 63.7 percent of titles. Cleveland and Horwitz alone were responsible for 41.9 percent of Australian novels published in the 1950s, and 60.8 percent of titles in the following decade.[13] Horwitz's prolificity has been noted.[14] But the comparable—indeed, greater—output of Cleveland, and the remarkable proportion of mid-century Australian novels produced by these companies, has not been adequately recognised.[15] Certainly, these findings show

---

[12] John Curtain, 'How Australian Publishing Won its Way Against the Odds', *Logos* 9.3 (1998): 143.

[13] These findings affirm Munro's observation that 'the fledgling postwar publishing industry ... was once almost exclusively Australian owned and controlled'. However, as regards novel publishing, control was not in the hands of the companies he nominates: namely, Angus & Robertson, Ure Smith and Cheshire. Munro, '2001 Publishing Report Card', in Munro and Sheahan-Bright, *Paper Empires*, p. 86.

[14] Anthony May and Frank Thompson argue that Horwitz 'dominated' (May) and 'was the local leader in' (Thompson) mass-market publishing. May, 'Horwitz', in Munro and Sheahan-Bright, eds, *Paper Empires*, p. 50; Thompson, 'Sixties Larrikins', in Munro and Sheahan-Bright, *Paper Empires*, p. 31.

[15] There are exceptions to this general oversight, including Toni Johnson-Wood's work on Australian pulp fiction. See Toni Johnson-Woods, 'The Mysterious Case of Carter Brown: Or, Who Really Killed the Australian Author?', *Australian Literary Studies* 21.4 (2004): 74–88; Toni Johnson-Woods, '"Pulp" Fiction Industry in Australia 1949–1959', *Antipodes* (June 2006): 63–67. Jason Ensor has also noted that 'Cleveland and Horwitz produced the greatest output of novels from 1954 to 1971 (respectively 1424 and 770 novels each), establishing them as undeniably the most prolific Australian publishers for the period'. It seems, however, that Ensor has not included imprints of Horwitz in this count, and has thus un-

that Australian publishers were responsible for a far greater proportion of Australian novels than has been assumed based on accounts that stress British domination of the industry.

The virtual invisibility of local companies like Cleveland, Horwitz and Calvert in histories of Australian publishing can be attributed to their production of mass-market or pulp-fiction novels. Although these companies have been considered unworthy of inclusion in histories of Australian publishing, attention to them yields valuable insights into industry trends. The success of these mass-market publishers suggests the productive as well as restrictive consequences of British control over book imports into Commonwealth countries. This control was formalised in 1947 in the British Traditional Market Agreement (BTMA), which ruled that:

> Australia-owned publishing companies were not permitted to acquire separate rights to British-originated books. A British publisher buying rights from an American publisher automatically obtained rights to the whole British Empire (except Canada); the US publisher was then obliged to cease supplying the book to Australia and could not sell Australian rights to any Australian publishers.[16]

The negative consequences of this agreement are frequently described. But when these mass-market companies are brought into view, the BTMA emerges as also responsible for the enormous number of Australian novels published locally in this period. Unable to 'acquire separate rights to British-originated books', or to American-originated books where British publishers were involved, these companies had little alternative but to use Australian authors. Ironically, then, most Australian

---

der-stated the output of that company. See Jason Ensor, 'Reprints, International Markets and Local Literary Taste: New Empiricism and Australian Literature', *JASAL Special Issue: The Colonial Present* (2008): 202.

[16] Magner, 'Anglo-Australian Relations', p. 8.

novels of the 1950s and 1960s were published because of the disadvantageous imperial organisation of the mid-twentieth century book market.

Much remains to be written about these mass-market publishers and the fiction they produced: for example, were these genres adapted and hybridised when written by Australian authors and published by Australian companies (as Wendy Griswold and Misty Bastian show was the case when Nigerian authors began writing romance novels[17])? Or should these publishers and this fiction be understood through a cultural imperialist framework (as is suggested by Cleveland's pretence of being an American company and Anthony May's description of Horwitz's output as 'American-style sensational fiction'[18])? And if a cultural imperialist interpretation is most appropriate, to what extent do these publishers displace the traditional colonial relationship—between Australian readers and writers and British publishers and authors—as the definitive or organising feature of Australian publishing until at least the 1960s?

Attention to these mass-market publishers also demonstrates the longstanding of certain marketing strategies considered entirely new to publishing. Dominant in accounts of the contemporary industry is the view that global media conglomerates have forced smaller publishers to adopt new, market-oriented strategies to remain competitive. These include, as Mark Davis summarises them, 'a shift in emphasis from backlist to frontlist titles' and 'marketing strategies that emphasise branding and market saturation', including 'increased emphasis on selling books to

---

[17] Rather than the traditional romance narrative—where a man and a woman fall in love—these Nigerian romances often included a number of men for each woman and/or a refusal of happy endings. Wendy Griswold and Misty Bastian, 'Continuities and Reconstructions in Cross-Cultural Literary Transmission', *Poetics* 16 (1987): 327–51.

[18] May, 'Horwitz', p. 50.

non-traditional outlets, such as discount and variety stores'.[19] The introduction of sales databases into Australian book publishing is seen as fundamental to this shift. As Davis writes: 'It was only with the availability of data from sources such as BookScan that publishers began to shift away from a top-down approach to managing culture to a bottom-up, consumer driven understanding of the market'.[20] Rather than being new, such approaches were foundational strategies of companies like Cleveland and Horwitz. These publishers emphasised their front list, and sold titles mostly in newsagents.[21] Branding and (as is evident from the proportion of Australian novel titles published by these companies) market saturation were also fundamental modes of operation. Even the availability of sales data, and the consumer-driven approach to the market that this enables, is not new. As May notes in his discussion of Horwitz's business strategies: 'Each month the returns figures provided by Gordon and Gotch enabled Horwitz to modify its future publishing in tune with the marketplace'.[22]

The fact that, in the mid-twentieth century, companies like Cleveland and Horwitz saturated the market with their titles and made publishing decisions based on sales data, shows that these approaches pre-dated the arrival of multinational conglomerates. Moreover, the dominance of these mass-market publishers—in terms of the number of titles published—reveals such market-orientation was a dominant trend in Australian publishing in the 1950s and 1960s.[23] These findings challenge

---

[19] Mark Davis, 'The Decline of the Literary Paradigm in Australian Publishing', in Carter and Galligan, eds, *Making Books*, p. 123.
[20] Ibid., pp. 125–26.
[21] May, 'Horwitz', p. 52.
[22] Ibid.
[23] I am not suggesting that, because they are longstanding, such strategies are productive ones in 'literary' terms, however we might define them. As many critics have argued, it is not unproblematic that a market orientation challenges

the view of publishing as newly commercialised—evident, for instance, in Frank Thompson's assertion that multinational corporations have ruined what was a 'gentlemanly'[24] pursuit with a focus on sales. Yet it is also apparent that these mass-market publishers operated in what was effectively a separate economy from the mainstream book trade. In terms of the types of books published, the production values and sales outlets, and even the contracts offered to authors, there was a clear distinction in the 1950s and 1960s between mainstream and mass-market publishers that has all but disappeared in the contemporary industry.

When noted, the success of companies like Cleveland and Horwitz is ascribed to specific historical conditions—including the interruption to book imports into Australia produced by World War II[25] and tariffs on American pulp fiction from 1939 to 1959.[26] Other accounts refer to the prevalence of mid-twentieth century mass-market publishing in the context of its decline, due to the arrival of television.[27] The fate of some Australian mass-market publishers suggests that these historical conditions were influential: Action Comics and Webster Publications—both in the top ten publishers of Australian novels in the 1950s—ceased operations in that decade. However, the continuing success of Cleveland and Horwitz challenges analyses that allow for the prosperity of these companies only under certain, limited historical circumstances. Cleveland and Horwitz remained the top two publishers of Australian novels in the 1970s, so dominant as to produce nearly half of that decade's novel titles.

---

the commercial viability of slower-selling literary titles that contribute in important ways to national and international culture.

[24] Thompson, 'Sixties Larrikins', p. 31.
[25] Munro and Sheahan-Bright, 'After the War', p. 4.
[26] Johnson-Woods, 'The Mysterious Case of Carter Brown', p. 74.
[27] May, 'Horwitz', p. 52; Tim Dolin, 'The Secret Reading Life of Us', in Brian Matthews, ed., *Readers, Writers, Publishers: Essays and Poems* (Canberra: Australian Academy of the Humanities, 2004), p. 115.

In the 1980s, Torstar (owner of Harlequin/Mills & Boon, another mass-market publisher) took the top position, a shift which reflects the relative decline of westerns and war novels and the rise of romance fiction. But Horwitz and Cleveland remained in second and third place respectively, still publishing a very substantial 19.1 percent of Australian novels. Although they slipped from the top ten in the 1990s—to positions twelve (Cleveland) and fourteen (Horwitz)[28]—only in the late 1980s did Horwitz cease publishing Australian novels. Cleveland published Australian novels (mainly westerns) until 2000.

Angus & Robertson is the only non-mass-market Australian publisher in the top ten publishers of Australian novels in the 1950s and 1960s, producing approximately seventy titles in the 1950s (3.65 percent) and forty-eight in the 1960s (1.81 percent). Given Angus & Robertson's high profile in histories of Australian publishing it is not surprising that this company appears as one of the top ten publishers in these decades. But the small percentage of titles produced by the company—particularly compared to the mass-market publishers—contrasts sharply with descriptions of Angus & Robertson as 'the major Australian publisher before and after the war,'[29] 'the most powerful force in Australian bookselling and publishing,'[30] and as 'so dominant that it exercised virtual monopoly power.'[31] Other Australian companies do appear in the top

---

[28] In the 1990s Cleveland and Horwitz published 3.35 percent of Australian novel titles. Horwitz shared the fourteenth ranking in this decade with Fremantle Arts Centre Press (later Fremantle Press).
[29] George Ferguson with Neil James as the authors, 'Flagship Angus & Robertson', in Munro and Sheahan-Bright, eds, Paper Empires, p. 11.
[30] Munro, 'A&R's Takeover Crisis', in Munro and Sheahan-Bright, eds, *Paper Empires*, p. 13.
[31] Mark Davis, 'Literature, Small Publishers and the Market in Culture', *Overland* 190 (Autumn 2008): 6.

twenty publishers of Australian novel titles in the 1950s and 1960s,[32] but the average number of titles produced is small. Given descriptions of Australian publishing at this time as British-dominated, it is also unsurprising that most of the other top ten publishers of Australian novels in the 1950s and 1960s were British-based: namely, Collins, Robert Hale, Hutchinson & Co., Heinemann, and Hodder & Stoughton. Yet as with Angus & Robertson, the output of these British publishers pales in comparison to that of the Australian mass-market publishers.

'National Awakening':[33] 1970s and 1980s

Beginning in the 1970s, the federal and state governments significantly expanded their support for Australian authors and publishers. State governments initiated a number of arts programs and literary awards,[34] while the Literature Board, established by the federal government in 1973, expanded and developed a previous program of 'grants to individual writers' and introduced 'financial incentives to publishers for creative writing programs'.[35] These incentives complemented the Book Bounty scheme, initiated in 1969, which subsidised the cost of printing books in Australia.[36] The 1970s also witnessed the end of the import of British colonial editions to Australia and the BTMA—historical components of

---

[32] These Australian publishers include, in the 1950s, Currawong (number twelve), Dymocks (number eighteen) and the Australasian Book Society (ABS) and Frank Johnson (equal number nineteen), and in the 1960s, Rigby (number fourteen) and ABS (number sixteen). Australian Consolidated Press (ACP) shares the sixteenth position with ABS in the 1960s, but given its international holdings, this company can more appropriately be considered as multinational.

[33] Munro and Curtain, 'After the War', p. 6.

[34] Ken Gelder and Paul Salzman, *The New Diversity: Australian Fiction 1970–88* (Melbourne: McPhee Gribble, 1989), p. 4.

[35] Ibid., p. 2.

[36] Craig Munro, 'Editing, Design and Production', in Munro and Sheahan-Bright, eds, *Paper Empires*, p. 176.

the international book trade that had maintained Australian publishers in a subordinate position in relation to their British and American counterparts.[37] In combination with a series of social and cultural shifts,[38] these political and economic initiatives are widely seen to have fostered literary production, and the development and expansion of the local publishing industry. According to Jim Hart:

> If the 1960s were the infancy of modern Australian publishing, then the 1970s was surely its adolescence—a time of life characterised by rapid growth, increased maturity and an urge for independence, together with experimentation, recklessness, high ideals and overactive hormones.[39]

And if the 1970s were the industry's adolescence, the 1980s were a coming of age. As Anne Galligan asserts, 'for many commentators today, the 1980s represent the golden age of Australian publishing, with the opening out of opportunities to embrace the diversity of Australian society and engage in many new public conversations.'[40]

---

[37] British colonial editions ceased being exported to Australia in 1972 (Magner, 'Anglo-Australian Relations', p. 7). Shortly after this, a court decision in the United States ended the BTMA by allowing Australian publishers 'access to rights for local editions of many US-originated books that had previously been locked into agreements with British publishers' (Jim Hart, 'New Wave Seventies', in Munro and Sheahan-Bright, eds, *Paper Empires*, p. 55).
[38] These include increased funding for Australian universities and the consolidation and teaching of Australian literature in schools and universities; an 'easing of censorship restrictions' (Kerryn Goldsworthy, 'Fiction from 1900 to 1970', in Webby, ed., *The Cambridge Companion*, p. 131); and 'escalating population, greater social and political complexity, widening economic structures and marked cultural diversity' (Delys Bird, 'New Narrations: Contemporary Fiction', in Webby, ed., *The Cambridge Companion*, p. 183).
[39] Jim Hart, 'New Wave Seventies', in Munro and Sheahan-Bright, eds, *Paper Empires*, p. 53.
[40] Galligan, 'The Culture of the Publishing House', p. 43.

This increased support for Australian literature and publishing produces no change in the number or names of the local companies in the top ten publishers of Australian novels in the 1970s: Cleveland, Horwitz and Angus & Robertson remain the only Australian companies in this list. But when the composition of the rest of the field is considered, the effects of this 'national awakening' are perceptible. Leaving aside the companies in the top ten, only six other Australian publishers in the 1950s, and four in the 1960s, produced five or more Australian novels.[41] Thirty or so Australian companies (thirty-two in the 1950s and thirty-one in the 1960s) published between one and four titles. Beginning in the 1970s, this 'tail' of Australian publishers of Australian novels both lengthened and expanded: in other words, there was noticeable growth in Australian publishers producing more than five Australian novels per decade, and in the number publishing between one and four titles. In the 1970s, the three Australian companies in the top ten are joined by ten others that produce more than five titles,[42] and a further sixty-eight that produced between one and four novel titles.[43] By the 1980s, the two Australian companies in the top ten are tailed by sixteen others that produce

---

[41] These companies are: Currawong, Invincible Press, Dymocks, ABS, Frank Johnson and Ure Smith in the 1950s; and Rigby, ABS, Cheshire and Ure Smith in the 1960s. I am not including self-publishers in this or any similar counts as they are not companies.

[42] Six of these companies (Wentworth Press, Alpha Press, Wren Books, Wild & Woolley, Outback Press and Spectrum) began publishing such novels in the late 1960s or early 1970s, while the others (Calvert, Georgian House and ABS) began such publishing in the 1950s or, in the case of Rigby, in 1960. I am not including university presses in this or any similar counts because this category is composed of a number of different publishers rather than a single company.

[43] This result affirms, in relation to the production of Australian novels, Galligan's description of the publishing industry as a whole in 1970s as characterised by the emergence of a number of small independent publishers. Galligan, 'The Culture of the Publishing House', p. 43.

five or more Australian novels,[44] and a further 168 that publish between one and four titles. Remarkably, the publishers responsible for five or more titles in the 1970s have disappeared from this category in the 1980s. With the exception of Hyland House and Hale & Iremonger, both of which began producing Australian novels in 1979, the companies responsible for five or more titles in the 1980s all began such publishing in that decade. While the significant growth in Australian publishers of Australian novels in the 1970s and 1980s lends support to claims of a 'golden age', this changing of the guard implies a significantly more complex and broken reality than that phrase implies.

In the 1980s, this expansion in Australian-based publishing of Australian novels begins to have an effect on the list of the top ten publishers—but in a different form to the publishing companies discussed to this point. At number seven in this decade is self-publishing and, at number eight, university presses. I have categorised novels as 'self-published' only when 'The Author' is listed as the publisher in AustLit, or the publisher is a small company established by the author to publish only that author's works; titles produced by subsidy or vanity presses, and individuals publishing other individuals' novels, are not listed as self-published. Catalogued individually, self-publishers would obviously not rank in the top ten producers of Australian novels: most are responsible for only one or two titles. I have grouped them together to demonstrate the prevalence of this publishing trend. Self-publishers continue to appear in the top ten publishers of Australian novels in all subsequent decades, and achieve their highest proportion of total titles (5.31 percent) in the 1990s. The

---

[44] These companies are: Hale & Iremonger, Hyland House, Fremantle Arts Centre Press, Pascoe Publishing, Boolarong Press, Dykebooks, Greenhouse Publications, Access Press, Animo Publishing, Cory & Collins, Rastar, Artlook Books, Aurora Press, Hudson Publishing, John Ferguson and Wobutoft Books. The number rises to seventeen Australian publishers if the co-publishing agreement between McPhee Gribble and Penguin is included.

relatively high proportion of self-published works since the 1980s shows that the 'explosion' of self-publishing, usually identified with the 'end of the century',[45] actually occurred earlier (indeed, self-publishers are the eleventh ranked publishers of Australian novel titles in the 1970s, producing more titles than the university presses, which are ranked thirteenth in that decade). The claim that self-publishing became popular in the late 1990s arises from the perception that it became increasingly difficult, from this time, for authors to attain publication through traditional avenues. If difficulty is the underlying cause of self-publishing, the earlier prevalence of this trend indicates that these difficulties preceded the 1990s.

Although self-publishing is frequently dismissed by scholars who take for granted that it is proof of lack of quality, it is a phenomenon deserving of attention, not only due to its prevalence, but for the challenge it poses to established ways of thinking about the relationship between market and literary value. High cultural forms are habitually distinguished from their low cultural others via supposed freedom from the market: a distinction is drawn, John Frow notes, 'between works founded in freedom and internal necessity, on the one hand, and in unfreedom and external (economic) necessity on the other'.[46] The complicated place of self-publishing in relation to this dichotomy is evident in the contradictory ways in which the activity is criticised. On the one hand, the relative separation of self-publishing from commodity production and the publishing market makes it all the more noticeable how often this activity is explained (and explained away) as a product of naïve economic self-

---

[45] Michael Webster, 'Into the Global Era', in Munro and Sheahan-Bright, eds, *Paper Empires*, p. 82.

[46] John Frow, *Cultural Studies and Cultural Value* (Oxford: Clarendon Press, 1995): pp. 17–18. As Frow notes, this 'binary logic is from the beginning undermined by the absorption of both "high" and "low" culture into commodity production' (17).

interest: these authors, it is routinely assumed, self-publish because they unwisely believe their novels will make them rich and famous. This association continues despite the fact that fame and fortune are rarely the outcome of self-publication. On the other hand, the assumption that self-published works are of dubious literary quality challenges the correlated association of escape from commodity culture with aesthetic value and literary achievement.

Like self-published authors, university presses would not rank in the top ten if listed individually.[47] However, as with self-publishers, I have grouped these presses together because they represent a particular type of publishing. Although their ranking has fluctuated (from position thirteen in the 1970s, to seven in the 1980s, to ten in the 1990s and back to seven in the 2000s), university presses have published an increasing proportion of Australian novels. But while the number of titles they publish has grown, it has remained a relatively small proportion of the Australian novel field. The remarkable contrast between the critical attention paid to university presses in histories of Australian publishing, and the proportion of titles produced by such presses, highlights both the critical focus on literary fiction and the small proportion of the publishing industry treated by academic analyses. The differing attitude towards university

---

[47] Oxford University Press is the only university press I have excluded from this category. I have done so due to the press's multinational profile. Only two of the university presses I have included in this category are not Australian: the University of the South Pacific published one Australian novel title in the 2000s, and the Institute of Papua New Guinea Studies published six titles in the 1970s and one in the 1980s. Unsurprisingly, the University of Queensland Press (UQP) is responsible for a significant majority of the titles in this category. UQP published ten of seventeen Australian novel titles produced by university presses (excluding OUP) in the 1970s (representing 58.8 percent of university press novel publications); forty-four of forty-nine titles in the 1980s (89.8 percent); ninety-five of 118 titles in the 1990s (80.5 percent); and seventy-five of 116 titles published up to 2007 (64.7 percent).

presses and self-publishers reinforces the challenge that self-publishing poses to the division of market and literary value. While university presses are more implicated in the market than self-publishers, self-publishers are accused of economic self-interest where university presses are imbued with a degree of cultural capital that supposes freedom from the market. The appearance of these alternative forms of publishing in the top ten publishers of Australian novels from the 1970s is particularly noticeable in the context of a parallel trend: the entry and growth of multinational publishing conglomerates.

Multinational Domination: 1990–

Throughout accounts of contemporary Australian publishing, the 1990s and 2000s are identified as an era of trade deregulation, economic rationalism, and the resulting rise and ascendancy of multinational conglomerates.[48] One of the most comprehensive of such analyses is Davis's account of how 'successive Australian governments have progressively "opened up" the Australian economy to international competition, ending industry assistance schemes, eliminating remaining tariffs and encouraging exports'. Davis identifies a series of decisions relating to this economic shift that particularly impacted the Australian publishing industry, including: 'changes to the copyright law to allow the parallel import of books from the United States in 1991, and the axing by the Howard government in 1996 of the Book Bounty ... [t]he introduction in 2000 of GST on all non-food retail products ... [producing] for the first time, a sales tax on books' and '[l]ow levels of government funding for literature'.[49] Due to these changes, '[s]ince the mid-1990s the industry has globalised and consolidated to become an information-based business,

---

[48] For example, David Carter and Anne Galligan, 'Introduction', in Carter and Galligan, eds, *Making Books*, p. 6; Munro, '2001 Publishing Report Card', p. 87.

[49] Davis, 'The Decline of the Literary Paradigm in Australian Publishing', p. 121.

beholden, in the case of nine out of ten of Australia's top companies, to global media giants'.[50] In relation to Australian novel publishing, however, multinationals were present well before the 1990s.

If one were to be pedantic, one could argue that multinational publishers have had a presence in the Australian book industry since the nineteenth century, when British-based companies like Collins and Macmillan established branches in Australia. Based on the *OED* definition of multinational—'Of a company or other organization: operating in several or many countries'[51]—the earlier presence of British publishers in Australia was multinational expansion. But these early multinationals differ in important ways from the conglomerates of contemporary publishing. Where these British-based companies opened branches in other countries, multinational conglomerates like News Corporation and Bertelsmann acquire other publishing companies (in fact, both Collins and Macmillan have now been subsumed in this way[52]). In particular, where these earlier multinationals were dedicated book publishers, today's conglomerates engage, as Galligan puts it, in 'publishing as part of the entertainment industry'.[53] This lack of specialism is seen to reflect an economic system where shareholder profits are privileged to the detriment of literary, and especially local literary, production.

Multinational conglomerates began appearing in the top ten publishers of Australian novels in the 1970s, with Torstar's acquisition of Harlequin/Mills & Boon, and the entry into the Australian market of Thomson, a Canadian-based media conglomerate with interests in pub-

---

[50] Ibid., p. 119.
[51] 'multinational, adj.' OED Online. Oxford University Press (June 2008), online, dictionary.oed.com/cgi/entry/00318191?single=1&query_type=word&queryword =multinational&first=1&max_to_show=10 [Accessed 23 February 2009].
[52] In 1989 News Corporation acquired Collins and, in 1999, Holtzbrinck acquired Macmillan.
[53] Galligan, 'The Culture of the Publishing House', p. 44.

lishing, travel and natural resources.[54] The presence and impact of these conglomerates increased in the 1980s: Torstar published the most Australian novel titles of any publisher; Pearson and News Corporation (the latter via the acquisition of Angus & Robertson) also entered the top ten in this decade. Including all multinational conglomerates involved in publishing Australian novels, from the 1970s to the 1980s the proportion of titles produced by these companies increased from 10 percent to 30.5 percent.[55]

While multinational conglomerates entered the Australian novel market earlier than is commonly acknowledged, it is the case that this trend was consolidated, as Davis and others suggest, in the 1990s and 2000s. With the exception of self-publishing and university presses, and of Allen & Unwin in the 2000s, the top ten publishers of Australian novel titles in the 1990s and 2000s are all either multinational conglomerates (Torstar, Pearson, News Corporation, Bertelsmann, Reed Elsevier and Hachette Livre) or companies that were soon to be subsumed into multinational conglomerates (Pan Macmillan, Random House, Hodder Headline and

---

[54] Thomson Organization, 'Company Research Guide', online (2009), www.123exp-orgs.com/t/00514212362/ [Accessed 4 March 2009].

[55] The multinational conglomerates I have counted in these decades are: 1970s—ACP, Bertelsmann, Granada, James Hardie Ltd, Pearson, Reed Elsevier, Thomson Organization, Time Warner and Torstar; 1980s—ACP, Bertelsmann, Fairfax, Granada, Hearst Corporation, James Hardie Ltd, News Corporation, Pearson, Reed Elsevier, Thomson Organization, Time Warner and Torstar. Other companies that are dedicated publishers rather than conglomerates could also have been included in this count due to their size and multinational holdings. For the 1970s and 1980s, these companies include Collins, Hodder & Stoughton, Macmillan, Pan Macmillan, Random House and Simon & Schuster. By this broader definition multinationals have been operating in Australia since the nineteenth century. Including these companies increases the percentage of Australian novel titles published by multinational companies to 16.8 percent (rather than 10 percent) in the 1970s and to 37.4 percent (rather than 30.5 percent) in the 1980s.

Lothian). From 30.5 percent in the 1980s, the proportion of Australian novels published by conglomerates (including those not in the top ten) increased to 38.7 percent in the 1990s and 43.2 percent in the 2000s.[56]

Viewed in this way—as a progressive domination of Australian novel publishing—this trend presents an apparently bleak outlook for local publishers. But this conclusion is complicated by a closer analysis of the activities of these conglomerates. For although they are commonly viewed as an homogenous group, they enter, operate in, and in some cases depart from Australian novel publishing in notably different ways. Some have not expanded their publication of Australian novels in the 1990s and 2000s—as might be expected based on the trend of overall growth—but have reduced their lists or vacated this part of the industry altogether. Simon & Schuster and Scholastic entered the market virtually cold—that is, not by acquiring companies with a significant previous involvement in publishing Australian novels—and after producing such titles for a few years, more or less abandoned the field.[57] Other corpora-

---

[56] The multinational conglomerates I have counted for these decades are: 1990s—ACP, Bertelsmann, Fairfax, Hachette Livre, Hearst Corporation, Holtzbrinck, News Corporation, Pearson, Reed Elsevier, Scholastic, Time Warner and Torstar; 2000s—Bertelsmann, Fairfax, Gale Group, Hachette Livre, Holtzbrinck, News Corporation, Pearson, Reed Elsevier, Scholastic, Time Warner and Torstar. As above, other companies that are not conglomerates but dedicated publishers could have been included in this count due to their size and multinational holdings. For the 1990s and 2000s these companies include Hodder Headline, Hodder & Stoughton, Pan Macmillan, Random House and Simon & Schuster. Including these companies significantly increases the percentage of Australian novel titles published by multinationals in the 1990s to 55.1 percent (instead of 38.7 percent), and slightly increases the percentage of titles published by multinationals in the 2000s to 47.3 percent (rather than 43.2 percent).

[57] Scholastic produced most of its Australian novel titles in the mid-1990s and Simon & Schuster, in the early 2000s. In the last few years, both companies appear

tions began producing Australian novels when they acquired a company or companies with a previous involvement in such publishing. But their subsequent manner of vacating, or reducing their involvement in, this part of the industry has differed. Reed Elsevier and, in particular, Torstar, greatly increased production of Australian novels before reducing their lists from the mid-1990s.[58] In contrast, Hachette Livre acquired a number of companies with significant involvement in publishing Australian novels—most particularly, Hodder Headline and the Australian publisher Lothian—only to reduce such publishing almost instantly. Other conglomerates have maintained or increased their production of Australian novels. After acquiring companies with an involvement in Australian novel publishing, Bertelsmann and Holtzbrinck published slightly fewer, but still a relatively stable number of Australian novels. Pearson and News Corporation have gone on to publish more Australian novels than the combined output of the companies they acquired in entering the market.

Many of these conglomerates, then, do not conform with the two approaches to publishing commonly ascribed to multinationals: that is, the grab and smash (à la Hachette Livre) or the unstoppable incursion (as

---

to be re-growing their Australian novel lists, but such growth has not continued for long enough to constitute a trend.

[58] George Paizis describes an overall decline in Torstar's 'sales … both in the main markets—USA and Europe—and elsewhere' since the mid-1980s. George Paizis, 'Category Romance in the Era of Globalization: The Story of Harlequin', in Anna Guttman, Michel Hockx and George Paizis, eds, *The Global Literary Field* (Cambridge: Cambridge Scholars Press, 2006), p. 128. The reduction in Australian novels published by this company has occurred in the context of an overall decline in Torstar's sales and market share. Interestingly, Paizis describes Torstar as both the product and the victim of globalisation: 'its thirty-five per cent share of world mass-paperback sales forced it to seek ever new markets: expansion into new areas is the only means of survival because a competitor will rush to fill a vacuum if and when prospects allow' (131).

may turn out to be the case with Pearson and News Corporation). It is not that these multinational corporations can be stopped—they may elect to stop. And although a departure of all multinationals from Australian novel publishing would undoubtedly make business easier for local (and small- and medium-sized overseas) publishers, it would not necessarily be positive for Australian authors. Torstar, for example, has enabled Australian romance novelists to attain international popularity and sales. In terms of Hachette Livre, the elimination of a venerable Australian publishing company like Lothian is regrettable, but this absence also opens up market space for smaller Australian publishers of Australian novels.

This brings us to the more than 50 percent of Australian novels not published by multinational conglomerates. While accounts of contemporary publishing stress the industry's increasing concentration—Michael Wilding asserts, 'sinister things are happening. More and more of the organs of communication are falling into fewer hands'[59]—in fact, Australian novel publishing today is far less concentrated than in the 1960s. The proportion of Australian novel titles produced by the top five ranked publishers has decreased from 70.2 percent in the 1960s to 62.7 percent in the 1970s, 43.6 percent in the 1980s, 39.7 percent in the 1990s, and 38.3 percent in the 2000s, despite the fact that, in this latter decade, the top five publishers were all multinational conglomerates. This decreasing concentration occurs not only because these multinational publishers produce fewer Australian novels than did companies like Cleveland and Horwitz, but because of the growing number of independent small- and medium-sized Australian companies publishing such fiction. The trend of the 1970s and 1980s, of an expanding 'tail' of Australian publishers of Australian novels, has continued in the 1990s and 2000s. The eighteen

---

[59] Michael Wilding, 'Australian Literary and Scholarly Publishing in its International Context', *Australian Literary Studies* 19.1 (1999): 57. Myers, 'Getting Published in Australia', p. 66; Hollier, 'Between Denial and Despair', p. 62.

Australian publishers that produced five or more Australian novel titles in the 1980s has increased to thirty-four in the 1990s; and the 168 local companies that produced between one and four titles in the 1980s has expanded to 322 in the 1990s. Between 2000 and 2007, thirty-three Australian publishers produced more than five Australian novels and 250 published between one and four titles. While this multiplication of small- and medium-sized Australian publishers could connote instability or stress in the system, it also indicates a healthy diversity, and the appeal of Australian novel publishing.

Among the trends discernible in the 1990s and 2000s is an expected growth in Australian companies either wholly or partially funded through subsidy publishing.[60] In the 2000s, a handful of Australian companies engaged in electronic and/or print-on-demand publishing entered the top fifty publishers of Australian novels.[61] But the more pronounced trend in this category is growth in Australian publishers of literary fiction. This group is comprised of a variety of publishers: some have been producing Australian novels since the late 1970s and 1980s, while others began in the 1990s and 2000s; the group includes relatively large, established presses like Allen & Unwin, ABC Books, Hale & Iremonger and

---

[60] Specifically regarding those companies in the top fifty publishers of Australian novel titles, the main Australian subsidy publishers of the 1990s were Seaview Press (number twenty-three), Boolarong Press (number thirty) and Wild & Woolley (number forty-five). Boolarong Press did not publish any Australian novel titles in the 2000s, but Seaview (number twenty) and Wild & Woolley (number thirty-six) were joined by a number of other such companies, including Sid Harta Publishers (number fifteen), and Black Pepper, Brolga Publishing and Peacock Publications (equally ranked number thirty-nine).

[61] These companies include Jacobyte Books (number nineteen), Interactive Press (number thirty-one), Equilibrium Books (number thirty-five) and DreamCraft (number forty-eight). The most prolific of these electronic publishers—Jacobyte Books—was acquired by the American e-publishing company BeWrite Books in 2005.

Fremantle Press; political or identity-based publishing houses like The Vulgar Press, Papyrus Press, Pascoe Publishing and Spinifex Press, as well as publishers with more explicitly literary aims, like Text Publishing, Ginninderra Press, Giramondo Publishing and Brandl & Schlesinger.[62] Considered in conjunction with the continuing prominence of self-publishing and university presses, Australian-based publishing of Australian novels appears to be diversifying rather than dying. Importantly, this growth contradicts the common assumption that the rise of multinational conglomerates supplanted and ended the national expansion of Australian publishing. Instead, at least in relation to the Australian novel, these two trends occur in concert through the 1990s and 2000s (and indeed, through the 1970s and 1980s).

In histories of Australian publishing, the 1950s and 1960s are seen as British-dominated, the 1970s and 1980s as a 'golden age' of government support and Australian publishing, and the 1990s and 2000s as the era of economic rationalism and the rise and domination of multinational conglomerates. Analysing the publishers of Australian novels contradicts the generalisability of this history. In the 1950s and 1960s, Australian novel publishing was dominated not by British companies (although these were certainly present) but by a handful of Australian mass-market publishers, who produced popular fiction and sold it using marketing techniques commonly identified as new to the publishing industry of the 1990s and 2000s. These mass-market companies continued to publish a significant proportion of Australian novels in the 1970s and 1980s, decades that also witnessed the beginning of growth in a more diverse range of Australian publishers of Australian novels, and the initial entry of multinational conglomerates into this industry. While the growth of multinational

---

[62] Other Australian companies in the top fifty publishers of Australian novel titles in the 1990s and 2000s include Duffy & Snellgrove, Indra Publishing, Scribe and Australian Scholarly Publishing.

corporations in the 1990s and 2000s is commonly seen as ending the era of national/ist publishing, in relation to Australian novels, these trends are concurrent (and have occurred in concert with the gradual decline of Australian mass-market publishing). Today, Australian novels are published by a significantly larger, less concentrated and more varied group of publishers than was the case in the 1950s and 1960s.

As always, the future is uncertain. But I would like to side with the optimists, and against those who foretell the imminent death of Australian publishing (and with it, the Australian novel) at the hands of multinational conglomerates. Current global economic conditions (as I write in March 2009) suggest the possible future contraction, rather than expansion, of these conglomerates. For instance, in February 2009, News Corporation (one of the major conglomerates involved in publishing Australian novels) reported enormous losses, necessitating 'record massive write-downs on its assets ... aggressive cost-cutting and layoffs'.[63] According to Simone Murray, multinational conglomerates have continued book publishing in the past not because it is profitable in and of itself—'Even with the introduction of managerial expertise and savage cost-cutting, the multinationals could not raise book publishing's profitability to the general region of the television and film subsidiaries'[64]—but in order to establish copyright that could be streamed into other, more profitable, media forms.[65] In these straitened times, these corporations may be forced to concentrate on immediate rather than potential ways of making a profit. Even if they do not, Kevin Rudd's recent proclamation that 'the great neo-liberal experiment of the past 30

---

[63] Melinda Peer, 'Bad News For News Corp', Forbes.com (5 February 2009), online, www.forbes.com/2009/02/05/news-corp-earnings-markets-equity-0205_advertising_52.html [Accessed 4 March 2009].
[64] Simone Murray, 'Generating Content: Book Publishing as a Component Media Industry', in Carter and Galligan, eds, *Making Books*, p. 62.
[65] Ibid., pp. 63–64.

years has failed'[66]—although almost certainly overly optimistic—holds out the possibility of a return to a 'golden age' of governmental support for Australian publishing and literature. Of course, economic conditions obviously affect small- and medium-sized Australian and overseas publishers as well as multinationals. However, the continual growth in Australian publishers in the last fifty years—and the difficult economic circumstances under which much of this growth has occurred—suggests that the local industry has both the will and capacity to take advantage of the current economic conditions.

---

[66] Kevin Rudd, 'The Global Financial Crisis', *The Monthly* (February 2009): 25.

Appendix

The Top Ten Publishers of Australian Novel Titles by Decade, 1950s to 2000s

1950s

	Publisher	#	%
1.	Horwitz	411	21.42
2.	Cleveland	393	20.48
3.	Action Comics	180	9.38
4.	Calvert	116	6.05
5.	Collins	82	4.27
6.	Angus & Robertson	70	3.65
7.	Robert Hale	47	2.45
8.	Hutchinson.	44	2.30
9.	Webster	41	2.14
10.	Heinemann	27	1.41

1960s

	Publisher	#	%
1.	Cleveland	987	37.11
2.	Horwitz	630	23.68
3.	Robert Hale	89	3.35
4.	Collins	83	3.12
5.	Calvert	78	2.93
6.	Thomas Tilling	61	2.29
7.	Harlequin/Mills & Boon	53	1.99
8.	Angus & Robertson	48	1.81
9.	Times Mirror	47	1.77
10.	Hodder & Stoughton	39	1.47

1970s

	Publisher	#	%
1.	Horwitz	536	26.99
2.	Cleveland	405	20.39
3.	Torstar	146	7.35
4.	Robert Hale	86	4.33
5.	Times Mirror	72	3.63
6.	Macmillan	58	2.92
7.	Angus & Robertson	57	2.87
8.	Collins	53	2.67
9.	Thomson	30	1.51
10.	Thomas Tilling	26	1.31

1980s

	Publisher	#	%
1.	Torstar	281	13.57
2.	Horwitz	244	11.78
3.	Cleveland	151	7.29
4.	Pearson	140	6.76
5.	News Corporation	87	4.20
6.	Robert Hale	72	3.48
7.	Self-published	64	3.09
8.	University presses	49	2.37
9.	Collins	44	2.12
10.	Macmillan	37	1.79

1990s

	Publisher	#	%
1.	Torstar	358	10.44
2.	Pearson	312	9.10
3.	Pan Macmillan	277	8.08
4.	News Corporation	233	6.79
5.	Self-published	182	5.31
6.	Reed Elsevier	140	4.08
7.	Random House	136	3.97
8.	Bertelsmann	124	3.62
9.	Hodder Headline	120	3.50
10.	University presses	118	3.44

2000s

	Publisher	#	%
1.	News Corporation	284	9.58
2.	Pearson	245	8.27
3.	Holtzbrinck	228	7.69
4.	Bertelsmann	199	6.72
5.	Torstar	178	6.01
6.	Allen & Unwin	164	5.53
7.	University presses	116	3.91
8.	Self-published	110	3.71
9.	Hachette	86	2.90
10.	Lothian	79	2.67

11
Squinting at a Sea of Dots: Visualising Australian Readerships Using Statistical Machine Learning*

Julieanne Lamond and Mark Reid

When we presented this chapter at the Resourceful Reading conference, a question was posed to us expressing concern that Australian literary studies faces the prospect of becoming lost in the data. Several papers at the conference argued for a shift in focus away from canonical texts and authors towards an examination of Australian literature as a field, a network, a broader structure. Our interlocutor suggested that such a bird's eye view results in a meaningless constellation of dots: we can make no sense of them. This question goes to the heart of an issue relevant to employing empirical methods in literary studies. One reason critics have been arguing for a more empirical approach to Australian literary studies is that we have access to new and much broader kinds of data than ever before. Data, however, are of little use in and of themselves. The key question when approaching literary studies with empirical methods is how to move between the generalisations involved in empirical research and the

---

* The authors would like to thank Tim Dolin for generously providing access to the ACRP database and Jason Ensor for his expertise and time answering technical questions about its organisation.

attention to the particular that characterises literary analysis: in other words, how such data could be made useful to literary analysis? This chapter examines one such approach. Specifically, it uses a collaboration between Australian literary studies and statistical machine learning to suggest how, in practice, empirical modes of research can speak to, enhance, or even help to direct more traditional modes of literary analysis.

As Katherine Bode has argued, the cultural materialist claims that tend to be made in Australian literary studies often imply a bird's eye view that is not always present in the research that generated them. There is an impulse within the discipline to make broad claims about the nation, the era or literary field based on close literary analysis of a few texts by a few authors and the rationale for basing these arguments on these texts and authors is not always clear.[1] Instead of focusing on a series of canonical authors and texts to make claims about the national literary field, Bode suggests we consider starting from the other end, to use the evidence of what was published and read, where and when, to determine which texts and authors might best warrant close critical attention. Instead of moving from the particular to the general, as has been our wont in the discipline, we should attempt the more methodologically sound approach of moving from the general to the particular: to use empirical evidence to direct our critical attention. We have some tools at our disposal to begin to approach this task: the AustLit database and the Australian Common Reader project are among them.

Large datasets raise new difficulties for literary critics and cultural historians—how do we make sense of these data? We know there must be useful information in this mass of data: how do we extricate it? There are two primary ways in which literary scholars use such databases: by

---

[1] Katherine Bode, 'Beyond the Colonial Present: Quantitative Analysis, "Resourceful Reading" and Australian Literary Studies', *JASAL Special Issue: The Colonial Present* (2008): 184–97.

making particular queries of the database or by creating summary statistics for the datasets as a whole. Each of these has its pitfalls. Specific queries are useful for viewing local relationships and small slices of the data but do not give us a sense of their relationship to the whole. Summary statistics such as average readership, books read and published over time offer us some insight but are 'coarse' summaries: they jettison a great deal of information in the extent of their generalisations. There are more sophisticated way of viewing a dataset as a whole without throwing away as much information, and this is where interdisciplinary collaboration becomes useful. One of the aims of this chapter is to draw attention to a field of research—statistical machine learning—that dedicates itself to doing what literary critics are not always very good at: drawing inferences from large datasets.

Collaboration

It is a cliché these days to say that we are overwhelmed by information. The recent and dramatic reduction in the cost of collecting, storing, copying, transporting and processing large amounts of data has meant individuals and organisations have had to rethink how they make sense of it.[2] The growing body of research within the field of statistical machine learning, and the increasing interest in it from outside its walls, are responses to this deluge of data.

Tom Mitchell, head of the recently formed Machine Learning Department at Carnegie Mellon University, describes the broader field of machine learning as 'a natural outgrowth of the intersection of Computer Science and Statistics'.[3] It is a large discipline that concerns itself with

---

[2] David J. Hand, *Information Generation: How Data Rule our World* (Oxford: Oneworld Publications, 2007), p. 3.
[3] Tom Mitchell, 'The Discipline of Machine Learning', Technical Report CMU-ML-06-108, School of Computer Science, Carnegie Mellon University (July 2006), p. 1.

questions of how to generalise, or 'learn', from examples in a computationally efficient manner. This encompasses problems in robotics, speech recognition and computer vision. *Statistical* machine learning is a subfield of machine learning that emphasises the theory and practice of statistical inference and so is primarily concerned with problems of prediction, modelling and hypothesis testing. Researchers within this discipline invent and study tools that help us to locate needles of knowledge in our ever-growing haystacks of information. Here we would like to provide a case history of the particular collaboration we used to explore the possible usefulness of statistical machine learning for Australian literary studies.

This project had its genesis in attempts to use a particular book history dataset, the Australian Common Reader project (ACRP), to think about how to make useful generalisations about Australian readerships in the late nineteenth century. The ACRP is a database collating loan records from six Australian libraries, kept intermittently for the period 1861 to 1912, alongside some biographical information about the borrowers. For our purposes, the database contains two main axes of information: about books—which libraries held them, how often were they borrowed, and by whom? And about borrowers—what did they borrow and when?

There are limitations to making generalisations from this kind of data. Whether a collection of data is suitable to support a generalisation made by a human or machine depends on its size, quality, how well it represents the subject of the generalisation and the validity of any assumptions made about it. As Tukey puts it, 'The data may not contain the answer. The combination of some data and an aching desire for an answer does not ensure that a reasonable answer can be extracted from a given body of data.'[4] For the purposes of generalising about Australian

---

[4] John W. Tukey, 'Sunset Salvo', *The American Statistician* 40 (February 1986): 74–75.

readerships, the data found in the ACRP database have some of these limitations. It is not comprehensive; it does not include all Australian libraries and the records for the periods covered are intermittent. It is a collection of records about borrowing, not reading. Although we deliberately conflate borrowers with readers in this chapter as a convenient shorthand, it is clear from the pattern of individual borrowers that some were likely to be borrowing for others. This is evidenced by records of individuals borrowing across a range of genres including, for example, children's books. However, the number of borrowers of a work seems a reasonable approximation to its readership. There is also a limit to how far we can generalise from such data, unless we are clear that we are generalising about particular, local, reading communities, and patterns that exist across these communities.

Julieanne began using the database to ask a narrow set of questions. She was interested in what the ACRP might reveal about the extent of Australian readerships for two particular authors, Rosa Praed and Steele Rudd. This involved making simple queries of the database and resulted in straightforward, quantifiable results: numbers of people who borrowed each of Praed and Rudd's books. From these data, she could ask whether these authors shared a readership. This involved some laborious searching and recording of data to cross-reference the borrowers of each but resulted in the interesting finding that these very different authors did, in fact, share a readership as defined in relation to these data. In doing so, she was taking up Tim Dolin's suggestion that such databases could be used to compile 'Amazon-style' lists of what works particular people borrowed in common: using his example, 'of the x readers who borrowed *Jane Eyre*, y also borrowed *The Mill on the Floss*, *Wuthering Heights* and so on'. Dolin continues: 'The outcome of this list is something more than a micro-canon, those works given special status by a particular reading community. What it shows up is a series of distinctive patterns and correspondences among literary works, patterns and correspondences that come into existence for that reading community at that time.'[5]

Dolin's use of the database is one means of going to the data to drive novel, contextualised close readings of particular texts by considering not only who read them and when, but what other works were read in common with them. In this methodology novels are analysed in relation to how they are read 'within the immediate horizon of other works'.[6] These patterns of readership provide the basis for 'locally situated re-readings' of novels: close analysis that is prompted by but not limited to the results of such quantitative data searches. For example, Dolin uses the ACRP data to consider a cluster of books 'within the horizon' of Dickens's *Great Expectations* in colonial Adelaide in 1861 and 1862. This results in a rereading of the novel in light of the circumstances of colonial Adelaide, and with an eye to resonances with the other novels that were popular with those who read *Great Expectations* in Adelaide at the time, including Eliot's *Silas Marner* and Bulwer-Lytton's *What Will He Do With It?*

This approach raises the possibility of using such databases to ask questions about reading communities: people who read similar books in similar geographical or temporal contexts. Dolin's method involves asking narrow questions of the data, driven by interest in particular texts. We began to think about how we could use the ACRP to think about reading communities more broadly: that is, how to look at the form and structure of reading communities across the whole database, or across particular libraries within the database, without bounding our queries with a narrow focus on particular texts or authors. Could we discern communities of readers or patterns of readership in these library records? Is

---

[5] Tim Dolin, 'First Steps toward a History of the Mid-Victorian Novel in Colonial Australia', *Australian Literary Studies* 22.3 (May 2006): 273–93.
[6] Ibid.

there another way, other than querying particular books or particular borrowers?

When Mark heard about the ACRP database and the types of questions Julieanne was asking of it, he saw an opportunity to apply methods from his research area to help refine and answer them. When faced with a new dataset that has been collected by a third party, standard statistical practice is to first perform what Tukey calls 'Exploratory Data Analysis'.[7] This typically involves creating various summaries of the data such as counts, averages, histograms and other graphs in order to extract a high-level overview. Of these, graphical summaries tend to provide the most insight. This is because, as Ware argues, 'the human visual system is a pattern seeker of enormous power and subtlety. The eye and the visual cortex of the brain form a massively parallel processor that provides the highest-bandwidth channel into human cognitive centers. At higher levels of processing, perception and cognition are closely interrelated, which is the reason why the words "understanding" and "seeing" are synonymous.'[8]

As Julieanne was most interested in questions of readership, an appropriate form of exploratory data analysis was to create a visual summary of the ACRP database that presented a map of the works within it so that proximity was indicative of shared readership. By doing so, visually apparent clusters of works in this map would immediately suggest micro-canons worthy of further examination.

---

[7] John W. Tukey, *Exploratory Data Analysis* (Reading, Mass.: Addison-Wesley, 1977).
[8] Colin Ware, *Information Visualization: Perception for Design* (San Francisco: Morgan Kaufmann, 2004), p. xxi.

Maps via Dimensional Reduction

At the time of writing, the database we had access to contained 99,692 loans of 7078 different works from six libraries by one of the 2643 people.[9] To make this more manageable, we focused on popular works that were borrowed at least twenty times and only considered loan records for these.[10] This distilled the database down to what we will call the *readership table*, with each row representing one of 1616 works and each column representing one of 2474 borrowers. Each cell in the readership table contains either a 1 or a 0, with a one indicating the work corresponding to the cell's row was lent to the borrower corresponding to its column.

The central insight that led to our method of visualisation is that this table of works and their borrowers summarises most of the information in the ACRP database pertaining to readerships. Our goal was to display the information in this table in a way that allows for both a general overview of all works in the database that suggested their shared readerships at a glance, and provides the ability to drill down to examine the details of specific works.

The machine learning technique we used to construct our map of the ACRP works is known as *dimensional reduction*. These are procedures that transform high-dimensional data into a low-dimensional representation while preserving salient information in the data. In the case of the ACRP data, each work has a high-dimensional representation as the sequence of 2474 1s and 0s appearing in its row in the readership table. For the purpose of visualising readerships, the salient information in this

---

[9] These are loans for which there is a valid library, work, borrower and loan identifier in the database. This means the numbers here are slightly lower than the number of entries (including incomplete ones) in the database.
[10] This number was chosen more or less arbitrarily with the aim to make data processing easier.

high-dimensional representation is the similarity of two works' readerships. This similarity is quantified as the number of common borrowers they have—that is, the number of columns for which both works' rows contain a 1. Mathematically, this is known as the *inner product* between the rows. To construct a map of the works that could be displayed on a screen, it was necessary to reduce this high-dimensional representation to a two-dimensional one that best preserved these inner products for all possible pairs of works.

The algorithm that performs the dimensional reduction is the recent t-distributed Stochastic Neighbour Embedding (hereafter t-SNE) algorithm developed by Laurens van der Maaten and Geoffrey Hinton.[11] This algorithm is particularly well suited for the visualisation of high-dimensional datasets. To interpret its results, the details of t-SNE are not as important here as a high-level understanding of what the algorithm does to the ACRP data. Consider the case of a simpler readership table where there are only three rows for the works A, B and C. Suppose each has 100 readers, and that A and B share thirty readers while A and C share ten. A good dimensional reduction will display the works A, B and C so that A and B are closer together than A and C. The actual location of each work on the screen is not as important as its relative position. Suppose we also know B and C share twenty readers. Then B and C should be displayed closer together than A and C but not as close together as A and B.

As we consider larger numbers of works and their overlapping readerships, the number of constraints on the relative distances between works grows rapidly, and determining an arrangement on the screen that respects all of these constraints becomes increasingly difficult. Dimensional reduction algorithms such as t-SNE use sophisticated

---

[11] Laurens J.P. van der Maaten and Geoffrey E. Hinton, 'Visualizing Data Using t-SNE', *Journal of Machine Learning Research* 9 (2008).

techniques to find good arrangements of the works that approximately satisfy a given set of constraints. It is necessary to emphasise that any visualisation produced by these techniques is only approximate and by no means the only one possible. In other words, different algorithms will layout the books in different ways and the particular layout used in our visualisation tool is but one possible way of visualising these overlapping readership relationships.

Using the Visualisation Tool

The arrangement of works produced by the t-SNE algorithm is nothing more than a collection of screen coordinates—one for each work in the database. In order to more easily interpret this output, Mark developed some software that allows a user to interact with this map of the database. The software he used is freely available over the web and works with most modern operating systems (Windows, Apple OS X, Linux). It can be accessed through a web browser at mark.reid.name/code/acrp/.

Figure 1 shows a high-level overview of the ACRP database. Each circle represents a literary work. The size and colour of each circle is intended to give a sense of the size of the readership for the corresponding work: larger, darker circles for works with larger readerships and smaller, lighter circles for those with fewer readers. As described above, two circles in close proximity is indicative of a high proportion of shared readers.

Hovering the mouse cursor over a circle will reveal the title of the corresponding work with the size of its readership in parentheses. Clicking on a circle—for example, (A) in Figure 1—will reveal details of the work in the location (B), including its author's surname and date of publication. Grey lines are also displayed, connecting the selected work to others that have a shared proportion of readers greater than the threshold controlled by the 'Similarity' slider (F). In the example in Figure 1 the threshold is 0.25, meaning grey lines are only drawn between

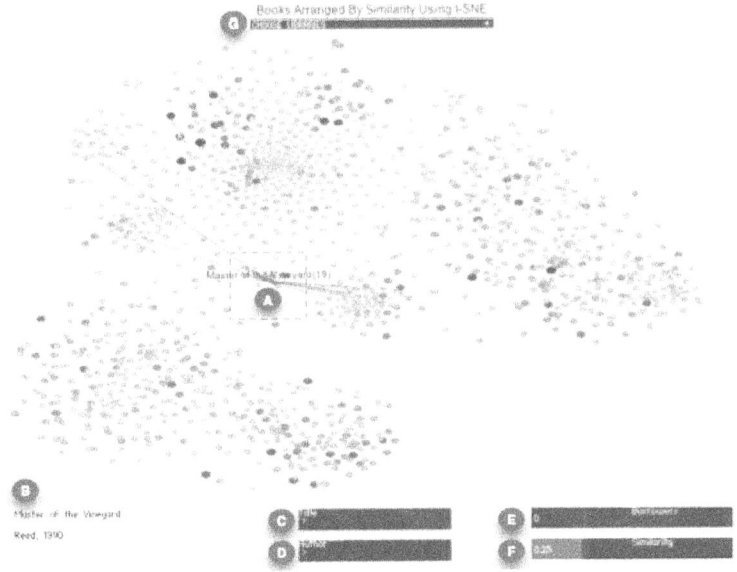

Figure 1 A Screenshot of the Visualisation Tool (Labels A–G highlight different aspects of the user interface that are described in the text)

the selected work and other works with more than 25 percent of their total readership in common.

There are several controls for filtering which works are displayed. Search terms can be entered into the 'Title' field (C) or the 'Author' field (D) restricting the displayed works with a title or author matching the term. The 'Borrowers' slider (E) sets a threshold for the minimum number of readers a work must have to be displayed. By increasing this, less borrowed works are hidden from view, allowing the user to quickly identify popular works. Finally, the drop-down list of libraries (G) can be used to restrict the visualisation to only those works that appear in a selected library. Figure 2 shows how this drop-down list can be used to show only those works appearing in the Port Germein Institute.

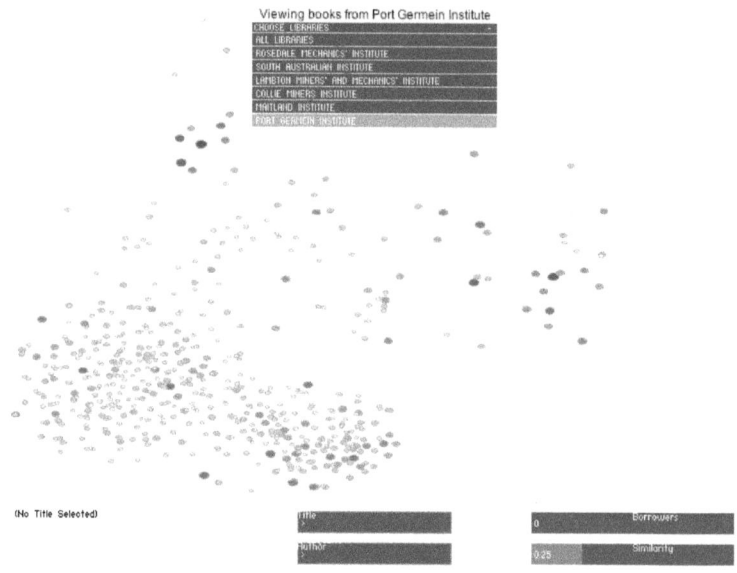

Figure 2 A View of the Books Contained in the Port Germein Institute Library (The drop-down list at the top is used to select which library is displayed)

Areas of the visualisation may be selected and zoomed in on by clicking and dragging the mouse over an area of interest. Figure 3 shows the result of selecting the region shown by the dashed rectangle in Figure 1. This zoomed area reveals a tight cluster of works connected by grey lines indicating a shared readership with Myrtle Reed's *Master of the Vineyard* of at least 35 percent. For later reference, the labelled circles represent the following works: (A) Waller's *Flamsted Quarries*, (B) Richardson's *The Lead of Honour*, (C) Williamson's *The Motor Maid*, (D) Stratton-Porter's *The Girl of the Limberlost*, (E) Barclay's *Through the Postern Gate*, (F) Bindloss's *Hawtrey's Deputy*, (G) Cooke's *The Girl who Lived in the Woods*, (H) Yorke's *Patricia of Pall Mall*, (I) Barclay's *The Mistress of Shenstone* and (J) Barclay's *The Rosary*.

This tour of the features of the ACRP visualisation is intended to demonstrate how it may be used to survey the ACRP database quickly and identify clusters of works with shared readerships. It is important to realise that visualising data in this way does not guarantee meaningful patterns will emerge, or that all apparent patterns are meaningful. We wish to emphasise that our ACRP visualisation tool is just that, a tool. Once an interesting pattern is identified careful inspection by a knowledgeable expert is still required to determine whether it is meaningful.

Using the Visualisation for Literary Analysis

This visualisation provides a methodology for approaching large datasets by moving between the general and the particular. Instead of asking particular questions of the data, or making broad generalisations about it, this tool enables us to spot patterns in the data which might then warrant further exploration. In other words, it enables us to do something like exploratory data analysis: to explore the data in order to come up with more specific questions or hypotheses we can investigate in more detail. Instead of asking, as Dolin does, what borrowers of *Great Expectations* also borrowed in common, the visualisation asks this one question—what other books were likely to be read by readers of this book?—of all the books in the database simultaneously. The aim, then, is to find interesting and unexpected relationships between books, or communities of readers. These relationships can then be queried in more qualitative ways, as Dolin has done with *Great Expectations*, or tested with other methods of quantitative analysis. The point is that our investigations will not be driven by interest in particular readers or texts, but by interest in patterns and relationships between books and readers. This kind of visualisation can enable us to begin using data to develop research questions, and perhaps begin to look at relationships between non-canonical books and authors in particular Australian reading contexts.

By allowing us to see how a book relates to other books in a reading community, this visualisation can be used to approximate the shape of a local readership, and to enable further questions, such as: are there patterns in the kinds of books people borrowed in common? Are there clusters according to genre, nationality of author, gender of borrower? How do these clusters pattern themselves temporally? Are there waves of readership of particular books or genres, or trailblazing readers? What is the relationship between the borrowing of periodicals and the books reviewed in them? Statistical machine learning enables us to ask such questions of the library data as a whole, rather than in relation to individual books and authors, and to look at more complex relationships between different aspects of the data.

The following examples of how the tool could be used by literary critics or cultural historians are introduced to raise questions rather than answer them. But this is the point—databases are not just a means of answering questions, but of posing them, or finding new questions to ask of the novels and their contexts. We might start with the visualisation of the data as a whole and look for patterns and clusters, then drill down to look at these in more detail. The pattern that is most immediately apparent in looking at the data as a whole (Figure 1) is the large clumping or clusters the books form. The first question to be asked of these is, do they relate to individual libraries? By selecting individual libraries on the visualisation we can quickly confirm that this is, to some extent, the case. Unsurprisingly, readership communities were bounded by the availability of books at particular libraries. More notably, holdings at the libraries in the database are relatively discrete. This finding takes us back to the data, further investigation of which reveals that nearly half the works in the database were found exclusively in a single library. About 30 percent had copies in two libraries, 14 percent were found in three libraries, 5 percent in four libraries, and less than 1.5 percent in five and less than 1 percent of works (five works in total) in all six libraries. This unequal spread could lead the book historian to ask questions about patterns and processes of distribution to such libraries in the period covered by the data.

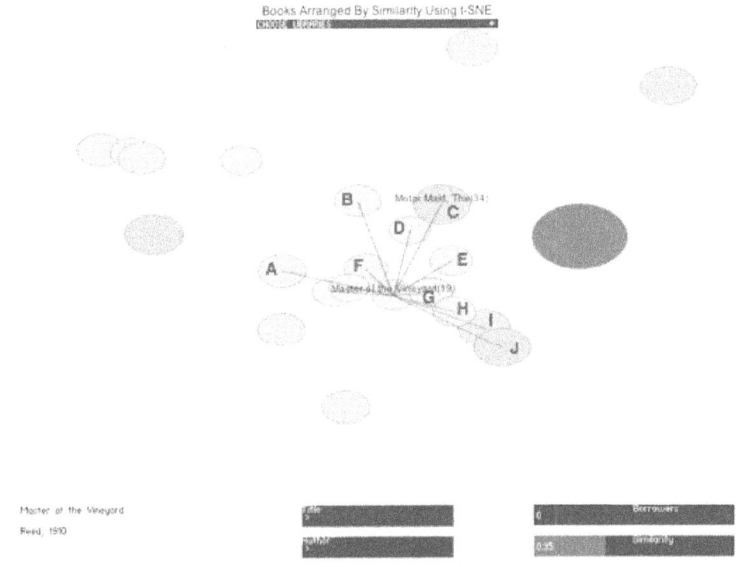

Figure 3 An Enlarged View of the Dashed Region in Figure 1 (Books corresponding to the labels A–J are discussed in the main text)

We can look at other clusters in more detail by zooming in on them, as described above. This method reveals some other expected clustering, for example, by author: it is unsurprising that readers who borrow works of one author are likely to also borrow other works by that author. For example, there is a cluster with a large degree of similarity and high number of borrowers of two of Anthony Trollope's novels, *Three Clerks* and *The Warden*. These texts also had a high degree of similarity with Eliot's *Silas Marner* (also not altogether surprising as these were popular and well-read texts). More interesting are clusters of books which, on first sight, appear to have little in common with one another: all three of these novels are clustered with *Paul Fane*, the only novel by American editor and poet Nathaniel Parker Willis. Why might these four novels have shared a readership? This is a question not easily answerable only by reference to the data: it sends us back to the texts themselves, and to their contexts.

Many of the clusters apparent in a brief glance at the visualisation involve texts not usually subject to literary analysis. However, the extent of their shared readership across borrowers in these data renders them interesting. One of the most readily apparent clusters which does not relate to a single author centres around Myrtle Reed's *Master of the Vineyard*, a domestic romance published in America in 1910 (Figure 3). In the Rosedale Library data, this book shares a high degree of similarity with an eclectic collection of novels: Harold Bindloss's *Hawtrey's Deputy* (1911) and *The Protector* (1919); adventure novels set in the Canadian Northwest; bestselling English romance novel *The Rosary* (1909) by Florence L. Barclay; *The Motor Maid*, a British motoring novel by Alice Muriel Williamson (1910); and *The Girl of the Limberlost* by American naturalist Gene Stratton-Porter (1909). The only common feature immediately apparent here is that these novels were all published between 1909 and 1911, confirming a high readership of contemporary work in these data as noted by Dolin.[12] But such clusters also raise the question of what else might account for these novels having a readership in common? Is it something to do with the texts, the circumstances of their publication or circulation, or the readers' circumstances? Again, answering such questions takes us back not only to the data but to the texts themselves and their particular contexts.

Conclusions

While such a visualisation tool lends itself to the shift in emphasis argued by proponents of empiricism away from a focus on canonical authors, it also offers a way around the simplistic opposite of this approach: that is, focusing on the most popular authors or texts. It offers another criterion

---

[12] Ibid.

for assessing the significance of a text that is not inherent either in the text itself or in the extent of its readership: its relationship to other texts and readers. Interdisciplinary collaboration of this sort can do more than provide methodological tools; it can suggest alternative conceptual frameworks for posing problems within our discipline. In this case, the emphasis in statistical machine learning on defining similarity has been particularly useful. Literary analysis tends to group texts according to categories such as period, author, genre, subject matter, nationality and form. This kind of data analysis can get us thinking about grouping books (thinking of them as similar) according to their readerships in more complex ways than simply looking at their relative popularity. We can look at relationships between local and temporal readerships, and readerships across time, as well as readerships grouped by class or gender, physical or temporal proximity.

If we are to make use of the data now available in relation to Australian literature and cultural history, we need to find ways to make them meaningful to our work. In order to do so, we may well need to venture outside our own discipline to seek help. This collaboration suggests that working with machine learning and other fields of statistical analysis can help not only to find answers to questions we might pose of the data, but to formulate questions and, further, to reconceptualise the kinds of questions we are able to ask of the data in the first place. It also suggests that co-opting scientists and scientific methods to our cause does not limit us to quantitative analysis alone. So although this visualisation does represent the Australian literary field, or at least one corner of it, as a sea of dots, it certainly does not reduce the field to the data, or result in meaningless generalisation. Rather, it provides a way for literary scholars to find patterns in the mass of data and use these patterns to return to the realm of the particular in which we are most comfortable: to the use of detailed literary and contextual analysis to seek explanations and find meaning in the patterns.

12
Is a Picture Worth 10,175 Australian Novels?[1]

Jason D. Ensor

[S]cience ... is rhetoric, a series of efforts to persuade relevant social actors that one's manufactured knowledge is a route to a desired form of very objective power. Such persuasions must take account of the structure of facts and artifacts, as well as of language-mediated actors in the knowledge game.[2]

If the poem's score for perfection is plotted along the horizontal of a graph, and its importance is plotted on the vertical, then calculating the total area of the poem yields the measure of its greatness. A sonnet by Byron may score high on the vertical, but only average on the horizontal. A Shakespearean sonnet, on the other hand, would score high both horizontally and vertically, yielding a massive total area, thereby revealing the poem to be truly great. As you proceed through the poetry in this book,

---

[1] '10,175 novels' refers to the number of first edition novels published in Australia during the period 1900–2000 (source: AustLit, 27 February 2009) and is represented graphically by Figure 3. I am indebted to Richard Nile, Tim Dolin and Rana Ensor for their feedback on an early draft of this chapter.
[2] Donna Haraway, 'Situated Knowledges: The Science Question in Feminism and the Privilege of Partial Perspective', *Feminist Studies* 14.3 (1988): 575–99, 577.

practice this rating method. As your ability to evaluate poems in this matter grows, so will your enjoyment and understanding of poetry.[3]

Drawing on an internet software development background where I was formerly a PHP (Hypertext Preprocessor)[4] and MySQL (Structured Query Language)[5] programmer, over the past two years it has been possible for me to engage with AustLit tagged-text data along the lines of enquiry suggested by Franco Moretti and William St Clair. In the absence of proprietary software suiting my research needs, this has meant building functions that enact specific analytical outcomes. These outcomes, presented within the context of new empiricism at ASAL and mini-ASAL conferences during 2007 and 2008, represent many hours of data mining, function programming and ... rendering. I deliberately use the word 'rendering' because I wish to suggest early on the practice of 3D computer graphic modelling and animation where an underlying mesh, in this case a vast resource of publication data legitimately downloaded from the AustLit website, is worked through a series of handmade, hand-coded tools to generate useable representations for academic debate. As these representations do not wear their underlying design on their sleeve, the resulting images of statistical analysis, deployed in my research for the purposes of discussing publication trends in Australian literary history, tend to elide their links with the technological labour that preceded their creation. In this sense, one might say—with apologies to Van Maanen who is writing about ethnography—that the 'fieldworker, having finished the job of collecting data, simply vanished behind a steady descriptive

---

[3] *Dead Poets Society*, Touchstone Pictures (1989). The quote is by a student reading out loud a class textbook to which Robin Williams's character, John Keating, responds: 'Excrement ... We're not laying pipe, we're talking about poetry.'
[4] See 'PHP: Hypertext Preprocessor', online (2009), au.php.net/ [Accessed April 2009].
[5] See 'MySQL: The World's Most Popular Open Source Database', online (2009), www.mysql.com/ [Accessed April 2009].

narrative justified largely by the respectable image and ideology of ... [new empiricist] practice'.[6] Which is to say, like the commonplace computer desktop or laptop screen, in using computer technologies to facilitate interpretative work my statistical graphs placed 'a premium on surface manipulation and thinking in ignorance of [their] underlying mechanism'.[7] Essentially, it asked viewers to suspend disbelief and become absorbed in, even seduced by, a 'certain kind of secular magic' that was being performed on the screen.[8] As Martyn Jessop claims, 'Images are seductive and there is a natural tendency to instinctively believe whatever one sees with one's own eyes but in the case of digital visualisations what is seen is entirely a constructed object'.[9]

This is an important observation because new empiricism and its related practices capitalise on the notion of computers employing neutral, carefully structured logic with an absence of poetics and felt emotion. Indeed, it is the ways that computers 'think' which is taken to be 'their most culturally important characteristic'[10] and contemporary social rhetoric surrounding technology encourages us to view computers as communicating (or 'thinking') in a logic that proceeds towards very specific ends. New empiricism, in denoting precise rational procedures linked with computing, seeks to be an expression of those ends and is connected with the production of digitally based visual texts, like my own statistical graphs, that seemingly 'speak for themselves' about Australian

---

[6] J. Van Maanen, *Tales of the Fields* (Chicago: University of Chicago Press, 1998), p. 46.
[7] S. Turkle, *Life on the Screen* (London: Weidenfeld & Nicolson, 1996), p. 35.
[8] Nigel Thrift, 'The Material Practices of Glamour', *Journal of Cultural Economy* 1.1 (2008): 9–23, 9.
[9] Martyn Jessop, 'Digital Visualisation as a Scholarly Activity', *Literary and Linguistic Computing* 23.3 (2008): 290.
[10] Julia Flanders, 'Data and Wisdom: Electronic Editing and the Quantification of Knowledge', *Literary and Linguistic Computing* 24.1 (2009): 55.

literary history. This might be because 'the kind of knowledge the computer encourages is rationalist, linear and analytic, mimicking the public communication of science',[11] and the possibility of objectivity which the humanities secretly desire.[12]

Yet information systems and information use are also highly 'sociotechnical in nature[:] ... they develop their own personality as determined through the initial design of the system and its ongoing human interface, and they reflect the politics of the organisational structure and its human actors'.[13] Perhaps new empiricism, in its perceived relevance to Australian literature and the humanities in general, is a system of analysis that represents what Fredric Jameson lamented as the 'depthlessness' of postmodernism,[14] privileging the consumption of visual images over deeper, critical forms of thinking. Indeed, does the move from 'close' reading to 'distant' reading parallel the loss of the felt authenticity of emotion and the rise of simulation and surface? Such questions are beyond the scope of this essay. However, if changes in 'technologies do not just expedite ... knowledge transmission, but deliver it in alternative ways which require different interpretative and behavioural skills',[15] then by considering the embodiment of the disciplinary space of Australian literature on a computer screen (through AustLit) as a type of 'cultural work', we might begin to take account of 'the representational logic of the

---

[11] Lynette Hunter, *Critiques of Knowing: Situated Textualities in Science, Computing and the Arts* (New York: Routledge, 1999), p. 86.

[12] Jessop, 'Digital Visualisation as a Scholarly Activity', p. 282.

[13] Robert Hutchinson, 'Knowledge and Control: A Marxian Perspective on the Productivity Paradox of Information Technology', *Rethinking Marxism* 20.2 (April 2008): 288–304.

[14] Frederic Jameson, *Postmodernism or, the Cultural Logic of Late Capitalism* (Durham: Duke University Press, 1991).

[15] Margery Mayall, 'Attached to their Style: Traders, Technical Analysis and Post-social Relationships', *Journal of Sociology* 43.4 (2008): 421–37, 422.

[computer] medium' in discussions of empiricism and modern-day forms of Australian literary knowledge production.[16]

This chapter will explore the work behind the charting. This will include the necessary apologetics and methodological uncertainties that contextualise analytic labour, and it will put forward an alternative reading of new empiricism which suggests that internet and computing technologies are shaping the cultural grammar of the domain of Australian literature in ways yet to be fully understood but which need to be corralled methodologically. It will propose that in the contemporary humanities environment new empiricism should continue to provide important 'reference points from which qualitative data can be understood'[17] and a way for literary scholars to visualise quantitative research but from within the framework of an Australian Charter for the Computer-Based Representation of Literary History. In so doing, I will draw upon standards from The London Charter. Established in relation to Cultural History, The London Charter has argued that 'computer-based visualisation methods' should be 'applied with scholarly rigour, and that the outcomes of research that include computer-based visualisation should accurately convey to users the status of the knowledge that they represent, such as distinctions between evidence and hypothesis, and between different levels of probability'.[18] This is not to adjudicate what shape and form an Australian Charter might take but rather to raise the

---

[16] Detlev Zwick and Nikhilesh Dholakia, 'Bringing the Market to Life: Screen Aesthetics and the Epistemic Consumption Object', *Marketing Theory* 6 (2006): 41–62, 42.

[17] Fiona Black, Bertrum MacDonald and J. Malcolm Black, 'Geographic Information Systems: A New Research Method for *Book History*', *Book History* 1.1 (1998): 13.

[18] 'Preamble', The London Charter for the Computer-Based Visualisation of Cultural Heritage (Draft 2.1), online (2009), www.londoncharter.org/ [Accessed April 2009].

possibility of an in-built scholarly apparatus for empiricism in Australian literary history.[19] It should also be noted that The London Charter is not the only feasible template: the Text Encoding Initiative (for scholarly editors) and the Electronic Cultural Atlas Initiative are other possible models for collective standards.[20]

Admittedly, the term 'new empiricism' has been made to carry much rhetorical weight thus far, and it needs further definition beyond its use here as an implied synonym for 'book history' or for quantitative analysis in the humanities via computing (though it can be these things). To begin with, new empiricism is not 'eResearch', 'e-Literature' or anything where the lower-case letter 'e' continues to 'operate as the value-added, universal signifier of the brave new wired world.'[21] It can, however, be linked with such projects, sometimes as an internet-hosted digital tool at the service of eResearch or e-Lit, other times as a particular mode of quantitative enquiry applied within the humanities to a dataset. The core attribute shared between both approaches is that new empiricism is—ideally—the theoretical position in Australian literary history and Australian print culture studies where information systems and information use merge with qualitative historiography in the discovery of new knowledge through data mining, data analysis and, often, digital visualisation.[22]

---

[19] The London Charter recommends that 'Each community of practice, whether academic, educational, curatorial or commercial, should develop London Charter Implementation Guidelines that cohere with its own aims, objectives and methods'. Ibid., p. 5.

[20] I am grateful to Tim Dolin for bringing to my attention the Text Encoding Initiative for scholarly editors (www.tei-c.org/index.XML) and the Electronic Cultural Atlas Initiative (www.ecai.org/).

[21] Rita Raley, 'eEmpires', *Cultural Critique* 57 (Spring 2004): 111.

[22] Digital visualisation focuses on 'arranging, formatting, or otherwise transforming the appearance of data'. Willard McCarty, 'Humanities Computing', in Miriam Drake, ed., *Encyclopaedia of Library and Information Science* (London: Taylor & Francis, 2003), p. 1230.

Representations or summaries of data as lists ordered according to a specific enumerative calculation, to graphs depicting various statistical correspondences, broadly indicate the kinds of combinations of data analysis and digital visualisation that can occur within the context of new empiricism.

In modern print culture studies, this is what Franco Moretti refers to as 'distant reading' or the 'quantitative approach to literature', in which a large collective system might be grasped as a whole through computing and graphical aids and where an individual text's relationship to the whole may be charted. It is also what Martin Mueller facetiously refers to as 'not reading'[23] in which, as Sculley and Pasanek equally claim, distant reading requires the researcher to 'trade in a close reading of the original text for something that looks like a close reading of experimental results—a reading that must navigate ambiguity and contradiction'.[24] While Moretti's and Mueller's terms are valid, neither in my view fully captures new empiricism. Though Moretti's term is an interchangeable referent for new empiricism, the word 'distant' as an antonym to 'close' implies 'objectivity' and therefore capitalises on this imported association as being a less 'intimate', less 'sentimental', more scientific type of reading without actually claiming it is so. Similarly, Mueller's 'not reading' obscures the irony that where 'we had hoped to explain or understand those larger structures within which an individual text has meaning in the first place, we find ourselves acting once again as interpreters'.[25] That is, through analysing charts and graphs, we engage in the kind of literary criticism

---

[23] Tanya Clement, Sara Steger, John Unsworth and Kirsten Uszkalo, 'How Not to Read a Million Books', online (2009),
www3.isrl.illinois.edu/~unsworth/hownot2read.html [Accessed April 2009].
[24] D. Sculley and Bradley M. Pasanek, 'Meaning and Mining: The Impact of Implicit Assumptions in Data Mining for the Humanities', *Literary and Linguistic Computing* 23.4 (2008): 417.
[25] Ibid.

and literary reading practices which new empiricism supposedly distances itself from.[26] Scholars need to take account of these stances, but new empiricism's relative youthfulness in Australian humanities departments means that there is a 'lack of in-built scholarly apparatus' such as an Australian Charter to provide an agreed theoretical position and methodological direction on what constitutes good information use and sound data visualisation.[27]

This motion for an Australian Charter is also intensified by a personal view that there can be something mildly suspect about new empiricism, in that its structure of representation can in some modes resemble economic rationalism whereby knowledge becomes most valuable when it is 'quantifiable and hence offers comparability'.[28] Economic rationalism of course, as literary culture's Other, is the 'belief that everything of value can be considered in economic terms'.[29] As the reader's experience might confirm, this has led to a 'dangerous equivocation' for the bureau-/techno-cratic class that administrates the quantifiable research contributions of humanities departments in Australian universities—'namely, thinking that since any x can be described in (more or less metaphorically) informational terms, the nature of any x is genuinely informational'.[30] (As an analogy, consider the impact that the introduc-

---

[26] Sculley and Pasanek ask whether there is anything that 'is not interpretable by the literary critic'. Ibid., p. 421.
[27] Jessop, 'Digital Visualisation as a Scholarly Activity', p. 288.
[28] Roger Beckmann, 'Literature, Science and Economic Rationalism', in Katherine Barnes and Jan Lloyd-Jones, eds, *Words for Their Own Sake: The Pursuit of Literature in an Economic Rationalist World* (Melbourne: Australian Scholarly Publishing, 2004), pp. 58–69, 63.
[29] Ibid., p. 63.
[30] Luciano Floridi, 'What Is the Philosophy of Information?' *Metaphilosophy* 33.1–2 (January 2002): 140.

tion of book sales data-monitoring software like Nielsen BookScan[31] had on Australian literature, igniting debates—continuing today—that link literary fiction's performance in the marketplace with questions targeting Australian literature's continuing relevance in modern education.)[32]

Given new empiricism is becoming an attractor in humanities scholarship and funding applications, reflecting the mathematical logic that is generally ascendant in advanced societies like Australia, and which marks a new theoretical position where modern literary research might usefully converge, this cautionary chapter about informational methodologies is timely. But it is not exhaustive, as the 'formal bias of socially rational artefacts and institutions is far more difficult to identify and criticise than inherited mythic and traditional legitimations.'[33] However, in common with much screen-based analysis is the tendency to consider only the screen's 'output and its particular relevance to one's purposes' [34] rather than interrogate the underlying systems—the 'technological unconscious'[35] as it were—which insist on the potency of screen-based analysis. The argument I put forward then, drawing on sociological and cultural studies readings of technology, is that through new empiricism the 'aesthetic qualities of a visual representation governed by the screen' is producing a 'new ontology' of Australian

---

[31] Nielsen BookScan Australia, online (2009), www.nielsenbookscan.com.au/ [Accessed April 2009].
[32] See Rosemary Neill, 'Who Is Killing the Great Books of Australia? Lits Out', *Australian*, 18 March 2006; Rosemary Neill, 'Is This the Most Feared Man in Australian Literature?—The Biblio Files', *Australian*, 22 July 2006.
[33] Andrew Feenberg, 'From Critical Theory of Technology to the Rational Critique of Rationality', *Social Epistemology* 22.1 (January–March 2008): 25.
[34] Karin Knorr Cetina, 'Sociality with Objects: Social Relations in Postsocial Knowledge Societies' Theory', *Culture and Society* 14 (1997): 1–30, 8.
[35] Ibid., p. 18.

literary history.³⁶ It is my view that an Australian Charter, progressively configured by the academy within the disciplinary context of Australian literature and built upon the principles established by The London Charter, might enable the application of new empiricism to cohere more critically with the aims, objectives and methods of Australian literary history. This would help ensure we take full account of the ideological or methodological shifts still unfolding within the discipline through the contemporary turn towards computer-based—and internet-hosted—visualisation techniques.³⁷

Necessary apologetics

Perhaps this chapter is projecting the methodological uncertainties that have become apparent in my own analytic work onto the discipline in general and repackaging them as scholarly revelation. Certainly, in my own case studies, applying methods of new empiricism to publication data drawn from the official Australian bibliographic record has been a particularly daunting process since 2006, complicated by issues of technology, questions of politics, problems of logic and limits to data. As a result, any published article about the application of new empiricism to Australian literary history has begun with the necessary apologetics. I say 'necessary' because as researchers we frequently work with materials that can be frustratingly incomplete or unfinished, and therefore it is considered good scholarly practice to situate the communication of our findings with disclaimers that address methodological gaps. This is so that others

---

[36] Zwick and Dholakia, 'Bringing the Market to Life: Screen Aesthetics and the Epistemic Consumption Object', p. 42.
[37] The London Charter recommends this activity for all subject areas. See 4.1, Richard Beacham, 'An Introduction to the London Charter', The E-volution of IC Technology in Cultural Heritage, papers from the Joint Event CIPA / VAST / EG / EuroMed Event (2006): 4.

may verify new knowledges, oppose them or even build on them, things that seem the core activities of humanities research.

As recent examples of this, Tony Johnson-Woods in her 2008 *JASAL* article on the Carter Brown Mystery Series describes in a 'data collection apologia' that '[t]he problems encountered during the course of ... [her] project', in the creation of a complete Carter Brown bibliography, 'are common in literary historiography'.[38] Priya Joshi, in her analysis of the English novel in India, notes that some data, 'pertinent to a sustained intellectual history of reading ... [remain] extremely elusive'.[39] Tim Dolin, through his Australian Common Reader project,[40] reveals an extraordinarily rich history of Australian reading based on the surviving loan records of seven community-based libraries,[41] but some data spans only eighteen months, prompting Roger Osborne to warn that '[g]eneral conclusions from this limited dataset must be cautious'.[42] Moreover, Carol Hetherington, in examining the American long-distance connection in Australian literature, has raised questions about the stability or incompleteness of book histories relying on legacy print-based bibliographic texts, materials which have traditionally been considered 'impeccable ... resources'.[43]

---

[38] Toni Johnson-Woods, 'The Promiscuous Carter Brown', *JASAL Special Issue: The Colonial Present* (2008): 167.

[39] Tim Dolin, 'The Secret Reading Life of Us', in Brian Matthew, ed., *Readers, Writers, Publishers: Essays and Poems* (Canberra: Australian Academy of the Humanities, 2004), p. 117.

[40] Australian Common Reader project, online (2008), www.australiancommonreader.com [Accessed April 2009].

[41] Ibid., 134.

[42] Roger Osborne, 'Australian Common Reader', Aus-e-Lit: Collaboration, Integration and Annotation, online (12 September 2008), aus-e-lit.blogspot.com/2008/09/australian-common-reader.html [Accessed April 2009].

[43] Carol Hetherington, 'London Calling? Long-Distance Connections in Australian Literature', in Tully Barnett, Nena Bierbaum, Syd Harrex, Rick Hosking and

Despite these gaps in the archival record, Tim Dolin's findings (along with Johnson-Woods's, Joshi's and Hetherington's) challenge assumptions that have informed previous histories of reading, publishing and literature. Yet in what seems shared methodological territory or interpretative strategies, there are strong reservations about new empiricism and what might be characterised as an early or premature adoption of it in Australian literature, particularly in the application of quantitative forms to publication data.[44] Central to these concerns is the empirically vast AustLit database[45] as it progresses towards significant milestones but which also leaves some information (at the time of writing) during this crucial maturing phase 'insufficiently comprehensive ... for statistical analyses'.[46]

This is a valid caution and it should signal the importance of being aware of the complexities and difficulties in any kind of empirical analysis that relies on datasets that, by their very nature, grow and change with the addition of new information. With reference to the Carter Brown Mystery Series and the Australian Common Reader project, this appears an implicit understanding of all research drawing upon archival and

---

Graham Tulloch, eds, *London Was Full of Rooms* (Adelaide: Lythrum Press, 2006), pp. 244–52, 245.

[44] This article draws on three years of independent consecutive data analysis conducted on a 'pre-clean' version of AustLit: The Australian Literature Resource database accessed through the Curtin University of Technology. This data analysis is located within the context of Richard Nile's CI-1 ARC Discovery grant 'Colonial Publishing and Literary Democracy in Australia: An Analysis of the Influence on Australian Literature of British and Australian Publishing'. For more details, please see Jason Ensor, 'Reprints, International Markets and Local Literary Taste: New Empiricism and Australian Literature', *JASAL Special Issue: The Colonial Present* (2008).

[45] For a background on the AustLit: The Australian Literature Resource, please visit www.austlit.edu.au:7777/presentations/index.html.

[46] AustLit, 'Coverage', online, www.austlit.edu.au/about/coverage [Accessed 27 February 2009].

bibliographic materials—even in those instances where the datasets appear to be complete. Therefore, as Joshi and Katherine Bode claim, 'rather than forcing a divide between ... statistics and cultural understanding, we should use one to enhance the other'.[47]

The Australian Literary Disciplinary Space

In Australia, any project intending to apply computational power to the analysis and visualisation of book history data must eventually turn its attention to AustLit: The Australian Literature Resource (formerly 'The Resource for Australian Literature', 2006, and 'The Australian Literature Gateway', 2002).[48] As the largest holder of information correlated with Australia literature, AustLit represents a growing 'structure of authority'[49] in the field of Australian creative and critical writing. Over time, it has established the cultural and institutional power to shape and set the legitimate definitions (and to influence the direction of bibliographic definition systems) for classifying Australian works and, more specifically, works as Australian. Collaborating with several Australian universities and the National Library of Australia, AustLit operates as a 'networked digital research environment' building a web-accessible 'comprehensive bibliographic record of the nation's literature'.[50]

---

[47] Katherine Bode, 'Beyond the Colonial Present: Quantitative Analysis, "Resourceful Reading" and Australian Literary Studies', *JASAL Special Issue: The Colonial Present* (2008): 189.
[48] Internet Archive Wayback Machine, online, web.archive.org/web/*/www.austlit.edu.au/ [Accessed April 2009].
[49] Pierre Bourdieu, *The Field of Cultural Production: Essays on Art and Literature* (Cambridge: Polity Press, 1993).
[50] Kerry Kilner, 'A Fool's Errand? Or, Ten Thousand Authors and the Madness of a National Bibliography', AustLit, online (2006), www.austlit.edu.au:7777/presentations/index.html [Accessed April 2009].

AustLit classifies works according to its own published scope policy, a process that might be described as the 'imposition of a form of thought'[51] on a representative regime of works or as a process, which assesses texts against specific 'frameworks of acceptance'.[52] AustLit's primary aim is to 'enhance and support research and learning in Australian literature'[53] and it achieves this through adapting online technologies to assist bibliographic discovery. So successful is this relationship between institutional power and the use of a web browser that AustLit's bibliographic ascriptions appear on the computer screen as properties of the texts or works it has inspected. That is, at the level of on-screen interaction, The Australian Literature Resource operates as a database responsive to queries and as a system that requires its users to view search results as possessing considerable paratextual authority and rigorously authenticated details. Just 'as the [colonial library] catalogue ordered society's body of knowledge within its card system',[54] today it might be argued that Australia's literary knowledge is being shaped and organised by a website search form. In this way, as an internet-based resource, AustLit associates the power to say with authority what is an Australian work—a power traditionally held by human literary agents—with an interactive licensed technology product in return for an annual subscription calculated 'under a range of pricing strategies'.[55]

---

[51] Jacques Rancière, *The Politics of Aesthetics* (London: Continuum International Publishing Group, 2006), p. 34.
[52] Edward W. Said, *Culture and Imperialism* (London: Chatto & Windus, 1993), p. 376.
[53] Tessa Wooldridge, 'Ensuring the Best—AustLit: The Resource for Australian Literature', Conference Paper (Melbourne: Australian and New Zealand Society of Indexers, 20 March 2005).
[54] Caroline V. Jones, 'The Influence of Angus & Robertson on Colonial Knowledge', *Journal of the Royal Australian Historical Society* 89.1 (2003): 26–37, 31.
[55] AustLit, 'How to Subscribe', online, www.austlit.edu.au/subscribe [Accessed 27 February 2009].

This distinguishes AustLit's 'canonical vision' as a 'product of privilege'[56] within what Ken Gelder might call the 'on-going canonisation of Australian literature through [a] well-funded, centralised editorial project'.[57] Certainly, literature from a researcher's perspective has always been in a sense a product of privilege. One has only to price rare print bibliographies of Australian novels in first-hand and second-hand bookstores to recognise that contemporary print bibliographies continue this tradition.[58] However, if a humanities researcher is affiliated with a university or a public library that absorbs the subscription, it is reasonable to assume that they would be familiar with AustLit's main website, or with what I describe as a virtual epistemic object constituted for academic consumption. This terminology is not to truncate AustLit's institutional and educational power, nor the oversight it exerts on the Australian literary disciplinary space, to an instrumental entity positioned within the national market. It must be clear by now to any user of the AustLit website that its layered structured depth represents knowledge work produced by specialists and experts who routinely inspect and interpret bibliographic materials. Instead, as one of many key stakeholders in—and primary producers of—the contemporary Australian literary disciplinary space, my intent is to signal AustLit's contemporary cultural grammar—that is, its user-centred metaphor of 'search'. Furthermore, this is to link

---

[56] Bourdieu, *The Field of Cultural Production*, p. 19.

[57] Ken Gelder, 'Recovering Australian Popular Fiction: Towards the End of Australian Literature', in Philip Mead, ed., *Australian Literary Studies in the 21st Century: Proceedings of the 2000 ASAL Conference* (Hobart: Association for the Study of Australian Literature, 2001), pp.112–20, 118.

[58] At the time of writing (April 2009), all four volumes of the *Bibliography of Australian Literature* were on sale as a complete collection at the University of Queensland Press for $499 AUD.

AustLit websites with broader postsocial[59] trends that aggregate information and expertise within a technological setting to produce a complex informational package, available online as a discrete object of knowledge in its own right.

Understandably, AustLit thus has an investment in being able to advise how useful its informational resource will be to particular forms of analysis, especially those conducted outside the 'singular symbolic surface'[60] of its websites, and the provenance of data available to this end. In this regard, on sustained reflection, the caution of a literary resource being 'insufficiently comprehensive ... for statistical analyses' should not be dismissed, at least not opportunistically.

Case Study: The Devil's Advocate Is in the Detail

The temptation in applying machine learning methods to humanities data is to interpret a computed result as some form of proof or determinate answer. In this case, the validity of the evidence lies inherent in the

---

[59] The term postsocial reflects 'the increased presence and relevance which non-human objects have assumed in contemporary life, and refer specifically to the kind of bonds which humans have developed with objects'. Mayall, 'Attached to their Style: Traders, Technical Analysis and Postsocial Relationships', p. 423. This is not to imply that scholars develop a relationship with an AustLit website though most Australian literary scholars will, at one point or another, turn to an AustLit website instead of a human expert. Rather, I wish to suggest more broadly that in the contemporary age scholars develop attachments to the virtual objects, online tools and internet-hosted information resources which help facilitate their particular brand of cognitive and interpretative labour. These 'attachments' can take the mild form of bookmarking internet favourites to the not-so-mild form of hoarding massive amounts of data (or quantifiable mass) for the potential next new breakthrough that such a quantity of information must surely be concealing.
[60] Mayall, 'Attached to Their Style: Traders, Technical Analysis and Postsocial Relationships', p. 425.

technology. This can be problematic when the methods are treated as a black box, a critic ex machina.[61]

Let me supplement this admission with two illustrations. Mimicking William St Clair's argument in *The Reading Nation in the Romantic Period* that the exercise of enumerative bibliography might prove useful for literary and cultural history, at the mid-year 2007 ASAL conference I presented a sequence of images that applied statistical methods to AustLit tagged-text data. Table 1 listed the top Australian novels reprinted internationally during the period 1890–2005. Drawing on the print-cultures logic that reprints can be a commercial indicator of demand, I presented this table alongside an argument that a picture, though oblique, could be built up of modern literary tastes and demands during the twentieth century through statistical analysis, specifically revealing which Australian novels publishers internationally reprinted or translated the most. My quest was not to solve or answer any particular problem about Australian publishing but rather—to retrospectively recast Willard McCarty's use of classicist Don Fowler as a redemptive personal motive—to make them worse, on the assumption that surprising and unusual results would create a context to ask new questions or refine existing ones.[62]

Over a two-week period in June 2007 where I was fully occupied with writing computer instructions and mining the AustLit database, I engineered an algorithm or what McCarty refers to as the 'black box' of 'unexamined or obscure process[es]' underpinning any humanities-based computing project.[63] As the algorithm behind the spreadsheet of ranks, authors, years, works and totals, it grouped manifestations or reprints of a

---

[61] Sculley and Pasanek, 'Meaning and Mining: The Impact of Implicit Assumptions in Data Mining for the Humanities', p. 421.
[62] McCarty, 'Humanities Computing', p. 1224.
[63] Ibid., p. 1230.

Table 1 Top Australian Works Reprinted Internationally (Outside Australia), 1890–2005 (Table generated from July 2007 AustLit data snapshot of 14,750 manifestation records)

Rank	Author	Year	Period	Work	Reprints
1.	Colleen McCullough	1977	1977–2005	The Thorn Birds	47
2.	Thomas Keneally	1982	1982–97	Schindler's Ark	39
3.	Colleen McCullough	1974	1974–2004	Tim: A Novel	28
4.	D'Arcy Niland	1955	1955–2001	The Shiralee	25
5.	Carter Brown	1958	1959–94	The Corpse	23
6.	Frederic Manning	1929	1930–2004	The Middle Parts of Fortune: Somme and Ancre, 1916	22
	Carter Brown	1959	1959–98	Walk Softly Witch!	22
	Murray Bail	1998	1998–2002	Eucalyptus	22
7.	Carter Brown	1958	1969–2004	The Blonde	20
	Carter Brown	1962	1962–2004	Angel!	20
8.	Christina Stead	1994	1941–2004	The Man Who Loved Children	19
	Patrick White	1957	1957–2002	Voss	19
	Carter Brown	1958	1958–2000	The Body	19
	Carter Brown	1959	1959–98	The Wanton	19
	James Vance Marshall	1959	1960–97	The Children	19
	Colleen McCullough	1987	1987–92	The Ladies of Missalonghi	19
	Garth Nix	1995	1996–2004	Sabriel	19

Rank	Author	Year	Period	Work	Reprints
9.	D.H. Lawrence	1923	1923–2000	*Kangaroo*	18
	Carter Brown	1959	1959–76	*The Dame*	18
	Carter Brown	1959	1959–2000	*The Passionate*	18
	Brown, Carter	1957	1959–75	*The Unorthodox Corpse*	18
	Brown, Carter	1961	1962–95	*The Tigress*	18
	McCullough, Colleen	1990	1990–2003	*The First Man in Rome*	18

work with their primary (first edition) title.[64] This formed many subsets of the kind where, for example, *La mochila* (1956), *Un sacre petit paquet: roman Australien* (1957) and *Shirali: roman* (1978) are correlated with their central (often English-language) first published title, which in this example is *The Shiralee* (1957) by D'Arcy Niland. The algorithm chronologically ordered the manifestations within each subset, allowing also for the identification of first and last years of publication, and then counted the number making up each set. The results were collated in a tabular format and arranged from highest to lowest through the application of a ranking system keyed to subset totals, which in turn suggested a hierarchy of decreasing significance with the international translation of Australian novels. In this way, rank one listed Colleen McCullough's 1977 work, *The Thorn Birds*, as having forty-seven manifestations during the years 1977 to 2005 and it could be reasonably interpreted to have more value (though what kind of value was not made explicitly clear) than, say, Carter Brown's *The Unorthodox Corpse* which inhabited rank nine with only eighteen manifestations internationally. This table was imported

---

[64] Ensor, 'Reprints, International Markets and Local Literary Taste: New Empiricism and Australian Literature', p. 208.

into that 'ubiquitous form of digitally assisted demonstration',[65] PowerPoint, the Microsoft software product researchers and academics regularly employ to add rhetorical power to their conference demonstrations. Within a larger narrative of seventeen images focusing on quantifiable outcomes, it was presented as slide number ten before a conference audience who shared scholarly interests in the disciplinary space of Australian literature.

These slides ranged from spreadsheets representing Australia's most productive authors, to line graphs indicating publishing outputs throughout the twentieth century, to a final image of a NASA world map dotted with places of publication that signalled via a kind of GIS (geographic information system) where Australian novels have been produced throughout the planet. Conjointly, this collection supported Stark and Paravel's claim that PowerPoint enables the bringing together of 'facts with different textures'[66] and its mention here is to invite awareness of the 'technical and rhetorical modalities of digital demonstrations' which often prop up 'the staging/screening of "facts", [and] their circulation'.[67] However, I see that this use of PowerPoint was also an attempt to satisfy a (as then unacknowledged and ambitious) personal drive to transport the ASAL audience to a 'distant imaginary'[68] of diverse mathematical virtuosity and empirical certainty.[69] This was in the service of

---

[65] David Stark and Verena Paravel, 'PowerPoint in Public: Digital Technologies and the New Morphology of Demonstration Theory', *Culture and Society* 25 (2008): 32.
[66] Ibid., p. 44.
[67] Ibid., p. 34.
[68] Ibid., p. 35.
[69] For data, as a component of methodology, 'can scarcely be deployed without implicitly stating the affiliation of the speaker, and not as a mere matter of fact but as a declaration of kinship, vested interest, antagonism, defensiveness and so forth.' Flanders, 'Data and Wisdom: Electronic Editing and the Quantification of Knowledge', p. 54.

constituting 'new genres for scholarship'[70] in Australian literature, of course, but it nevertheless blurred the analytic labour conventionally divided between scholars and technicians.[71] A version of slide ten was later published with the (necessary) apologetic that it was to be considered 'provisional ... upon the completion of the AustLit database in the future and [antecedent to] the findings of a follow-up statistical analysis'.[72]

I did not think much more about slide number ten until February 2009 when I returned to the topic of Australia's top reprinted novels and conducted another analysis using the same algorithm (Table 2). Though some changes were expected, most surprisingly the only novels which remained familiar to both tables in the uppermost ranks were *Schindler's Ark*, transitioning from rank two to rank eight, and *The Thorn Birds*, usurped from rank one to rank five by Morris West's *The Devil's Advocate* (with an impressive-looking sixty-five manifestations). If I was still seeking a context to pose new questions, I had certainly found one in the lack of correspondence between these two tables. Such a lack would command any researcher to ask what happened between July 2007 and February 2009 to initiate such a dramatic reconfiguration of the publishing facts covering 115 years of Australian literary history and to

---

[70] McCarty, 'Humanities Computing', p. 1230.
[71] On the traditional separation between scholars and technicians (since academics often employ RAs with the informational and database skill sets they themselves may not possess), Julia Flanders asks: 'If the computer merely displays knowledge to a post-production society, what might this imply about our mechanisms for generating new (as opposed to retrieving and redeploying old) expert knowledge? How real is the danger that the scholar-worker, whose origins lie in a nineteenth-century conception of learning as heroic endeavour, will be transformed into the scholar-technician?' Flanders, 'Data and Wisdom: Electronic Editing and the Quantification of Knowledge', p. 61.
[72] Ensor, 'Reprints, International Markets and Local Literary Taste: New Empiricism and Australian Literature', p. 201.

Table 2 Top Australian Works Reprinted Internationally (Outside Australia), 1890–2005 (Table generated from February 2009 AustLit data snapshot of 18,954 manifestation records)

Rank	Author	Year	Period	Work	Reprints
1.	Morris West	1959	1959–2005	*The Devil's Advocate*	65
2.	Nevil Shute	1957	1957–2005	*On the Beach*	56
3.	Nevil Shute		1950–2001	*A Town Like Alice*	55
4.	Morris West	1963	1963–2003	*The Shoes of the Fisherman*	48
5.	Colleen McCullough	1977	1977–2005	*The Thorn Birds*	47
6.	Morris West	1973	1973–95	*The Salamander*	46
7.	Patrick White	1957	1957–2000	*Voss*	41
8.	Nevil Shute	1942	1942–2000	*Pied Piper*	39
	Nevil Shute	1952	1952–2000	*The Far Country*	39
	Thomas Keneally	1982	1982–97	*Schindler's Ark*	39
9.	Morris West	1971	1971–94	*Summer of the Red Wolf*	37
10.	Morris West	1968	1968–99	*The Tower of Babel*	36
11.	Morris West	1965	1965–99	*The Ambassador*	34
	Morris West	1974	1974–2005	*Harlequin: A Novel*	34
	Morris West	1979	1979–93	*Proteus*	34
12.	Nevil Shute	1944	1944–2001	*Pastoral*	33
13.	Nevil Shute	1947	1947–2000	*The Chequer Board*	31
	Nevil Shute	1948	1948–2000	*No Highway*	31
	Nevil Shute	1955	1955–2000	*The Breaking Wave*	31
	Nevil Shute	1960	1960–2000	*Trustee from the Toolroom*	31
	Morris West	1981	1981–2003	*The Clowns of God: A Novel*	31

ask, perhaps more significantly, what the methodological implications might be for future statistical analyses of this kind.

One immediate answer is that the foundational dataset upon which the enumerative bibliography was conducted had changed significantly with the addition of new information, enough not only to reorder the original 2007 findings but to replace them with a significantly different list of works. (In fact, 4202 manifestation records and 2107 first edition records were added to the database for the period under analysis, 1890–2005. However, as an aside, to contextualise these numbers, according to the daily report that appears on the front page of its website, it is worth noting that AustLit reported 558,591 works in its database on 22 June 2007,[73] compared to 626,376 works on 4 April 2009. This suggests that the whole database grew by 67,785 works, of which the additional manifestation and first edition records under discussion represent only 10 percent or less of AustLit's total bibliographic growth between July 2007 and February 2009.)

This creates quite a paradox. On the one hand, it remains reasonable to stand by my claim that the empirical certainty reflected in each table is nonetheless accurate for the scope of data available *at the time of analysis*. From a data-mining perspective, the statistical results were calculated in a valid manner. On the other hand, the table for July 2007 (which reflects the processing of over 14,750 manifestations, a not insignificant amount) is correct—and yet now obviously incorrect—and the table generated in February 2009 (representing the processing of 18,954 manifestations) is also correct *as of this moment*. It too, however, will eventually cycle through its 'half-life' of certainty much like its 2007 predecessor. Borrowing a term from the glossary of nuclear physics, by 'half-life' its definition refers to the time in which half the conclusions of a particular set of aca-

---

[73] Internet Archive Wayback Machine, online, web.archive.org/web/*/www.austlit.edu.au/ [Accessed April 2009].

demic findings disintegrate. This half-life is a characteristic property of all research including the hard sciences, which are often popularly considered incontrovertible.

However, as might be becoming clear to the reader, this half-life is a particularly important caveat in enumerative bibliography. Here, the perception of change in knowledge may be measured in briefer timeframes than, say, traditional scholarship which relies on archival documents (whose retrieval and synthesis into new historical facts requires a period of activity considerably longer than the time it takes to unleash an algorithm on updated datasets). The underlying difficulty is that most scholars function within university environments hungry for quantifiable research contributions. It is a generally accepted working condition that academics publish their findings as soon as practically possible and therefore typically it is an unsatisfactory situation to refrain from being issued in print format. But, in light of the above paradox—where the half-life of new empiricist analysis is likely in some modes to be less than the time which passes between the acceptance of an article by an editor and its actual publication—is presenting one's conclusions as subject to qualification and ongoing work (again, those necessary apologetics) sufficient insurance against the risk of one day being out of date but not out of print?

Necessary Lessons

It is appropriate at this point to refer back to Jessop who writes that the incomplete record is:

> a significant weakness of digital visualisation which will have to be addressed if its scholarly status is to be ensured. Visual sources present the viewer with a complete, and convincing, picture that is often derived from an incomplete record but the nature of the media used requires that the gaps be filled during its creation and thus concealed. If the applications of representation and abstract secondary sources are to be regarded as anything more than mere entertainment it must be ensured that view-

ers are aware of not only what is present but also what is omitted and the levels of uncertainty of that which is present.[74]

The case study above illustrates the ease with which this kind of problem can be encountered in a quantified analysis of Australian publication data. While the availability of PowerPoint, statistical analysis packages, internet-hosted empirical tools, and online database resources confer a level of scientific authenticity to humanities knowledge production and outcomes, the foreshortened half-life of some computer-based research should encourage caution and an overarching method to contextualise findings. One way to guard against such gaps is to create a set of standards reflecting good practice under an Australian Charter for the Computer-Based Representation of Literary History, within whose context new findings would be presented. This would be achieved through an open debate using The London Charter as a template. It would: 'provide a benchmark having widespread recognition among stakeholders, promote intellectual and technical rigour ... ensure that computer-based visualisation processes and outcomes can be properly understood and evaluated by users, [and] enable computer-based visualisation authoritatively to contribute'[75] to the study of Australian literary history and Australian print cultures. It would also respond to what Sculley and Pasanek identify as a 'need to find an articulate consensus on meaningful standards for experimental evidence provided by data mining'.[76] Additionally it is my hope, should an Australian Charter (or London Charter Implementation Guidelines for Australian Literature) eventuate, that it would respond to the following five issues that are specific in my view to Australian literature:

---

[74] Jessop, 'Digital Visualisation as a Scholarly Activity', p. 287.
[75] 'Objectives', The London Charter, p. 4.
[76] Sculley and Pasanek, 'Meaning and Mining: The Impact of Implicit Assumptions in Data Mining for the Humanities', p. 421.

1. There are two 'black boxes' embedded within any humanities computing project analysing publication data. One is the code employed to process the analysis, the other is the dataset used in the analysis, both of which can be difficult to release to the public or a shared disciplinary / methodological commons but which need to be more open in order to be tested, challenged and incorporated by alternative, even competing projects. As Beckmann notes, part of the success of the hard sciences is that they 'subsidise opposing voices'.[77] Thus, if technical questions are entangled with political questions over data ownership and access then it is perhaps beneficial to address both kinds of questions in parallel in order to advance methods of (and to encourage a healthy ecology of) quantitative analysis for Australian literature. That means debating sensitive issues of ownership, independent testing, reproducible methods and gatekeeping practices regarding data retention and knowledge creation, at least within the context of creating a shared disciplinary / methodological commons or online archive.[78] It follows, as McCarty suggests, that humanities computing 'challenges issues of ownership, which is to say, reveals that many [source materials] are held in common and there is much to be gained from sharing them. If its real potential is understood, humanities computing can be quite threatening to the status quo.'[79]

2. The creation of a data source is cultural work and especially so with data that are centred on culture or nation as its core organising con-

---

[77] Beckmann, 'Literature, Science and Economic Rationalism', p. 69.
[78] See point '6.3.4 Make data available and methods reproducible', Sculley and Pasanek, 'Meaning and Mining: The Impact of Implicit Assumptions in Data Mining for the Humanities', p. 423.
[79] Willard McCarty quoted in Stuart Moulthrop, 'Computing, Humanism, and the Coming Age of Print', Seminar: Is Humanities Computing an Academic Discipline?, online (3 December 1999), iat.ubalt.edu/moulthrop/essays/uva99/ [Accessed April 2009].

cept (even though intellectually we would argue that the nation state is no longer obsessively maintained as a 'categorical foundation or operational centre').[80] Although Australian literature is a rather friendly environment for works and authors from around the world (mirroring on the one hand the 'sign of the postcolonial',[81] and on the other hand, the de-centred and de-territorialising logics of capitalism), there is no escaping the key disciplinary conceit that every entry in the AustLit database is taken to be importantly correlated with Australia. Yet in assessing a book's suitability for inclusion, 'we "don't just peer" ... [w]e must also "interfere" with the incoming data based on what we know we are trying to observe'.[82] In this way, books and authors, as Andrew Hassam claims for celebrities, 'can be regarded as Australian despite one's citizenship, place of birth or where one lives: the important factor is one's association with Australia'.[83] Thus, while close readings of an AustLit record would unpack a work's sometimes invisible or even obscure connection to Australian literature, a distant reading of the database does not have this cognitive power and therefore cannot account for the bibliographer's judgement behind the creation of the data entry. This can distort some historiographic conclusions derived from quantitative analysis. For an Australian literary database, as Ramsay claims for software, 'cannot be neutral ... since

---

[80] Raley, 'eEmpires', p. 126.
[81] Graham Huggan, *Australian Literature: Postcolonialism, Racism, Transnationalism* (Oxford: Oxford University Press, 2007), p. 150.
[82] Willard McCarty, 'Digitising Is Questioning, or Else', Long Room Hub Lecture Series, Trinity College Dublin, staff.cch.kcl.ac.uk/~wmccarty/ [Accessed April 2009].
[83] Andrew Hassam, 'From Ned Kelly to Don Bradman: India, Australia and the Incongruities of Globalisation', in C. Vijayasree, R. Azhagarasan, Bruce Bennett, Mohan Ramanan, R. Palanivel and T. Sriraman, eds, *New Bearings in English Studies: A Festschrift for C.T. Indra* (Hyderabad: Orient Longman, 2008).

there is no level at which assumption disappears' nor where a 'demonstrably non-neutral act of interpretation can occur'.[84] Ways then need to be discovered to reveal this stored labour of bibliographic assignment (which endows Australian literature with much of its power). As Stuart Moulthrop remarks: 'Data is past participle, that which is given, but in the humanities we tend not to accept the given without scepticism or inquiry'.[85] Indeed, should we take such things at their word and be done with critical inquiry?[86] By identifying and evaluating research sources in a 'structured and documented way', future studies incorporating new empiricism may explore how Australian literary data and 'visual sources may be affected by ideological, historical, social ... and aesthetic' factors.[87]

3. Tufte, Stark and Paravel contend that academia has become comfortable with Microsoft PowerPoint as a mode of presentation and that any scholarly use of it needs to take account of the affordances and rhetorical modalities PowerPoint encourages within a conference or audience setting.[88] This means being critically attuned to PowerPoint's standardised style of post-synchronisation (its presentation templates, bullet-pointing, subtitling, etc.) which, like empirical reporting services, can delimit a focus only on outcomes, making it challenging 'to convey processes of reasoning' that are not 'co-authored, [and] shepherded toward a certain, quite minimalist, frame of mind'.[89] (Andrew Feenberg extends this notion further, holding that technology 'based

---

[84] S. Ramsay, 'In Praise of Pattern', *TEXT Technology* 2 (2005): 182.
[85] Stuart Moulthrop, 'Computing, Humanism, and the Coming Age of Print'.
[86] A question posed by a reader of an earlier version of this chapter.
[87] 'Research Sources', The London Charter, p. 7.
[88] See Edward Tufte, 'The Cognitive Style of PowerPoint: Pitching Out Corrupts Within', *Beautiful Evidence* (Cheshire: Graphics Press, 2006).
[89] Stark and Paravel, 'PowerPoint in Public: Digital Technologies and the New Morphology of Demonstration', p. 37.

on calculation and optimisation ... shapes not just technical devices and social systems but individual consciousness'.)[90] Progress might be made by considering that though 'the projector might malfunction' the 'presenter controls every aspect of the presentation'. In retrospect, much like my own ASAL talk that used PowerPoint to narrate seventeen slides, 'displays of virtuosity are about *lock in*. The fix is in, outcomes are locked up, [and] contending interpretations are locked out'.[91] Documenting the rationale behind selecting one method of research dissemination or visualisation over another would need to be considered by an Australian Charter.[92]

As with the history of print, which took centuries to stabilise into the forms we exploit today, we must be highly conscious of the 'newness' of new empiricism because, as is also claimed about PowerPoint and which I apply to computing in Australian literature, we are using 'technology in its early moments of adoption, during which there are important questions about when and, if so, how it becomes stabilised'.[93] While it is useful to link contemporary humanities computing to previous projects of exemplary empirical studies that pre-date information technology, this can have the effect of naturalising computational variants of empirical research before they have finished unfolding within humanities disciplines, leaving critical

---

[90] Andrew Feenberg, 'From Critical Theory of Technology to the Rational Critique of Rationality', *Social Epistemology* 22.1 (January–March 2008): 12.
[91] Ibid., p. 48.
[92] The discussion about Microsoft PowerPoint may seem an awkward companion to this essay's main argument. However, its inclusion is to invite speculation about whether humanities' gravitation towards template-driven visualisation technologies in the past has been uncritical and, if so, whether this provides significant context for the present 'computational turn'.
[93] Ibid., p. 36.

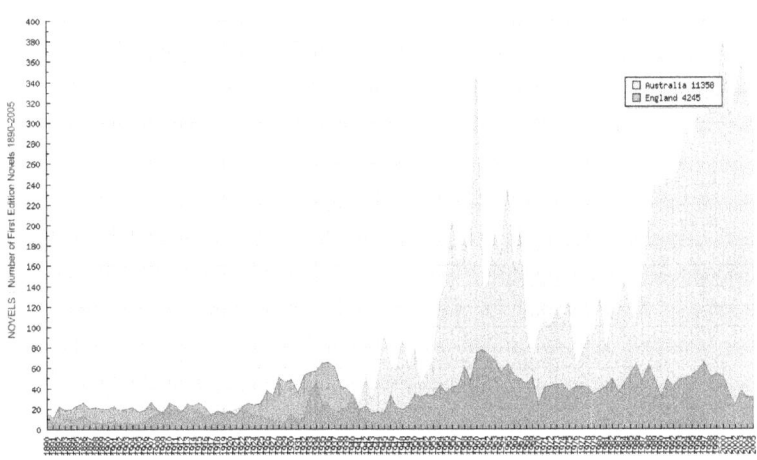

Figure 1 First Publication of Novels in Australia and England, Plotted for 1890–2005 (Graph generated from July 2007 AustLit data snapshot of 19,140 first edition records)

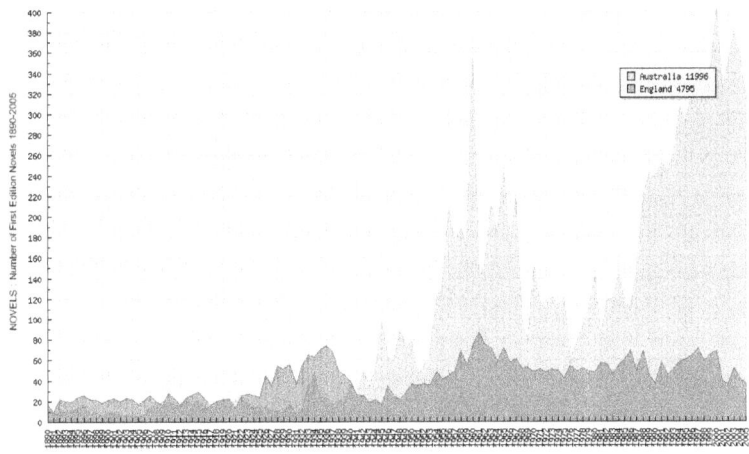

Figure 2 First Publication of Novels in Australia and England, Plotted for 1890–2005 (Graph generated from February 2009 AustLit data snapshot of 21,247 first edition records)

awareness of the influence of technology—of its orchestrated effects—on methodologies a little weak.

4. As discussed above, conclusions drawn via the computational turn can be prone to having a much shorter half-life (that is, the lapse of time before new findings are presented which challenge and overturn previous knowledge claims) than traditional scholarship preoccupied with archival materials. Documenting knowledge claims would make clear to other scholars what a particular visualisation of quantified analysis is seeking to represent, and the extent of any factual uncertainty. Connected with this point, different levels of scale in distant reading have proportional effects on claims of certainty when the foundational dataset is still maturing. A macrocosmic form of distant reading that interprets trends (as in Figures 1 and 2) can be reasonably expected to outlive a microcosmic form that parses 'top-ten'-type enquiries. Figures 1 and 2, though also generated from the same Aust-Lit snapshots taken nineteen months apart as the top Australian reprint lists under discussion, show very little observable difference in their representation of Australian novel production—certainly nothing that overturns the July 2007 reading of Australian versus English publication trends—and therefore are findings still in print that have not yet disintegrated. (But, it should be noted, there is still a significant difference of 1188 first edition titles between the totals of Figures 1 and 2 which would impact other kinds of analysis comparing Australia with England.) Microcosmic enquiries like 'top ten' lists, though intriguing, can be a kind of secondary instrumentalisation which is brought about when a dataset's *stabilised-for-now* status is taken to be broadly indicative of a future unchanging or *stabilised-enough* nature.[94] As my own experience testifies, not accounting for secondary

---

[94] I would argue that 'top-ten'-like enquiries are generally susceptible to this kind of problem when working with datasets that have not stabilised. For example,

instrumentalisation invites the possibility of a foreshortened half-life in the presentation of any microcosmic research outcomes. Additionally, other kinds of microcosmic enquiries and reports—like 'how many times does etc?'—run the risk of being received as quick-and-dirty journalistic facts with short-lived historical resonance, even though they may remain what Priya Joshi says of all statistics—'lies that tell a truth that would not otherwise be evident'.[95] Such lists and reports, if orphaned from critical thinking, should be revealed as a naïve form of new empiricism. Indeed Sculley and Pasanek caution professional readers like literary scholars that 'just because results are statistically valid and humanly interpretable does not guarantee that they are meaningful … [For] we can give a gloss or a paraphrase for all varieties of nonsense'.[96] The core issue then is to recognise that 'some representations are better than others … in the sense of

---

with the 2007 dataset used in my ASAL presentation, I found that the top ten publishers of first-edition Australian novels worldwide for the period 1960–2005 were: (1) Cleveland, (2) Horwitz, (3) Mills & Boon, (4) Penguin, (5) Allen & Unwin, (6) Angus & Robertson, (7) Scripts, (8) University of Queensland Press, (9) Robert Hale and (10) Pan Macmillan Australia. In 2009, the same analysis applied to the most recent data snapshot yielded: (1) Cleveland, (2) Horwitz, (3) Mills & Boon, (4) Penguin, (5) Scripts, (6) Robert Hale, (7) Angus & Robertson, (8) Allen & Unwin, (9) University of Queensland Press and (10) Pan Macmillan Australia. Though minor, in comparing the analysis applied to data snapshots nineteen months apart, there were nonetheless shuffles in order for ranks five, six, seven, eight and nine. While this does not negate the overall illustrative and indicative value of this kind of enquiry, it does confirm that caution should be exercised in its presentation within an argument.

[95] Priya Joshi, 'Quantitative Methods, Literary History', *Book History* 5 (2002): 264.

[96] Sculley and Pasanek, 'Meaning and Mining: The Impact of Implicit Assumptions in Data Mining for the Humanities', p. 420.

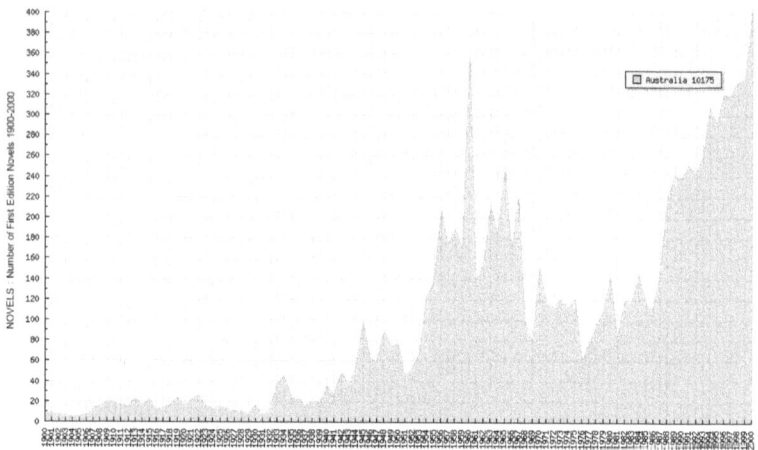

Figure 3 First Publication of (10,175) Novels in Australia Only, Plotted for 1900–2000 (Graph generated from February 2009 AustLit data snapshot of 21,247 first edition records)

providing a more useful analytical model'[97] for cases where the dataset may not be relatively stable.

Conclusion: What Then Is the Worth of a Picture?

In *Principles of Literary Criticism*, I.A. Richards, credited with pioneering the literary movement of New Criticism, begins with, 'A book is a machine to think with'.[98] Today, eighty-five years since the first publication of *Principles of Literary Criticism*, we use machines to think about books but, to contemporise the second half of Richards's opening formulation, these need not usurp the humanities scholar. In view then of the above

---

[97] Flanders, 'Data and Wisdom: Electronic Editing and the Quantification of Knowledge', p. 56.
[98] I.A. Richards, *Principles of Literary Criticism* (London and New York: Routledge, 2001), p. vii.

points and with reference to Figure 3, this chapter appears to insist on a lot of groundwork before answering its title question, 'Is a picture worth 10,175 Australian novels?' Perhaps an answer is finally possible, but only within the context of an Australian Charter for the Computer-Based Representation of Literary History. Through this, though I would be unable to make any claims to truth or historical fact with my answer, I would nonetheless be able speak it with a greater level of confidence in the face of datasets being 'insufficiently comprehensive', as a better-founded hypothesis, with some probabilities of certainty.

13
Voices from the Past: Gender, Politics, and the Anthology*

Gillian Whitlock

Twenty years ago, my literary anthology of Australian women's writing *Eight Voices of the Eighties* appeared in the UQP Australian Authors series; these days remaining copies are hard to recognise on the shelf, with the ochre cover faded to a pale wash. In this chapter I return to that edited selection of stories, journalism and criticism by Kate Grenville, Barbara Hanrahan, Beverley Farmer, Thea Astley, Elizabeth Jolley, Jessica Anderson, Olga Masters and Helen Garner to re-engage with my former self at work as an editor, critic and anthologiser. I will be using data which has the potential to bring a different approach to bear on Australian women's writing in what, I see, I confidently described as 'a phase in the national literary history when women writers and readers entered the mainstream.'[1] In one of the few extended critical essays that addresses

---

*Thanks to my colleagues in the Resourceful Reading project; to Robert Thomson for his research assistance and advice; and to David Carter, for his patient 'wise idiot' questions.
[1] Gillian Whitlock, *Eight Voices of the Eighties* (St Lucia: University of Queensland Press, 1989), p. xi.

Australian short story anthologies,[2] Steve Holden begins with the observation that 'anthologies of any kind of writing serve as monuments': they *describe* a group of texts as though selecting them from a larger body of possibilities, they *constitute* and then *consecrate* that group of texts as the best examples drawn from the larger body of possibilities according to the terms that the anthologiser dictates.[3] The monumental, the constitutional, the dictat: the anthologist as the gatekeeper of the 'museum of literature', the practitioner of constitutive practices that remain submerged: it is no wonder I return to *Eight Voices* and the earlier practice of the anthologist from a distance now, and tentatively, to explore its contents and the meanings of its current condition.

Gender-based interpretation and feminist critiques of Australian literature in particular have rapidly emerged as a focus of debate as literary criticism takes an empirical turn. In her germinal article 'Along Gender Lines' Katherine Bode uses the AustLit database to develop a quantitative analysis of the relationship between gender, genre and Australian novels from the 1930s to 2006.[4] Bode's article contests what she characterises as an iconic account of contemporary Australian literary history: during the 1970s Australian literature emerged from a period of masculinist conservatism into a golden age for authors, scholars and readers. Turning to the

---

[2] Holden selects the following as a random group of short story anthologies for his article: Cecil Hadgraft and Richard Wilson's *A Century of Australian Short Stories* (1963), Harry Heseltine's *The Penguin Book of Australian Short Stories* (1976), Kerryn Goldsworthy's *Australian Short Stories* (1983), Leonie Kramer's *My Country: Australian Poetry and Short Stories* (1985) and Laurie Hergenhan's *The Australian Short Story* (1986). Steve Holden, 'Short Story Anthologies and "the Solid Body of Australian Fiction"', *Australian Literary Studies* 19.3 (May 2000): 279–94.
[3] Ibid, p. 279.
[4] Katherine Bode, 'Along Gender Lines: A Quantitative Study of the Relationships between Australian Novels, Gender and Genre from 1930s to 2006', *Australian Literary Studies* 24.2 (2009), forthcoming.

work of Elizabeth Webby, Ken Gelder and Paul Salzman, Kerryn Goldsworthy, and my own essay on Australian women's writing 1970–90 in the second edition of Carole Ferrier's *Gender, Politics and Fiction*, Bode identifies the shaping of this grand narrative by a generation of scholars and critics whose academic careers and intellectual roots are associated with the institutionalisation of Australian literature and the political liberalism of the 1970s, and with the emergence of literary scholarship informed by theory—feminism, postcolonialism, poststructuralism. Alternatively, Bode's empirical approach challenges gender-based interpretations of this period: it questions the relationship between women's writing and feminism; it incorporates a more expansive field that argues for the importance of male-authored genre fiction to a dramatic increase in the publication of Australian novels in the 1950s and 1960s; it argues that feminist-inflected critique has been essentially conservative in its failure to conceptualise the literary as only one category or genre within the field of fiction. Paul Eggert also uses the more empirical turn of recent textual and book-historical research to critique feminist scholarship, most particularly feminist accounts of literary canon formation in Australian literature in the 1890s.[5] Like Bode, Eggert is contesting accounts that emerged in the 1980s. Returning to Susan Sheridan's classic feminist essay first published in 1985, "'Temper Romantic; Bias Offensively Australian": Australian Women Writers and Literary Nationalism',[6] Eggert argues that feminist critiques of gender and canon formation in the 1890s focus on ideology with insufficient attention to empirical evidence about the availability and affordability of Australian fiction in the colonies; the

---

[5] Paul Eggert, 'Australian Classics and the Price of Books: The Puzzle of the 1890s', *JASAL Special Issue: The Colonial Present* (2008): 130–57.
[6] Susan Sheridan, '"Temper, Romantic; Bias, Offensively Australian": Australian Women Writers and Literary Nationalism', *Kunapipi* 7.2-3 (1985): 49–58.

role of publishers in shaping the trajectory of books and reading; and the effects of the marketplace more generally in canon formation.

New empiricism historicises and interrogates the moment that produced *Eight Voices* late last century as a time when ideologically driven critiques shaped new canons and communities of interpretation. To review these critiques now as conservative (as Bode suggests) or uninformed about histories of reading and the book (as Eggert proposes) raises important questions about feminist critiques of Australian literature and culture in a recent past and (interestingly) now, at a time of generational change when those who contributed to that iconic narrative begin to leave the academy. My argument here will be that the anthology might be a particularly useful tool to address some of these issues about gender, writing and empirical critique. Although the anthology is, as Holden suggests, fundamental to institutions of canon formation, quantitative analysis using the AustLit database suggests it is one of the most readily available gateways for the dissemination of writing of all kinds through small and intimate networks. This lends substance to Jane Tompkins's suggestion that the anthology is more transient than monumental, and it is only by reading *across* a series and producing a history of anthologies that the shifting ideoscapes of literary value and its historical and cultural locations come into view. Tompkins's mapping of multiple volumes of American literary anthologies indicates that they are engaged in a constant rewriting of literary history, in which entire periods, genres and modes of classification disappear, the fate of individual authors remains uncertain, and preoccupations with gender, race, regions and class are unstable. The anthology, she concludes, is an index of the variable social and historical circumstances within which anthologists work, and of the changing definitions of literary excellence:

> the evidence of the anthologies demonstrates not only that works of art are not selected according to any unalterable standard, but that their very essence is always changing in accordance with the systems of description

and evaluation that are in force. Even when the 'same' text keeps turning up in collection after collection, it is not really the same text at all.[7]

From this perspective, the production and reception of anthologies is one indicator of the dynamic relationship between literary values and historical conditions. Moving out from *Eight Voices*, this chapter will look to anthologies more generally and literary anthologies in particular in Australian letters late last century with a view to mapping the spaces they occupied, and the locations they made available to writers, readers and critics.

Scanning the Body of Australian Anthology

The AustLit data confirms that in the last three decades of the twentieth century there was a surge in the publication of literary anthologies. Anthologising in general and short story anthologies in particular, peaked in the 1990s (Table 1).

Conventionally defined as 'a collection of stories, poems, or nonfiction pieces by more than one author,'[8] separating the literary anthology from other collections and editions listed at the database raises difficult issues. For example anthologies have been selectively indexed in AustLit, and many are not yet included although 'anthology' is a category available for selection under 'work type'. Some anthologies are not all Australian, and these have been excluded from the count here, as have Australian anthologies published overseas. Anthologies are composites, and although many in the Australian literary archive are compilations of short stories, to the extent that 'literary anthology' is sometimes taken as

---

[7] Jane Tompkins, *Sensational Designs: The Cultural Work of American Fiction 1790–1860* (New York: Oxford University Press, 1985), p. 196.
[8] Lewis Turco, *The Book of Literary Terms* (Hanover NH: University Press of New England, 1999), p. 168.

Table 1 Anthologies (figures in brackets are literary anthologies featuring short fiction)

1800–1899	29 (5)
1900–1909	9 (3)
1910–1919	13 (2)
1920–1929	7 (5)
1930–1939	17 (8)
1940–1949	30 (11)
1950–1959	21 (14)
1960–1969	67 (34)
1970–1979	99 (40)
1980–1989	300 (104)
1990–1999	615 (194)
2000–2008	354 (174)

coextensive with 'short story' genre in Australian criticism, others (such as *Eight Voices*) are multi-genre and feature journalism, interviews or poetry as well. Yet the database evidence suggests clear trends and relationships that can be read to indicate that the field of anthologies in general burgeoned late last century, increasing almost tenfold from 1960 to 2000, and so did the publication of the subset of literary anthologies like *Eight Voices*, although as a proportion of anthologies in general, literary anthologies dropped from 50 percent to 30 percent over the same period. In his study of the emergence and decline of literary forms and their historical context, Franco Moretti speculates that genres and types exhaust their potentialities, no longer capable of representing the most significant aspects of contemporary reality; literary cycles, he suggests, remain in place for twenty-five years or so.[9] Moretti is concerned with the history of the novel, but his comments are suggestive as we survey the surge of anthologies in Australian writing late last century and note that it does, in fact, accord with Moretti's notion of the tenure of 'generic' cycles.[10]

Although the anthology is characteristically associated with regulation and consecration of a national cultural formation, the anthology in Australian letters late last century is a democratic, regional, and unregulated form. AustLit data brings to light a diverse array of texts and contexts, and the coexistence of very different kinds of anthology that resist any simple codification. The body of anthologies is larger and less shapely than we might think. For example, in 1989 alone the fifty anthologies listed in the AustLit database suggest the anthology makes publication available to collectives that share various identities, affiliations and needs. Consider, for example: *Fancy Seeing You Here*, a collection of writings by residents of nursing homes in Launceston and the Tamar region; *Fitting Into My Skin*, a collection of young women's writings and artworks about health, relationships and sexuality published by the Young Women's Writings Collective in Canberra; *Ink Slingers Inc.*, an anthology of poems and short stories published by the Kensington and Norwood Writers Group; *Here We Are*, an anthology published by the Migrant Women Writer's Group in East Ormond, Victoria. In this one year alone, regional and communally based collectives of writers creating their own publications (a significant number subsidised by the Fellowship of Australian Writers) account for 30 percent of the titles. By comparison, 20 percent were published by major trade publishers, such as Penguin, UQP, Hodder & Stoughton. One, an anthology of women's

---

[9] Franco Moretti, *Graphs, Maps, Trees: Abstract Models for a Literary History* (London: Verso, 2005), p. 20.
[10] Thanks to my colleague David Carter for discussions on this point.

novellas from Women's Redress Press, is published by a specialist feminist press. Changes in technology, increasing literacy, and a turn to creative writing and life writing as recreation, therapy, and/or a means of community engagement all underpin a proliferation of anthologies as an assertion of the local: regional or community identities that bring together small collectives of writers and readers. *Eight Voices* is one of the 15 percent of publications that take up gendered issues specifically; however it is clear that women are active in anthologising of all kinds: where editors are named in anthologies for that year, 45 percent are edited by women. Here Bode's point that women's writing and women's involvement in writing is not necessarily feminist in its inspiration and motivation is a useful caution. A feminist agenda is specifically signalled in few of the anthologies published in 1989 (5 percent), nevertheless it is evident that the anthology functions as a means of engaging with institutions of writing, reading and publication for numerous women—as writers and editors and proofreaders, as well as, no doubt, proficient contributors to the labour of self-publishing using the rapidly changing technologies of word processing and publication in the late 1980s.

Extending the survey across the two decades where there was a marked increase in the production of anthologies allows some clearer perspectives on the trends evident in the 1989 cross-section discussed above. It sharpens the argument that the anthology of late last century is a composite, and open to ephemera, to region, and to interest groups that incorporate various axes of identity, difference and affiliation. There is an exponential growth in the numbers of anthologies published in the 1970s, 1980s and 1990s, and some shifts in the key coordinates that allow us to describe this heterogeneous field of publications (Table 2).

These figures are broad brush strokes derived from the AustLit database. Some books record several entries—for example *Women's Words: A Local Anthology* published by the Northcote Christian Women's Book Project triggers both 'regional' and 'women-centred' categories—and others none—such as Carmel Bird's *Red Hot Notes*, published by UQP.

Table 2 Categories of Anthologies, 1980s and 1990s

	1970s	1980s	1990s
Number of anthologies	90	300	615
Trade publishers	30%	28%	20%
Regional focus	11%	18%	30%
National focus	22%	22%	30%
Woman-centred	1.5%	9%	8%
Multicultural	5%	6%	9%
Indigenous	5%	1.5%	6%
Woman/women editors	16%	40%	40%
Writing communities (guilds, collectives and fellowships)	7%	16%	25%
Young adult	5%	4%	16%
Generational	9%	5%	22%

This is an overview that does not account for scale and impact, such as print run, or distribution and readership. An increasing percentage of anthologies are produced by local and regional communities of writers rather than trade editions addressing the national community appealing to nation-based identities. However composites that lay claim to national representativeness and historical range, such as *Best Australian Stories* and *The Penguin Book of Australian Short Stories,* are usually produced by trade publishers with large print runs and expansive distribution networks that tap into institutional readerships organised through tertiary and secondary curricula. Possibly anthologies record both the surge of interest in 'making it national' that occurred around and about the bicentenary celebrations of 1988, and its aftermath. In any event, a survey of the proliferation of anthologies in the period using AustLit suggests a decentred and localised impetus rather than a concerted process of canonising and nationalising. A specific association of anthologies in general with marginal, oppositional and vanguard movements (feminism, Indigenous activism, multiculturalism) is not strong. We see a slight increase in multicultural concerns across the period, yet these anthologies (a few bilingual) remain concerned with European immigrant writing, and there is little recognition of Asian writing. There is a marked increase in attention to Indigenous writing across the period, and although this includes notable early anthologies from trade publishers such as *Paperbark: A Collection of Black Australian Writings,* edited by Jack Davis, Stephen Muecke and Adam Shoemaker and published by UQP in 1990, numerically the increase in this category records the activities of small collectives and specialist presses. Most notably late last century we see an increase in anthologising that taps into generational identities and markets, overwhelmingly this responds to the emergence of a young adult market.

This shift, a major feature of the peak of anthologising in the 1990s, emerges more clearly if we use the AustLit database categories and expand the field chronologically to map the generic affiliations of anthologies across four decades (Table 3).

Here again there are convergences across categories. For example the emergence of genre writing—most notably sci-fi and fantasy—overlaps with the young adult category, as during the period we see a convergence of genre and a specific readership. This happens too in the crime, mystery and detective categories, where the gendered uptake of genre fiction by women writers in particular comes into play. The interpretation of these figures needs to incorporate other kinds of information about market and impact. So, for example, the turn to fantasy and young adult markets is not just numerically significant; we see the investment of trade publishers such as HarperCollins entering these fields in the 1990s with titles such as *Fantastic Worlds* (1998), or unexpected convergences within genre writing such as Damien Broderick's hybrid anthology of sci-fi and travel stories, *Not the Only Planet* (1998), published by Lonely Planet and *Cybertales: An Anthology of Fantasy and Science Fiction by Young Writers*

Table 3 Generic Categories of Anthologies 1970–2008[11]

	1970–79	1980–89	1990–99	2000–08
Adventure		1		
Crime		4	28	12
Detective		1	7	6
Dreaming story		3		
Fantasy			15	40
Historical fiction			1	2
Horror			6	17
Humour	10	32	10	
Indigenous story	2	3	4	4
Mystery	1	2	7	9
Romance			3	1
Satire	12	9	18	3
Sci-Fi		10	25	42
Thriller			1	
Travel	1	3	13	4
War	1	5	1	3
Young adult	6	10	48	5

(1999, FourW Press). Time and again the composite nature of the anthology is telling; the form is agile and adaptable, able to incorporate hybrid formulations and in a constant process of change, as we see from the generic categories above. No single ideological impulse explains the generic shape-shifting of anthologies, and so for example the influence of feminism is limited if we chronicle the number of anthologies that openly signal an affiliation to the politics of gender and sexuality (1 percent in

---

[11] Thanks to Robert Thomson of AustLit for his work on this table. These are AustLit database genre categories.

the 1980s; 5 percent in the 1990s). However in these decades 'women's writing' was a popular identification, running around 10 percent, and if we consider the presence of women as writers, editors and readers, a survey of anthologising indicates that it was an activity where women played a major role in literary culture broadly conceived.

What then of what we now know to be a relatively small and reducing component of the body of anthologies: the fictional short story anthology? In the 1980s, anthologising was a lively industry in Australian literary criticism, and it opened opportunities for younger academics, writers and critics to publish and engage in debates about gender, writing, and the national literature. In May 1989, for example, Susan Sheridan reviewed two major new anthologies and two author-based studies of Australian women writers of the nineteenth century, a bibliography of Australian women's fiction, and a major feminist critical study, all published in 1988. As Sheridan drily remarks, it is hard to say whether the interest in the long-neglected field of nineteenth-century women's writing is a sign of publishers' participation in the bicentennial patriotic delirium, feminist entrepreneurship, or enlightened readers who have hitherto been complacently or aggressively satisfied with the male separatist tradition of Ozlit.[12] What can be said with more certainty is that anthologising was an important part of emerging feminist critiques of the organisational and institutional formations of Australian literary and cultural studies more generally at this time.

Another sign of a vibrant and self-conscious industry of anthologising in the 1980s and 1990s are editors' comments on sequence, companionship and dialogue emerging intertextually across different volumes. For example, Don Anderson suggests in the Introduction to his edition *Transgressions: Australian Writing Now* (1986) that it might profitably be read alongside Frank Moorhouse's anthology of contemporary Australian

---

[12] Susan Sheridan, 'Review', *Australian Literary Studies* 14.1 (May 1989): 118–22, 118.

short stories *The State of the Art* (1983). For the first time in the 1980s women played a major role as editors (the most notable earlier Australian example of female editorship is Beatrice Davis's co-editorship of *Best Australian Short Stories* [1967 rep. 1986], with Douglas Stewart). The response to Craig Munro's *The First UQ Story Book*, published in 1981, indicates some of the sexual politics that came into play in the production and reception of contemporary anthologies. Munro's selection was controversial, and it triggered a debate that is a useful sign of how anthologising engaged in debates about gender, identity politics, and writing at the time. Munro offered a selection of stories by Murray Bail, Peter Carey, Frank Moorhouse, Michael Wilding, Barry Oakley, among others, but included no women authors. The reception of *The First UQ Story Book* made the point that the author could no longer be taken as generically male, although a quick glance over the contents of other anthologies, both contemporary and historical, indicates that this was a rare case where an editor selected only male writers without using a cautionary subtitle. Brian Kiernan's *The Most Beautiful Lies* (1977) evaded a similar critique, perhaps because the subtitle signalled its selection more overtly: *A Collection of Stories by Five Major Contemporary Fiction Writers: Bail, Carey, Lurie, Moorhouse and Wilding*, as did John Barnes in *An Australian Selection: Short Stories by Lawson, Palmer, Porter, White and Cowan* (1974). Nevertheless the implicitly gendered association of the 'Australian' and 'major' with male writers remains.

As we have seen, the publication of literary short stories increased with the rise of anthologising more generally. Although literary anthologies comprise a decreasing proportion of the whole output of anthologies in this period, they carry a disproportionate influence. It is here that the literary and canonising processes of selection and interpretation that Holden comments upon come into view. Oxford, Penguin, Faber & Faber, and UQP published collections of stories selected in macroscopic sweeps organised in terms of epochs (for example 'century', or 'modern', 'contemporary' and 'new') and values ('Australian', 'best').[13] The major trade publishers continued to invest in anthologies that staked large chronological or national claims, monumental and retrospective, and these continued to be edited by authoritative male writers and academics, by and large. Yet at the same time publishers also invested in anthologies that claimed to revise, reformulate or (in the case of *Eight Voices*) produce an alternative canon. It is here that the genre of anthologies informed by feminist literary criticism came into play.

These began to emerge and in fact peaked numerically in the 1980s.[14] Less visible in anthologies at this stage are Indigenous writers[15] and mul-

---

[13] For example *The Penguin Book of Australian Short Stories* (Heseltine, ed., 1976), *Classic Australian Short Stories* (Waten, ed., 1974), *An Australian Selection* (Barnes, ed., 1974), *Best Australian Short Stories* (Stewart and Davis, eds, 1971), *The Australian Short Story: An Anthology from the 1890s to the 1980s* (Hergenhan, ed., 1986), *Cybertales: An Anthology of Fantasy and Science Fiction by Young Writers* (Anderson, ed., 1986), *The Faber Book of Contemporary Australian Short Stories* (Bail, ed., 1988), *Australian Short Stories* (Goldsworthy, ed., 1983), *The State of the Art: The Mood of Contemporary Australia in Short Stories* (Moorhouse, ed., 1983) and *The Oxford Book of Australian Short Stories* (Wilding, ed., 1994).

[14] They include *Feeling Restless: Australian Women's Short Stories* and *Eclipsed: Two Centuries of Australian Women's Fiction* (Burns, ed., 1989; 1988), *From the Verandah: Stories of Love and Landscape by Nineteenth Century Women* (Giles, ed., 1987), *Happy Endings: Stories by Australian and New Zealand Women Writers 1850s-1930s* (Webby and Wevers, eds, 1987), *Room to Move: The Redress Press Anthology of Australian Women's Short Stories* (Falkiner, ed., 1985), *Australian Women's Stories: An Oxford Anthology* (Goldsworthy, ed., 1999), *Falling for Grace: An Anthology of Australian Lesbian Fiction* (Snow and Taylor, eds, 1993), *Sisters* (Mosjeska, ed., 1993), *Wilder Shores: Women's Travel Stories of Australia and Beyond* (Lucas and Forster, eds, 1992), *Heroines* (Spender, ed., 1991).

[15] Three editions of Indigenous writing were published in this period: *Paperbark: A Collection of Black Australian Writings* (UQP, 1990), *Us Fellas: An Anthology of Aboriginal Writing* (Art Books, 1987), *Message Stick: Contemporary Aboriginal*

ticultural writers; of the emergent literary theories of the time, it was feminism that shaped anthologies. A notable exception is *Beyond the Echo: Multicultural Women's Writing* (1988), Sneja Gunew and Jan Mahyuddin's volume in the UQP Australian Authors series. This edition indicates that multicultural writing posed a serious challenge to the politics and aesthetics of contemporary Australian literature, and it is a reminder that more oppositional or vanguard writing was emerging from writers affected by both gendered and ethnic difference. The turn to realist and semi-autobiographical forms that characterised the 'female naturalism' of Helen Garner, Olga Masters and Jessica Anderson, was challenged by the experimental forms and language of Ania Walwicz, Rosa Cappiello and Antigone Kefala, for example. Gunew and Mahyuddin present their anthology as an act of making visible, in positive ways, a difference which has existed covertly in the compilations of Australian literature:

> To describe the making of an anthology as an act of 'positive discrimination' is, quite deliberately, to position this particular text in relation and opposition to some prevailing and much-contested notions about reading, writing and criticism: namely that a text can be produced and received as if outside any socio-political context; as if the text itself, and those involved in the process (writer, reader, and particularly here, editor) were free of any considerations of class, race and gender, of subordinate or dominant cultures, of political, or indeed, rhetorical positions.[16]

The coexistence of *Eight Voices* and *Beyond the Echo* in the UQP Australian Authors series suggests that, in a phase of prolific anthologising

---

Writing (IAD Press, 1997). Individual Indigenous writers such as Bruce Pascoe, Archie Weller, Oodgeroo, Alexis Wright and John Clark were included in various anthologies organised in chronological, national or regional terms.
[16] Sneja Gunew and Jan Mahyuddin, eds., *Beyond the Echo: Multicultural Women's Writing* (St Lucia: UQP, 1988), p. xiv.

activity, there is space for composites to present alternative interpretations of gender and difference within a strong market. Laurie Hergenhan points out that the production of the 'AA series' deliberately addressed institutional and individual interests, and was fuelled by an expansive period in Australian literature and Australian literary scholarship.[17]

Reading across the contents of anthologies in this way recalls Tompkins's attention to anthologies as signs of instability within a literary formation; an index of variable social and historical circumstances and their effects on determinations of literary value. It is the work of editors to introduce and naturalise their selection, to establish the terms and conditions which suture the composite. Distant reading across an array of anthologies published during the 1980s suggests how varied and tenuous these judgements of value can be. With the exception of Majorie Barnard's 'The Persimmon Tree'[18] there is little consensus in story selections across the editions, which stand as a sign of the differing systems of de-

---

[17] Laurie Hergenhan, 'On an Australian Selection', in Craig Munro, ed., *UQP: The Writer's Press 1948-1998* (St Lucia: UQP, 1998), pp. 159-70, 168-69.

[18] Tompkins suggests that even if the same text keeps turning up in collection after collection, it is not really the same text at all. If we read across the series of literary anthologies edited and published in the 1980s there is one story in particular that makes this point. Marjorie Barnard's short story 'The Persimmon Tree' is the most frequently anthologised short story, and yet the company it keeps suggests different thematic and aesthetic interpretations. So, for example, it appears in Laurie Hergenhan's *The Australian Short Story: An Anthology* (1986) amidst a broad sweep that begins with Henry Lawson and Barbara Baynton and concludes with Fay Zwicky and Barry Hill, and it is similarly placed in Hadgraft's *A Century of Australian Short Stories* and the Davis and Stewart edition *Best Australian Short Stories*. On the other hand for Murray Bail in *The Faber Book of Contemporary Australian Short Stories* it begins the turn to the modern, a point where the Australian short story takes a decisive turn and breaks with the past. 'The Persimmon Tree' is a rare instance of consensus in Australian literary anthologies of the 1980s, and the company it keeps alters significantly from one edition to another.

scription and evaluation in force. The Introduction to *Eight Voices* works to shape an interpretive community informed by feminist critique, and one of its definitive features is a deliberate and self-conscious attention to institutional realities that determine the processes of selection, interpretation and dissemination and shape the recognition of women's writing in Australia. Eggert's point that literary critical arguments about aesthetic objects, discursive analysis of ideological formations, and bibliographical-editorial explanations are all necessary finds no argument with feminist literary critique. To the contrary, this formulation of politics and aesthetics is familiar. New empiricism and book history generate new data and new insights, and on this basis they can (to use Rita Felski's phrase) 'speak back to feminism'.[19] But to the extent that they engage in debates about value, for example recognition of genre fiction and discourses of masculinity, and examine texts as 'commodities which are ... produced and marketed and consumed like much less hallowed objects',[20] they continue the materialist orientation of the feminist criticism emergent in Australia in the 1980s. Quantitative studies and eResearch generally remain embedded in the insights that have shaped the discipline over the past three decades.[21]

A Feminist Counter-Sphere

Recently, in her polemical review entitled *Literature after Feminism*, Rita Felski approaches feminist literary criticism of the 1970s and 80s in a spirit of generosity, as a flawed but necessary precursor of contemporary criticism: 'How could I ever have thought *that*? a critic may wonder,

---

[19] Rita Felski, *Literature after Feminism* (Chicago: University of Chicago Press, 2003), p. 21.
[20] Whitlock, p. xiv.
[21] Katherine Bode, 'Beyond the Colonial Present: Quantitative Analysis, "Resourceful Reading" and Australian Literary Studies', *JASAL Special Issue: The Colonial Present* (2008): 184–97, 184.

looking back at what seems in retrospect like a lacklustre set of ideas. The canon of feminist criticism is not just a history of changing politics but a revealing record of the rise and fall of metaphors.'[22] By the late 1980s Gilbert and Gubar's *The Madwoman in the Attic* and Elaine Showalter's *The Female Malady* had introduced an influential discourse on female authorship, and a feminist poetics that drew on metaphors of enclosure, entrapment and dis-ease to re-read women's writing. In 1989 Felski's first monograph, *Beyond Feminist Aesthetics: Feminist Literature and Social Change*, an astute study of the relations between literature, aesthetics and second wave feminism, was an important departure in shaping a materialist feminist critical practice. At a time when Toril Moi's influential survey characterised feminist literary theory as preoccupied with the reflectionist and instrumental approach of Anglo-American feminist criticism on the one hand, and the text-based aesthetics of French feminism on the other, *Beyond Feminist Aesthetics* turned to the broader ideological constructs and institutional locations framing textual production and reception. Felski, at that time writing and teaching in Australia, does not address Australian women's writing specifically in this book. Nevertheless she does open up perspectives that situate the work of feminist literary scholarship in the 1970s and 1980s institutionally, as a key element in the formation of a global feminist counter-public sphere. It is, I would argue, an approach that characterises the work of Australian feminist criticism in the 1980s. Adapting the model of the bourgeois public sphere theorised by Habermas, Felski describes the feminist counter-public sphere as a discursive space that politicises culture and seeks to relate literature to the specific interests and experiences of an explicitly gendered community; it offers a materialist critique of cultural values from the standpoint of women as a marginalised group within

---

[22] *Literature after Feminism*, p. 71.

society.[23] The language of new empiricism and book history now, with its concerns for institutions of production and publication, distribution and consumption, appreciation and certification and the kinds of value attached to reading and writing in the marketplace or public culture, finds a precursor in this materialist turn of feminist literary criticism in the 1980s. In the Australian context, this recognition of the public life of literary texts marked a radical departure from the ethico-formalist tradition of Australian literary criticism.

Felski separates two different yet vitally interconnected levels of activity. Firstly there is the level of *organisation*: the material apparatus of publishing houses, the book trade, libraries and bookshops through which books are produced and distributed (173). This includes the infrastructure of literary grants, schemes and prizes. Secondly there is the level of *institutionalisation*, the various forms of discourse about literature such as reviews, criticism, literary theory and feminist pedagogy in secondary and tertiary classrooms. Anthologising is part of this process. Using these terms, it is clear that both organisationally and institutionally the shaping of a feminist counter-public sphere was well underway in Australia by the late 1980s.[24] Felski's analysis returns some of the colour

---

[23] Rita Felski, *Beyond Feminist Aesthetics: Feminist Literature and Social Change* (Cambridge, Mass.: Harvard University Press, 1989), p. 167.

[24] A number of organisational elements promulgated both contemporary and earlier Australian women's writing: alternative presses such as McPhee Gribble, Sisters, Sybylla, Everywomen, Hecate and Redress, and mainstream presses such as Angus & Robertson, Penguin, Collins and the University of Queensland Press. A network of women's bookshops—some specialising in generic forms such as crime fiction—flourished in major Australian cities during the 1970s, and changes to the infrastructure of funding, from writer-in-residence schemes to literary prizes, and federal and state grants. Di Gribble notes, for example, that McPhee Gribble developed a reputation as 'virtually an offshoot of the Literature Board' (109), one sign of how women's writing prospered with the more general recognition of Australian Literature as a major cultural industry following the

to *Eight Voices*. It emerged from a rich and energetic context where the infrastructure for a feminist counter-public sphere was established rapidly in Australia and elsewhere—it was only towards the end of the 1970s that a surge of 'new writing' began to be parsed in gendered terms, and the production and reception of women's writing began to be shaped in frameworks and networks of feminist cultural politics. As editor I do, I notice with some relief, anticipate the normative functions of anthologising: 'It seems both disingenuous and misleading to deny notions of a canon when dealing with these eight writers who have so obviously represented the accepted and popular face of women's writing in Australia.'[25] *Eight Voices* confirmed literary celebrity, and elaborated the organisational and institutional canonisation of some women writers. The politics whereby a white Anglo-Celtic cultural hegemony might be sustained within the feminist counter-public sphere come into view, and this is a reminder of Felski's point that endemic to the operation of a public sphere is a disparity between its ideal and real status—in this case, a tension between its self-understanding as a representative forum for all women and an actual practice which remains dominated by white mid-

---

establishment of the Literature Board in 1975. Institutional elements include women's studies courses which boomed in the 1970s, a network of feminist conferences such as the Women & Labour events; specialist journals such as *Hecate*, *Refractory Girl* and *Australian Feminist Studies* were established and feminist criticism emerged in mainstream literary journals such as *Meanjin*, *Australian Book Review* (particularly under the editorships of Judith Brett and Kerryn Goldsworthy respectively) and the review pages of major weekend papers published by Murdoch and Fairfax; a series of canonical works of Australian feminist criticism by Dixson (1974), Summers (1975), Modjeska (1981) and Schaffer (1988), editions by Ferrier and Gilbert (1988), and an array of journal articles explored the terms for a distinctively Australian approach to women's writing. Finally, bibliographies of Australian women's writing expanded the field of research exponentially (Adelaide 1988).

[25] Whitlock, p. xiv.

dle-class interests and deeply implicated in existing power structures.[26] The selection of stories, journalism and criticism anthologised in *Eight Voices*, with its strong preference for realism and woman-centred narrative, is a reminder of the importance of symbolic fictions in the shaping of second wave feminism in Australia and elsewhere. Yet, I have been arguing here, the self-conscious attention to the normative functions of editing, anthologising, shaping (which, as we have seen, appears in the Gunew and Mahyuddin's 'Introduction' too) and an awareness of the role of feminism and writing in a contested public sphere, are signs of a strong awareness of organisational and institutional literary formations in Australian feminist criticism of the 1980s.

Inevitably, to return to the work of twenty years ago produces the 'how could I ever have thought *that*?' moment. Yet it is also an opportunity to re-encounter and reassess an earlier time in Australian feminist criticism as its artefacts fade into shabby chic. The work of anthologising is always controversial; as I noted in 1989: 'one sends an anthology out to sea with little control over what cargo it brings back to port'.[27] Although the anthology has been associated with 'the solid body of Australian fiction', the AustLit database suggests otherwise: anthologies were essential to the presence of a diverse array of creative writing, which circulated in local communities, affiliations and associations, and below the radar of the 'Australian' 'major' and 'modern'. Equally, empirical research reveals a vibrant period of anthologising in Australian literary criticism. Quantitatively speaking, feminism fades into minor significance and contributes little to either of these spheres of anthologising if we reckon its influence: the outputs of feminist presses, or a specific 'feminist' brand, or explicit

---

[26] In fact, Thea Astley's 'Home Is Where the Heart Is', included in *Eight Voices*, is signalled as a reflection on the limitations of white middle-class liberalism and its understanding of Indigeneity.

[27] Whitlock, p. xix.

identification with organised feminism, are insignificant. However qualitatively speaking the feminist literary criticism that emerged in the 1980s is essential to the politics of reading, writing and criticism; gender, as David Carter argues, was the key revisionary concept for the first wave of reconstructing Australian literature in the 1970s and 1980s.[28]

The questions emerging from new empirical research now develop further insights into the implication of gender, politics and fiction in Australian literary studies. These call for more attention to the value of genre fiction and books aimed at women readers; the circulation of the book as a commodity and the presence of the author as both aura and brand; the historical and cultural production of masculinities and femininities; and the gendered operations of literary ethics and aesthetics in the reading nation. However these concerns of distant reading and book history do not enter a vacuum, and they are not new. These engagements are firmly located in the precincts of literature after feminism.

---

[28] David Carter, 'Publishing, Patronage and Cultural Politics: Institutional Changes in the Field of Australian Literature from 1950' in Peter Pierce, ed., *The Cambridge History of Australian Literature* (Melbourne: Cambridge University Press, 2009), pp. 360–90, 386.

Section 3

Project Reports

14
AustLit: Creating a Collaborative Research Space for Australian Literary Studies

Kerry Kilner

In a recent article discussing the current state of digital humanities research practice, Willard McCarty, Professor of Humanities Computing at King's College London and one of the leading voices on the influence of new technologies on the humanities, suggests that we have reached a point in the evolution of humanities scholarship where 'new thinking and new institutional structures' are required to support, facilitate and reward eResearch practice in the humanities. 'Computing's trajectory,' he says, 'calls upon us to rethink the craft of our own research and to connect it up with whatever informs its goals'.[1] For this to occur, McCarty believes we need both the technological and institutional environments where imaginative explorations of the uses of digital technologies in the humanities can occur. In other words, the explorations in 'rethinking the craft' of research practice currently occurring at many sites across the humanities will only bear fruit if they are supported by the combined facilitators of technical and institutional support.

With McCarty's ideas in focus, this chapter discusses some of the requirements these layers of support impose upon the emerging landscape

---

[1] Willard McCarty, 'What's Going On?', *Literary and Linguistic Computing* 23.3 (2008): 258.

of eResearch practice, especially as it relates to contemporary studies in literary and other narratives, and considers some of the larger, global issues around scholarly communication within the research sector. Finally, it will outline the innovative ways that AustLit: The Australian Literature Resource[2] is trying to address the emergent eResearch needs of scholars of Australian literary culture through the Aus-e-Lit project,[3] funded by the National E-Research Architecture Taskforce, an NCRIS[4] Platforms for Collaboration program.

Digital Scholarship Means New Communication Methods

Empirical research practice involving text mining, dataset analysis and visualisation is becoming increasingly common in literary studies. Unlike purely text-based research where the close reading of a single text, or group of texts, can be undertaken by a lone scholar with reference only to the text/s themselves and the work of other scholars, the use of new technologies and emerging forms of digital scholarship requires different skill sets and often benefits from interdisciplinary collaborations between humanities scholars and computer scientists.

The enormous changes under way in scholarly communication on a global level suggest a need to reconceptualise what scholarly outcomes might actually be. Are we nearing a time when a research outcome comprised of a web-based artefact which takes a highly detailed but visual approach to the analysis of an author's oeuvre might be formally recognised as a top-level publication? Could a piece of scholarship comprising an exegesis with an interoperable dataset be understood as of high a value

---

[2] See www.austlit.edu.au [Accessed 30 June 2009].
[3] See www.itee.uq.edu.au/~eresearch/projects/aus-e-lit/ [Accessed 30 June 2009].
[4] National Collaborative Research Infrastructure Strategy, ncris.innovation.gov.au/Pages/default.aspx [Accessed 2 March 2009].

as a 5000-word essay published in *JASAL* or *ALS* or even a single authored monograph? It is very likely that these types of scholarship already being developed across many humanities disciplines will begin to be regarded as at least as valuable as traditional forms.

Literary scholar, bibliographer of nineteenth-century literature and digital theorist, Jerome McGann, believes that it is now simply impossible to 'refuse' the digital environment and, given that reality, 'we must learn by going where we have to go'.[5] He suggests that we now face two inevitabilities:

> First, integrating digital technology into our scholarship will have to be pursued on as broad a scale as possible. Circumstances are such that this work can no longer be safely postponed. Second, we have to restore textual and bibliographical work to the center of what we do.[6]

Based on the AustLit experience the need for improved research training in the fields of textual and bibliographical studies in Australia is apparent and this topic is discussed in this collection by Carol Hetherington, AustLit's Content Manager. However, restoring the centrality of such training has even wider ramifications when considering the fundamentally transformed research and information-seeking practices wrought by the impact of the internet in the education and research sectors, at least in technologically advanced countries. While bibliographical and textual studies relating to the pre-digital age retain validity in the digital era, the discipline will have to somehow take into account the entirely different chain of production and consumption that exists today because the internet is increasingly the vehicle for both production and reproduction of textual artefacts.

---

[5] Jerome McGann, 'Information Technology and the Troubled Humanities', *TEXT Technology* 2 (2005): 105–21.
[6] Ibid., pp. 106–07.

John Hartley argues that that arrival of the digital age, which has interactivity and participation at its core, means that the nature of reading and writing and communication on all levels has fundamentally changed and that audio-visual (digital) literacies must now be recognised.[7] The era of relatively uni-directional communication is over and the one-to-many relationship of past publishing and formal communication channels is becoming less and less relevant as the distance between reading and writing, author and reader narrows sharply due to the networked approach to communication that underpins the structure of the internet. It is this network structure that will increasingly underpin and shape contemporary communication practices across society and within the research sector.

The new communication paradigm is one whereby 'centralised control must in fact be abandoned'[8] because the production of web-based content (read 'literary or narrative-based object' in this context) is exploding at such a rapid rate that new mechanisms of information management must be conceptualised. This explosion has major implications both for those who collect the physical (or digital) artefacts produced (libraries, museums, etc.) and for those who record the history of those artefacts (bibliographers, literary historians, etc.). The distance between writer and reader is narrowing as digital media make 'publication' so much easier and reduce the role of mediator, previously undertaken by publisher or proprietor. This shift has profound implications for scholarship. There is no guarantee, for example, that the quality metrics of the print era will operate in the digital age. Investigations of new quality metrics are beginning and involve the use of computational methodologies for analysing quality and community assessment.

---

[7] John Hartley, *The Uses of Digital Literacies* (St Lucia: University of Queensland Press, 2009).
[8] Ibid., p. 47.

New Literacies Required

A significant challenge to the changing communication landscape and the integration of digital technologies and research practices into current activities is that many literary scholars remain unversed in the languages required for communicating and working within an eResearch environment. McGann comments that, 'digital *illiteracy* puts many of us on the margin of conversations and actions that affect the centre of our cultural interests (as citizens) and our professional interests (as scholars and educators)'.[9]

Overcoming these shortcomings in digital literacy is increasingly important for a full engagement with the opportunities becoming available as the digital age matures. Humanities scholars must begin to learn the languages and use the theoretical approaches of digital research in order to enhance their engagement. This might occur by taking courses in information technologies, web development or human–computer interaction and by incorporating these skills in the educating of the next generation of scholars. At the moment, for example, hands-on workshops for contemporary scholars wanting to work with digital humanities practices are rare in Australia. Judging by activities on numerous bulletin boards and announcement lists in Europe and North America, there are more opportunities for scholars in the fields of literary studies or history to learn such skills as textual mark-up and encoding practices for digital scholarly editing or the use of data for visualisation where competencies in the use of many aspects of digital technologies are built.[10]

---

[9] McCarty, 'What's Going On?', p. 109. Original emphasis.
[10] For example, workshops and summer schools are regularly run at the Institute for Advanced Technologies in the Humanities at the University of Virginia, USA (www.iath.virginia.edu/), the University of Victoria, British Columbia, Canada (www.dhsi.org/), the Digital Humanities Observatory at the Royal Irish Academy, Dublin, Eire (www.dho.ie/) and at The Centre for Humanities Computing at

The recent uptake of empirical research methods in literary studies, currently occurring under the influence of the work of, for example, Franco Moretti and William St Clair,[11] is changing the skill sets of some contemporary scholars as they begin to work in, or build, online environments or compile and statistically analyse large sets of data relating to particular fields or genres of study especially relating to publishing history.[12] There do, however, remain some large gaps in these areas and a growing need for the development of digital era skills in Australia.

Innovative Practices and Challenges for Scholarly Communication

Information and communication technology (ICT) is now a part of every aspect of the scholarly communication cycle and the internet is now a central platform for many aspects of scholarly activity. The result of this reality is that the very nature of the *practice* of research is changing. Many research projects in the fields of literary and narrative studies are now regularly collaborative with those collaborations made up of groups of researchers who may be geographically distributed but united through web-based communication. They often involve the collection, annotation and analysis of digital material, both born digital and digitised data, and textual content; and the results and sometimes the processes[13] of that

---

King's College London (www.kcl.ac.uk/schools/humanities/depts/cch) [All accessed 2 March 2009].

[11] Franco Moretti, *Maps, Graphs, Trees: Abstract Models for a Literary History*, (London: Verso, 2005); William St Clair, *The Reading Nation in the Romantic Period* (Cambridge: Cambridge University Press, 2004).

[12] For example, recent work by Katherine Bode, David Carter, Richard Nile and Jason Ensor, and Tim Dolin.

[13] By 'processes' I mean that researchers are more often working in a way that puts their data and the things they are doing in the course of their work out in the public arena. The building of a dataset within AustLit for example means that a

research are frequently disseminated via the internet. The primary outcome of a research project is no longer likely to be only a book or article/s; a dataset, website, database or archive of digital material is also quite likely to be produced and made available to end users and readers. And when distributed via the web the dimensions and kinds of audience change. All this marks a radical departure from early forms of scholarly activity.

This changing landscape of scholarly communication and research activity coupled with the growing influence of the open access movement across the research sector, which is underpinned by the principle of making publicly funded research outcomes across the disciplines publicly available, suggest (perhaps demand) that we need significant changes to the current system of reward and recognition for scholarship in universities and that the mechanisms for dissemination also need restructuring.

Currently, the recognition of, and reward for, scholarly outcomes remain bound to old technologies. The recognition hierarchy remains a steep descent from the single-authored book at the pinnacle of scholarship, followed by jointly authored books, articles in peer-reviewed journals, refereed book chapters and conference papers and so on. Meanwhile, regardless of the amount of work involved, the achievements of editors of scholarly editions of previously published texts, anthologies, major bibliographies and academic journals are usually not valued sufficiently enough to generate the all important research quantum that underpins academic advancement. Where does the scholar working in the online environment stand in this hierarchy?

The work involved in sharing the processes of research, whether that's the creation of a website, the participation in the building of a dataset, the engagement with the public through blogs or other communicative

---

researcher is incrementally releasing scholarly content before the completion of a project and the articulation of a particular analysis. This has not happened before.

strategies should be recognised as formal indicators of successful academic engagement and points awarded in the measuring of an academic's contribution to scholarly life. In addition, the institutional support structures for enabling ongoing communication and engagement with the diversified audiences that result from digital-era scholarship need to be changed so that use-by dates on digital research activity don't expire before the value of the content is outlived. Managing the ramifications of the changes being wrought by the web on research processes is fundamental here. Building digital repositories that act as a dump for research data is not a solution though it is one step towards the building of a new research ecology to suit the new environment.

There are examples of early adopters and innovators engaging with 'the possibility space[s]'[14] emerging in the digital humanities that may lead the way in the new thinking required. In the field of literary studies, the University of Virginia's Institute for Advanced Technologies in the Humanities (IATH) is one such innovator. The recently (re)developed NINES project[15]—Nineteenth-Century Studies Online—has the not trivial goal of 're-engineering' the study of nineteenth-century literature to 'expose the rich hermeneutic potential of the electronic medium'.[16]

NINES is attempting to build a platform upon which the discovery, collection and creation of data and information can inform the annotation, analysis, interpretation, peer-review and publication of nineteenth-century literary scholarship. This should, according to NINES's underpinning principle, all occur within a robust, accessible, electronic

---

[14] Albert Borgman, 'The Habitat of Information: Social and Organisation Consequences of Information Growth', London School of Economics lecture (2008), www.lse.ac.uk/collections/informationSystems/newsAndEvents/2008events/SSIT 8/borgmannVideo.htm [Accessed January 2009].
[15] Nineteenth-century studies online, www.nines.org/ [Accessed 22 February 2009].
[16] McGann, 'Information Technology and the Troubled Humanities', p. 116.

medium that is freely available to all. These aims are transformative in intent and, if successful, would begin to lay down the institutional and digital environment that McCarty envisions as necessary for our imaginative exploration of new forms of scholarship. The major challenges for such projects lie both in the uptake, and in the sustaining of the intellectual and physical/digital infrastructure.

AustLit: A Possibility Space for Scholars of Australian Literature

Like NINES, and in its own discipline-specific way, AustLit is attempting to create an environment where, in McCarty's words, scholars change from being 'end-users to end-makers'. AustLit is successfully meeting its responsibility as a widely accessible source of dependable information on most aspects of Australian narrative culture, and its emerging role as a platform for independent eResearch and teaching activities by discipline scholars is currently being developed.

Although not directly influenced by the NINES initiative, AustLit has similarly transformative aims in building on its foundation of biographical, bibliographical and specialist research projects to establish an environment where scholars can progress through the many phases of a research project—from search to data creation and collection, annotation, analysis, and the publication of datasets with accompanying essays, peer-review and scholarly editions of literary texts. These tools also have the potential to assist scholarly editors by providing a work-space and repository to visualise the most complex textual transmissions.[17] Like NINES, AustLit developers recognise the value of engaging with emergent scholarly practice that results in divergent scholarly outcomes. We aim to be a part of the solution to the perceived 'Crisis in Scholarly

---

[17] Terminology used by Roger Osborne in the description of the process of scholarly editing (unpublished).

Communication'[18] and to offer mechanisms for new forms of scholarly communication.

The need to support Australian social sciences and humanities research infrastructure has been recognised in the 2008 revision of the roadmap to the National Collaborative Research Infrastructure Strategy[19] which, when first published in 2006, overloooked the needs of the humanities and social sciences sector, focusing mainly on big science. The revision has led to new funding streams to assist with the development of eResearch infrastructure.[20]

AustLit has recently (2008) been the recipient of some funding under the National eResearch Architecture Taskforce to develop new generation tools and services for the transformation of Australian literature studies. This three-year project, titled Aus-e-Lit,[21] is a transformative, platform-building project. It has the potential to influence research practice and scholarly communication mechanisms for our discipline and, ultimately, the way web-based scholarship in our field is perceived and rewarded in Australia.

The Aus-e-Lit project will change the AustLit experience by extending the services currently delivered to demonstrate what can be achieved when scholars of Australian narrative cultures are able to work within a

---

[18] This term has entered the lexicon of the research sector and relates to the problem of rising prices and commercial control of the outcomes of scholarly research. See, for example, www.library.cornell.edu/colldev/StatementOnCrisis.htm and www.caul.edu.au/cisc/aboutCISC.html [Accessed 2 March 2009].
[19] ncris.innovation.gov.au/Pages/SRARI.aspx [Accessed 22 February 2009].
[20] Unfortunately, the 2009 federal government budget has not committed any funds for specific infrastructure for the HASS sector.
[21] Aus-e-Lit website (www.itee.uq.edu.au/~eresearch/projects/aus-e-lit/), led by Professor Jane Hunter (www.itee.uq.edu.au/~jane/) and Kerry Kilner. The team is made up of Dr Roger Osborne (project manager), Anna Gerber (senior software engineer) and Christopher Davoren (software engineer). See www.itee.uq.edu.au/~eresearch/projects/aus-e-lit/people.php.

specially adapted eResearch environment. On one level it will take traditional scholarly activities—biographical and bibliographical compilation and annotation, textual annotation and comparison, scholarly editing—and adapt them to the digital environment; on another level the Aus-e-Lit project will open up opportunities for as yet unknown research involving data analysis and interpretation, text mining and visualisation, collaborative annotation and authoring, and will assist with in the creation of new forms of scholarship.

The key elements of the Aus-e-Lit project are:

- the creation of a federated search function, within AustLit, to facilitate the discovery of relevant content in other data sources such as AusStage, various National Library services, the Australian Dictionary of Biography, the Australian Digital Thesis database, Google Scholar and other appropriate sources as identified;
- the easier delivery of empirical reporting against AustLit data and the opportunity to create graphs, maps and other visualisations in the course of research and publication;
- the establishment of support services for eResearch subcommunities so that private research groups can work collaboratively on a scholarly outcome of their choosing—this will be an enhancement of the current AustLit Research Communities;
- the development of collaborative scholarly mark-up and annotation services to enable the creation and publication of scholarly editions of literary or critical works;
- the development of a ground-breaking tool, the AustLit LORE, based on the OAI-ORE standard,22 that enables the creation of a

---

[22] 'The Open Archives Initiative Object Reuse and Exchange (OAI-ORE) is an international collaborative initiative that aims to support the creation, management and dissemination of the new forms of composite digital resources being produced by eResearch and to make the information within these compound

graphically formatted, web-based resource that collects, annotates and presents an articulation of, for example, the lineage of derivative works based on a common concept or idea or relates disparate objects on a theme or for teaching purposes.

The development and delivery of these new services and tools within a trusted resource such as AustLit has the potential to transform some of the standard research practices undertaken by scholars in the field of Australian literary and other narrative studies and, perhaps, to engage other discipline scholars as well. What it will eventually mean to the communities of researchers, teachers and students exploring and writing about Australian literary culture is a question that will be examined as the uptake of these transformative practices begins.

Scholarly activity, digital humanities scholar Martyn Jessop says, is 'about the discovery, exchange, interpretation, and presentation of knowledge'.[23] The ability to engage with this activity using non-traditional methods across the humanities—that retain, and make transparent, the standards of scholarship required to gain institutional and collegial approval—is necessary for the incorporation of new forms of scholarly communication into standard practice. This requires new forms of peer

---

digital objects discoverable, machine-readable, interoperable and reusable.' Kerry Kilner, Anna Gerber and Jane Hunter, 'Transforming the Study of Australian Literature through a Collaborative eResearch Environment', paper delivered at the Oxford eResearch Conference, October 2008, ora.ouls.ox.ac.uk/objects/uuid:42f51e07-3034-4533-abdd-f44e36236a98 [Accessed 20 February 2008]. See also C. Lagoze and H. Van de Sompel, Compound Information Objects: The OAI ORE Perspective (2007), www.openarchives.org/ore [Accessed 20 February 2008] and the Aus-e-Lit project site, www.itee.uq.edu.au/~eresearch/projects/aus-e-lit/publications.php, for other publications on the LORE.

[23] Martyn Jessop, 'Digital Visualization as Scholarly Activity', *Literary and Linguistic Computing* 23: 3 (2008): 281–93.

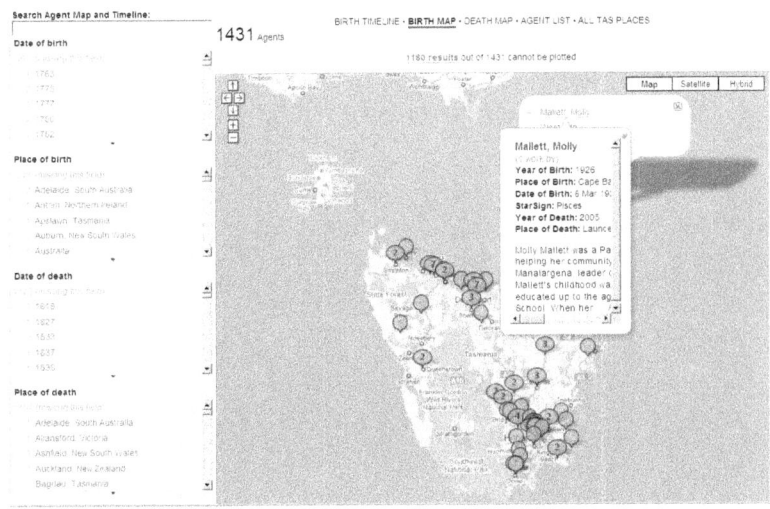

Figure 1 The Mapping of Author Information onto the Map of Tasmania

review to be put into place, which will rely in turn upon developing the competencies to undertake that peer review.

Jessop's interest in the recognition of divergent scholarly outcomes such as 3D visualisation is predicated on an understanding that 'visualisation departs from being an illustration when it becomes the principal medium of communication'.[24] Citing the London Charter for the computer-based visualisation of cultural heritage,[25] a 2006 statement relating to the validity of visualisation to contemporary scholarship, Jessop discusses the challenges that new methods and methodologies make to accepted practice. There is, as a part of engaging with digital scholarship, a need to '[o]pen a debate on methodological and theoretical issues to

---

[24] Ibid., p. 283.
[25] The London Charter for the Computer-based Visualisation of Cultural Heritage, www.londoncharter.org/ [Accessed 29 February 2009].

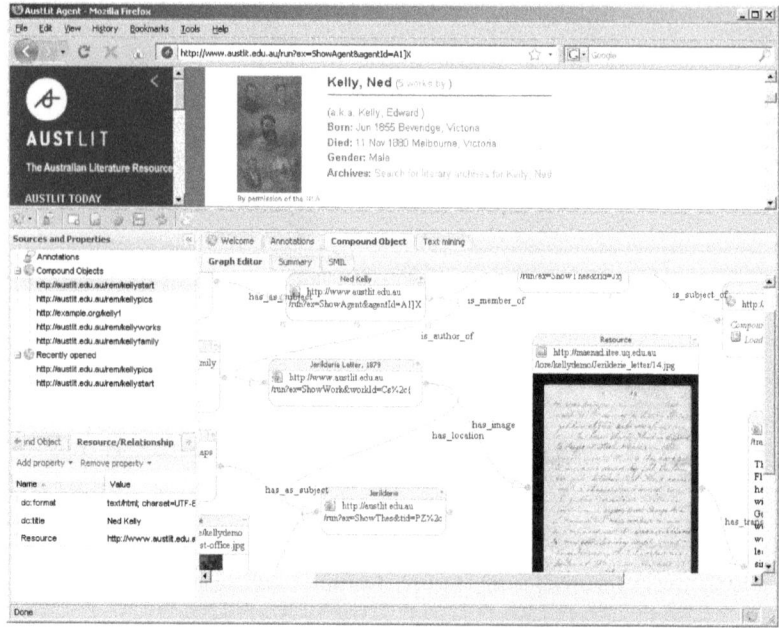

Figure 2 Draft Format of the LORE Tool Using Ned Kelly's Jerilderie Letter as a Way into a Range of Related Texts, Images, Objects and Annotations[26]

compensate for the lack of a framework similar to that that has evolved over many hundreds of years for other research methods. This is complicated further by the collaborative and interdisciplinary nature of research in the digital humanities.'[27]

This challenging situation is not dissimilar to the one the AustLit community of scholars will need to deal with, and the broader ramifica-

---

[26] See the Aus-e-Lit project site for demonstrations of the LORE tool, www.itee.uq.edu.au/~eresearch/projects/aus-e-lit/ [Accessed 30 June 2009].
[27] Jessop, 'Digital Visualisation as Scholarly Activity', p. 291.

tions of this include recognising the value of diverse outcomes that seek to communicate scholarship in ways outside of currently accepted formats. Proving that the Aust-e-Lit innovations will meet the high standards set by humanities scholars will be vital. It is hoped that providing these new spaces for scholarly activity will stimulate uptake by researchers and result in the required debate and discussion that will encourage excellence and thereby facilitate acceptance. By encouraging contemporary scholars to become 'end-makers' and, as McCarty says, providing access to 'the scholarly equivalent of Tinker Toys',[28] we will hopefully see transformed activity and outcomes.

Sustaining Resourceful Reading

Creating tools with the potential to transform research practices raises some issues around sustaining services such as AustLit. While the NCRIS review provided the opportunity for positive statements from the current federal government and its ministers about the importance of supporting appropriate infrastructure for the humanities, AustLit and projects like it continue to be vulnerable to the vagaries of the yearly funding cycle. This is why building digital, web-based resources at this moment engages us in the debate around scholarly communication.

This situation is not unique to Australia. Like many innovative organisations and projects developed over the last decade or so, IATH and the projects it supports, such as NINES, are dogged by the problem of sustainability; of achieving sufficient ongoing support to enable a full engagement with the digital revolution. And that struggle is intensified by the lack of formal recognition of the scholarship involved in creating such resources. Even relatively well-supported projects, like AustLit, are inevitably 'born into poverty', as McGann says, unless the long-term institutional mechanisms exist to support them and thereby enable the

---

[28] McCarty, 'What's Going On?', p. 255.

full engagement of discipline researchers. Embedding the tools and services into the research practice of current researchers and teachers will hopefully keep at bay the risk of institutional abandonment once the initial funding cycle is over. But, in addition, a change of attitude towards the support required for the outcomes of digital research practice is necessary. Disappointingly, the internet is littered with projects that did not reach their full potential and, losing institutional and funding support, have become static and degraded.

AustLit is not immune to this reality and with the increasing demand for open access to research resources, and the potential that digital lodgement of research data in open access repositories will be mandated, we are facing a serious struggle to maintain our core activities alongside a full engagement with research trends. Without this engagement our ongoing relevance to literary scholars may be undermined.

The inevitable changes to scholarly communication that the digital era is creating demand new business models and new support mechanisms; without them Australia's engagement with the digital era will not be as pervasive as it should be. To be able to read resourcefully we need to be certain that the resources being read are available, robust, of high quality and deeply engaged with current and emerging scholarly practice in both the humanities and the field of information and communication technology.

15
A Place in Stories: A Report on the Literature of Tasmania Subset of the AustLit Database

Tony Stagg and Philip Mead

This is a preliminary report on an experiment within an AustLit database subset about the literary representation of place. The Literature of Tasmania subset is one of the regionally or sub-nationally defined research communities of the AustLit database. From the beginning the subset team was aware of numerous definitional complexities of regional bibliographical work, including the question of regional and subregional descriptors and the taxonomy of spatial terms within existing database structure. As we undertook more extensive indexing, though, new patterns in the spatial markers of colonial and modern literary publications have emerged. The subset team has worked with the methodology of the database and the subset structure to design quantitative categories that begin to enable analysis of various spatial markers—like Composition Place, Place of Publication, thematic spatial reference.

The original vision of the subset was to identify a body of literature by its geopolitical parameters. And then to record it bibliographically. The model here was Cheryl Taylor's pioneering work with the Writing the Tropical North subset. On the face of it, this aim might appear easier for Tasmania than any other 'region' of Australia, given that Tasmania is the only conventionally geographically defined region, colony or state. All the other regions have latitudinal, meridian or cadastral boundaries as well as geographical ones. Islands and continents are natural and indivisible; states, provinces and territories are historical and geopolitically contingent. More theoretically, the subset is motivated by a kind of critical regionalism that draws the specific, the singular, the (imagined and historical) places of literary texts and locational perspectives on authors, oeuvres, production and reception to the centre of critical attention.[1] As such, it is part of a disciplinary trajectory that emphasises the locational singularities of literary texts and their production; new knowledge about Australian literature as Katherine Bode expresses it.[2] This is a direction, perhaps, counter to the other axis of empirical research and quantitative methodology represented by the AustLit database: the ambition to be comprehensive about the 'collective [literary] system' (as Moretti expresses it [quoted in Bode, p. 186]). The Literature of Tasmania spatialisation project suggests the way a bibliographical version of the 'collective system' might be used to identify patterns in specific locational representations.

There is a well-recognised, and rhetorically complex, thematics of islandness that the literature of Tasmania contributes to, with one point of origin in Abel Tasman's map of 1642 and its inclusion in a speculative, fantastic map as a frontispiece to Jonathan Swift's *Gulliver's Travels* (1726). The back-story to this history of insularisation haunts the litera-

---

[1] 'Critical regionalism' is a term from Gayatri Spivak, who uses it to describe her activist academic work in a more purely political context of North-South differences but who nevertheless understands there is no 'clear-cut distinction between self-determination and nationalism, [between] regionalism and nationalism'. See Judith Butler and Gayatri Chakrovorty Spivak, *Who Sings the Nation-State? Language, Politics, Belonging* (London: Seagull, 2007), p. 214.

[2] Katherine Bode, 'Beyond the Colonial Present: Quantitative Analysis, "Resourceful Reading" and Australian Literary Studies', *JASAL Special Issue: The Colonial Present* (2008): 194.

ture of Tasmania in various ways: Van Diemen's Land (as it was for more than 200 years, longer than it has been Tasmania) has not always been an island, in geological time, or Aboriginal time, or even in European maritime history (there's every reason to think Tasman believed his Van Diemen's Land was part of a large southern landmass). As late as the bicentennial of white settlement in 2003/04 the Premier Jim Bacon was complicating Tasmania's history of insularity, and sense of place, by referring to it as an archipelago of one large island surrounded by 300 other islands. The asynchronous history of Tasmania's insularisation, its representation in the pre-discovery European imagination and its cartographical history all inflect the representation of Tasmania.

Van Diemen's Land became Tasmania, officially, in January 1856 and after the cessation of transportation, but our sample indexing of pre-1855 newspapers suggests that the idea of Tasmania, as a place, was widely shared by the colonial population from at least twenty years earlier.[3] The further indexing of these newspapers using the spatial categories of the subset would allow us to chart more extensively this consciousness of place, an unexpected result of our research in Tasmanian literature. The mapping of a spatial consciousness as represented in a geopolitically

---

[3] See, for example, J.S., 'Lines to Tasmania', *Hobart Town Magazine* 2 (12 February 1834): 306–07:

> A song for the land where the kangaroo bounds—
> A song for the land which the ocean surrounds,
> Where the hills are so green, and the vales are so fair,
> That the emigrant gazes with boundless delight,
> As the shores of Tasmania rise on his sight ...
>
> Rapid is the progress Tasmania has made
> By science and commerce uniting their aid,
> But the dawn of her glory is scarcely begun,
> Like the eagle, she'll soar with her eyes on the sun;
> Till Britain her likeness shall marvel to see,
> And Europe acknowledge the land of the free.

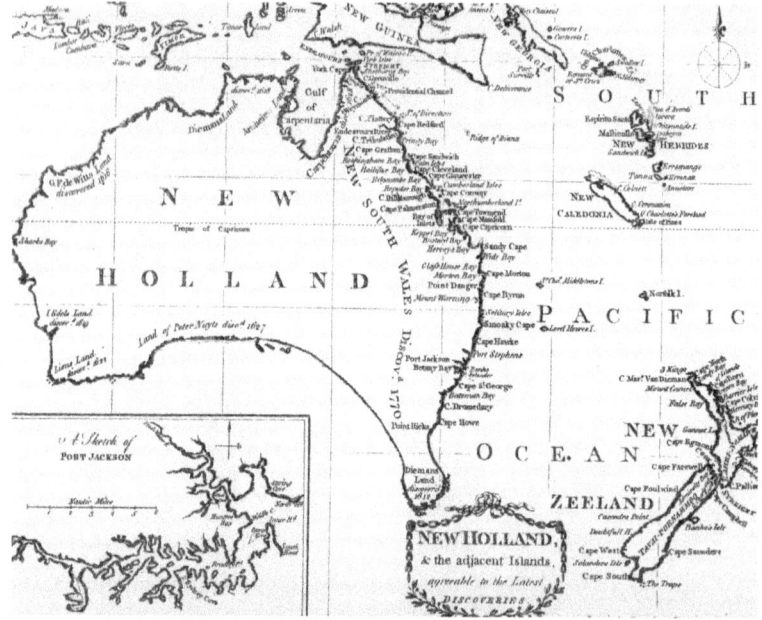

Figure 1 Map of New Holland by T. Kincade, 1790 (R.V. Tooley plate XIV)

defined set of literary texts is reliant, then, on theoretical perspectives, historical inflections, database methodologies and limitations, visualisation technologies, cognitive mapping and insider knowledge. The space that constitutes Tasmania is easier to imagine from the outside than to define spatially from within.

During the three years of compiling the Tasmanian subset for AustLit, we have encountered many strange appropriations of the island; from Bessie Marchant's bucolic interpretation of the Southwest Wilderness in her 1908 children's story *The Apple Lady*, to Nevil Shute's creative reinventions of the West Coast in *The Rainbow and the Rose* (1958), to Candice Proctor's convict romance *Whispers of Heaven* (2001), to 1970s rock star Graham Parker's rediscovery of the Tasmanian Tiger in *The*

Other Life of Brian (2003). Marchant never left England, but conducted her research on exotic locations through various libraries, including the Bodleian in Oxford. Her source material generated some interesting results. In *The Apple Lady*, two of Marchant's characters trek—stroll really—through the Southwest from Port Davey to Mount Picton, stopping off for the night at a town called Craycroft. There is no town called Craycroft, indeed there are no towns in Southwest Tasmania at all. Yet for Marchant, the town existed because it appeared on a map in Walch's *Almanac*. For years, Walch's *Tasmanian Almanacs* included a map of the state that displayed not only existing towns but also gazetted settlements. These 'towns' were habitations planned for the future. Craycroft was one

Figure 2 The 'Town' of Craycroft, just to the Right of the Arthur Range (Walch's *Tasmanian Almanac*, 1896)

Figure 3 Butlers Gorge Town Site (Google Maps)

such place. The fact that the location was wilderness, and still is, meant nothing to Marchant. Craycroft perfectly suited the narrative requirements of her story.

If Craycroft never existed, Butlers Gorge, by contrast, only exists as a memory and as a place in a story. Enter the term 'Butlers Gorge' into an online mapping resource and you'll be presented with a location somewhere in the Tasmanian Central Highlands, near Lake King William. Zooming in a little closer reveals Clark Dam and a canal (leading to Tarraleah). But this isn't Butlers Gorge. Careful examination of the surrounding area reveals the spectral gridlines of an abandoned settlement.

This is the trace of a town—a hydroelectric construction village that flourished between 1940 and 1955 when the last residents left and the site was slowly rehabilitated. Butlers Gorge now exists as a memory, and as an important setting for Richard Flanagan's novel *The Sound of One Hand*

Clapping (1997). As such, this 'ghost town' represents a significant Tasmanian literary site.

This phantom that is Butlers Gorge raises other issues concerning spatial representation: how to indicate places that may have otherwise been forgotten? Butlers Gorge exists in memory and in the fiction of Richard Flanagan (and others) but there are numerous other sites which now exist only in words—old mining and logging camps, other hydro construction villages, subsumed farms, huts in the forest—all of which are difficult or impossible to locate on any map or database. Representing such places requires a creative and flexible approach to the integration of other datasets. Beneath conventional geography lies a phantom map, filled with ghostly spaces of literary significance.[4]

Indexing the textual material that constitutes the Tasmanian subset has entailed determining and ascribing specific settings to particular works: spatial indicators enabling users to trace works by place. This indexing process is often not entirely straightforward. In its physical area Tasmania may only be 63,000 square kilometres, but it contains numerous micro-regions, the dimensions of which exist beyond the scope of conventional geography. These regions are often fluid and organic, rather than fixed, as they are produced by a lived sense of place rather than topographical features alone. They may also be sensitive to historical shifts.

Any credible understanding of literary geography is not necessarily predicated upon easily established and visible boundaries. Such understanding is often very subjective as it derives from a lived sense of place. The kinds of cognitive maps we all carry around with us generate literary

---

[4] For a spatialised reading of Tasmanian mining and hydro towns in relation to their dereliction and absence, see Elizabeth McMahon, 'Wasted Memory and Generational History: Tasmania's Abandoned Places', in Elizabeth McMahon and Brigitta Olubas, eds, *Women Making Time: Contemporary Feminist Critique and Cultural Analysis* (Perth: UWA Press, 2006), pp. 43–61.

geographies. A database, however, requires more tangible parameters. One of the challenges of the Literature of Tasmania subset project has been to translate what are in fact collectively produced cognitive maps into more concrete spatial definitions. When we refer to the literature of Tasmania's West Coast, for instance, we aren't referring literally to works produced on the coastline. Virtually no one lives on the actual West Coast; the main settlements are inland but the term 'West Coast' has become the accepted regional designation for anything that emanates 'from the west'.[5]

Part of our project led to a reconsideration of the AustLit spatial thesaurus in relation to its representation of Tasmania and to our modifying it in accordance with our interpretation of Tasmanian regionality. This led us into a re-examination of local taxonomies of place. For the purposes of the AustLit Tasmanian subset, we eventually considered the following spatial taxonomy the most appropriate:

Tasmanian Subset Regions
- Bass Strait Islands
- Central Highlands
- East Coast
- Macquarie Island
- Midlands
- Northeast Tasmania
- Northwest Tasmania
- Southeast Tasmania

---

[5] European exploration invariably moved west from a line between the major colonial settlements of Launceston in the north and Hobart in the south, as the eastern regions of the island were more readily accessible from the early days of settlement. In *Explorers of Western Tasmania*, Binks illustrates how, in the colonial imagination, most of Tasmania was west. C.J. Binks, *Explorers of Western Tasmania* (Devonport, Tas.: Taswegia, 1989), p. xii.

- Southwest Tasmania
- Van Diemen's Land (1803–56)
- Western Tasmania (including the West Coast)

In the taxonomy these terms serve as subregions of Tasmania; layers beneath this level contain micro-regions such as the Derwent Valley, the Fingal Valley, the Northern and Southern Midlands and the Far North-West; these in turn contain specific places. We are not suggesting that any of these spatial terms rather than regional determinations are set in stone. At some future date other researchers may choose to vary the boundaries of inclusion, or to create entirely new regions. For the purposes of the current project, however, this arrangement is satisfactory.

One particular research outcome that drove this spatial reorganisation arose from certain textual elements that presented themselves while we were indexing, aside from the spatial subjects relative to the setting of individual works. These spatial elements had more to do with production and composition than with thematic or referential content. While indexing various issues of nineteenth-century newspapers, in particular the *Tasmanian Mail*, we noticed that some items of poetry and prose contained additional published information, relating to their place of composition. In consideration of the ways in which future researchers may be able to use this information, we sought ways to incorporate it usefully into the dataset. We accomplished this through the use of the Composition Place node, thus generating a further spatial dataset, offering new perspectives on the relationship between text and place.

While regions exhibit parameters that are inherently flexible, spatial data are also subject to and influenced by historical change: the name of a particular place may undergo a series of changes over time. The challenge is to be able to record historically specific spatial data in order to track how the terms of this dataset change in relation to changes in spatial nominations. For instance, the spatial designation 'Tasmania' occurs very early in local colonial literature, and is well established long before the nomenclature of Van Diemen's Land is officially abandoned. Similarly, it would be useful to chart the literary evolution of Hobart Town through Hobarton to its current incarnation of Hobart. Other places also offer interesting case studies. After 1877, Port Arthur briefly transforms into Carnarvon before reverting to its original designation, convict baggage and all. A number of works bearing the Composition Place 'Carnarvon' occur during this period. In the dataset these redundant names may be absorbed under the synonym 'Port Arthur', yet it is of historical significance—and of value in terms of future research—to note their deviation in provenance.

Most of our work over the past three years has been dedicated to compiling the core of the Tasmanian subset. The sheer depth and scope of this core has meant that our work has allowed us less time than we would have liked to consider broader issues concerning the representation of literary geographies. Such questions of spatial interpretation have arisen, along with many others, throughout the course of this process; however, they remain largely issues for future researchers to ponder. How does one represent ephemeral and transient places in a dataset? What information that is not now considered to be bibliographically standard might be of significance for future researchers? Consideration needs to be given to compiling a dataset that presents the maximum potential for future research outcomes. We should also add that these are not issues or questions that are unique to the Tasmanian subset; indeed they apply to any project attempting to translate such abstract concepts into some form of tangible and accessible data.

16
AusStage: From Database of Performing Arts to a Performing Database of the Arts

Neal Harvey, Helena Grehan and Joanne Tompkins

Researching the performing arts in Australia remains a difficult practice. Apart from very popular productions or those that tour the world, performing arts events are largely forgotten in a matter of months. Traces may remain in various collections, but few collecting agencies (whether libraries or performing arts museums) catalogue each flyer or program individually, let alone the various reviews or photographs that are associated with a production. The recapture of such arguably ephemeral[1] resources is a task of researchers in the performing arts. While performance is fleeting, it is crucial that those traces that do exist be documented so that future scholars and practitioners can draw on this body of knowledge. The new empiricism for theatre studies rests on contemporary researchers' ability to document the existing empirical evidence *as well as* the methods that were used to document that evidence. Hence, unless one knows that an event took place at a certain time in a certain place, finding relevant material regarding that event and engaging with that material as part of a research project is often a matter

---

[1] For a fuller argument about ephemerality and performing arts research, see Diana Taylor, *The Archive and the Repertoire: Performing Cultural Memory in the Americas* (Durham: Duke University Press, 2003).

of chance. AusStage, a freely accessible database devoted to performance, aims to address this situation through the creation of an online database of live Australian performance and event-related data. This chapter briefly outlines the history of AusStage before articulating the ways in which it has attempted to provide new ways to intersect with its community of researchers and contemporary technological developments. We envisage that as AusStage both increases its number of entries and broadens the ways in which its information can be accessible, the nature of research in the performing arts will also become more dynamic and far-reaching.

AusStage (www.ausstage.edu.au) records information on live performance in Australia, as a wealth-producing creative industry, a generator of social capital and an indicator of the nation's cultural vitality. It is different from AustLit (www.austlit.edu.au) in the sense that it treats the production of a particular text as the 'work' in question—though the database uses the term 'event' instead of 'work'—and not the text upon which the work might presumably be based. Whereas AustLit creates a bibliographic record that catalogues particular *versions* of a text (translations, editions, etc.) in a manner that groups them in order that they be understood as branches of the original text, AusStage catalogues events that might not necessarily be based on published texts, or on any texts at all. AusStage does have the functionality to reverse engineer a catalogue, similar to AustLit—that is, it is possible to search out and connect authors or contributors to particular texts (or 'works' in AusStage's case), but it does not rely on bibliographic terms like 'version' or 'publication'.

AusStage is used by researchers and students to develop new knowledge about live performance in Australia and to assess the contribution that live events make to the nation's cultural vitality and international image. It is intended to be a resource capable of recording information about live events that will allow researchers to access information about that event long after it has occurred. Companies, artists and reviewers use

AusStage to find out who's doing what in the live performance industry. Librarians, archivists and performing arts museum staff use AusStage as a source of information on items in their collections and to assist the public with enquiries.

AusStage continues to be developed in terms of database technology, breadth of data, user interface and server technology, but to date AusStage contains the following data:

Events: 40,298
Venues: 4009
Contributors: 67,296
Organisations: 7849
Articles: 34,435.

Data continue to be entered into the AusStage database, chronologically, in two directions—today towards the future and working backwards from 2001. AusStage has attempted to create a comprehensive listing of live events with a dramatic content from January 2001, covering all of Australia (excluding music in the form of concerts, rock bands, etc., but including music theatre). Inevitably, however, there are gaps in this data. In particular, not all regions have been covered, while other regions, including some capital cities, have not yet been brought fully up to date.

Since the project's inception AusStage has continued to evolve the manner in which it catalogues performing arts data. The scope and range of what can be indexed in AusStage is growing, but initially the AusStage team resolved that the minimum data listed for each event were to be:

- the name (title)
- the venue
- the date
- the production company
- the primary genre.

Allowance was made to collect and enter a number of other relevant details, including the origin of the data, linked articles and reviews (where easily discernable), details on contributors and organisations, but it was decided that such data could not be mandatory.

Among the significant developments in AusStage documentation in 2008 are the integration of blogging and event-related critical material. In order to build links with digital sources in online repositories and begin cultivating an eResearch capacity by developing the interactive potential of AusStage, the project has begun associating event-related data with relevant critical material. This task also makes theatre researchers' jobs somewhat easier as it offers an introductory point for scholars seeking critical information about particular productions.[2] Critical material relevant to Australian performing arts events comes in a variety of forms. We divided the available material into two categories: traditionally published critical material and new media or self-published material. Traditionally published material consists of books, articles, newspaper or magazine reviews and interviews, while new media content is probably best exemplified by the growing theatre-blogging community. This chapter examines the integration of this first type of published material, but it is worth emphasising that the project's plans to integrate performance-related blog writing intersects with a form of theatre commentary and research that is yet to be examined as thoroughly as it deserves.[3]

The integration of 'traditional' research data—that is, articles and books—into the database takes the supporting documentation for the

---

[2] We stress that it is an introductory point. While this stage of the project is still in development, it would be unrealistic to assume that all relevant critical material associated with a particular event could be considered catalogued by AusStage.
[3] The blogging tool, not the focus of this paper, is a web-based project attempting to engage with the emerging discourse of performance-related blog writing in Australia. More information about this project can be found at www.ausstage.blogspot.com.

crucial events that AusStage records well beyond the theatre reviews that were the original focus of data collection. To achieve this next step of developing a shared resource with much more detail and accuracy than any one researcher's archive, the AusStage team charged with expanding the critical stream of data on theatre and performance identified three specific sources of data to use as a proof of concept trial for entering:

- Australian book publications from the year 2002 onwards
- *Australasian Drama Studies* journal articles from the same period
- *RealTime Stage and Screen* magazine articles from 2006 onwards.

Obviously this data scope is only a sample of the possible range of material. Financial, time and staff constraints forced the team to select a range of critical material that could be surveyed in the time-period available for this stage of the project.

The first step was to audit each of the data ranges and list all the event or contributor associations that each particular article or book contained. The goal in associating each article or book with existing AusStage data was to find the 'least number of most substantial links' for each critical source. That means that a critical decision had to be made about what data from the article constitute 'most relevant'. In most cases, this is a relatively straightforward decision: many articles discuss specific productions at a specific venue staged by specific individuals or companies. In the case of books, though, it is not always possible to index the thematic or critical argument of the book in a database such as AusStage. Decisions have to be made regarding books that could be considered so general in their association to an event as to render the cataloguing of them with that particular event as redundant. For example, Helen Gilbert and Joanne Tompkins's book, *Post-Colonial Drama*,[4] could theoretically

---

[4] Helen Gilbert and Joanne Tompkins, *Post-Colonial Drama: Theory, Practice, Politics* (London: Routledge, 1996).

be associated with every event in the AusStage index since the argument can be made that all Australian theatre is postcolonial; but to catalogue it with anything other than those events that it specifically mentions could be more misleading than helpful.[5] Once these audits were completed, information on relevant critical material was entered into the database.

Now that this process has been completed, AusStage users will find relevant bibliographic information concerning published material pertinent to particular performance events. The database entry for Legs on the Wall's production of *Homeland*[6]—a show that was staged outside the AMP building in Sydney for the bicentennial celebrations, and which also toured different locations in Australia—now includes a reference for Joanne Tompkins's *Unsettling Space*[7] which discusses this production.[8]

One of the great hurdles in traditional theatre research has always been the absence of performative data once a production has closed. As we identified earlier, the difficulty in locating or accessing information regarding a past performance means that a resource such as AusStage is critically important for theatre scholars: while it does not offer the tangible source that a book manuscript might provide, it does record the event's existence and the response it generated, slowing that event's otherwise inevitable journey from happening to memory. AusStage offers

---

[5] The association of this type of critical material with the database is a future goal of the project and one dependent upon the successful completion of phases 2 and 3 of the present project.

[6] *Homeland*, Legs on the Wall (AMP Building, Sydney, 1998).

[7] Joanne Tompkins, *Unsettling Space: Contestations in Contemporary Australian Theatre* (Basingstoke: Palgrave Macmillan, 2006).

[8] Reviews discuss productions in a very different manner to books and articles. A review is obviously brief and is written shortly after a performance and engages with a general audience whereas an article or book mounts a more sophisticated argument that is based on lengthier consideration of the production and includes other supporting research materials that are generally not relevant or possible in a review.

researchers the chance to begin to unearth a new empiricism for theatre studies that incorporates event-related data *and* the wider sociological and historical context in which the event existed. Theatre studies is just as susceptible as other humanities disciplines to what William St Clair calls 'the parade of authors' and the 'parliament of texts'[9] and what Robert Dixon summarises as the past being represented by great names or organised as a series of connections between great texts—or in this case productions.[10] Working towards a new empiricism, AusStage offers scholars the chance to document the changing nature of production and production practices and begin to interrogate the causes and consequences of such changes. Theatre practice and production are not static—one production of Shakespeare's *Hamlet* isn't the same as another production of the same text—and without a resource like AusStage, the productive elements that shape Shakespeare's texts' continual reinterpretation and re-imagination are difficult if not impossible to articulate. Tracing the evolution of a particular production, its genealogy (where it played, who performed in it, who directed it, etc.) is now a possibility for Australian theatre researchers who can use AusStage to chronicle a production's evolution; its company and personnel changes; its venue associations (and hence, to a certain extent, its geographical exposure); its directorial evolutions (through reviews and associated literature) as well as its theatrical offspring. Being able to make such performative and productive connections quickly and accurately gives researchers the chance to begin mapping other sociological and cultural factors that a

---

[9] William St Clair, 'The Political Economy of Reading', online (2005), learn.creativecommons.org/wp-content/uploads/2008/09/stclair.pdf [Accessed 6 January 2009], p. 3.

[10] Robert Dixon, 'Australian Literature and the New Empiricism: A Response to Paul Eggert, "Australian Classics and the Price of Books"', *JASAL* 9 (2008): 158–62, 158.

'close reading' of any one particular production would not be able to provide.

AusStage gives researchers the chance to study performative patterns of production and reception that formerly would have been nigh on impossible to determine. Researchers can unearth theatre's homologising elements for the first time and begin to investigate how and what brings work to the Australian stage. In undertaking research like this, theatre scholars have the opportunity to help nurture the performing arts sector of Australia, to assist an industry that is constantly changing its productive and performative models in accordance with funding models as well as public response. As the Australia Council continues to adapt and mould its funding practices, so too will companies adapt the way that they produce theatre. Such changing practices demand new methods of recording, archiving and studying performance. An important first step in articulating and defining these new methods is documenting the search for those methods. Anecdotal and 'water-cooler' research have long been staple methods of data gathering for performance theorists, methods that often yield data and results that are as ephemeral as the event they describe. A resource like AusStage allows future generations of researchers the opportunity to interrogate the same data as previous scholars. This repeatability, of methodology and of research, represents one defining aspect of the emerging empiricism for performance studies. AusStage plays an important role in this process as it documents and archives production-related material—including public and expert response to that material—in a manner that was not possible before. In such a manner electronic databases like AusStage are well positioned to document the shifting nature of performance practices and their accompanying research.

The work undertaken during this phase of AusStage's development has paved the way for the future directions of the project. Building on the success of incorporating critical literature into the database, AusStage will begin further expanding the scope and appeal of a new empiricism for performance studies by installing a suite of font-end tools for the database that take full advantage of recent developments in ICT. By embracing practices that 'crowdsource' data, engage with a 'popular intelligence' and further enhance AusStage's platform for 'collaboratory' based research the database will continue to test what will and what won't contribute to performance studies' new empiricism.

17
Constructing APRIL: The Australian Poetry Resources Internet Library

John Tranter and Elizabeth Webby

APRIL: The Australian Poetry Resources Internet Library aims to increase the circulation, reading and understanding of Australian poetry within Australia and internationally by providing reliable reading texts of a wide range of poems by contemporary and earlier writers as well as much contextual and critical material, including interviews, photographs and recordings. Since mid-2007, a team at the University of Sydney, based in the English Department and Fisher Library, has been developing this site, with funding provided by a large Australian Research Council (ARC) Linkage Grant and industry partner the Copyright Agency Limited (CAL). Collaboration with CAL and use of new Digital Object Identifier technology will allow authors to receive payment for material still in copyright, thus solving the major problem associated with making this material accessible on the internet.

The inspiration for the APRIL project came from poet and editor John Tranter who, in the early 1990s, with Philip Mead, had compiled the *Penguin Book of Modern Australian Poetry*. Penguin had allocated 300 pages for the book but the manuscript eventually handed in came to 475 printed pages, which they graciously accepted. Even so, there were no notes on the authors, since this would have meant leaving out a dozen or so poets. Some readers of the book were disappointed by this, and reviewers rightly mentioned the lack of biographical and other information.

Five years after the *Penguin Book* appeared, John began publishing *Jacket*, an internet-only free poetry and review magazine. It immediately achieved a large audience and a wide international reach. After ten years and thirty-six issues, the home page had recorded over three-quarters of a million visits. Inspired by *Jacket*'s success, John applied in 2000 (with the assistance of the English Department at the University of Sydney) for a small ARC grant to publish an internet edition of his first book of poems, *Parallax* (1970), which had gone out of print. The appearance in 2004 of the text (with several reviews and other secondary material) on the SETIS pages of the site managed by the University of Sydney Library again found a wide readership. While the physical book had been borrowed from Fisher Library perhaps thirty times since 1970, the electronic edition received 15,000 visits in the first year.

Would the work of earlier Australian poets find an equivalent response on the internet? John secured a grant (for typesetting and payment of copyright clearances) from the Literature Board of the Australia Council and, with support from Australian Literary Management and the University of Sydney Library, three books of poems were typeset and published on this site in 2004: substantial collections of poems by Christopher Brennan (1870–1932), Kenneth Slessor (1901–1971) and Lesbia Harford (1891–1927).

Next, John thought of those missing author notes; to put them on the internet would make this useful information freely available to a large, worldwide audience. Furthermore, the notes could be considerably expanded, to include poems and reviews as well as bibliographical and biographical information, so giving the poets (and their critics and reviewers) more space to address their public in different ways, as well as supplying readers with extra background material to enrich their responses to the poems. This would be particularly helpful for teachers and students. In 2004 John began placing material on some seventy poets on the internet site run by Australian Literary Management, who kindly made it available for the purpose. In late 2004 the Literature Board offered a grant to enable Australian Literary Management to publish samples of the writing, as well as author notes and extensive background material, for sixteen Australian poets, with a fee payment to each of the poets. This part of the project was completed in June 2006. By then, the material available ran to over a thousand printed pages, making it the largest anthology of poetry and secondary material yet published in Australia. But why limit the range of poets to those eighty-six who had been fitted into the procrustean bed of the *Penguin Book of Modern Australian Poetry*? The internet makes page limits, printing and distribution costs and retail price irrelevant. Surely several hundred poets would be a more useful number?

Of course it was too much for any one person to take on. Again John approached the English Department at the University of Sydney. Professor Margaret Harris suggested that an application to the ARC for a Linkage Grant, which would involve a commitment of financial and other support from an industry partner, would be more likely to succeed than a request for a Discovery Grant. Elizabeth Webby agreed to lead the research project and the University of Sydney Library enthusiastically joined in with a promise of staff and facilities. All that remained was to find a partner.

John had been on the board of the Australian Society of Authors when CAL was founded in 1974 to manage the collection and redistribution of photocopying fees to authors and publishers. Nearly three decades later he attended a seminar organised by CAL at the University of Sydney to promote the understanding and use of digital object identifiers (DOIs) as a means of tagging and identifying pieces of text on the internet, so that fees similar to photocopying fees could be efficiently collected and remitted to copyright owners when texts were used or printed out. As the Australian licensee for the system, developed in Europe, CAL was the ideal business partner for an ARC Linkage Grant application for the poetry project. DOIs would provide an essential means of managing the material we wished to publish on the internet.

The grant application was successful, with just over $580,000 received from the ARC, as well as additional funds and in-kind support from CAL and in-kind support from the University of Sydney, especially the Library. There was a long delay, however, between confirmation of the grant in July 2006 and the final signing of the contract between CAL and the university in May 2007. This effectively set the project back almost twelve months, so we anticipate finishing it now in late 2010 rather than 2009 as originally planned.

In the period since funding began, members of the team have been busy designing and constructing the website, signing up the 170 poets with work still in copyright who were selected for inclusion in the first stage of the project, sourcing and preparing each author's collections of poetry for digitisation, and researching and writing the biographical and bibliographical entries for each poet as well as more general thematic essays. Once the poets are signed up we will also be carrying out interviews with them and making recordings of them reading their work, probably in association with the National Library's Oral History unit.

A key issue in establishing protocols for APRIL was deciding what type of searches would be of most benefit to users of the site, especially researchers. As the full texts of the poems will be searchable we decided not to attempt any subject indexing, which is in any case already available on AustLit. We are, however, providing researchers with the opportunity to search by genre, so that anyone who wishes to trace the use by Australian poets of forms such as the sonnet, ode or epic will be able to do so.

Excellent progress was made during 2008 in contacting the selected poets, or their literary executors in the case of deceased poets, and arranging for them to become members of CAL and to participate in the project. One hundred and twenty of the 170 selected poets have now agreed to participate; six have declined for a variety of reasons. The remaining authors are mainly deceased and in some cases it has proved very difficult to discover who owns the copyright to their work. However, nearly all major Australian poets whose work is still in copyright, or their estates, have now agreed to participate, and the site will include work by John Tranter, Robert Adamson, Les Murray, Dorothy Porter, Judith Wright, A.D. Hope, James McAuley and John Forbes, among many others.

Excellent progress has also been made in arranging the digitisation of the published works of the participating poets. The seventy-one collections by forty-six Australian poets whose work is now out of copyright, earlier digitised by Sydney Electronic Text and Imaging Service, have been split into 3400 individual poems which are now ready for adding to the final database. As well, 7670 poems by authors whose work is still in copyright have been fully processed and are ready for addition to the database. This represents 120 collections by fifty-one poets that have been scanned, converted to XML and checked for systematic errors such as completeness, accuracy of the number system and correct bibliographic information. The poems have not been individually proofread, since the digitisation process involves a system of double-keying to locate input errors. A significant aspect of the checking is to make sure that the finished product faithfully replicates the often very complex layout of the published versions of the poems. In difficult cases an image file will sit alongside the digital version. Images are also supplied for illustrations included in the published works, especially where these specifically accompany the poems or are created by the poet.

A further 554 volumes representing the works of 106 poets are currently being digitised while another 300 volumes representing the work of eighty-three poets are currently being checked after digitisation. It is estimated, on the basis of library records and the AustLit database, that the final number of poems included on APRIL will be well over 110,000. Seven video interviews with and readings by poets made in the 1970s and 1980s by the University of Sydney's then Television Service have also been digitised together with aural tapes of interviews carried out by Erica Bell during the 1990s for her PhD thesis. By the end of 2009, digitisation of works by the selected poets should be completed and the development and testing of the website will be well under way, with a launch planned for 2010.

18
An Australian Reading Experience Database, 1788–

Patrick Buckridge

An Australian reading experience database has the potential to unite the benefits of large-scale historical synthesis with those of intensive qualitative analysis of the act of reading.[1] What follows is an account of the present state of the project, together with some consideration of the questions of design and definition that have already come to light.

The British Reading Experience Database 1450–1945 (henceforth RED) was launched in 2006. It is a fully searchable database, with open internet access, containing written records of specific reading experiences that have occurred in Britain from 1450 to 1945. At present it contains over 21,600 such records; the short-term aim is to have 25,000 by the middle of 2009; and the long-term objective is for the database to keep growing forever, funds permitting. It is an open-ended project. As records of reading experiences are discovered, they are submitted to the RED where they are verified and edited by RED staff, and finally released

---

[1] Very few studies of reading unite the macro and micro perspectives. A recent exception might be Jonathan Rose, *The Intellectual Life of the British Working Class* (New Haven: Yale University Press, 2001), but this book—though received with great enthusiasm in some quarters—was elsewhere felt to lack coherence and cogency.

to the public database, which has both basic and advanced search functions.[2]

Early in the gestation of the RED a decision was taken to restrict the readers to persons of British nationality, wherever in the world their reading experience occurred, and to persons of any nationality whose reading occurred in the United Kingdom. Residents of former British colonies were not included unless they were born in Britain.[3] Hence, if Australia wants a similar database for Australian reading experiences it will need to build its own. The Centre for Public Culture and Ideas at Griffith University, in collaboration with the Public Memory Research Centre at the University of Southern Queensland, are jointly providing internal start-up funds to produce a prototype for an Australian reading experience database (henceforth AusRED), beginning in 2009.

To realise its potential the AusRED will need to be interoperable not just with the British RED but with other national REDs, if and when they come into existence. To that end, arrangements are in place to involve RED staff as technical and content consultants during the process of building the prototype. Plans are also afoot for including New Zealand in the next phase of the AusRED's development, and further down the track links will be actively forged with whatever other countries establish comparable databases. (South Africa is certainly moving in a RED-ward direction, and Germany and Canada are rumoured to be doing likewise.)

That is the larger vision, and whatever its shortcomings and naïvetés it is genuinely global in scope. One looks forward to the day—still some way off—when a scholar in Brisbane can find out what people in Sydney, Hamburg, Toronto and Tokyo had to say about the novels of Dostoevsky in the 1930s. Meanwhile, back on *terra firma*, what will the AusRED

---

[2] www.open.ac.uk/Arts/RED/.
[3] Simon Eliot, unpublished conference presentation, 'The History of Reading', Napier University, Edinburgh, 2000. (Unstated on the RED website, but subsequently confirmed.)

prototype look like? And in particular, how might it differ from its British parent?

Generally speaking, the intention is to adhere fairly closely to the British format—the linked relationship dictates that in any case—but there is one inescapable difference between the British and Australian contexts, and that is the almost 350 years between 1450 and 1788 (realistically the earliest possible start date for an AusRED). That chronological difference has two consequences relevant to the final shape of an AusRED. The first is the pressure it exerts to bring the terminal year covered by the database much closer to the present than 1945 (the terminal year of the British RED). If you only have 220 years of reading history, you can't really afford to pass up sixty-four of them! And that internal pressure is reinforced by nearly every external institution with a potential interest in supporting the development of an AusRED: publishers, booksellers, large libraries and various state and federal government departments and semi-government agencies. For all of these, the notional payoff is access to information about recent reading habits on which to base projections about emerging tastes and niche markets, which in turn might influence commissionings, author-profiling, print runs, etc.—or in the case of non-profit public bodies, access to data relevant to achieving more efficiently targeted resourcing of schools and public libraries, or a more equitable allocation of arts project funds. In this sense—to put the case slightly cynically—the AusRED would be doing free client-survey work for organisations that would otherwise have to pay for it themselves.

Indeed, some potential clients or sponsors would urge no fixed terminal date at all, but rather a continuous updating—in effect a constant monitoring—of the reading experience of the Australian community. If such a service were financially or technologically feasible, one can readily understand its appeal to an 'industry partner', but it would not be without interest to reading historians either. It would be interesting, for example, to track the effects on Australian reading habits of changes in government policy such as the proposed lifting of the ban on parallel book imports.

Clearly an open-ended RED would entail a very different data-collection methodology from that used for earlier periods, at least for the years since the explosion of online discussion groups and blogs in the mid-1990s. The astronomical increase in the sheer quantity of reading-experience data in those locations raises the question of whether a RED could afford to devote resources to reading, selecting and transferring large quantities of information between websites? Machine-searching or 'harvesting' of blogs and databases like ADB Online is a possibility, but in the end it might make more sense to declare the last ten or fifteen years a kind of borderless information zone, to which the RED would supply map references in the form of annotated links to the main sites on which Australian readers will have recorded their own reading experiences. Indeed the AusRED could even enter the zone with its own modest blog—just one among many—inviting Australians to record (and thereby submit) their reading experiences directly then and there. The 'mapped zone' concept would presumably also avoid copyright problems, since no actual reproduction of texts would be involved. Whether such a zone could share a platform with an edited AusRED is uncertain at this stage.

Not all the challenges occur at the recent end of the proposed database. A question that has to be addressed, at whatever point on the historical time-line, is: 'What do we mean by an Australian Reading Experience?' The British RED defines a 'reading experience' as: 'A recorded engagement with a written or printed text—beyond the mere fact of possession'.[4] This definition, it seems to me, conforms to common sense, meets the likely expectations of the typical searcher, and can be easily understood by the volunteers who will no doubt do much of the work of

---

[4] 'What Is a "Reading Experience"?', on RED website, www.open.ac.uk/Arts/RED/.

populating the database in the longer term. The definition of a reading experience, however, like the terminal date, is a point at which stakeholder pressure might well be applied, but I would be reluctant to move away from the base notion of a transaction with a written or printed text. Expand the definition to include the reading of faces, films, landscapes, paintings and social situations, and I fear the whole project becomes unworkable: it will have become the 'Australian Life Experience Database' and we will have lost the possibility of documenting, exhaustively, the continuing history of a distinct and determinate cultural practice. The British formulation of the larger phenomenon being recorded, with a different national adjective, will serve the project well: 'What British [sc. Australian] people read, where and when they read it and what they thought of it'.[5]

Further definitional problems will arise, of course, with 'Australian'. Picture a young English backpacker spending a gap-year in Australia, travelling around the country, reading a series of fantasy paperbacks in bed at night. He writes letters home, in one of which he describes his reading to a parent or a kindred spirit. Does his description constitute an Australian reading experience? It is certainly a British one, but it would not be captured by the British RED with its terminal date of 1945; so it would be the AusRED or nowhere for this young man's reading experience—and it does seem a pity to exclude it, and to ignore the salience of the environment in which the experience occurred.

A somewhat different question arises at the other end of the time line, in relation to the great number of British and other immigrants and transportees to the early colonies whose reading experiences took place there and are recorded in Australian archives (or, more rarely, in overseas archives). In principle, such records will find their way into the British RED, as they should; but should they also appear in the AusRED? There

---

[5] Ibid.

seems no good reason why not, but it would surely be desirable to avoid duplication of labour and data storage space.

The question of colonial immigrant readers leads naturally to a related, possibly somewhat contentious question, that of fictional accounts of reading—or, as I would rather put it, accounts of reading in fiction. Australian colonial fiction, like British Victorian fiction, is particularly rich in such accounts,[6] and nobody could doubt their great interest and value to historians of reading. One thinks in this context of the work of recent British reading historians like James Raven, Helen Small, Naomi Tadmor and Kate Flint—but also of an older figure like Amy Cruse—as having all made sophisticated use of fictional scenes of reading.[7]

But even if fictionalised reading is granted a legitimate place in monographs, a real question remains as to whether it belongs in a RED. The British RED have said in effect, 'No, fictional accounts of reading are not evidence of actual reading performances. *Ergo*, they do not belong in an historical database.'[8] Personally, I incline to the view that if the available data stoarge space, research time, and financial resources are all adequate, and if in addition there are good intellectual reasons to include fictional reading experiences in the AusRED, then one may as well do it. *Are* there such reasons? To this I would say a guarded and qualified Yes,

---

[6] For examples, see my 'Bookishness and Australian Literature', *Script and Print* 30.4 (2007): 223–36.

[7] James Raven, Helen Small and Naomi Tadmor, eds, *The Practice and Representation of Reading* (Cambridge: Cambridge University Press, 1996); Kate Flint, *The Woman Reader 1837–1914* (Oxford: Clarendon Press, 1993); Amy Cruse, *The Shaping of English Literature* (London: Harrap, 1927); Amy Cruse, *The Englishman and His Books in the Early Nineteenth Century* (London: Harrap, 1930); Amy Cruse, *The Victorians and Their Books* (London: G. Allen, 1936); Amy Cruse, *After the Victorians* (London: Allen & Unwin, 1938).

[8] 'What Sort of Data Are We Looking For?', on RED website, www.open.ac.uk/Arts/RED/.

mainly on the grounds that fictional representations of reading, whether they be seen as reflections, imitations, idealisations or hypotheses of actual reading performances, do reveal much about the assumptions, attitudes and values of the reading culture that produces them. Furthermore, if one thinks of an AusRED not just as a repository of information, but as an active driver of new research projects in the historiography of reading—and why would we not?—then the range of project types that a RED could serve would, I think, be significantly wider *with* fictional content than *without*. Clearly though, fictional examples need to be clearly tagged as fictional, and perhaps 'quarantined' as a separate subset of the database.

A similar case to that for including fictional material could of course be made for including visual images of reading and readers. Images of all kinds—drawn, painted, sculpted, engraved and photographed—have been much used, sometimes quite intensively, by British reading historians such as Kate Flint and Adrian Johns, and indeed by Martyn Lyons in the second volume of *The History of the Book in Australia*.[9] But images of reading, like fictional representations of reading, are specifically excluded under the British RED protocol.[10]

I would certainly be inclined, *pace* the British, to include images in an AusRED if it proved to be technically feasible. Social facts about the history of reading cannot be simply read off from images, even photographic images, any more than they can from fictional descriptions of reading; but the interpretative activity necessary for understanding all

---

[9] Kate Flint, *The Woman Reader*; Adrian Johns, *The Nature of the Book: Print and Knowledge in the Making* (Chicago: University of Chicago Press, 1998); Martyn Lyons and John Arnold, eds, *The History of the Book in Australia, 1891–1945: A National Culture in a Colonised Market* (St Lucia: University of Queensland Press, 2001).
[10] 'What Sort of Data Are We Looking for?' on RED website, www.open.ac.uk/Arts/RED/.

such highly mediated sources is properly the task of the user, not the builder, of a database. And it is precisely this kind of nuanced and context-aware cultural reflection and synthesis that a reading experience database, with its wide—indeed potentially limitless—historical and international scope, combined with its intensive focus on the act of reading texts, can promote.

Index

A
Abbey, Sue, 151, 162, 165, 169, 172, 174
ABC Books, 216
Aboriginal Studies Press, 161, 164, 188
Academy Editions, 54, 62–64, 68
Access Press, 207
Action Comics, 197, 202, 220
Adams, J.R., 127, 140
Adamson, Robert, 147, 338
Adelaide Mail, 117
Advertiser (Adelaide), 121, 123, 131, 133
Afro American (US), 116
Age, 117, 121, 130–32, 134, 137, 152
Allen & Unwin, 161, 165, 186–88, 212, 216, 222, 271
Allen, Louis A., 187
Alpha Press, 206
America Publishes Australia project, 25, 76, 105
American Book-Stratford Press, 118

American Literature, 2
Anderson, Benedict, 124, 138
Anderson, Don, 285
Anderson, Jessica, 148, 274, 288
Anderson, Warrigal (Edward), 167
Angus & Robertson, 51, 108, 114, 129, 135–37, 146–47, 149, 161, 185, 187, 197–98, 203, 206, 212, 220–21, 271; Arkon series, 149
Animo Publishing, 207
anthologies, nature of, 274–95
anti-essentialism, 48, 49
Antipodes, 94, 100, 103, 118
Apter, Emily, 20, 88, 90, 95, 97, 104
Argonauts, 129
Argus, 121, 126, 131, 134, 136–38
Aristarchus of Samothrace, 53
Armidale Express, 121, 131, 133
Arthur, Paul Longley, 1, 2, 9, 11, 23
Artlook Books, 207

Asian literature, 283; *see also* University of Queensland Press
Association for Computing in the Humanities, 10
Association for Literary and Linguistic Computing, 10
Association for the Study of Australian Literature (ASAL), 7; Aust-e-Lit, 313; mini-conference (2007), 71; Wollongong conference, 71, 152
Astley, Thea, 145, 274
Atherton, V., 110
Aurora Press, 207
AusRED (Australian Reading Experience Database), 13, 24, 26, 340–47
AusStage, 13, 24, 26, 309, 327, 325–33
Austen, Jane, 67
AustLit: The Resource for Australian Literature, 12–13, 22, 24–26, 61, 70, 74–83, 99, 106, 120–21, 125, 195, 207, 224, 241, 243, 251–57, 260–62, 266, 269–70, 272, 275, 277–78, 280–83, 294, 300–01, 307–10, 312–16, 318, 322, 326, 337–38; Literature of Tasmania, 24, 26, 315–24
Australasian Book Society (ABS), 204, 206

Australasian Drama Studies, 329
Australia Council, 99, 332; Literature Board, 152, 160, 166, 204, 335–36
Australian Academy of the Humanities, 12
Australian Charter for the Computer-Based Representation of Literary History, 244, 247, 249, 264, 268, 273
Australian Common Reader Project, 226–29; database, 227, 229–30, 232, 235
Australian Consolidated Press (ACP), 212–13
Australian Defence Force Academy (ADFA), 61, 62
Australian Dictionary of Biography (ADB), 309, 343
Australian e-Humanities Gateway, 12
Australian Government Trade Commissioner, 109
Australian Literary Management, 335–36
Australian Literary Publishing and its Economies project, 25, 157
Australian Literary Studies (ALS), 13, 25, 72–73, 75, 103, 124, 138, 223–24, 226, 301

Australian National University (ANU) Press, 177
Australian Poetry Resource Internet Library (APRIL), 13, 24, 26, 334–39
Australian Research Council, 12, 25, 61, 88, 334, 336
Australian Scholarly Editions Centre, 62
Australian Scholarly Publishing, 217
Australian Society of Authors, 336

B
B.P. Magazine, 132
Babidge, Sally, 189
Bacon, Premier Jim, 317
Bail, Murray, 145, 257, 286
Bairds (store), 135
Ballarat Courier, 121, 132, 134–35
Barclay, Florence, 234, 238
Bardon, Geoffrey, 185, 187
Barker, Nicolas, 7
Barnard, Majorie, 289
Barnes, John, 286
Barrymore, Freda, 135
Barthes, Roland, 49, 159
Bartoloni, Paolo, 90, 97, 99
Barwell, Graham, 62
Battarbee, Rex & Bernice, 186
Beavan, Gordon, 123–24
Beaver, Bruce, 147

Beckmann, Roger, 265
Behrendt, Larissa, 167
Beier, Ulli, 164
Bell, Diane, 186
Bell, Erica, 338
Bellear, Lisa, 174
Bendigo Advertiser, 121, 133
Bennett, Bruce, 119
Berne Convention (1886), 107
Berrie, Phill, 63, 64
Bertelsmann Media Worldwide, 211–14, 222
Best Australian Short Stories, 286
Best Australian Stories, 282
BeWrite Books, 216
bibliographic record, Australia, 249
bibliography, 4, 6, 8–9, 12, 17, 70–71, 73–74, 77, 81–82, 250, 256, 262–63
Bicentenary (1988), 165, 169, 282, 285, 317, 330
Bindloss, Harold, 234, 238
Bird, Carmel, 2871
Bjelke-Petersen, Joh, 164
BlackBooks, 161
Blainey, Geoffrey: *A Land Half Won*, 179; *Triumph of the Nomads*, 185
Blanchot, Maurice, 49
Blocksidge, Peter, 142
Boans (store), 135

351

Bobbs-Merrill Company, 113
Bode, Katherine, 43, 224, 252, 275–77, 281, 316
Bodey, John, 167
Bodleian Library, 319
Boldrewood, Rolf, 54–55
Book Bounty scheme, 204, 210
book history, 6, 8, 16, 21–22, 32–36, 38–40, 42, 48–52, 70–72, 75, 79, 81–82, 89, 105–06, 117–18, 226, 245, 250, 252, 268; book historians, 6, 8, 105
Book History Reader, 6
Booker Prize, 148
Book-of-the-Month Club, 114
BookScan, 201, 248
Boolarong Press, 207
Border Morning Mail, 121, 133
Boston Post, 116
Bourdieu, Pierre, 32, 44, 49–50, 104
Boyd, Robin, 178
Boys' and Girls' Own, 126
Brennan, Christopher, 147, 335
Brennan, Frank, 185
Brennan, Noëlle (literary agency), 109, 110
Brisbane Courier, 121, 131, 134
Britain, 110–11, 115–16, 128–29, 197, 269–70, 319, 340–41; control over Commonwealth imports, 199; London, 21, 80, 105–08, 111–13, 117–18, 182, 244–45, 249, 264, 299, 311; publishing network of empire, 128
British Library, 79, 128
British Reading Experience Database, 27, 340–46
British Research Council, 12
British Traditional Market Agreement (BTMA), 199, 204
Brontë, Charlotte, 227
Brontë, Emily, 227
Broome, Richard, 186
Brophy, Kevin, 166
Brown, Carter, 114, 250, 257–58; *Carter Brown Mystery Series*, 250–51
Brown, Curtis (literary agent), 108, 113, 118
Buckley, Vincent, 147
Bulletin, 51, 110, 114, 117, 122, 132, 139
Bulwer-Lytton, George, 228
Burnum Burnum, 185
Burrows, John, 10
Buzo, Alex, 148
Byron, Lord, 240

C
Calvert, 197, 199, 206, 220
Campbell, David, 146
canons and canon formation, 11, 18, 21, 23, 35, 43, 51–52, 92, 120, 141, 157, 174, 192, 223–24, 227, 238, 254, 276–

77, 282, 286–87, 291, 293; anti-canonical, 47; 'classics', 157; denaturalisation of, 3; non-canonical, 43, 235
Cappiello, Rosa, 22, 151–55, 159, 288; Premio Calabria award, 151; reviewed by Franco Schiavoni, 152
Carey, Peter, 103, 145, 148, 159, 286; *Illywhacker*, 164; *Living Together*, 148; *Oscar and Lucinda*, 80, 148; *Fat Man in History*, 148
Carnegie Mellon University, 225
Carrick & Evans Inc., 113
Carter, David, 13, 71, 76, 295
Cartland, Barbara, 127
Casanova, Giacomo, 90, 94
Casanova, Pascale, 87
Cassell & Co. Ltd., 128, 181
Chapman, R. W., 67
Chatwin, Bruce, 90
Cheshire, 185, 198, 206
Christian Socialist Movement, 106
Clarke, Marcus, 63, 135
Clayton, Jay, 2
Cleary, Jon, 109
Cleveland Publishing, 197–202, 206, 215, 220–21, 271
Cleven, Vivienne, 167
close reading, 14, 17–18, 35, 45, 69, 89, 97, 246, 300, 332

Clousten, Brian, 159
Coast to Coast, 110
Cody, Chris, 98
Coetzee, J.M., 50, 102
Cohen, Philip, 73
Cole, Keith, 187
Colebrook, Joan, 109
Composition Place node, 323
Computer Assisted Scholarly Editing (CASE), 62
computing, 9–11, 23, 25, 242–47, 256, 265, 268; 3D visualisation, 311; Apple, 63, 232; JITM, 64–65; Linux, 232; Microsoft, 232, 259, 264, 267–68; MIX System, 142, 144–45; MySQL, 241; OCR, 60; PHP, 241; SGML, 63; t-SNE algorithm, 231; XML, 56, 338; *see also* internet
copyright, 40, 78, 80, 102, 107–08, 113, 128, 157, 159, 210, 218, 334–38, 343; Copyright Agency Limited (CAL), 334, 336–37; copyright law, 107, 108, 128, 210
corporate publishing models, 179
Cory & Collins, 207
Cowlishaw, Gillian, 189
Cronin, Kathryn, 164
Cruse, Amy, 345
Cubis, Dorothy, 109

cultural history, 16, 32, 35–36, 40–42, 48, 50–52, 239, 244, 256; depoliticisation of culture, 191
cultural industries model, 43
cultural pathology, 31
cultural studies, 16, 26, 32, 42, 73, 248
Currawong Press, 204, 206
Currency Press, 148, 161
curriculum, 22, 76, 147–48, 160, 181, 282; High School Certificate (HSC), 151, 163
Cybertales, 283

D
Daily Examiner, 121, 132, 134
Daily Guardian, 121, 133
Daily Mercury, 121, 133
Dalley, John, 128
Dante, 91, 92, 95
Dark, Eleanor, 109, 113
Darnton, Robert, 7
Darrell, George, 148
data analysis, 18, 229, 235, 239, 245, 309
databases, 12–13, 15, 71, 201, 224, 227–28, 236, 332, 341, 343
data mining, 13, 15, 18, 20, 24, 71, 193, 241, 245, 262
David Jones (store), 172
David Unaipon Award winners, 167

Davidson, Cathy, 2, 13
Davis, Beatrice & Douglas Stewart, 114
Davis, Colin, 19
Davis, Jack, 165–66, 168, 171
Davis, Mark, 176, 200
Davison, Frank Dalby, 117
de Man, Paul, 35
Department of Education, Employment and Workplace Relations (DEEWR, formerly DEST), 12
Depression, the, 125
Derrida, Jacques, 49
Dessaix, Robert: *A Mother's Disgrace*, 98–100, 104; Chevalier dans L'Ordre des Arts et Lettres, 100; *Night Letters*, 90–100; Ninette Boothroyd and Michelle Royer's essay, 97–101
Dick, Charlotte, 132
Dickens, Charles, 228
Digital Object Identifier technology, 334
digital repositories, 306
Digital Thesis Database, 309
digitisation, 337, 338
dimensional reduction, 230–31
Dingle, Tony, 186
distant reading, 9, 14–15, 20, 36, 89, 104, 246, 266, 270, 289
Dixon, Graeme, 166–67, 174

Dixon, Robert, 39, 52, 71, 157, 331
Dixson, Miriam, 187
Docutech, 174
Dodd, Bill, 167, 170
Dolin, Tim, 44, 51, 227–28, 235, 238, 250–51
Doubleday Doran, 113
Doyle, Fiona, 167
Dransfield, Michael, 145–47, 159; *Streets of the Long Voyage*, 146, 150; *Inspector of Tides*, 146, 150
DreamCraft, 216
Duell, Sloan & Pearce, 113
Duffy & Snellgrove, 217
Duguid, Charles, 186
During, Simon, 45, 46, 145, 318
Duwell, Martin, 163
Dykebooks, 207
Dymocks, 135–37, 140, 172, 204, 206

E
economic rationalism, 247
e-editions, 64
Eggert, Paul, 5, 11, 44, 71, 276–77; Colonial Texts Series, 17, 68
Eight Voices of the Eighties, 274–79, 281, 287–90, 293–94
Electronic Cultural Atlas Initiative, 245
Eliot, George, 227–28, 237

Elkin, A.P., 185
Ellis, Malcom Henry, 114
empirical literary studies, 8–9
empirical turn, 3, 14, 19, 38
Equilibrium Books, 216
eResearch Australasia conference, 12
eResearch or e-Lit, 1, 3, 11, 13–15, 17–18, 23–27, 65, 245, 299–300, 303, 307–09, 328
e-texts, 53
ethico-formalism, 292
Evans, H.A. (bookseller), 136
Evans, Raymond, 164
evolutionary theory, 44
Examiner, 121, 123, 134, 135
Exploratory Data Analysis, 229

F
F.W. Cheshire Publishing, 197
Faber & Faber, 286
Facey, A.B., 148
Fairfax, 212–13
Fantastic Worlds, 283
Farmer, Beverley, 274
Feenberg, Andrew, 267
Fellowship of Australian Writers, 280
Felski, Rita, 290–92
feminism, 163, 171, 178, 275–76, 281, 283, 285, 288, 291, 294; masculine bias, 152, 275, 286
Ferguson, J.A., 5

Ferres, Kay, 32
Ferrier, Carole, 276
film, 113, 125, 152, 172, 218
Fish, Stanley, 49
Fitzgerald, Ross, 164
Fitzgibbon, Rosanne, 159
Flanagan, Richard, 321
Flint, Kate, 345, 346
Fontana Press, 181
Forbes, John, 338
Forster, Clare, 169, 173
Foucault, Michel, 159, 171
Fowler, Don, 256
Foy & Gibson (store), 135, 136
Frank Johnson Publishing, 204, 206
Franklin, Miles, 139
Freeman, Cathy, 190
Fremantle Arts Centre Press, 161, 188, 207, 217
Frow, John, 38, 40, 41, 208
Functional Requirements for Bibliographic Records (FRBR), 75

G
Galligan, Anne, 205–06, 211
Garner, Helen, 153, 274, 288; *Monkey Grip*, 148; response to Rosa Capiello, 153
Gaskell, Philip, 63
Gee, Valda & Rosalie Medcraft, 167, 170

Geelong Advertiser, 121, 132, 134
Gelder, Ken, 254, 276
genre writing, 283
Georgian House, 206
geo-spatial mapping, 13, 15
Gerard, Dominique, 98
Gibbons, Anthony, 25
Gilbert, Helen & Joanne Tompkins, 329
Gilbert, Kevin: *Because a White Man'll Never Do It*, 185; *Living Black*, 184, 190; *People Are Legends*, 160
Gilbert, Sandra M. & Susan Gubar, 291
Ginibi, Ruby Langford, 170, 173; *Don't Take Your Love to Town*, 185; *Haunted by the Past*, 170, 185, 189; *My Bundjalong People*, 170; *Real Deadly*, 185
Ginninderra Press, 217
Giramondo Publishing, 217
globalisation, 179, 200, 214
Golden Age of Australian publishing, 145
Goldsworthy, Kerryn, 276
Gollancz, Victor, 112
Goods and Services Tax (GST), 210
Google Scholar, 309
Gordimer, Nadine, 102

Gordon & Gotch, 136, 201
Graham, Mary, 169, 173
Granada Media, 212
Grant, Stan, 190
Grassby, Al & Marji Hills, 185
Grattan, C. Hartley, 111
Gray, Robert, 147
Green, H.M., 5
Greenhouse Publications, 207
Greetham, David, 41
Greg-Bowers method, 62
Grenville, Kate, 80, 152, 274
Griffith University, 341
Grimmett, Clarrie, 127
Griswold, Wendy & Misty Bastian, 200
Guha, Ranajit, 182
Gunew, Sneja & Jan Mahyuddin, 288, 294

H
Hachette Livre, 212–14, 222
Hadow, Lyndall, 110
Haebich, Anna, 189
Hale & Iremonger, 207, 216
Hall, Michael, 145
Hall, Robert, 186
Hall, Victor, 186
Hancock, W.K., 127
Hanrahan, Barbara, 145, 152, 159, 274
Hardie Ltd., James, 188, 212
Hardy, Bobbie, 187
Hardy, Frank, 187

Hardy, Thomas, 66
Harford, Lesbia, 335
HarperCollins, 113, 188, 190, 204, 211–12, 220–21, 283
Hart, Jim, 205
Hartley, John, 302
Harvard University, 162
Hassall, Tony, 165
Hausler, Art, 110
Hawkins, Ann, 81
Headon, David, 161
Hearst Corporation, 212–13
Hegarty, Ruth, 167
Heinemann, 149, 204, 220
Heiss, Anita, 161, 188
Henricksen, Noel, 90
Herald (Melbourne), 121, 131, 134
Herbert, Xavier, 108
Hergenhan, Laurie, 289
Hetherington, Carol, 5, 250, 301
Hibberd, Jack, 148
high culture, 76, 208
high theory, 31, 58, 61
History of the Book in Australia project, 6
History of the Book in Canada, 37
Hockey, Susan, 9
Hodder & Stoughton, 204, 212–13, 220, 280
Hodder Headline, 212–14, 222
Hodgson, Elizabeth Eileen, 167
Holden, Steve, 275, 277, 286

357

Holt, Yvette, 167
Holtzbrinck Publishing Group, 213–14, 222
Hooker, John, 190
Hooper, Chloe, 190
Hope, A.D., 147, 338
Horne, Donald, 178
Hornibrook, Mrs, 136
Horwitz Publications, 197–202, 206, 215, 220–21, 271
Hospital, Janette Turner, 159
Houghton Mifflin Harcourt Publishing Company, 113
Howard government, 210
Hubble, Gregory, 76; *A Title Checklist 1900–1970*, 73; *The Australian Novel*, 73
Hudson Publishing, 207
Huggan, Graham, 88
Huggins, Jackie, 189
Hughes, Robert, 178
Hutcherson, Gillian, 189
Hutchinson & Co., 204, 220
hybridity, 90, 97
Hyland House, 207

I
IMPAC Dublin Literary Award, 101, 103–04
Indigenous Australians: Aboriginal Week, 166; activism, 191, 283; Black Rights movement, 162; cosmology, 157; Deaths in Custody (Royal Commission), 164; economic disparity with whites, 171
Indigenous literature, 283, 287; Arts Board, 165; bicentennial fund, 165, 169; commercial publishing, 184; criticism of, 158; declining sales, 185; *see also* under individual authors' names, Aboriginal Studies Press, BlackBooks, Institute for Aboriginal Development Press, UQP
Indra Publishing, 217
Information and Communication Technology (ICT), 12, 304, 333
Institute for Aboriginal Development Press, 161, 188
institutional histories, 23, 45–52
institutionalisation, 292
Interactive Press, 216
International Society for the Empirical Study of Literature and Media, 8
internet, 26, 56, 241, 244–45, 249, 253, 264, 301, 304, 314, 334–37, 340; structure, 302; Web 2.0, 13
intertextuality, 164
Invincible Press, 206
Isaacs, Jennifer, 164
ISIT Milan, 102
Ives, Maura, 81

J
Jacaranda Press, 159
Jacket Magazine, 335
Jacobyte Books, 216
James Cook University, 180, 183
Jameson, Fredric, 243
Jeffery Farnol, 141
Jenkin, Graham, 187
Jessop, Martyn, 242, 310
John Ferguson Publishing, 207
Johns, Adrian, 346
Johns, Brian, 181
Johnson-Woods, Tony, 250
Johnston, Grahame, 73
Johnston, John, 127
Johnston, Martin, 145
Jolley, Elizabeth, 145, 152, 159, 274
Jose, Nicholas, 148
Joseph, Michael, 112
Joshi, Priya, 250, 271
Journal of the Association for the Study of Australian Literature (JASAL), 250, 301

K
Kalgoorlie Miner, 121, 130, 132–33
Kansas City Star, 116
Kefala, Antigone, 288
Keneally, Thomas, 103, 257, 261
Kenna, Peter, 148
Kennedy, Gayle, 167

Kensington and Norwood Writers Group, 280
Kidd, Rosalind, 189
Kiernan, Brian, 286
Kincaid, Jamaica, 102
Knight, Stephen, 76
Knopf Publishing Group, 113
Koch, Christopher, 80

L
Lamond, Henry, 108
Lane, Allen, 178
Langley, Eve, 108, 114
Lawler, Ray, 148
Lawrence, D.H., 90, 257
Lee, Alwyn, 111
Legs on the Wall, 330
Lehmann, Geoffrey, 147
Lermontov, Mikhail, 91
Lever, Susan, 3
Lindrum, Walter, 127
Lindsay, Norman, 109
Lippincott Publishing, 113
literary criticism, 4, 8, 14, 17, 88, 124, 130, 246
literary scholarship, 11, 16–17, 20, 53, 71, 97
literary theory, 11, 43, 70, 78
Lithgow Mercury, 121, 131, 133
Little Brown Book Group, 113
Lockwood, Douglas, 186
London Charter, 244, 249, 264, 311
London Missionary Society, 182

359

Lonely Planet, 283
Longman Publishing, 177
Loos, Noel, 182
Lothian Publishing, 213–15, 222
Loukakis, Angelo, 145
Lowe, Robert, 167
Lurie, Morris, 286
Lyons, Martyn, 36; *A History of the Book in Australia* (John Arnold), 6, 105, 346; *Australian Readers Remember* (Lucy Taska), 6

M
Mabo, Eddie, 182
Macartney, Frederick, 72–73, 76
MacClellan & Co, 136
Macdonald, D.P., 132
MacDonald, Rowena, 189
Macmillan Publishers, 113, 116, 126, 136, 211–12, 221, 271
Maddock, Kenneth, 184
Magabala Books, 161, 188
Magarey, Susan, 189
Magner, Brigid, 194
Maiden, Jennifer, 147
Malouf, David, 89, 101–04, 145, 150, 159–60; *An Imaginary Life*, 101, 103; *Bicycle*, 150; *Dream Stuff*, 102–03; *Fly Away Peter*, 103, 148; Cavangnoli's translations, 102–03; *Johnno*, 148;

Spinucci's translations, 102; *Remembering Babylon*, 101, 103–04; Dormagen's translation, 103; Pepin's translations, 101–03; *Conversation at Curlew Creek*, 102; *Great World*, 101, 103
Mann, Cecil, 111
Mann, Thomas, 91, 111
Manning, Frederic, 257
Marchant, Bessie, 318
marketisation, 51, 179, 200–01
Marshall, Alan, 187
Marshall, James Vance, 257
Marxist criticism, 42, 43
Maryborough Advertiser, 122, 133
Maryborough Chronicle, 121, 133
Massola, Aldo, 186
Masters, Olga, 145, 152, 159, 274, 288
May, Anthony, 200
McAuley, James, 338
McCarthy, Steven, 167
McCartney, Charlie, 127
McCarty, Willard, 256, 299
McCullough, Colleen, 257–58, 260–61
McDonald, Peter, 37, 40, 48–50, 142, 145
McDonald, Roger, 150

McGann, Jerome, 72, 77–8, 83, 301, 303, 313
McKay, Edith, 110
McKenzie, D.F., 71
McLaren, Philip, 167, 172
McPhee Gribble Publishers, 186, 187
McPhee, Hilary, 178
McQueen, Humphrey, 176, 180, 181, 184
Mead, Philip, 334
Meanjin, 178
Mears, Gillian, 165
Meggs, Ginger, 126
Melbourne University Press (MUP), 197
Mercer, Jan, 187
Mercury, 122, 131, 133
Meridian editing debate, 7
Merrill & Company, Charles E., 109
metadata, 57
Migrant Women Writer's Group (Vic), 280
Miles Franklin Award, 148
Miller, E. Morris, 5, 70, 72–74, 76
Miller, James, 185
Mills & Boon, 203, 211, 220, 271
Milton, John, 82
Mitchell, Tom, 225
Mode 2 research, 25
Modern Language Association (MLA), 78, 81

modernism, 46
Modjeska, Drusilla, 125
Moi, Toril, 291
Moorhouse, Frank, 285–86
Moretti, Franco, 8, 14–15, 32, 33, 35, 38, 40, 44, 89, 241, 246, 279–80, 304, 316
Morgan, Sally, 162
Morning Bulletin, 132, 134–35, 141
Morrison, Toni, 102
Moulthrop, Stuart, 267
Mountford, Charles P., 185; & Ainslie Roberts, 186
Mudgee Guardian, 122, 128, 133
Mudgeroo, 165, 168, 172
Mudrooroo, 165–66, 169, 174
Muecke, Stephen, 165, 168
Mueller, Martin, 246
Muk Muk Burke, John, 167, 174
Mullens (bookseller), 136
Muller, Laurie, 154, 159, 162
multicultural literature, 288
multiculturalism, 283
multinationals, 23, 194, 201, 209, 210–19, 211–13, 215, 217–18
Mulvaney, John, 164
Mundine, Djon, 98
Munkara, Marie, 167
Munro, Craig, 144, 146, 159, 161, 164–65, 169, 286
Munro, Craig & John Curtain, 197

361

Murdoch, Nina, 128, 132
Murnane, Gerald, 22, 149, 151
Murray Island, 182
Murray, Les, 338; *Ethnic Radio*, 147; *People's Otherworld*, 147; *Vernacular Republic*, 147
Murray, Simone, 218
Muswellbrook, 107
Myer (store), 136, 172

N
Naipaul, V.S., 102
National Aeronautics and Space Administration (NASA), 259
National Collaborative Research Infrastructure Strategy (NCRIS), 61, 300, 308, 313
National Endowment for the Humanities (US), 12, 62
National eResearch Architecture Taskforce, 308
National Library of Australia, 106, 252; catalogue, 187; People Australia, 75
National Times, 176, 180
nationalism, 196; crisis in, 192; nationalist publishing, 218
New Bedford Standard Times, 116
New Bibliography, 62
New Criticism, 66, 272
New Media, 51, 328

New South Wales, 106, 116, 122, 125, 128, 151, 169; Sydney, 21, 80, 98, 105–06, 108–09, 118, 122, 128–29, 135, 137, 151, 172, 330, 341
New York Times, 116
News (Adelaide), 122, 133
News Corporation, 211–15, 218, 221–22
Niland, D'Arcy, 257–58
NINES project, 11, 306–07
Nix, Garth, 257
Noble, M.A., 127
Noonuccal, Oodgeroo, 159, 166, 169, 171; *Stradbroke Dreamtime*, 185
Northcote Christian Women's Book project, 281
Not the Only Planet, 283

O
O'Connor, V.J.A., 110
Oakley, Barry, 286
Office of War Information, 109
Olympic Games (Sydney), 98
Orczy, Baroness, 127, 129
Osborne, Roger, 41, 250, 307
Outback Press, 206
Outhewaite, Ida Rentoul, 127
Overland, 178
Oxbridge Catholics, 158
Oxford English Literary History, 34

Oxford University, 319
Oxford University Press, 286

P
Palmer, Nettie, 76, 135, 196; essays in Rockhampton's *Morning Bulletin*, 135
Palmer, Vance, 76, 127, 159, 196
Pan Macmillan, 212–13, 222, 271
Paperbark, 168, 283
Papyrus Press, 217
parallel imports, 210
Park, Ruth, 148
Parker, Graham, 318
Pascoe Publishing, 207, 217
Pearson Australia, 212–15, 221–22
Penguin Book of Australian Short Stories, 282
Penguin Book of Modern Australian Poetry, 334–36
Penguin Books, 23, 50, 148, 161, 176–81, 183–85, 187, 190, 271, 280, 286, 334–36; British board, 190; Penguin Aboriginal, 190
Penn Publishing, 113
Perkins, Elizabeth, 80
Phillips, Sandra, 168
Pilkington, Doris: *Caprice*, 167, 170, 173; David Unaipon Award, 170; *Follow the Rabbit Proof Fence*, 170
Pinker, James (literary agency), 108
Pinney, Mary, 110
Pivot, Bernard, 98
PLMA (journal of the Modern Language Association of America), 37
Poland, Louise, 168
political economy of reading, 15, 89
political influence of books, 193
Polo, Marco, 90, 94
Port Fairy Gazette, 122, 133
Port Germein Institute Library, 234
Porter, Dorothy, 338
postcolonialism, 276
postmodernism, 243
postnationalism, 88, 95
poststructuralism, 16, 42–44, 48, 58, 276
post-theory, 14, 16, 32–33, 41–42, 48
postwar period, 68
Potts, Marion, 98
Praed, Rosa, 227
Presland, Gary, 186
Press Development Plan, 146
Price, Leah, 40
Prichard, Katharine Susannah, 121

print culture, 264
print-on-demand publishing, 216
Proctor, Candice, 318
Project Gutenberg, 54
Putnam Publishing Group, 113

Q
Queensland, 122, 125, 158, 164, 170; Brisbane, 135, 159, 341

R
Radiola, 123
Rainey, Lawrence, 46
Ramsey, Stephen, 266
Rando, Gaetano, 152
Random House, 212–13, 222
Rastar, 207
Raven, James, 345
Read, Peter, 189
RealTime Stage and Screen, 329
Reed Elsevier, 188, 212–14, 222
Reed, Myrtle, 234, 238
Reflet, 99
regional centres, 121–22, 130
Resourceful Reading project, 13, 18, 25, 89, 119, 141, 223, 313; conference, 27, 71, 223
Reynolds, Henry: *The Other Side of the Frontier*, 23, 176, 178–79, 182–84, 187, 191, 193
Reynolds, Paul R. (literary agency), 108

Richards, I. A., 272
Richardson, Henry Handel, 111, 140; *Fortunes of Richard Mahony*, 140; *Ultima Thule*, 128, 140
Rigby, 161, 186–88, 204, 206
Robert Hale Publishing, 204, 220–21, 271
Roberto Busa Award, 10
Robinson, Roland, 185
Rodriquez, Judith, 159
Roe, Jill, 139
Romeril, John, 148
Rose, Jonathan, 7
Rossetti Archive, 58
Roughsey, Elsie, 186
Rowe, Nicholas, 53
Rowley, C.D., 177, 181, 183; *Destruction of Aboriginal Society*, 184; *Outcasts in White Australia*, 184; *Recovery*, 184; *Remote Aborigines*, 184
Rudd, Keivn, 218
Rudd, Steele, 159, 227
Ryan, Lyndall, 164

S
Salzman, Paul, 276
Sankey, Margaret, 98
Sarao, Frank, 110
Saunders, Kay, 164
Schmidt, Siegfried J., 8

Scholarly Communication, 308
scholarly editions, 4, 8–9, 11, 17, 53, 56–58, 62, 65–66, 71, 77, 303, 305, 307, 309
Scholarly Editions Centre, 80; website, 64
Scholarly Electronic Text and Imaging Service (SETIS), 13, 54, 63, 335
Scholastic Australia, 213
Scribe Publishing, 217
Sculley, D. & Bradley Pasanek, 246, 264, 271
self-publishing, 207–09, 212, 217, 328
Shakespeare, William, 66, 240
Shann, Edward, 127
Shapcott, Tom, 145
Shawcross, John T., 82
Sheridan, Susan, 276, 285
Shillingsburg, Peter, 62
Shoemaker, Adam, 165, 168–69, 172, 173
Showalter, Elaine, 291
Shute, Nevil, 261, 318
Simon & Schuster, 212–13
Simon, Ella, 187
Simpson, Colin, 185
Sinclair, Murray, 140
Sirius Publishing Company, 114
Skipper, Mervyn, 127
Skrzynecki, Peter, 22, 145, 150–51
Slessor, Kenneth, 147, 335

Small, Helen, 345
Snow, C.P., 2, 9; Rede Lecture, 1
South Australia, 122; Adelaide, 127, 131, 186, 228
Spectrum, 206
Spencer, A.H. (bookseller), 136
Spinifex Press, 217
St Clair, William, 15, 32, 39, 41, 44, 89, 241, 256, 304, 331
Stark and Paravel, 259, 267
Statistical Machine Learning, 24, 224–26, 239
Stead, Christina, 257
Steinbeck, John, 115
Sterne, Laurence, 90, 94
Stopes, Marie, 136
Stow, Randolph, 148
Strange Sequence, 111
Stratton-Porter, Gene, 234, 238
Summer, Anne, 187
Sun (Sydney), 122, 126, 131, 132, 134
Sun Books, 185
Sunday Guardian, 121–22, 132, 134–35
Sutherland, Kathryn, 66
Swift, Jonathan, 316
Sydney Morning Herald, 110, 122, 131, 134, 136, 140
Sykes, Roberta, 162–63, 169, 173

T
Tadmore, Naomi, 345
Tasman, Abel, 316

Tasmania, 122, 311, 321–22; Butlers Gorge, 320–21; Central Highlands, 320; Craycroft, 319–20; Hobart, 122, 322, 324; Lake King William, 320; nursing homes anthology, 280; Port Arthur, 324; subset regions, 322; Van Diemen's Land, 317, 324
Tasmanian Mail, 323
Tatz, Colin, 189
Taylor, Cheryl, 315
Tebbutt, Geoffrey & 'Plum' Warner, 127
Telegraph (Brisbane), 122, 134
television, 47, 98–100, 104, 172, 202, 218
Tennant, Kylie: *Foveaux*, 112, 115; *The Battlers*, 21, 106, 109, 112–18; compared with J.B. Priestly, 116; criticised by Frank Swinnerton, 115; criticised by George Orwell, 115; trans-Atlantic crossing, 113
Terry, Michael, 187
Texas A&M University, 81
Text Publishing, 217
Text-Encoding Initiative (TEI), 62, 63
textual analysis, 15, 35
theatre-blogging community, 328
Thomas Tilling, 220, 221

Thompson, E.P., 182
Thompson, Frank, 146, 158, 202
Thomson (now Thomson Reuters), 121, 211–12, 221
Thorpe, Bill, 164
Tiffin, Chris, 62
Time Warner, 212–13
Times Mirror, 220–21
Toer, Pramoedya Ananta, 164
Tolstoy, Leo, 91
Tompkins, Jane, 277, 278, 289
Tompkins, Joanne, 330
Toowoomba Chronicle, 122, 133, 140
Torstar Corporation, 203, 211–15, 221–22
Townsville Daily Bulletin, 122, 134–35
Toyne, Phillip & Daniel Vachon, 186
trade barriers, 108
trade fairs, 97
Transcontinental, 122, 133
translation zone, 20, 88–89, 95, 97, 99–100, 104
transnationalism, 158; transnational corporations, 194
Tranter, John, 334–38; *Parallax*, 335; *Red Movie*, 147
Trollope, Anthony, 237
Tsaloumas, Dmitris, 145
Tufte, Edward, 267

Tukey, John, 226, 229
Turnbull, Clive, 185

U
United States of America, 3, 12, 41, 76, 79–81, 100, 105–11, 113–18, 128, 139, 152, 199–200, 202, 205, 210, 250; New York, 21, 80, 106–09, 111–14, 116, 118
University of Kentucky, 82
University of New South Wales (UNSW) Press, 188
University of Newcastle (Australia), 10
University of Queensland Press (UQP), 22, 142, 144–48, 150, 151–66, 168–69, 171, 173–74, 187–88, 271, 280–81, 283, 286; Asian and Pacific Writing, 145, 164; Australian Authors series, 274, 288–89; Black Australian Writers (BAW) series, 22, 156, 169, 172–74; Contemporary Russian Writing, 145; *Writer's Press*, 144, 159
University of Southern Queensland, 341
University of Sydney, 4, 99, 109, 334–38; Fisher Library, 54, 334–36; Television Service, 338
University of Virginia, 58, 306

University of Wollongong, 153
Unwin, Stanley, 107
Upfield, Arthur, 108
Ure Smith Publishing, 198, 206

V
van der Maaten, Laurens & Geoffrey Hinton, 231
Van Maanen, John, 241
Venuti, Lawrence, 88, 97
Victoria, 122, 163, 169; Melbourne, 90, 105, 108, 127, 136–37, 180
Victorian Fiction Research Guides, 73
Vidiikas, Vicki, 145
Viking, 113
Virtual Research Environments (VRE), 13
Vogel Prize, 165
Vulgar Press, 217

W
Waks, Nathan, 98
Walker, Cheryl, 171
Wallace-Crabbe, Chris, 147
Waller, Mary E., 234
Walwicz, Ania, 288
Warwick Daily News, 122, 133
Watego, Cliff, 173
Watkins Inc., A. (literary agency), 109
Watkins, Armitage, 109, 110, 111

Watson, Samuel Wagan, 167
Watt & Son, A.P. (literary agency), 108
Wearne, Alan, 145
Webby, Elizabeth, 55, 124, 276, 336
Webster Publications, 197, 202, 220
Wentworth Press, 206
West Australian, 122, 131, 134–35, 137
West, Morris, 260–61
Western Australia, 122; Perth, 127, 135, 137
West-Pavlov, Russell, 90, 92, 94
Wevers, Lydia, 160, 174
White, Patrick, 103, 178, 257, 261; *Aunt's Story*, 109
Whitebeach, Terry, 170
Whitlam era, 160, 190
Wild & Woolley, 206
Wilding, Michael, 145, 148, 215, 286
Wilkes, G.A., 4
William Blake Archive, 58
William Morrow Publishing, 113
Williams, Magdalene, 189
Williamson, Alice Muriel, 234, 238
Williamson, David, 149
Willis, Nathaniel Parker, 237
Winch, Tara June, 167
Windschuttle, Keith, 191
Winton, Tim, 148
wissenschaftlich, 58
Wobutoft Books, 207
Women's Redress Press, 281
Wood, James, 19
Woolf, Virginia, 141
World War II, 108–09, 116, 186, 202
Wren Books, 206
Wright, Judith, 147, 163, 338

Y

Yale University, 109
Yass Tribune-Courier, 122, 133
Young Women's Writings Collective (Canberra), 280
Yowell, Jackie, 181

Z

Zagar, Cilka, 189
Zenodotus of Ephesus, 53
Zwicky, Fay, 145

www.ingramcontent.com/pod-product-compliance
Lightning Source LLC
Chambersburg PA
CBHW061509180426
43194CB00057B/2897